Android Apps for Absolute Beginners

Second Edition

RaceData

Wallace Jackson

Apress·

Android Apps for Absolute Beginners

ISBN-13 (pbk): 978-1-4302-4788-3

ISBN-13 (electronic): 978-1-4302-4789-0

President and Publisher: Paul Manning
Lead Editor: Steve Anglin
Developmental Editor: Douglas Pundick
Technical Reviewer: Chad Darby
Editorial Board: Steve Anglin, Ewan Buckingham, Gary Cornell, Louise Corrigan, Morgan Ertel, Jonathan Gennick, Jonathan Hassell, Robert Hutchinson, Michelle Lowman, James Markham, Matthew Moodie, Jeff Olson, Jeffrey Pepper, Douglas Pundick, Ben Renow-Clarke, Dominic Shakeshaft, Gwenan Spearing, Matt Wade, Tom Welsh
Coordinating Editor: Kevin Shea
Copy Editor: Judy Ann Levine
Compositor: SPi Global
Indexer: SPi Global
Artist: SPi Global
Cover Designer: Anna Ishchenko

Distributed to the book trade worldwide by Springer Science+Business Media New York, 233 Spring Street, 6th Floor, New York, NY 10013. Phone 1-800-SPRINGER, fax (201) 348-4505, e-mail orders-ny@springer-sbm.com, or visit www.springeronline.com.

For information on translations, please e-mail rights@apress.com, or visit www.apress.com.

Apress and friends of ED books may be purchased in bulk for academic, corporate, or promotional use. eBook versions and licenses are also available for most titles. For more information, reference our Special Bulk Sales–eBook Licensing web page at www.apress.com/bulk-sales.

Any source code or other supplementary materials referenced by the author in this text is available to readers at www.apress.com. For detailed information about how to locate your book's source code, go to www.apress.com/source-code.

Contents at a Glance

Contents

About the Author

Wallace Jackson is the CEO of Mind Taffy Design, a new media content design and production company founded in 1991. Mind Taffy specializes in leveraging free for commercial use open source technologies to provide extremely compact data footprint, royalty-free, digital new media advertising and branding campaigns for leading international brands and manufacturers worldwide.

Wallace has been pushing the leading-edge of i3D and Rich Media Application Design via viral digital content deliverables, using under 1MB of Total Data Footprint, for over two decades. He has worked for leading international brands and manufacturers to create custom new media digital campaigns for industry-leading companies, including projects targeting brand marketing, PR, product demonstration, digital signage, e-learning, AdverGaming, product marketing, 3D logo design, and end-user training.

Wallace has produced cutting-edge new media projects in a number of digital media "verticals" or content deliverable areas, including: interactive 3D [i3D], Rich Internet Applications (RIA) content production, virtual world design, user interface (UI) design, user experience (UX) design, e-book design, multimedia production, 3D modeling, sound design, MIDI synthesis, music composition, image compositing, 3D animation, game programming, mobile application programming, BrandGame creation, website design, CSS programming, data optimization, digital imaging, digital painting, digital video editing, special effects, morphing, vector illustration, IPTV programming, iTV application design, interactive product demos, and tradeshow multimedia.

Wallace has created new media digital campaigns for leading international branded manufacturers, including Sony, Samsung, Tyco, Dell, Epson, IBM, Mitsubishi, Compaq, TEAC, KDS USA, CTX International, ADI Systems, Nokia, Micron, ViewSonic, OptiQuest, SGI, Western Digital, Sun Microsystems, ProView, Sceptre, KFC, ICM, EIZO, Nanao, Digital Equipment [DEC], TechMedia, Pacific Digital, ArtMedia, Maxcall, Altrasonic, DynaScan, EZC, Smile, KFC, Krillogy, and Kinoton GMBH.

Wallace holds an MSBA postgraduate degree in Marketing Strategy from the University of Southern California (USC), an MBA degree in Management Information Systems Design and Implementation from the USC Marshall School of Business, and a Bachelor's degree in Business Economics from the University of California at Los Angeles (UCLA) Anderson School of Management. He is currently the number 2 ranked All Time Top Expert on LinkedIn, out of more than 200,000,000 executives that currently use that business social media website. You can read Wallace's blog at www.WallaceJackson.com and follow him on Twitter @wallacejackson as well.

About the Technical Reviewer

Chád Darby is an author, instructor, and speaker in the Java development world. As a recognized authority on Java applications and architectures, he has presented technical sessions at software development conferences worldwide.

In his 15 years as a professional software architect, he has had the opportunity to work for Blue Cross/Blue Shield, Merck, Boeing, Northrop Grumman, and a handful of startup companies.

Chád is a contributing author to several Java books, including Professional Java E-Commerce (Wrox Press), Beginning Java Networking (Wrox Press), and XML and Web Services Unleashed (Sams Publishing).

Chád has Java certifications from Sun Microsystems and IBM. He holds a BS in Computer Science from Carnegie Mellon University.

You can read Chád's blog at www.luv2code.com and follow him on Twitter @darbyluvs2code.

Acknowledgments

Steve Anglin, my lead editor, for his patience and thoughtful guidance in shaping this second edition of *Android Apps for Absolute Beginners*. Steve, thanks for guiding me as a returning Apress author, and I look forward to many future collaborations with you.

Chád Darby, my esteemed technical reviewer, for his hard work and insightful suggestions in shaping this second edition of this best-selling book.

Douglas Pundick, my Development Editor, for all his hard work helping me to write the best introductory Android book. I wouldn't have been able do it at all if it were not for you!

Kevin Shea, my Coordinating Editor, for listening to all of my miscellaneous and sundry problems during the writing of this book, and for helping to get them all sorted out.

Judy Ann Levine, my Copy Editor, for her excellent editing and book-polishing skills, and for all the great suggestions for making this a fantastic Android book.

Plus to the many loved ones and clients who patiently awaited my return to i3D content production from the "professional sidetracker" commonly known as writing an Android 4.1 programming book – I thank you for your patience...

—Wallace Jackson

Introduction

Over the last three years, Google's Android operating system (OS) has gone from a virtually unknown open source solution to the current mobile OS market leader among all mobile handsets, with over one-half of the market share and still climbing. Android has even started to dominate the tablet OS marketplace, and is also the foundation for the popular iTV OS known as GoogleTV as well as for e-book e-readers from Sony, Amazon (Kindle), and Barnes and Noble (Nook). There seems to be no end in sight for Android's rocketing success, which is great news for the owners of this book.

I've heard a great many people say, "I have a really phenomenal idea for a smartphone and tablet application! Can you program it for me!?" Rather than sit back and code all of these cool applications for everyone, I thought it might be a smarter idea to write a book about how an absolute beginner could code an Android application using open source tools that cost nothing to download and that are free for commercial use, and then leverage that new found knowledge to reach their dream of making their application idea a revenue-generating reality.

Thanks to open source tools and formats and Google's Android development environment, Oracle's Java programming language, Linus Torvalds' Linux operating system, the Eclipse code editing software, and to this book of course, vaporizing a software product out of thin air and at no production cost other than your PC and "sweat equity," is now a complete reality.

The Target: The Programming Neophyte

As you may have inferred from the title, this book assumes that you have never programmed before in any programming language. It is written for someone who has never written a single line of code, and who is thus unfamiliar with object-oriented programming (OOP) languages such as Oracle's Java and markup languages such as XML. Both of these open source languages are used extensively in creating Android applications and will be taught thoroughly in this book.

There are a lot of Java and Android books out there, but all of those books assume that you have programmed before and know all the OOP and programming lingo. I wanted to write a book that takes readers from knowing absolutely nothing about programming; not even knowing about how to install a software development kit (SDK) or an integrated development environment (IDE), all of the way from Ground Zero to being able to program useful Android applications using Java and XML and new media assets such as images, audio, and animation.

The Weapon: Android—An Innovative Internet 2.0 Coding Environment

Android is my Internet 2.0 development weapon of choice because it allows me to develop highly advanced applications for the primary Internet 2.0 devices, including the primary four consumer electronics product "verticals" where revenue potential is by far the greatest:

- Smartphones
- Tablets
- e-book e-readers
- iTVs or interactive television sets

The other reason I place my bets on Android is because it is open source and uses open source technologies and is therefore free from royalties and politics. It includes advanced new media "engines" (tools) such as OpenGL, ON2 VP8 (WebM and WebP), Java, XML, CSS, HTML5, PNG, and JPEG. I do not have to submit my Android application to any company and ask for permission to publish it, as long as it is not harmful in any way to others. For this reason, and due to the free for commercial use nature of open source software, there is little external risk involved in developing an application for the Android Platform.

How This Book Is Organized

Because this is a book for absolute beginners, we start at the very beginning—showing where to download, and how to install, the various Android, Java, and Eclipse environments. We also show how to configure these environments, and how to set them up for application development and testing. We even show how and where to download the other leading-edge new media tools (GIMP, for instance) that you will use in conjunction with the primary Android development tools.

We essentially show you exactly how to put together a complete and professional-level Android New Media Content Production Workstation, and at zero cost to yourself to boot. This in itself is no easy task, and must be done correctly, as these professional tools provide the foundation for all of our Android development, debugging, and testing for the remainder of the book.

Next we provide you with an overview of where Android came from, why, how, and when Google acquired it, and how it is uniquely structured among software development platforms. We introduce XML, Java, OOP, and Android concepts soon after that, as well as covering how Android manages its screen layout. We then move these concepts into use in later chapters in the second half of the book; these chapters explain the most important concepts in Android, in their most logical order, as they pertain to your applications development.

In that second half of the book, we start getting into developing a user interface (UI), as that is the front-end or interface for your end-users to your Android application. Soon after that we cover how your UI talks to your application via events processing. To spice up your application's visual appearance, we'll get into graphics, animation, and audio, and then into even more advanced topics after that, such as databases and communications.

Finally, we will look at some of the advanced features of Android that you will want to visit after finishing the book; these are topics that are too advanced for a first book on Android, but which provide some of the coolest features to be found in smartphone, iTV, and tablet software development today.

We'll walk you through all of these topics and concepts with screenshots of the IDE and visual examples, and then take you through step-by-step examples reinforcing these concepts. Sometimes we may even repeat previous topics to reinforce what you have learned and apply these programming skills in new and different ways. This enables new programmers to reapply key development skills and feel a sense of accomplishment as they progress.

The Formula for Success

Learning to develop an Android application is an interactive process between you and the tools and technologies (Eclipse, XML, Java, Android, GIMP, and so on) that I cover in this book. Just like learning to play a sport, you have to develop these skills and practice them daily. You need to work through the examples and exercises in this book, more than once if necessary, to become comfortable with each concept and proficient in their execution.

Just because you understand a concept, that doesn't necessarily mean you will know how to apply it creatively and use it effectively. That takes practice and it ultimately will happen when the "ah-ha" moment occurs, when you understand a concept in context with the other concepts that interconnect with it.

You will learn quite a bit about how Android works from this introductory book. You will glean a lot of insight into the inner working of Android by working through all of the exercises in this book. But you will also learn new things not specifically mentioned in this book when you compile, run, and debug your programs. Spending time experimenting with your code and trying to find out why it is not working the way you want, or trying to add new features, is a learning process that is also very valuable.

The downside of debugging is it can sometimes be quite frustrating to the new developer. If you have never wanted to put a bullet in your computer display, you will soon. You will question why you are doing this, and whether you are savvy enough to solve the problem. Programming can be very humbling, even for the most experienced of applications developers.

As with an athlete, the more you practice, the better you will become at your skill. You can do some truly amazing things as an Android programmer. The world is your oyster. It is one of the most satisfying accomplishments you can have, seeing your app in the Google Play (Android App) Store. However, there is a price, and that price is time spent practicing your coding.

Here is our formula for success:

- Trust that you can pull it off. You may be the only one who says you can't do this. Don't tell yourself that.

- Work through all the examples and exercises in this book, twice if necessary, until you understand them.

- Code, code some more, and keep coding—don't stop. The more you code, the better you'll get.

- Do further research via Google Search as well as the Developer.Android.com website into areas of the Android OS that interest you, and that you want to master.

- Be patient with yourself. If you were fortunate enough to have been a star pupil who could memorize material simply by reading it, this will probably not happen with Java and XML coding. You are going to have to spend a lot of time coding to come to understand what exactly is happening inside the Android OS Environment.

- Whatever you do: DON'T GIVE UP!

Required Software, Materials, and Equipment

One of the great things about Java, Android, and Eclipse is they are available on all three primary operating systems that are in use today:

- Windows

- Macintosh

- Linux

The other great thing about Java, Android, and Eclipse is that they are completely free. For equipment, any modern dual-core or quad-core computer will do. Fortunately computer workstations are only $200 to $400 brand new on www.PriceWatch.com or you can walk into WalMart and buy an HP or Acer tower with a fast quad-core processor for $300 to $500 including Windows 7 or 8. There are also open source OSes such as SUSE Linux, which is free and an amazing development operating system. SUSE Linux V12 can be downloaded at www.OpenSUSE.com and is currently at version 12.2 and is very stable.

Operating System and IDE

Although you can use Android on many platforms, the Eclipse integrated development environment (IDE) that developers use to develop Android apps is most commonly used on an Intel-based Windows or Linux PC. The Eclipse Juno 4.2 for Java EE IDE is free, and is available on the Internet at www.eclipse.org. The operating system should be Windows XP SP3 or later, or SUSE Linux 12.2 or later, to run Eclipse most effectively. Note that as of Android 4.2 API Level 17, developers can now develop using a 64-bit "clean" Android IDE environment, so the Windows 7 64-bit or Windows 8 64-bit OSs may be the best way to go if you want to develop using a 64-bit platform.

Software Development Kits

You will need to download the Eclipse Juno 4.2 for Java EE IDE from Eclipse.org and the Android 4.1 or later SDK from Google. This is available at http://developer.android.com/SDK/. This is another area that changed significantly with the release of Android 4.2, as there is now an ADT Bundle that can be downloaded for either 32-bit or 64-bit OSs which makes installation much easier than it used to be. We cover this in Chapter 3, and do the install in both ways, so that you can see the long-form installation (and see how everything goes together in the process) as well as the streamlined installation that emerged along with the Android 4.2 Level 17 API in the end of 2012. Also note that wherever we reference Android 4.1 or Android 4.1.2 you can now substitute Android 4.2, as we have updated several chapters with the new 4.2 features. Whew! Caught that one just in time!

Dual Displays

It is highly recommended that developers have a second display connected to their computer. It is great to step through your code and watch your output window and Android emulator at the same time on dual, independent displays. Today's PC hardware makes this easy. Just plug your second display in to the second display port of any Intel-based PC or laptop, with the correct display port adapter, of course, and you're able to have two displays working independently from one another. Note it is not required to have dual displays. You will just have to organize your open windows to fit on your screen if you don't. I am using a Philips 32" HDTV 1920 by 1080 LCD display to code on, so that my code is very readable. With 40" HDTV displays at $250 at WalMart, having a big widescreen or two to use for your Android application development workstation is a great idea!

Chapter 1

Preliminary Information: Before We Get Started

This chapter introduces the Android operating system, giving you a little background information to help put things into perspective. We'll visit just how expansive this platform has become in today's Internet 2.0 environment of portable consumer electronic devices. *Internet 2.0* here refers to the consumption of the Internet over a wide variety of different types of data networks using highly portable consumer electronic devices, including smartphones, tablets, e-book readers, and even new emerging consumer electronic products such as interactive television (iTV).

As this is an introductory book on the subject not all of the advanced new media-related areas, such as 3D and video streaming, will be covered. Some specifics of what the book will and will not cover are outlined in this chapter.

At the end of the chapter, you'll learn which tools you will need to obtain to develop for the Google Android platform, with instructions on how to download them.

Those of you who already recognize the significance of the Android revolution and know which tools are needed to develop Android applications development may want to skip this chapter. However, there may be some tidbits in here that could spawn development ideas—so skip over it at your own risk!

Just a bit of fair warning: developing reliable applications for Android is not in any way a trivial task. It takes a fair amount of knowledge of both high-level programming languages such as Java and markup languages such as XML. Building useful and engaging new media applications also requires a deep knowledge of related new media technologies such as 2D imaging, 3D rendering, audio processing, video streaming, GPS localization, and database design.

Don't expect to learn all of this at one sitting. Becoming a top-notch Android programmer will take years of dedication and practice as well as diligent research and trial and error. In this book, you will gain the foundation that you need to build future expertise as well as learn the work process for eventually building your own Android masterpiece.

Some History: What Is Android?

Android was originally created by Andy Rubin as an operating system for mobile phones, around the dawn of this twenty-first century. In 2005, Google acquired Android Inc., and made Andy Rubin the Director of Mobile Platforms for Google. Many think the acquisition was largely in response to the emergence of the Apple iPhone around that time; however, there were enough other large players, such as RIM Blackberry, Nokia Symbian, and Microsoft Windows Mobile, that it seemed a salient business decision for Google to purchase the talent and intellectual property necessary to assert the company into this emerging space, which has become known as Internet 2.0.

Internet 2.0 allows users of consumer electronics to access content via widely varied data networks through highly portable consumer electronic devices, such as smartphones, touchscreen tablets, and e-book e-Readers, and even through not so portable devices, such as iTVs, home media centers, and set-top boxes. This puts new media content such as games, 3D animation, digital video, digital audio, and high-definition imagery into our lives at every turn. Android is one of the vehicles that digital artists will increasingly leverage to develop new media creations that users have never before experienced.

Over the past decade, Android has matured and evolved into an extremely reliable, bulletproof, embedded operating system platform, having gone from version 1.0 to stable versions at 1.5, 1.6, 2.0, 2.1, 2.2, 2.3, 3.0, 3.1, 3.2, 3.3, 4.0, and recently, 4.1. Here are the latest stats from the Android website at: http://developer.android.com/about/dashboards/index.html

VERSION	CODENAME	API LEVEL	MARKET SHARE
1.5	Cupcake	3	0.2 %
1.6	Donut	4	0.4 %
2.1	Eclair	7	3.7 %
2.2	Froyo	8	14 %
2.3.2	Gingerbread	9	0.3 %
2.3.7	Gingerbread	10	57.2 %
3.1	Honeycomb	12	0.5 %
3.2	Honeycomb	13	1.6 %
4.0.2	Ice Cream Sandwich	14	0.1 %
4.0.4	Ice Cream Sandwich	15	20.8 %
4.1	Jelly Bean	16	1.2 %

An embedded operating system is like having an entire computer on a chip small enough to fit into handheld consumer electronics, but powerful enough to run applications (commonly known as *apps*). Like today's computers, Internet 2.0 devices such as smartphones, tablets, e-readers, and iTVs now feature dual-core and even quad-core computer processing power as well as one or two gigabytes of system memory.

Android has the power of a full-blown computer operating system. It is based on the Linux open source platform and Oracle's (formerly Sun Microsystems's) Java, one of the world's most popular programming languages.

Note   The term *open source* refers to software that has often been developed collaboratively by an open community of individuals, is freely available for commercial use, and comes with all of its source code so that it can be further modified if necessary. Android is open source, though Google develops it internally before releasing the source code; from that point on, it is freely available for commercial use.

It is not uncommon for an Android product to have a 2GHz processor and 2GB of fast, computer-grade DDR2 memory. This rivals desktop computers of just a few years ago and netbooks that are still currently available. You will see a further convergence of handheld operating systems and desktop operating systems as time goes on. Some examples are the new Windows 8 operating system and Linux platform.

Once it became evident that Android and open source were forces to be reckoned with, nearly 100 major companies—including HTC, Samsung, LG Electronics, and T-Mobile—formed and joined the Open Handset Alliance (OHA). This was done to put some momentum behind Google's open source Android platform, and it worked. Today, more brand manufacturers use Android as an operating system on their consumer electronic devices than any other operating system.

The development of the OHA is a major benefit to Android developers. Android allows developers to create their applications in a single environment, and the support by the OHA allows developers to deliver their content across dozens of major branded manufacturer's products, as well as across several different types of consumer electronic devices: smartphones, iTV sets, e-book e-readers, home media centers, set-top boxes, and touchscreen tablets. Exciting possibilities—to say the least.

So, Android is a seasoned operating system that has become one of the biggest players in computing today, and with Google behind it. Android uses freely available open source technologies such as Linux and Java, and standards such as XML, to provide a content and application delivery platform to developers as well as the world's largest consumer electronics manufacturers. Can you spell O-P-P-O-R-T-U-N-I-T-Y? I sure can … it's spelled *ANDROID*.

Advantage Android: How Can Android Benefit Me?

There are simply too many benefits of the Android platform to ignore Android development.

First of all, Android is based on open source technology, which was at its inception not as refined as paid technologies from Apple and Microsoft. However, over the past two decades, open source software technology has become equally as sophisticated as conventional development technologies. This is evident in Internet 2.0, as the majority of the consumer electronics manufacturers have chosen Linux and Java over the Windows and Macintosh operating systems. Therefore, Android developers can develop not only for smartphones, but also for new and emerging consumer electronic devices such as tablets and iTVs that are network compatible and thus available to connect to the Android Marketplace, recently rebranded by Google as Google Play. This translates into more sales onto more devices in more areas of the customer's life, and thus more incentive to develop for Android over closed technologies such as Windows and iOS and over less popular and less prolific PC operating systems.

In addition to being free for commercial use, Android has one of the largest, wealthiest, and most innovative companies in modern-day computing behind it: Google. Add in the OHA, and you have more than a trillion dollars of megabrand companies behind you supporting your development efforts. It seems too good to be true, but it's a fact, if you are an Android developer (which you are about to be, in about a dozen chapters) then you've got a great support team behind you!

Finally, and most important, it's much easier to get your Android applications published than those for other platforms that are similar to Android (I won't mention any names here to protect the not so innocent). We've all heard the horror stories regarding major development companies waiting months, and sometimes years, for their apps to be approved for the app marketplace. These problems are nearly nonexistent on the open source Android platform. Publishing your app on the Google Play Android marketplace is as easy as paying $25, uploading your *.apk* file, and specifying free or paid download.

The Scope of This Book

This book is an introduction to developing applications for Android. It's intended for absolute beginners—that is, people who have never created an application on the Android platform for a consumer electronic device. I do not assume that you know what Java is or how XML works.

What's Covered

This book covers the basic and essential elements of Android development, including the following

- The open source tools required to develop for this platform.
  - Where to get these free tools.
  - How to properly install and configure the necessary tools for application development.
  - Which third-party tools are useful to use in conjunction with the Android development tools.
  - Which operating systems and platforms currently support development for the Android using these tools.
- The concepts and programming constructs for Java and XML, and their practical applications in creating Android applications.
- How Android goes about setting up an Android application.
  - How it defines the user interfaces.
  - How it writes to the display screen.
  - How it communicates with other Android applications.
  - How it interfaces with data, resources, networks, and the Internet.
  - How it alerts users to events that are taking place inside and outside the application.

- How Android applications are published.

- How Android applications are ultimately sold, downloaded, and updated automatically through the Google Play Android marketplace.

You should realize that Android has more than 44 Java packages that contain over 7,000 pieces of programming code functionality to allow you to do just about anything imaginable—from putting a button on the screen to synthesizing speech and accessing advanced smartphone features like the high-resolution camera, GPS, and accelerometer.

> **Note**   A *package* in Java is a collection of programming utilities that all have related and interconnected functionality. For example, the java.io package contains utilities to deal with input and output to your program, such as reading the contents of a file or saving data to a file. Later chapters describe how to organize your own code into packages.

What does this mean? It means that even the most advanced Android books cannot cover the plethora of things that the Android platform can do. In fact, most books specialize in a specific area in the Android APIs. There is plenty of complexity in each API, which ultimately, from the developer's viewpoint, translates into incredible creative power. "What's the price?" you might ask. Your time spent in mastering each API is the only price you will pay, as Android is otherwise free for commercial use.

What's Not Covered

So, what *isn't* covered in this book? What cool, powerful capabilities do you have to look forward to in that next level book on Android programming?

On the hardware side, we will not be looking at how to control the camera, access GPS data from the smartphone, and access the accelerometer and gyroscope that allow the user to turn the phone around and have the application react to phone positioning. We will not be delving into advanced touchscreen concepts such as gestures, or accessing other hardware such as the microphone, Bluetooth, and wireless connections.

On the software side, we will not be diving into creating your own Android SQLite database structure, or its new media codecs for digital video and digital audio, and its real-time 3D rendering system (called OpenGL ES 2.0). We will not be exploring speech synthesis and recognition, or the universal language support that allows developers to create applications that display characters correctly in dozens of international languages and foreign character sets. We will not be getting into advanced programming such as game development, artificial intelligence, and physics simulations. All of these topics are better suited to books that focus on these complex and detailed topical areas.

Preparing for Liftoff: SDK Tools to Download

In Chapter 3, you'll learn how to set up a complete Android development environment. We focus on Windows 7 because that's what the vast majority of developers use to develop for Android, but the process on Mac and Linux systems is similar, and I'll make sure you can follow along if you prefer either of those systems. Also, because the Android r20.0.3 SDK, known as the Android Jelly Bean 4.1 environment, uses a 32-bit programming environment, we will be using the latest Java 6 update 37 in its 32-bit version, and the Eclipse 4.2.1 Juno for Java EE 32-bit integrated development environment (IDE) software, both of which work perfectly on 32-bit Windows OSs (such as XP, Vista, and Win7) as well as on the 64-bit Windows 7 and Windows 8 OSs.

Here, we'll look at where to go to download the tools you'll need, so that you are ready for action when the time comes to install and configure them. This is because each of these development tools is hundreds of megabytes in file size, and depending on your connection speed, may take anywhere from ten minutes to ten hours to download.

There are three major components of an Android development environment:

- Java
- Eclipse
- Android

In Chapter 3, when you install and configure the packages you are downloading now, you will see that Eclipse requires the Java package to be installed in order to install and run. Therefore, we will walk through downloading them in the order of installation, from Java to Eclipse to Android.

Java

Let's start with the foundation for everything we are doing, the Java 6 Platform, Standard Edition (Java SE) 32-bit version. Java 6 SE contains the core Java programming language. Note that Android 4.1 does not yet support the use of Java 7.

To download Java 6 SE, simply go to the Java SE Downloads section of Oracle's web site, which is in the Technology Network section under the Java directory, at this URL:

`http://www.oracle.com/technetwork/java/javase/downloads/index.html`

Figure 1-1 shows the Java SE Downloads site. Be sure and download Java 6 and not Java 7.

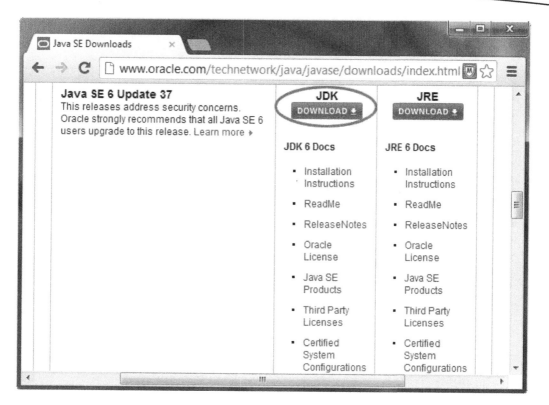

Figure 1-1. *Download the Java SE 6 JDK*

Click the Download Java 6 JDK button to start downloading the Java 6 SE Java Development Kit (JDK). This will take you to a second page shown in Figure 1-2 where you need to Accept the License Agreement by selecting the shown radio button option and then download the Windows 32-bit version of the Java 6 software also highlighted in the screenshot below by clicking on the link shown in red.

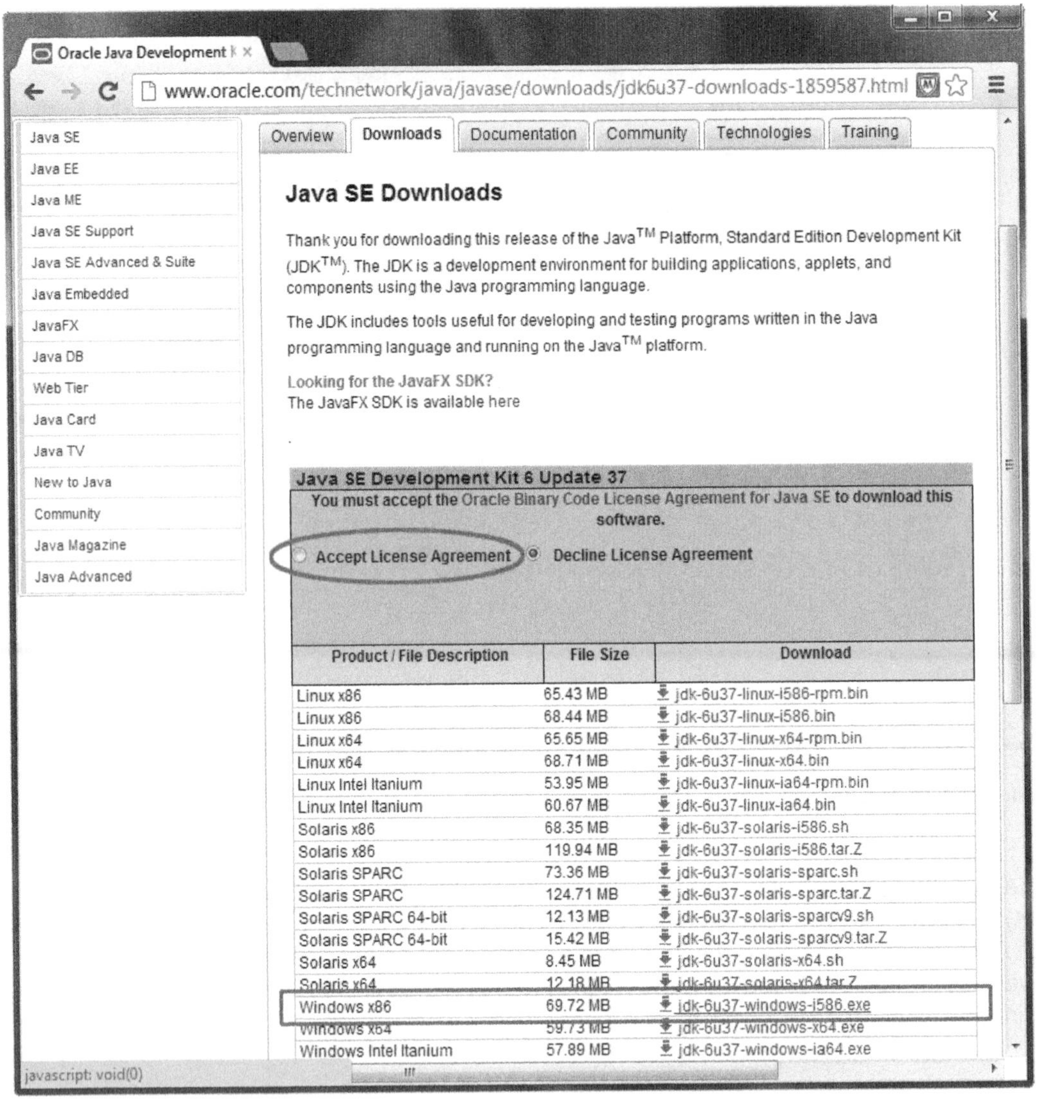

Figure 1-2. Accept License Agreement and Download Windows x86 version of Java 6

Note   Make sure *not* to download Java 7 Platform, Enterprise Edition (Java EE), JavaFX 2.2, or Java with NetBeans. These are the buttons on the top of the first download page. Scroll down to the bottom and find Java 6 (shown in Figure 1-1).

Eclipse

Eclipse is an *integrated development environment* (IDE), which is a piece of software dedicated to allowing you to easily write programming code and run and test that code in an integrated environment. In other words, you write all your code into its text editor, before running and testing that code using commands in Eclipse, without ever needing to switch to another program.

Currently, Android requires the Eclipse IDE, and I recommend the Eclipse Juno Version 4.2 for Java EE. You should download a version of Eclipse that supports Java—such as the Eclipse Juno 4.2 IDE for Java EE shown in Figure 1-3. Go to the Eclipse website Downloads section at this URL:

`http://www.eclipse.org/downloads/`

Figure 1-3 shows the Eclipse Juno 4.2 for Java EE software package that you should download.

Click the Windows 32-bit version link in the right-hand column, and your download begins.

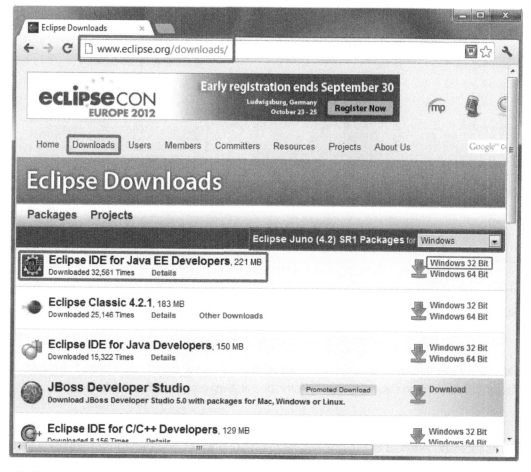

Figure 1-3. *Choose to download the Eclipse 4.2.1 Juno for Java EE IDE for Java Developers*

Android SDK

The Android software development kit (SDK) is a collection of files and utilities that work hand-in-hand with the Eclipse IDE to create an Android-specific development tool.

To download the latest Android 4.1 SDK, go to the Android developers' web site, located at this URL:

`http://developer.android.com/sdk/index.html`

Figure 1-4 shows the Android download page. Click on the Big Blue Button to download the latest SDK for the Windows platform.

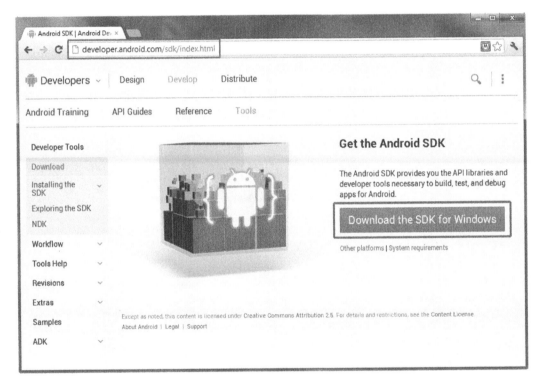

Figure 1-4. Download the Android SDK

> **Note**   We will walk through installing the other minor packages (shown on the left side of Figure 1-4) using Eclipse in Chapter 3. For now, you don't need to worry about anything except downloading the main SDK.

Once the Eclipse and Android SDKs are installed and configured, you can further enhance them by installing phone emulators and other add-ins, which are covered in Chapter 3. In that chapter, we will go through the detailed setup of the Eclipse Juno 4.2.1 for Java EE IDE for Android 4.1 development.

Summary

Andy Rubin's creation called Android was purchased by Google in 2005 and made freely available to developers to create mobile device applications using Java and XML. Since then, the Android phenomenon has grown to encompass an open industry alliance of the leading manufacturers and has become the fastest growing mobile platform today. It is the horse to bet on for the future of not only mobile devices, but also other types of consumer electronic devices, including tablets, e-Book e-Readers, and iTVs.

What you will learn about in this book spans from the how and where to get the Android development environment to how to set it up properly, how to configure it optimally, and how to use it to create applications that employ many of the powerful features of Android.

The three basic components you'll need for Android development are Java 6, Eclipse 4.2.1, and of course, Android. You can download these various components for free, as described in this chapter. Once the Android r20.0.3 SDK (Android 4.1.2 AKA Jelly Bean) is installed in Eclipse, that IDE becomes a comprehensive Android application development environment.

The next chapter provides an overview of what you will learn in this book, and then we'll get started with setup in Chapter 3.

Chapter 2

What's Next? Our Road Ahead

Before getting into the details of Android applications development, we'll take a look at our "road ahead." This chapter provides an overview of what is covered in this book, and why it's covered in the order that we will cover it in.

You will see the logical progression throughout the book of how each chapter builds on the previous ones. We'll move from setting up the Eclipse IDE in Chapter 3, to learning how Android works in Chapters 4 and 5, to adding exciting visuals and user interfaces (UIs) in Chapters 6 through 8, to adding interactivity and complexity in Chapters 9 through 11. The final chapter inspires you to keep learning about the more advanced features of the Android platform, as it continues to expand to encompass applications development for emerging consumer electronics platforms such as interactive television sets (iTVs), tablets, and e-book readers.

Your Android Development IDE

In Chapter 1, you downloaded the Java SE, Eclipse, and Android SDK packages you need to build an applications development environment for creating Android applications. In Chapter 3, you'll learn how to set up these tools as a cohesive Android development environment, and then you'll use this development environment throughout the rest of the book to create applications, or "apps." You'll do this by creating, step-by-step, from scratch, the very latest Android IDE out there—right on your very own development workstation.

Note that the latter part of this process must be done while online, so be sure to have your Internet connection active and firing on all cylinders. We'll be connecting in real time, via Google's Android developers website, to the latest Android application development tools, plug-ins, drivers, and documentation. We'll even set you up with some other related new media tools such as the new GIMP 2.8.2 Digital Imaging software.

Although it might seem to you that the setup of Java SE, Eclipse IDE, Android's SDK, and an Android Virtual Device (an emulator that mimics the behavior of a real Android smartphone or tablet) is a topic too trivial for an entire chapter, this task is actually one of the most critical in this book. If your Android IDE does not work 100% perfectly, your code will not work 100% perfectly. In fact, without a robust and properly configured IDE, you may not be able to develop any code at all!

The Eclipse IDE is a sophisticated programming environment that features code highlighting, device emulation, logic tracing, debugging, and a plethora of other advanced features. Figure 2-1 shows an example of working in Eclipse, and Figure 2-2 shows an Android Virtual Device in action.

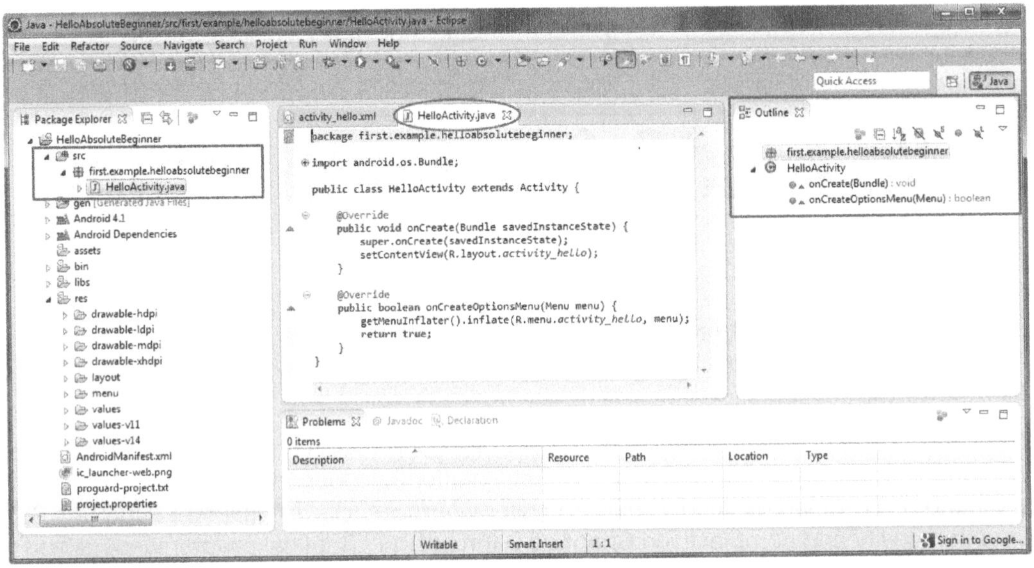

Figure 2-1. The Eclipse IDE

Note An *Android Virtual Device* is a software-based emulator that mimics the behavior of a real Android smartphone or tablet, as shown in Figure 2-2.

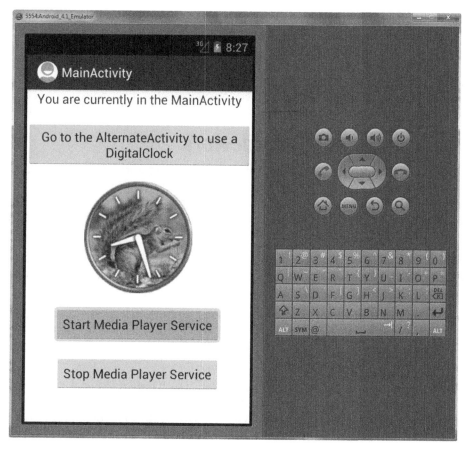

Figure 2-2. *An Android 4.1 Virtual Device (AVD) in action*

In Chapter 3, you will learn how to customize the Eclipse Juno 4.2.1 for Java EE IDE with Android plug-ins, which will morph the Eclipse IDE tool into one that is tailored to the particular needs of an Android developer like yourself. As you will see, setting up the Eclipse Juno 4.2.1 for Java EE IDE for your specific Android development goals is not a trivial undertaking by any means.

Java, XML, and How Android Works

As you'll learn in Chapter 4, an Android application is "stratified." Its functionality is spelled out via Java code, its design via XML markup, and its privileges via the Android Manifest XML file in a way that is truly unique, modular, and powerful. This modularity adds a great deal of extensibility, or development flexibility, to applications.

Android makes heavy use of an XML-based markup language to define the basic component design of an application, especially its visual and user interface components. XML "markup" is not technically code, but rather consists of tags, similar to the HTML tags that web developers use to format their online documents. XML is used in Android to define everything from UIs to animation to data access, and even programmatic constructs such as Java object definitions and parameter configurations.

XML markup tags are easier for beginners to comprehend than a complex programming language like Java. For this reason, you'll use XML throughout this book whenever possible, as Google recommends. Here, you'll get a basic beginning knowledge of Android application development, yet this will still give you the ability to make your apps look very elegant and professional. I call it getting the maximum return on your investment, and XML makes this possible for the absolute beginner, and thus we will leverage it wherever and whenever possible within this book.

The Android Application Framework

By the time you reach Chapter 5, you'll have built a rock-solid integrated Android application software development environment. You also will have acquired a basic understanding of the components that make up an application development project (images, text, layout, buttons, code, audio, video, animation, XML, etc.), built your very first Android application, and run it in the AVD emulator as an Android 4.1 app.

In Chapter 5, you'll learn the unique lingo of Android application design—that is, what the various components of an Android application are called, and some background regarding how the Java programming language works.

I'll outline how Java programming logic or code and XML, along with any new media resources, are compiled, compressed, and bundled into Android's signature *.apk* file type (APK stands for *Android PacKage*), and how the various Android application components "talk" to each other inside your application.

Chapter 5 also provides an overview of Android *activities*, which define the user experience on the screen, and explains how they operate. You'll learn about Android *services* as well, which run in the background, separate from the application's activities, and provide the user with advanced functions through the UI.

You'll also take an initial look at *broadcast receivers,* which alert an Android application to events of interest, such as the activation of a camera on an Android device, or an incoming phone call. In fact, your app can even send out its own broadcasts, if there is some reason to let other applications know of a change in state in one of your application's data constructs.

The chapter finishes up with a look at *content providers*, which are often databases filled with information, such as a contact list, that applications may want to access to provide functionality of their own. Android ships with a number of preconfigured content providers, and you can also write your own.

Screen Layout Design

By Chapter 6, you will have a better idea of how the Android operating system works internally, and how it wants to see applications put together. You'll be ready to design visual graphics, user interfaces (UI), and ultimately user experiences for your Android applications.

You'll do all of this using screen constructs called *views* and *view groups* (grouped views) which are flexible *layout* containers, which can be nested inside each other to create any custom UI for your application needs.

Chapter 6 explains how the display screen—the way most users interact with an Android application—is handled in Android, using a mixture of Java code and XML markup that controls the hierarchy of View and ViewGroup objects and Layout containers. You can also "extend" these Java classes by adding your own custom code to create your own custom View objects and Layout containers, when you need a more complex design. These ViewGroup layout containers ultimately hold the other visual and UI content in your application in its proper place, and thus are the foundation of your application design. You'll want to learn these screen view and layout concepts thoroughly, as they are core concepts to implementing everything else that Android can do. After all, without a proper user interface, your software functionality cannot be accessed by your end-users in the first place!

You'll revisit XML yet again in Chapter 6, and learn how it allows you to define complex screen layouts and UI designs *without writing a single line of Java code*. You'll learn about the different types of layout containers, and how each can be useful in different UI design scenarios, and even code a really cool application that is written almost completely with XML (eXtensible markup language).

User Interface Design

In Chapter 7, we'll start building usable UI designs, using the XML foundation of the previous chapters, via your screen layout and view controls, and Eclipse's powerful Graphical Layout Editor.

We'll cover the primary or mainstream screen resolutions for you to design UIs for Android, and which options you have for providing extra-high-, high-, medium-, and low-resolution graphics that allow Android to fit your application to each common device screen size and device type, such as smartphone, tablet, e-reader, or iTV. We'll also cover the creation of standardized Android icons for use in your UI designs for each of these primary four screen densities.

Android has a large number of UI elements, such as buttons, text fields, radio buttons, check boxes, menus, alert dialogs, and all of those familiar controls that allow users to interface with application software functions. These items can be implemented both in Java as well as in XML.

In Chapter 7, we'll again design and code another usable Android application. We'll design views, layouts, and UI elements as well as attaching their XML design elements to Java code that performs some simple functions when the UI elements are used by the application's users.

We'll look at the differences between option menus and context-sensitive menus as well as submenus for both of these types of menu constructs. We'll also review different types of dialog boxes such as alert dialogs, progress dialogs, and dialogs for picking dates and times.

Graphics and Animation Design

In Chapter 8, we'll start adding application new media elements through images and animation. These new media elements are key to making your application look great across all Android devices.

The Android smartphone Active-Matrix Organic Light-Emitting Diode (AMOLED) half-size video graphics array (HVGA) and the wide video graphics array (WVGA) screens on current Android tablet and e-reader products are impressive enough these days to allow some amazing experiences to be created, so this is where it starts to get interesting, as far as the application visuals are concerned.

In Chapter 8, we'll explore the following

- How to use bitmap images in Android applications.

- How to animate bitmaps and vectors to create some pretty realistic effects.

- The different screen sizes and how to create icons and graphics that scale between widely varying screen resolutions.

- The concept of an alpha channel that allows transparency, which allows image compositing to be accomplished in Android.

- Basic color theory and imaging concepts, and how to optimize image quality with the smallest data footprint.

- How Android allows you to control images directly.

- How to cross-fade two images to create powerful image transition effects.

Interactivity

In Chapter 9, we'll talk about adding interactivity to your applications, so that they respond to user input and actually do something useful. You will do this by handling UI *events*. We'll look at the most efficient way of handling events that are triggered by your users using the UI elements (Views) that are attached to the ViewGroups (UI layout containers) that you have defined within your XML files.

The following topics are covered:

- *Event listeners* that execute the proper code in response to an event that is triggered when a UI element is used by the user (e.g., you can run some code when a user touches a UI element, or presses a key on the keyboard).

- Default event handlers that allow you to build event handling right into your UI elements.

- Touch mode and navigation via the directional keys and the trackball and the differences between these, mainly having to do with a concept called *focus.*

- How focus movement is handled in Android.

- How the operation of focus in Android can be controlled via Java code.

- How focus preferences can be set in your XML files.

Content Providers

In Chapter 10, we'll be ready to get into the complexity of accessing data structures and Android *content providers*. These content providers allow you to access databases of system information that are available through the Android operating system as well as your own databases of information.

Content providers are the primary method Android provides for sharing stored data across applications, which is why they are important enough to merit their own chapter. We'll take a close look at the features of Android that allow you to query data regarding items common to the Android platform such as images, video, audio, and contacts.

In addition, you can create your own content providers or add data to an existing one. You'll see how to create a *content resolver* so that you can interface with whichever content providers you choose (and for which you have permissions to access).

You'll learn about how content providers expose their data via data models similar to SQL databases, and about how to use cursors to traverse the Android SQLite databases in various ways.

Finally, we'll investigate URI objects, and how to use them to identify and access data sets. Each set of data in the database will have its own uniform resource identifier (URI), which is similar to an HTTP URL.

Intents and Intent Filters

In Chapter 11, we are going to tackle one of the more complex concepts in the Android development environment: intents. *Intents* are asynchronous messages (members of the Intents class) that travel between Android's activities, services, and broadcast receiver components. *Asynchronous* means they are not synchronized; that is, the messages can be sent and received independently (not in sync, but without any pattern or order) from each other.

Using intents allows you to take your current Android applications to an entirely new level of complexity. Prior to this chapter, you'll have added functionality to your application by accessing the cool functions that Android provides. But all easy things must come to an end, so they say.

Armed with intents (no pun intended), you can create advanced programming logic of your own that ties together everything you have learned in the previous chapters. This allows for far more powerful and useful programming constructs, and takes you from an absolute beginner to an intermediate level.

You'll learn how to spawn Intent objects that can carry highly customized messages back and forth between your Android UI (activities) and your programming logic (services), for instance, as well as to and from broadcast receiver components.

We'll also look at *intent resolution* and *intent filters*. These allow you to filter out events that your apps do not need to be concerned with, allowing you to optimize the processing of internal communications.

The Future of Android

In the final chapter, I expose you to all of those fascinating areas within the Android development environment that we did not have the bandwidth to cover in this book, as well as to some troubleshooting techniques. There may be a lot of unfamiliar names and acronyms in this chapter, but that's the nature of the future of Android.

The 3D engine inside of Android is called OpenGL ES 2.0, and OpenGL ES 3.0 is right around the corner as well. You'll see how it allows you to create amazing real-time rendered 3D games and applications. And I'll give you some great resources to find out more about this powerful 3D engine.

The SQLite database exists right inside the Android operating system, in fact, it has its own library of classes. We'll uncover the power it offers in allowing client-side databases to be created and used as content providers inside your applications.

Smartphone hardware such as the high-definition camera, GPS, accelerometer, touchscreen, and microphone can be used to capture and digitize real-world events around us as images, audio, and gestures, and turn them into data that can be used inside your applications. Computer programming has never been so powerful and so highly innovation oriented.

Inter-Android communication is another hot area, especially because Android devices can be used as wireless hubs, giving access to many. We will look at Android's integrated Bluetooth and NFC APIs, which allow Android applications to wirelessly connect with any Android device nearby, and even provide for multiple connections, or allow applications to talk to each other between Android hardware devices such as iTVs, Smartphones, Tablets, and e-Readers.

Have you seen that TV commercial where the Android users touch phones to transfer files? This is Inter-Android Communication APIs at work.

We'll cover the concept of creating app *widgets*, or miniature applications that can be embedded in other applications (think: the Android home screen) and receive real-time updates (for widgets like clocks, radios, and weather stations).

Finally, we'll consider the popular area of locations and maps using the Android location package and Google Maps as an external data library. These tools are valuable for Android application development, due to the mobile nature of the smartphone, tablet, and e-readers, and the fact that most have a built-in GPS.

Summary

As you can see from this chapter, this book will take you on a wild journey through the various parts and components of the Android operating environment—from UI design, to new media assets, to database access, to more complicated background services and interapplication messaging. We'll be dealing with adding some pretty cool elements to Android applications, mainly by leveraging the power of "design via XML" and many of Android's powerful built-in features.

In the next chapter, you'll build an Eclipse-based Android IDE using the open source applications development software packages that you downloaded at the end of Chapter 1. After that, you'll learn about how the Android development environment is modularized as well as how to set it up to create Android applications using this diverse mobile operating system. You'll also get some new media related software packages set-up that you can use to take your Android development to an entirely different (visual) level, some of which are actually used in this book.

Enough excitement and anticipation! Let's get right into turning your workstation into an Android app development machine!

Chapter 3

Setting Up Your Android Development Environment

It's time to get your hands dirty. In this chapter, starting from scratch, you'll equip a computer system to develop Android applications. You'll first install Oracle's (formerly Sun's) Java 6 SE JDK and the Java 6 Runtime Environment, then the Eclipse for Java EE IDE, and finally the Android SDK, the tool set that provides Eclipse with the tools you'll need to create Android apps. Sound convoluted? It is. After all, this is high-end software development, remember. What these Software Development Kits (SDK) are, and how exactly they relate to each other will become evident as you proceed through this chapter.

Once the installation process is complete, you'll finish up by fine-tuning your Android Development environment within Eclipse to include smartphone and tablet emulators, which let you test your app with a representation of an Android phone or tablet on your workstation. You'll also have USB driver support, which makes it possible for you to test your applications on a real-live Android smartphone or tablet. With these tools in place, you'll be ready to rock and roll, and you can begin to explore exactly how Android does things.

Installing Java, Eclipse, and Android

If you have not downloaded the required software as described in Chapter 1, you will need to do that before proceeding, so those packages are ready to install. Here, we will walk through installing Java 6 SE and the Java 6 JRE, Eclipse Juno 4.2 for Java EE, which is the IDE that is currently best suited for the Android SDK, the Android SDK itself, and the Android Development Tools (ADT). For the examples in this chapter (and book), we will install the software using 32-bit versions on a Windows 7 system, however you can also use Windows XP, Vista, or Windows 8, as long as you have them upgraded to their latest service pack versions. Android SDK is 32-bit, and looks for 32-bit Java 6 and 32-bit Eclipse on installation, but if you have a 64-bit workstation (as I currently do) don't worry a bit, as 64-bit workstations will run 32-bit software environments perfectly well. Because Android OS is currently 32-bit, we will develop for it using a 32-bit development environment, even if that development environment is running on top of a 64-bit operating system.

Note that Android 4.2 now supports a full 64-bit Android development environment, so we added a section at the end of this chapter covering that support via a new ADT Bundle installation that is now available on the Android Developer web site. Luckily, we were able to add this information before the book went to print!

Note   Versions of the Java 6 JDK and Runtime Environment, the Eclipse Juno Java EE IDE, the Android SDK, and the Android Eclipse plug-in are also available for Macintosh and Linux computers. The steps to install them are nearly identical to those described in this chapter, and you will have no problems following along. For more information, click on the "other platforms" link on the left just underneath the big blue "Download the SDK for Windows" button on the Android Download screenshot in Chapter 1. If you are using Linux or Macintosh computers, then the Big Blue Button should instead say "Download the SDK for Linux" or "Download the SDK for Macintosh" instead!

Java 6 SE and JRE: Your Foundation for Application Development

In Chapter 1, you downloaded the latest Java 6 JDK from the Oracle website, so the file *jdk-6u37-windows-i586.exe* (or a similarly named file with later version numbering) should be on your desktop (or in your My Documents/Downloads/Folder) and ready to install.

The installation includes the Java 6 Runtime Environment (JRE), which is the environment that allows Java programs such as Eclipse to run, or execute, under the Java runtime engine. Indeed, this is the reason it is called a *runtime*—it is the environment, or software process, that is active while a Java application is running. Java Applications or "Apps" can be said to run "on top of," or with the support of, this Java Runtime Environment. Note that each Java JDK has its own associated JRE, so be sure not to "mix and match" different Java revision SDKs (also known as JDKs) with other Java version JREs. JDK stands for: Java Software Development Kit, and thus saying JDK is the same as saying "Java SDK."

Oracle has made the installation of the Java 6 SE environment relatively painless. The installation package is itself a software program (an executable, or *.exe* file type) that will create the necessary folder structure on your hard disk drive and install all the Java 6 SDK files precisely where they need to go and where other software, such as the Eclipse for Java EE IDE, will be looking to find them.

Follow these steps to install the Java 6 SE SDK and its associated JRE:

1. Double-click the JDK 6 install icon on your desktop (or in whatever folder you downloaded it to) to launch the JDK 6 setup application; at the time of the writing of this book, the current version was Java 6u37, or the 37th update of Java revision 6. If your operating system asks if it is OK to run the installation software, tell it to go right ahead.

2. The next dialog tells you which files and features will be installed, and lets you turn off features that you do not wish to include. We are not going to touch anything in these set-up dialogs, so simply click Next to copy the more than 300MB of development files onto your hard drive, as shown in the installation screen sequence shown in Figure 3-1.

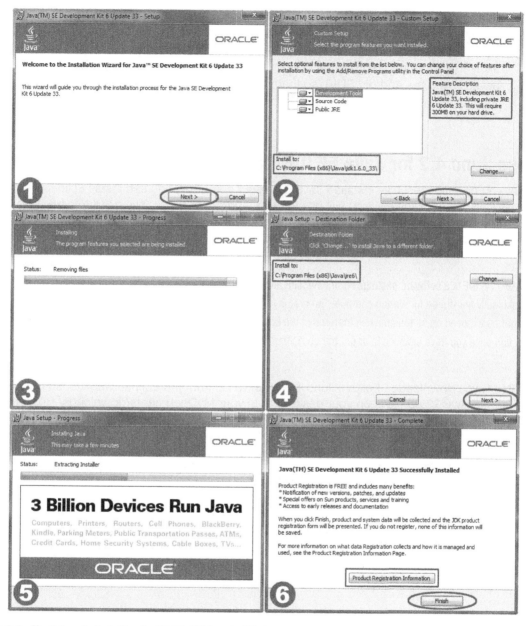

Figure 3-1. *Six dialogs for installing the 32-bit JDK 6 under Windows*

3. After installing the JDK 6 files, the installer will suggest a folder for the JRE, usually something like *C:/Program Files/Java/jre6.* Or if you have a 64-bit workstation, it will be C:/Program Files (x86)/Java/jre6. Simply hit the Next button to accept the default setting, as the JDK6 installer will find and use the correct folder names for you.

4. Once the JDK 6 and JRE 6 have finished installing, the final screen will let you know of a successful installation, and provide a button for you to register the product online if you are currently connected to the Internet. It is most likely a good idea to register the JDK 6 (as well as the Eclipse Juno 4.2 for Java EE and the Android SDK), so that you can receive updates regarding their future development progress.

Eclipse Juno 4.2 for Java EE IDE: The Development Environment

Now that you have successfully installed Java 6 on your computer, you can install Eclipse Juno 4.2 for Java EE, which is the IDE you will use for your Android projects. You need to have Java 6 installed before you install and run Eclipse Juno for Java EE, because Eclipse Juno 4.2 for Java EE is written in Java, and thus requires the Java Runtime (JRE), which is part of the JDK install.

> **Note**   An IDE is a software package somewhat like an advanced text editor, but with features specifically fine-tuned for writing computer programs rather than publishing text documents. If you want to get up to speed on all the amazing features of the Eclipse Juno IDE, run through the Help or Tutorials section once you have installed it, or get the book *Android Apps with Eclipse* from Apress.

In Chapter 1, you downloaded Eclipse Juno 4.2 for Java EE from the Eclipse website, so the *eclipse-jee-juno-win32.zip* file is on your desktop or in your MyDocuments/downloads/ folder and ready to install. Eclipse is a little harder to install than Java because it does not have an installation program (an *.exe* file, in the case of Windows), but instead has a folder structure of files inside a *.zip* archive. The trick is to extract this file structure properly onto your hard drive, so that Eclipse for Java EE can find the files that it needs, and so that they are in the folders where Eclipse and Android Development Tools (ADT) are going to look for them.

Follow these steps to install Eclipse for Java EE:

1. Right-click the *eclipse-jee-juno-win32.zip* file in your Downloads folder, and select the option "Extract All. . ." to launch the WinZip extractor, as shown in Figure 3-2 (notice that the Extract All menu selection is highlighted in light blue, as well as circled in red).

> **Tip**   If you don't have WinZip, a free alternative called PKZIP is available for Windows, Mac, and Linux. Simply Google "PKZIP" or "ZIP File Utility" and download the free version for your operating system type now. Got it? Good. If you have Windows Vista or Windows 7, you can also open *.zip* files natively, using the Windows Explorer application, so you don't need to download an extractor utility unless you want to.

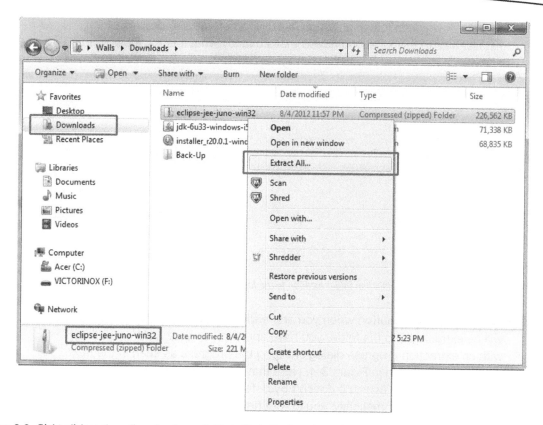

Figure 3-2. Right-click on the eclipse-jee-juno-win32.zip file in the Downloads folder to access the Extract All function

2. Once you click on the Extract All menu selection, you will need to edit the default location to extract the Eclipse file structure into, so that it is in the root of your *C:* disk drive, as shown in the second dialog in the middle of Figure 3-3. This will put Eclipse into a folder structure (defined in the *.zip* file) under *C:\eclipse-jee-juno-win32*, which is exactly where other software (in this case, the Android SDK) is going to look for (and find) it. Because the Eclipse Zip file is in your Downloads folder, the initial dialog for the Eclipse for Java EE IDE extraction will assume that that is where you want to install Eclipse (this is shown in the first dialog in Figure 3-3 in blue). So that it will be more prominent (and so you can find it at a later date) on your hard disk drive, we are going to move this up a few directory (folder) levels, by placing our editing cursor right before the word Eclipse, and backspacing over the "Users\YourName\Downloads\" part of the filename specifier. Once you are done, the folder name should read "C:/eclipse-jee-juno-win32" as it does in the second dialog shown in Figure 3-3. Note that if you wanted to leave the default install path (and thus install) Eclipse under your Downloads folder, that other software could still find it there, and that it would still function from that location, it's just not a best practice to install your software under

(in) your downloads folder, although it is a good practice to download the installer files to this location (indeed that's exactly what it is for: Downloads).

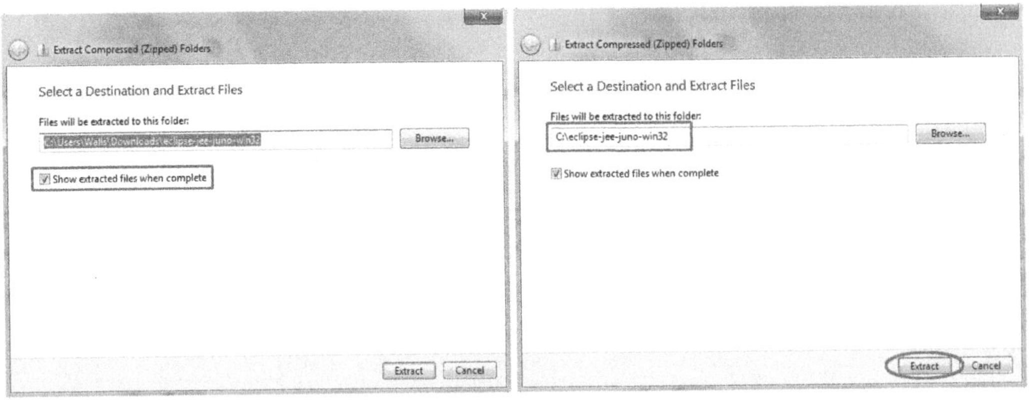

Figure 3-3. *Renaming your Eclipse installation folder location to the top of your C: Drive*

3. Click the "Extract" button when you are ready and Eclipse 4.2 for Java EE will be extracted into the folder you have specified on your hard disk drive, with an extraction progress dialog showing the progress as seen in the next dialog screen shown in Figure 3-4. Note that if this folder does not exist on your hard disk drive (which it doesn't by default) the extraction process will create it for you automatically, you do not have to create this folder before running this step!

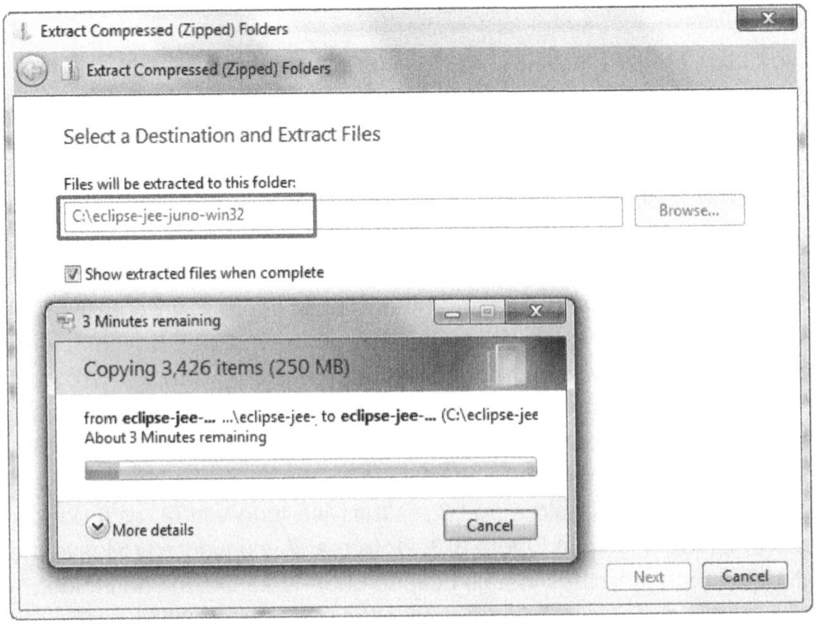

Figure 3-4. *Progress Dialog showing 3,426 items totaling 250 megabytes being installed on your HDD*

4. Next, go to the Windows Explorer application and click on the *c:\eclipse-jee-juno-win32* folder to view its file structure. Look for a folder called "eclipse" and in that folder a file called *eclipse.exe*, which is the actual Eclipse program "executable" (hence .exe) file that you will want to use to launch the Eclipse 4.2 for Java EE IDE each time you wish to use it to develop software.

5. Right-click on the *eclipse.exe* file and select the **Pin to Taskbar** option, as shown in Figure 3-5.

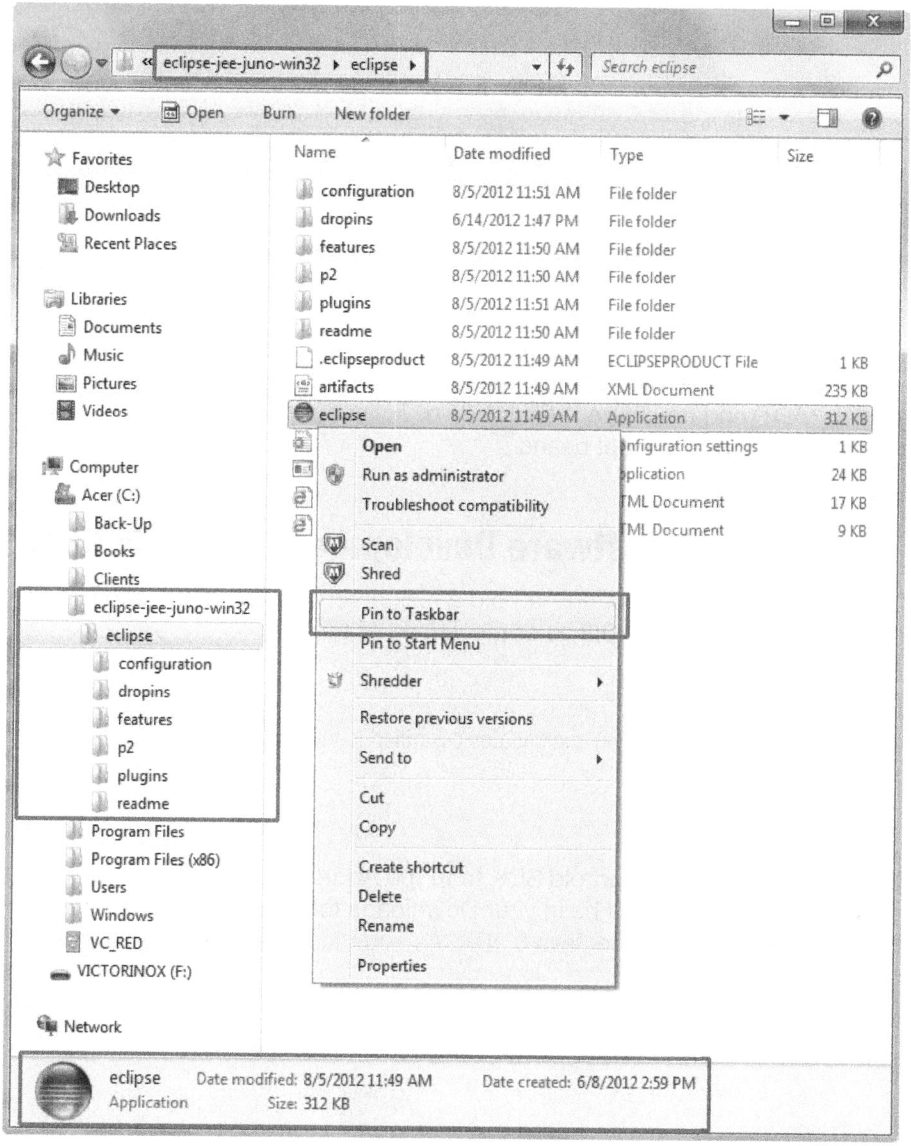

Figure 3-5. Creating a shortcut for Eclipse using the Windows 7 Pin to Taskbar Function via a right-click menu

6. Selecting the Pin to Taskbar option will install the *eclipse.exe* shortcut icon onto your Quick Launch bar, and *voila*, you now have an icon that requires only a single-click to launch the Eclipse 4.2 Java EE IDE, as shown in Figure 3-6.

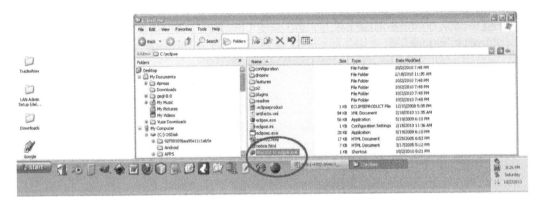

Figure 3-6. *Result of Pinning the Eclipse shortcut icon onto the Quick LaunchTaskbar in Windows 7*

Congratulations, you now have one of the most powerful open source IDE software packages ever written, installed on top of Java 6 SE, ready to launch at a moment's notice and use to develop Java or Android applications software. Now, all you need to do is install the Android SDK and Android Development Tools (ADT) and configure them inside of Eclipse, and you'll be ready to develop Android applications *ad infinitum*. Cool beans.

Android SDK: Android Software Development Kit for Eclipse

The last major step in putting together an Android development environment is to install the latest Android SDK (currently at version 20.0.3 as of the writing of this book).

> **Note**   To perform the SDK configuration and updates described in this chapter, you need to be connected to the Internet.

In Chapter 1, you downloaded the Android SDK from the Android website, so the file *installer_r20.0.3-windows.exe* should be in your Downloads folder and ready to install. This process is quite similar to the installation of the Java 6 JDK. As you did with Java 6, install the Android SDK now, as shown in Figure 3-7.

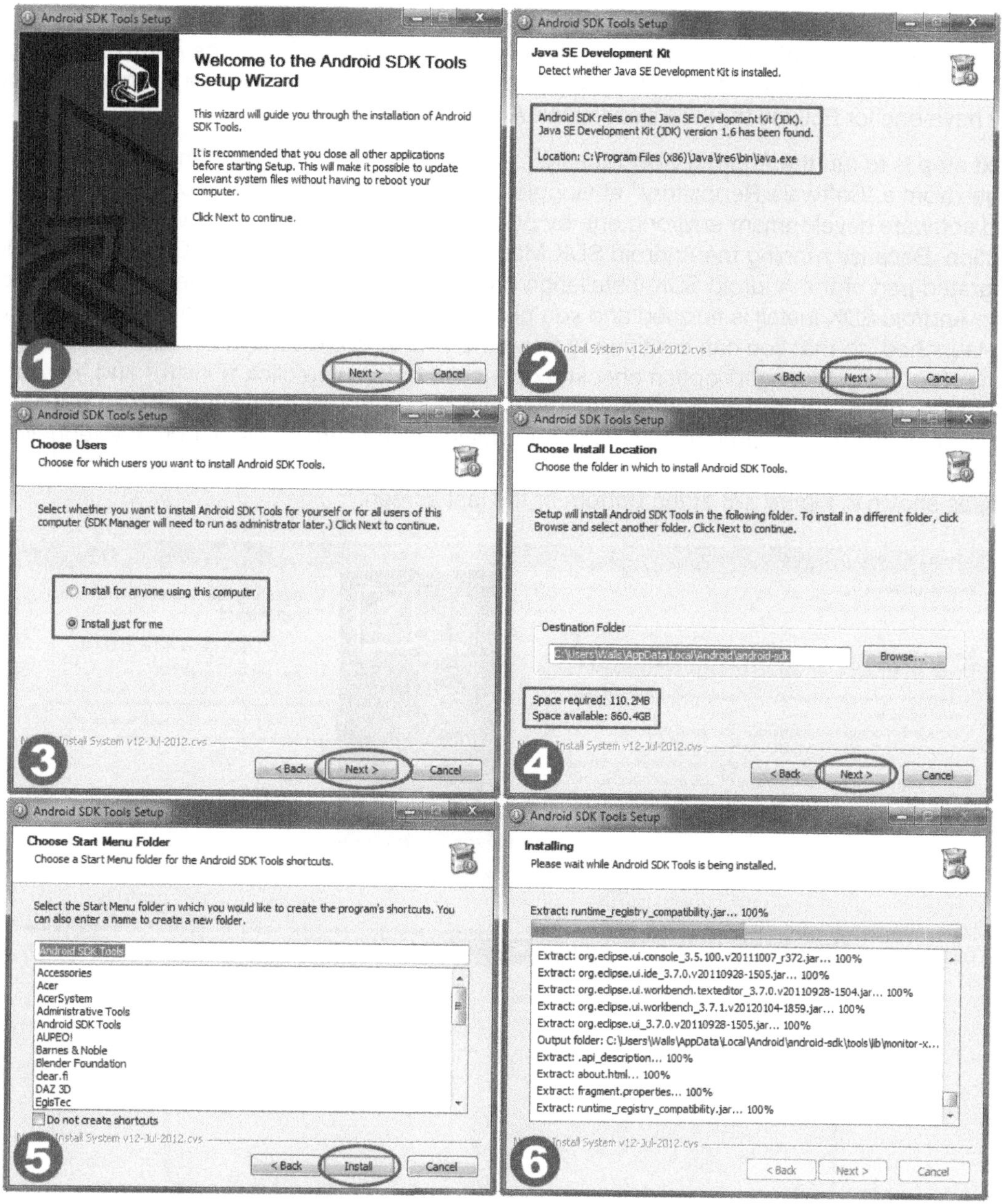

Figure 3-7. Installing the Android r20.0.3 SDK onto your hard disk drive

Notice that the SDK software installs into a Start Menu folder called *Android SDK Tools*. This is the folder where other software, such as Eclipse Juno 4.2 for Java EE, will look for the Android SDK, so it is best to use the default folder name that Google already has defined for Android inside the *.exe* installer file.

The Android SDK environment is now installed on your system. Because the Android Software Development Environment will run inside of the Eclipse 4.2 for Java EE IDE (the Android SDK needs to become an integrated part of Eclipse), you don't need to create a shortcut for it—because you already have one for Eclipse that will also launch Android development.

The next step is to run the Android SDK Manager, which pulls over additional Android SDK Packages from a "Software Repository" at Google. This will add even more functionality to your Android software development environment, by pulling additional SDK assets over your Internet connection. Because running the Android SDK Manager is such a critical step, Google has made it an integrated part of the Android SDK installation process. As you can see in the next screenshot, after the Android SDK install is finished and you click the "Finish" button, the Android SDK Manager is auto-launched, so that you can continue to fine-tune your Android SDK installation. Be sure to leave the "Start SDK Manager" option checkbox checked before you click "Finish," and the Android SDK Manager dialog will appear, showing that Android r20.0.3 is installed. Note also (at the bottom of the dialog, in the status bar) that it will look for additional software to install from the repository. You must be connected to the Internet for this process to occur, as the repositories are on Google's servers, as shown in Figure 3-8 at the bottom of the last screen.

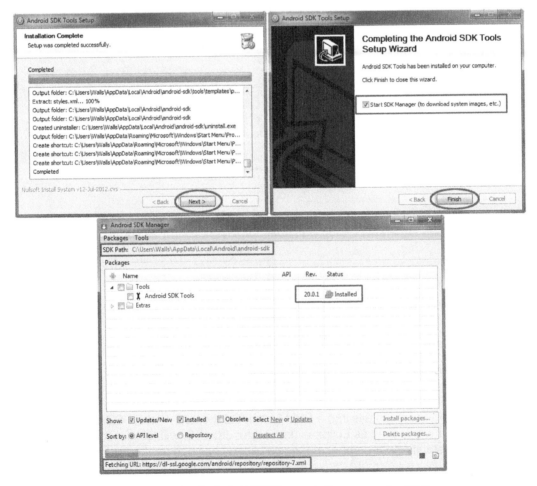

Figure 3-8. Ending the SDK install and starting the Android SDK Manager in the same work process

Once the Android SDK Manager has finished communicating with the Google Android Repositories, a screen will appear as shown in Figure 3-9 that lists the Android Packages and software application programming interface (API) versions that are not currently installed on your system. Because this is a fresh install, this would be all of the Android versions from 1.5 through 4.1. The screen, which should show up next, is shown in Figure 3-9 with the recommended latest Android "Jelly Bean" 4.1 API tools shown checked and ready for installation. Note at the bottom that the SDK Manager is finished talking to the Google Android Repositories. Also note that there are two boxes that I recommend (as does Google) that you also check, so that you have the Android SDK Platform Tools and the Android Support Library, which gives the 4.1 Jelly Bean API backwards compatibility with the previous APIs to a large extent (but not completely, according to Google).

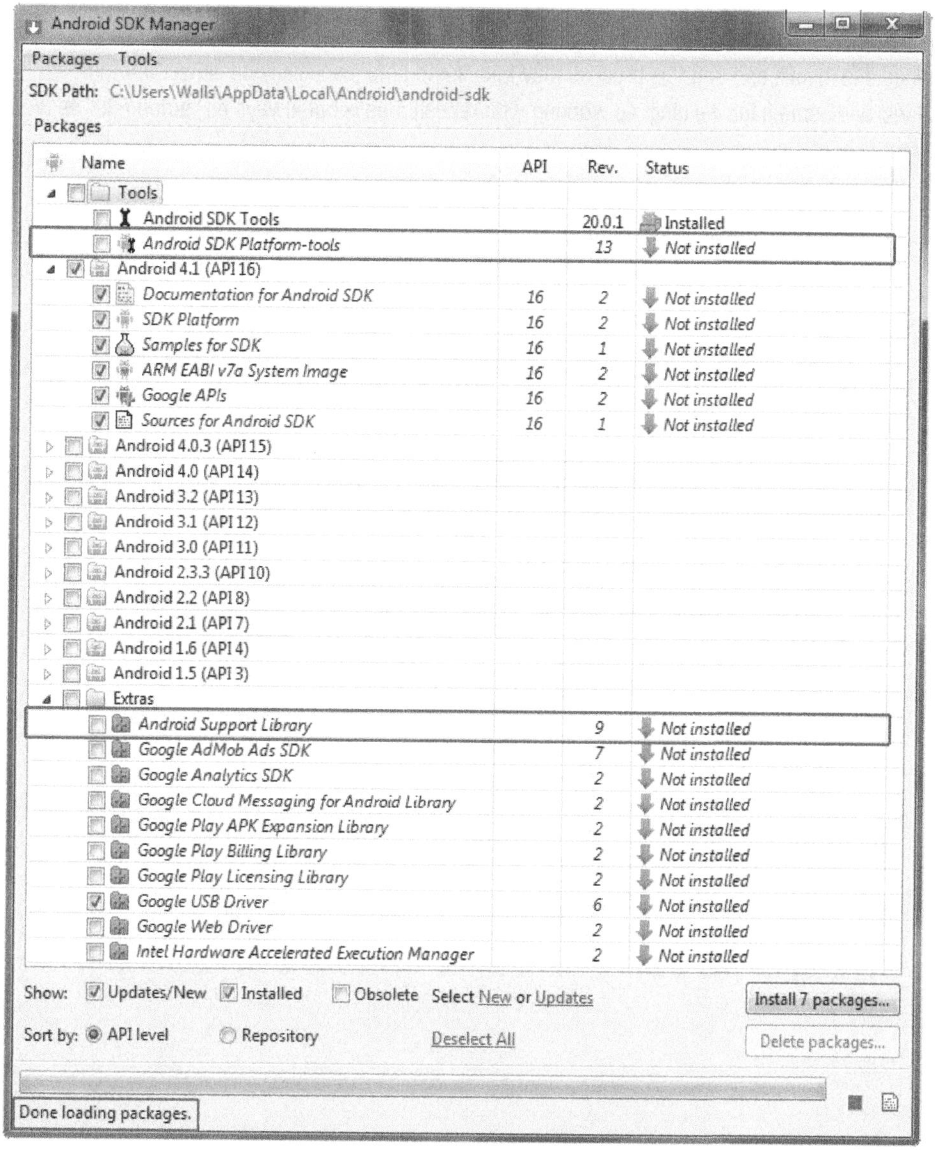

Figure 3-9. Selecting the unchecked SDK Platform Tools and Android Support Library options

Once these nine options are all checked and selected for installation, click the button at the bottom on the right that says "Install 9 Packages" and the Android 4.1 API Level 16 tools will be installed into your Eclipse IDE. Note that because I show you the two that are unchecked (that you need to check), the button in the screenshot in Figure 3-9 says: Install 7 Packages. Once you check the additional two packages, this will update to: Install 9 Packages.

If you want to install the API packages for any previous API versions of Android, there are ten prior API revisions, three through fifteen, that can also be checked for installation. This is shown on the next screen in Figure 3-10, and if you are going to develop apps for hardware devices that run and support earlier versions of the Android OS, you may wish to install these as well.

> **Note**   Beware that installing all of these APIs and documentation may represent gigabytes of data to download and install, and that this process may take some time (especially on slower Internet connections) and some hand-holding, as working with repositories is not always as "automatic" as we would like it to be!

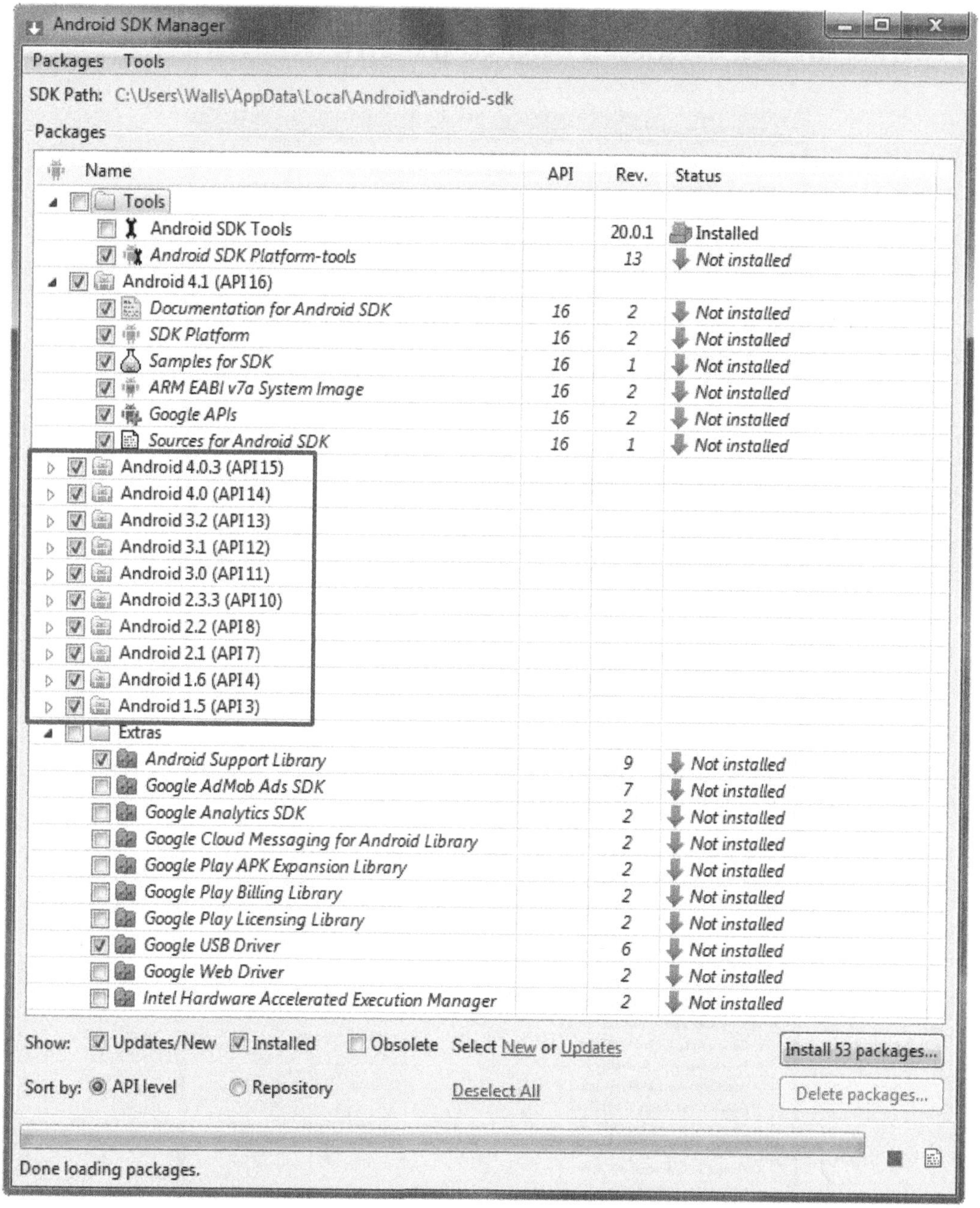

Figure 3-10. Selecting other Android APIs to install for the maximum cross-platform API development

Note that now that these other APIs are selected, that the Install Packages button says "Install 53 Packages," so each API level has an average of about 5 packages associated with it. I recommend that for now that you just install Android 4.1, but I wanted to show you how to install all of the Android OS Platform API versions, in case you had a fast connection and are fearless in general regarding software installation. In any event, once you click the Install Packages button, regardless of which API levels you have chosen to install, you will get one more screen that confirms which packages you wish to install. This screen is shown in Figure 3-11.

Figure 3-11. Selecting the "Accept All" option instructing that all packages be installed in Eclipse

At the bottom of this dialog, you will see a Radio Button option labeled "Select All," and once you select that, all of the packages in the list (53 in this case) will be enabled for download from the Google Android Development Software Repository. Then, once you click on the "Install" button, as shown circled in red, you will begin the download process, and add all of this additional Android OS functionality to the "base" Android SDK that you have installed already.

What you need to do next is show Eclipse 4.2 for Java EE where the Android SDK is located, so that Eclipse can make the Android SDK functionality an integrated part of the Eclipse IDE. This is done by installing the Android Development Tool plug-in for Eclipse, which we will do in the next section.

Android Development Tool: Android Tools for Eclipse

It's time to fire up Eclipse and add the Android Development Tool (ADT) plug-in to the IDE.

Follow these steps to perform the installation:

1. Click the Eclipse Quick Launch bar icon to start Eclipse.

2. Accept the default workspace location (it will be under your *C:\Users\ YourName\workspace* folder).

3. From the main Eclipse menu, select **Help ➤ Install New Software…,** as shown in Figure 3-12.

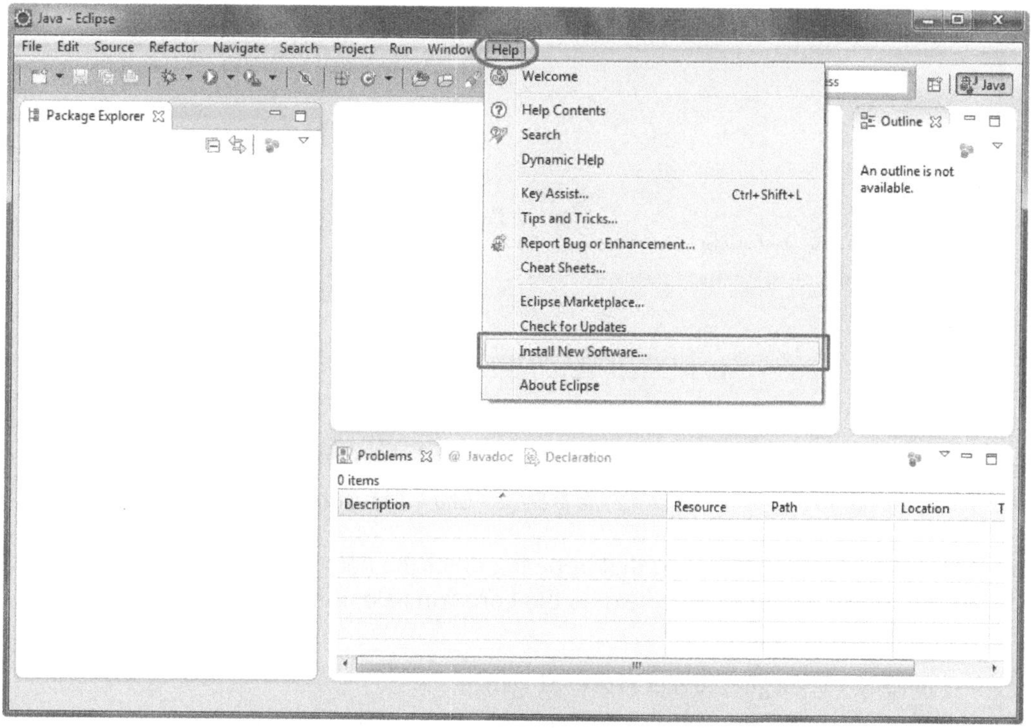

Figure 3-12. Selecting the Install New Software option on the Eclipse Help Menu

4. In the Install dialog that appears, click the Add button at the upper right, as shown in Figure 3-13.

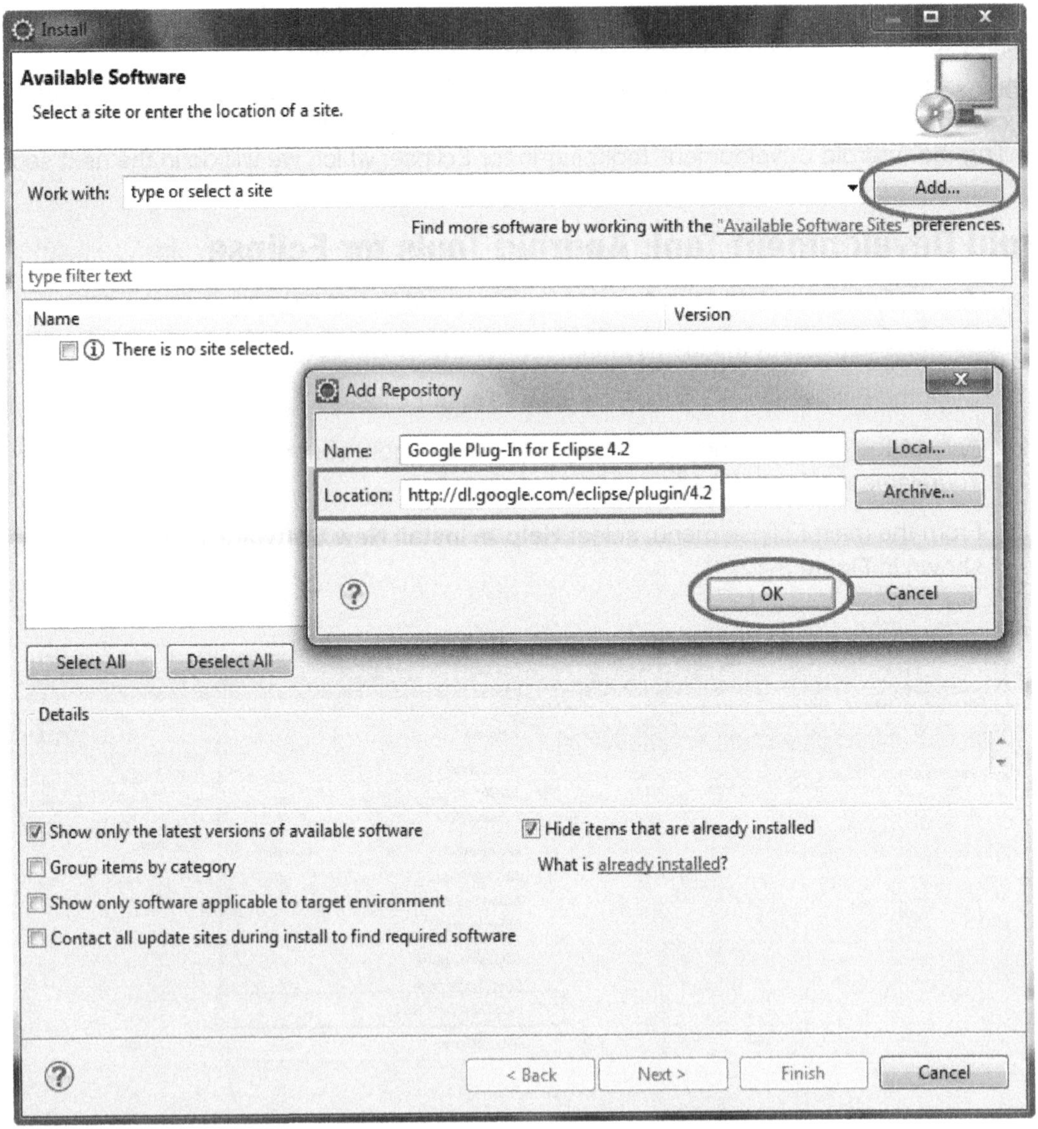

Figure 3-13. Adding the Google plug-in for Eclipse 4.2 site to Eclipse Juno 4.2 for Java EE

5. In the Add Repository dialog that appears, enter the name **Google Plug-In for Eclipse 4.2** in the Name field. In the Location field, enter the following, as shown In Figure 3-13:

    ▪ `http://dl.google.com/eclipse/plugin/4.2`

    Figure 3-13 shows the HTTP site address entered in the Add Repository dialog's Location field. Click OK to add the site.

6. Once you've added the new Google Eclipse 4.2 plug-in option, its name appears at the top of the Install dialog, and after a few moments, a hierarchy of Developer Tools options populates the center of the Install dialog. Select the first (highest) level, called Developer Tools (which will select them all), and the Google Plug-In for Eclipse (required) as shown in Figure 3-14. Then click Next to continue with the ADT installation. The plug-in proceeds to calculate installation requirements and dependencies for several seconds, so hang on!

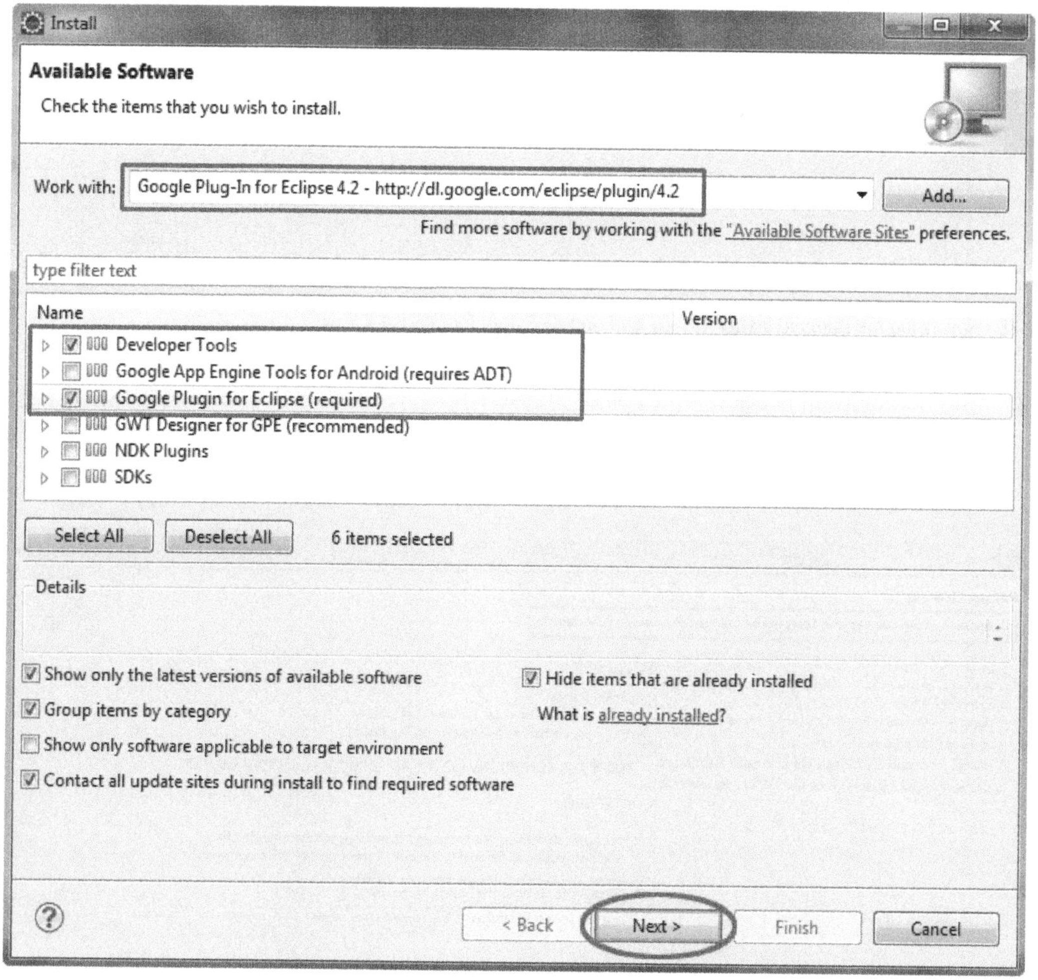

Figure 3-14. Installing Android Developer Tools and Google Plug-In for Eclipse 4.2 plug-ins in Eclipse

7. The next screen shown in Figure 3-15 lists the Android Development Tools, Android Dalvik Debug Monitor Server (DDMS, which is a debugging tool), Google Plug-In for Eclipse 4.2, and some other useful Android development utilities. Click Next to accept these items.

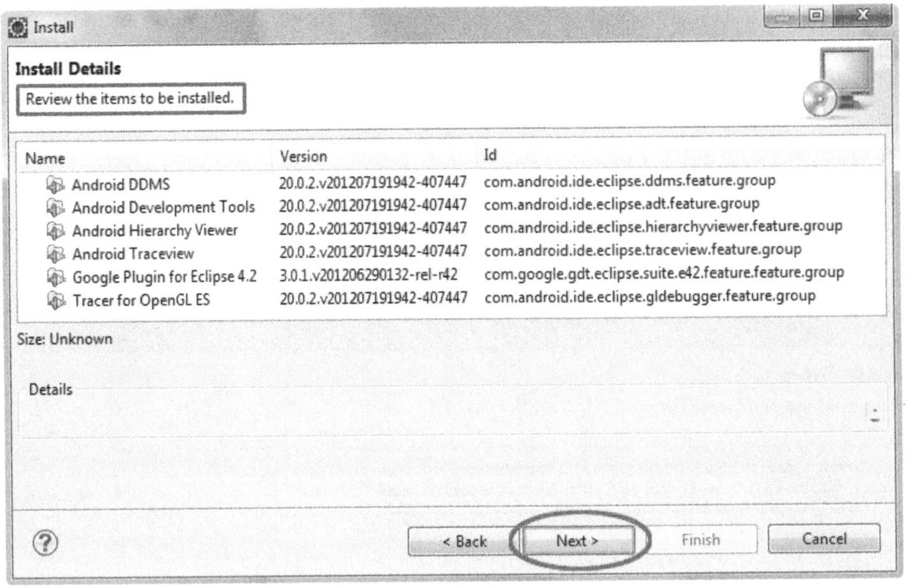

Figure 3-15. Reviewing the items to install for ADT and Google Plugin for Eclipse 4.2

8. The next screen is agreeing to all of the ADT and Related Software Licensing Agreements; select the "I Accept the Terms of the License Agreements" radio button, and then click Finish as shown in Figure 3-16.

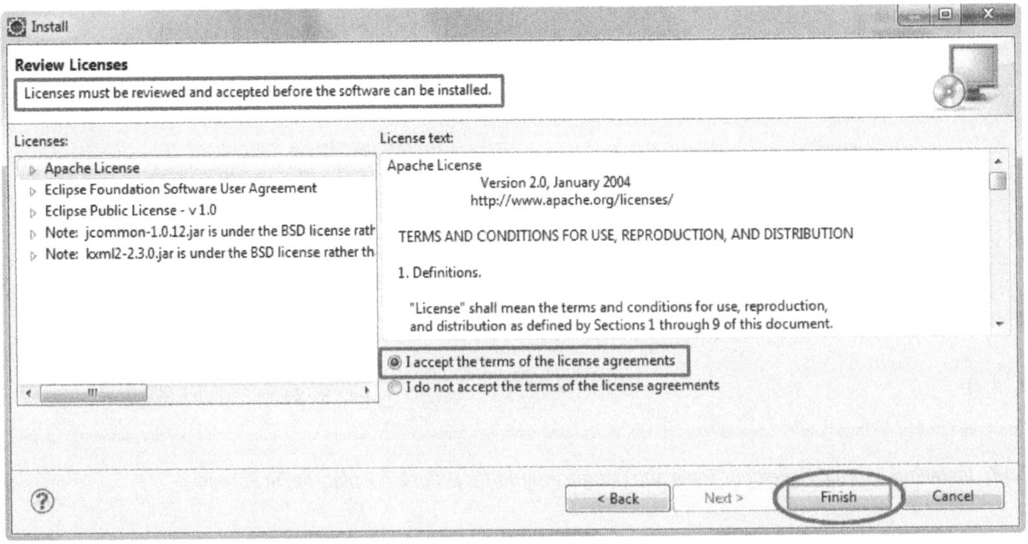

Figure 3-16. Approving the software licenses for the Android Developer Tools

9. The Android development environment will be installed and updated from the Google Android website. If a message appears asking you to approve an unsigned certificate, click OK to continue the installation, at which point you will see an installation progress screen like the one shown in Figure 3-17.

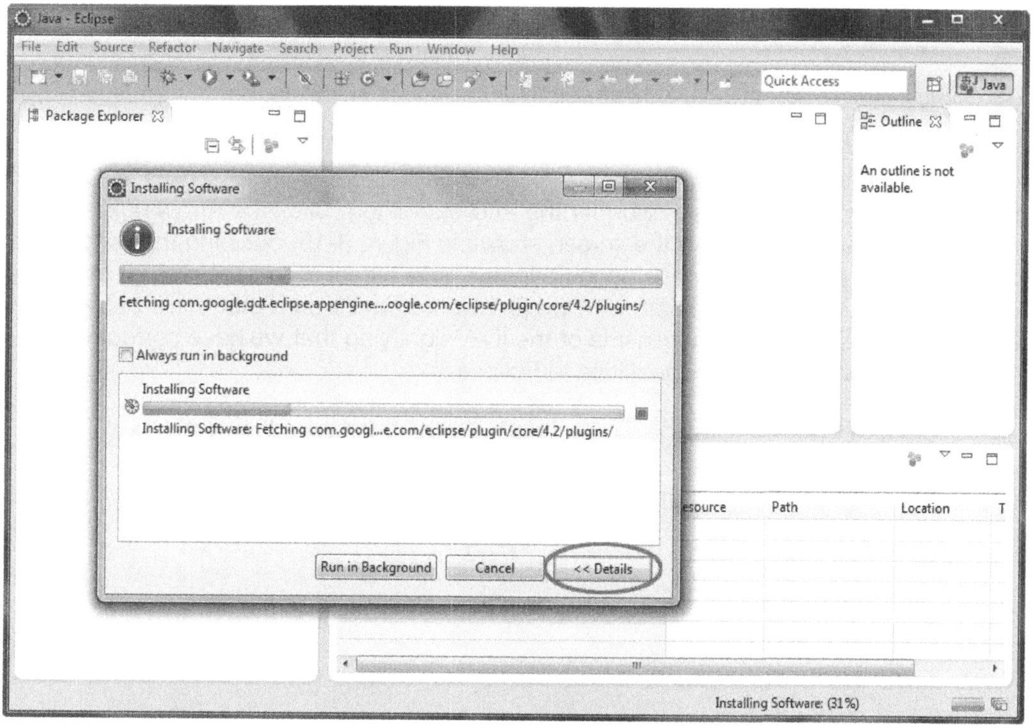

Figure 3-17. Software installation progress bars outlining software being installed via the repository

10. At this point the Android Development Tools and Google Eclipse 4.2 Plug-Ins will install as shown in Figure 3-17. If you want further installation files detail, use the Details button as shown in the screenshot (circled in red).

11. A dialog appears, asking you to restart Eclipse to allow the changes you have just made to be installed into memory, and thereby take effect in the IDE (which runs from system memory, not from your hard disk drive). Select Yes, as shown in Figure 3-18.

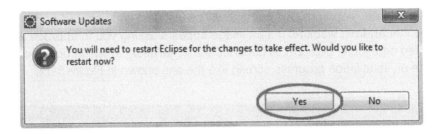

***Figure 3-18.** Opting to restart Eclipse to reload software installation changes into system memory*

To make sure the Android Development Environment is now actually installed correctly, once Eclipse restarts go to the File ➤ New ➤ Project… Menu Sequence, and you should see an Android Application Project Type listed (inside or under the Android folder). Click the Arrow next to the Android folder, and it should look like the screen shown in Figure 3-19, outlining the various types of Android Projects that you can now develop in Eclipse. Click Cancel to exit the dialog, as we are not going to develop an Android Application now, we just wanted to confirm that there was an Android folder filled with Android Project types inside of the IDE, signifying that we have correctly added Android Application Development capabilities to Eclipse.

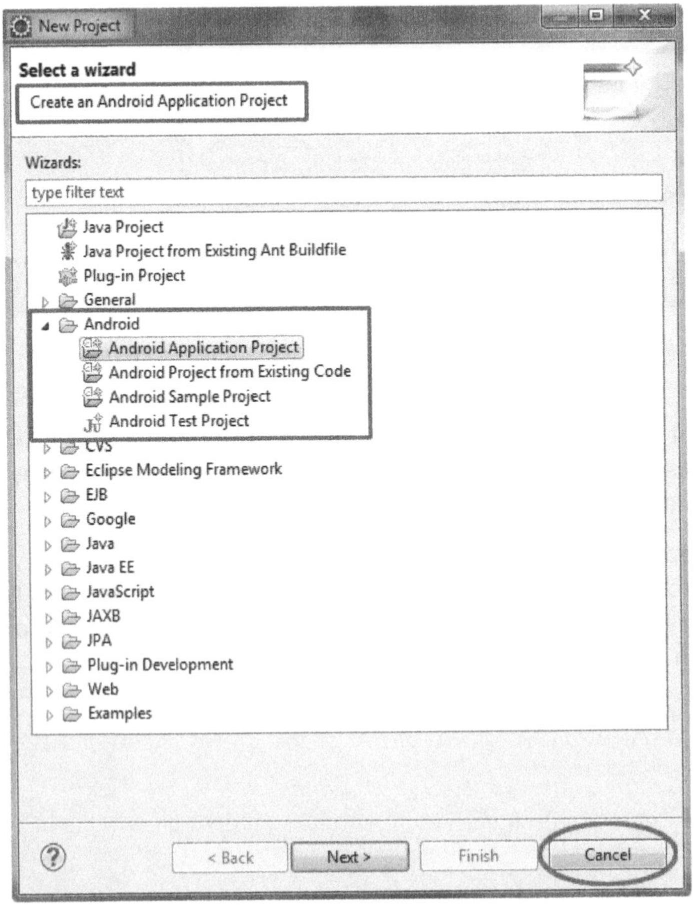

***Figure 3-19.** Testing to see if ADT is installed in Eclipse by seeing if the New Android Application Project is there*

Configuring the Android Environment Inside of Eclipse

Once Eclipse restarts and you confirm that you can now add new Android Application Projects, the final step is to configure the ADT plug-in, which should have already found your Android SDK installation. Let's check and make sure, so you can see how this is done. Follow these steps:

1. In Eclipse, select **Window ➤ Preferences**. Click the Android node on the left to select the Android Preferences option. A dialog shown in Figure 3-20 will pop-up, asking you to share your usage information with Google, so that they can improve their product. You can choose to send usage info (or not to) via a checkbox in this dialog, as shown below. Click on the Proceed button to continue.

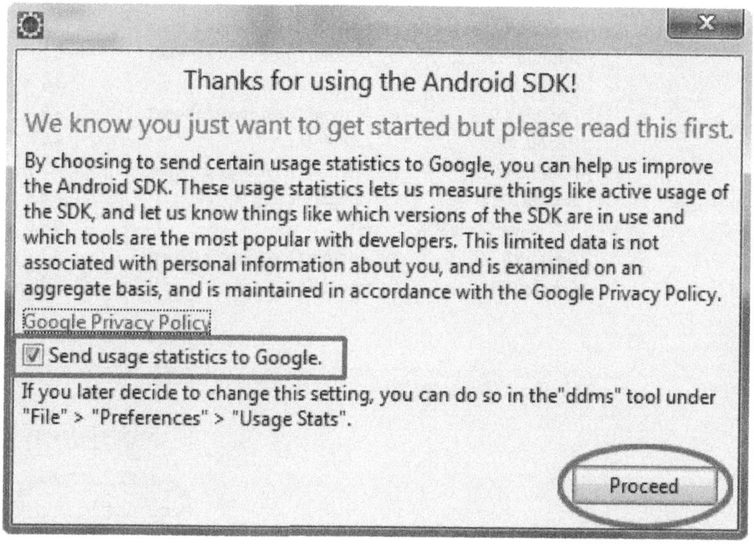

Figure 3-20. Sending your Android Development Tools usage statistics to Google

2. In the Preferences window, you will see that Eclipse has already found your Android SDK installation via the ADT plug-ins that you installed, as shown in Figure 3-21. It also shows the API versions that you added beyond Version 4.1, in my case, I added 2.3.3 and all of the 3.x and 4.x versions, as shown in the screenshot in Figure 3-21. Click on the Apply or the OK button, and the Android SDK will be updated as part of Eclipse (if it isn't already), meaning that the Android development environment within Eclipse 4.2 will be configured.

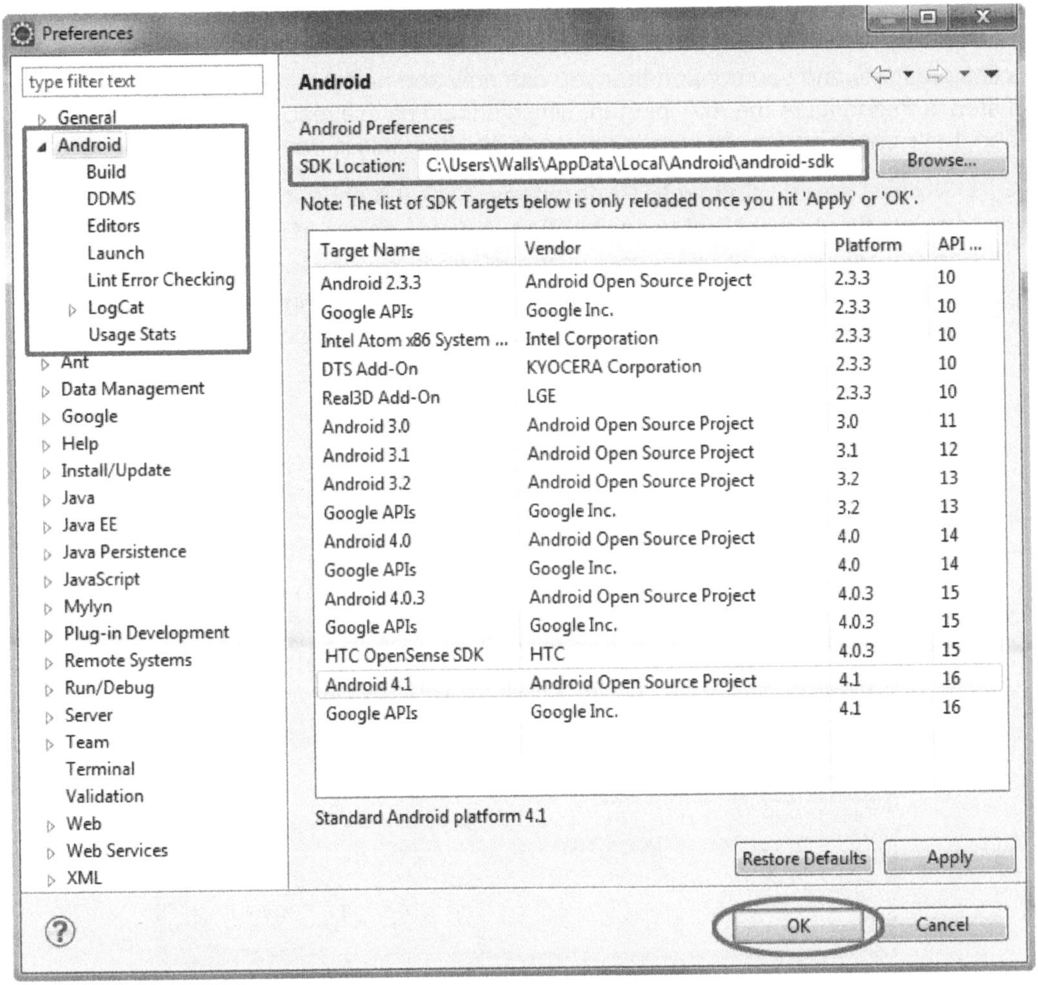

Figure 3-21. Viewing the Android Preferences dialog and installed SDK Targets and Android SDK location

Note   You do not need to restart Eclipse again for the Android SDK to become a part of it because all the SDK needs is to be referenced in Eclipse, in case any of the SDK tools need to be called (used) by Eclipse.

3.   Select **Help ➤ Check** for Updates just to make sure you have the very latest versions of everything, as shown in Figure 3-22.

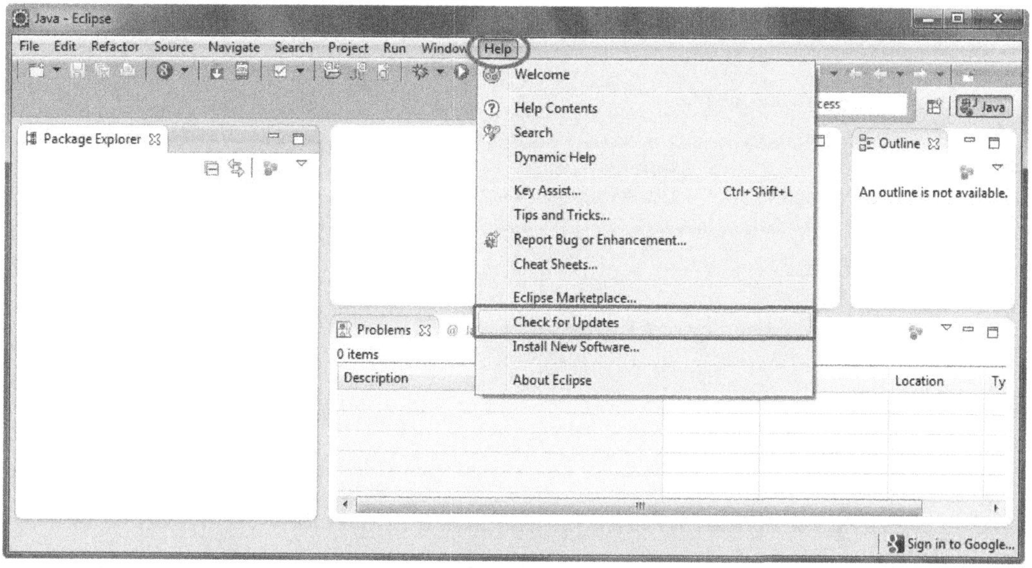

Figure 3-22. *Instructing Eclipse to check for any IDE updates to make sure we have the latest versions*

Your Android development environment will now check for updates to the Eclipse software to make sure that you have the most recent release available, as shown in Figure 3-23.

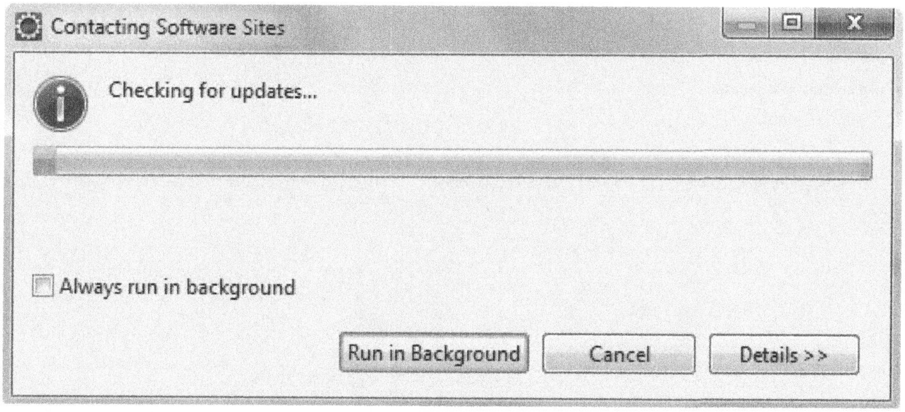

Figure 3-23. *Checking for any further updates for Eclipse that might be out there*

If the Check for Updates routine finds any updates, which it did in my installation, it will show a dialog called "Available Updates," and allow you to select which available updates you wish to install. In my case, there was a new version of the Google Plug-In for Eclipse 4.2, which is a critical component in the chain between Java ➤ Eclipse ➤ ADT, so I selected it for Installation, as shown in Figure 3-24.

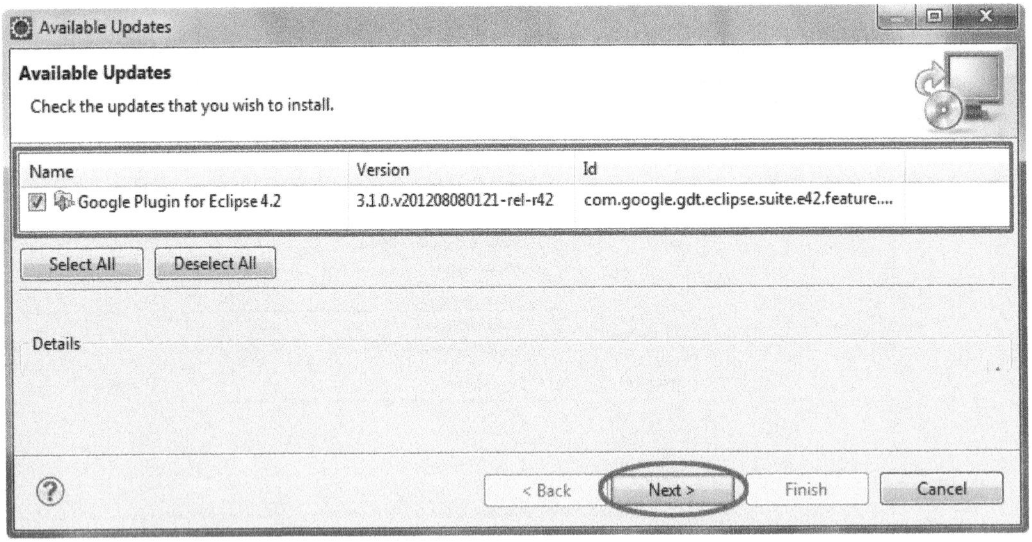

Figure 3-24. Selecting the latest available updates to install to make our environment as current as possible

Once you select the updates to install, and click on the Next button, you will get the Update Details dialog, as shown in Figure 3-25, which tells you the name, version, and repository location for the updates that you are about to install. Hit the Next button to proceed with the update process.

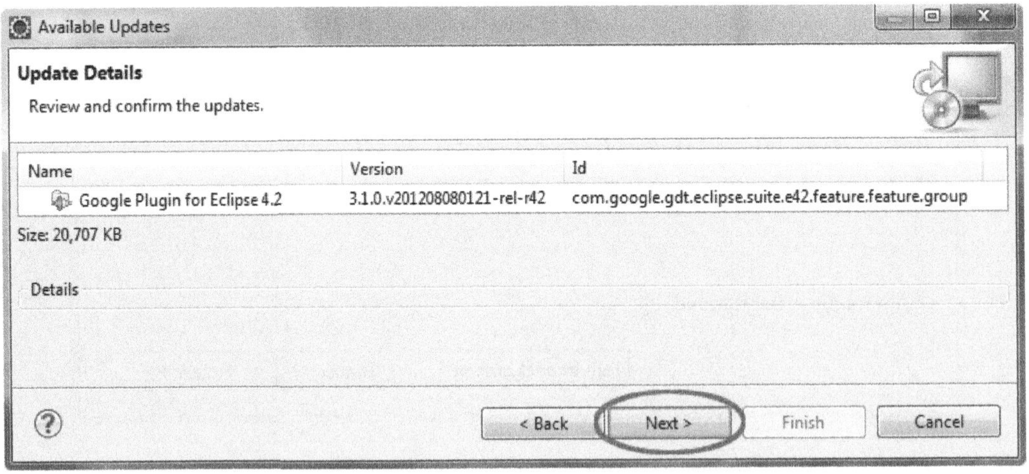

Figure 3-25. Reviewing and confirming updates to install

The next dialog Is the Licensing Review and Acceptance dialog shown in Figure 3-26, where you need to select the radio button that states that you accept the terms of the license agreement for the update that you are about to install. Once you review the license and agree to it, click on the Finish button, and updating process will begin.

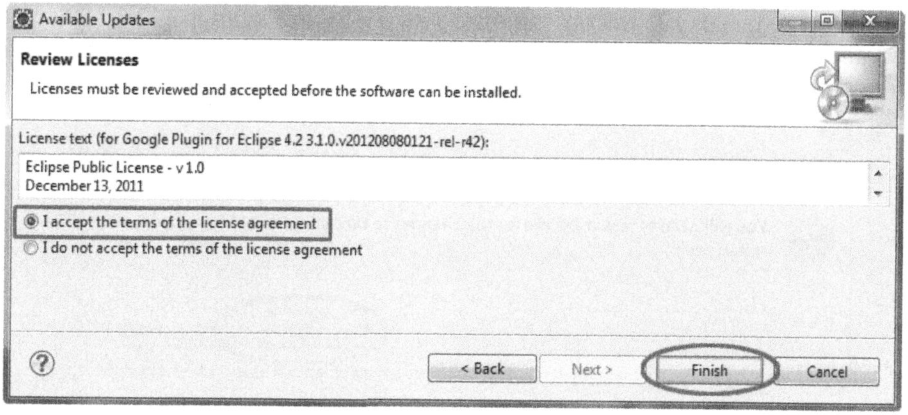

Figure 3-26. *Accepting the terms of the license agreement*

Figure 3-27 shows the Updating Progress dialog that you will see once you agree to the licensing terms.

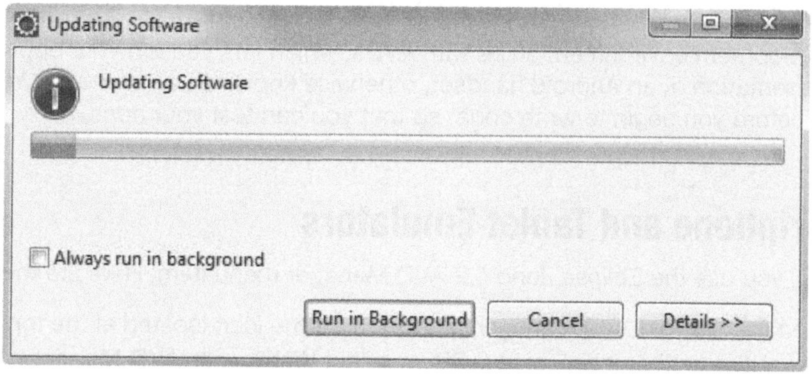

Figure 3-27. *Updating progress bar for software installation*

After the software update download process is complete, you will get a dialog as shown in Figure 3-28 that warns that you are about to install software that contains unsigned content. Click OK to proceed with the installation.

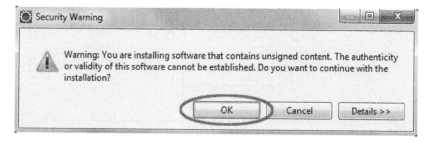

Figure 3-28. *Unsigned software installation warning*

Once the software is installed, you will get the dialog as shown in Figure 3-29 that tells you that for the newly updated version of Eclipse to be run (from system memory) that it must be restarted (to load the new updated code from your hard disk drive into system memory for use).

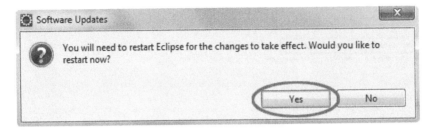

Figure 3-29. Restarting Eclipse to install the latest software updates into your system memory

Now that we have updated the Eclipse Juno 4.2 for Java EE to its latest version, it's time to set-up Android Virtual Devices (AVDs), so that we can test the applications that we write in this book.

Setting Up AVDs and Smartphone Connections

The Android development environment ships with AVDs, which lets you run your applications on a graphical representation of an Android handset, otherwise known as an *emulator*. You'll want to install one now, before you begin to write code, so that you can test your apps.

AVDs: Smartphone and Tablet Emulators

To install an AVD, you use the Eclipse Juno 4.2 AVD Manager menu item. Here are the steps:

1. To open the Android AVD Manager window, click the icon located at the top left of the Eclipse toolbar (see Figure 3-30) or select **Window ➤ AVD Manager**.

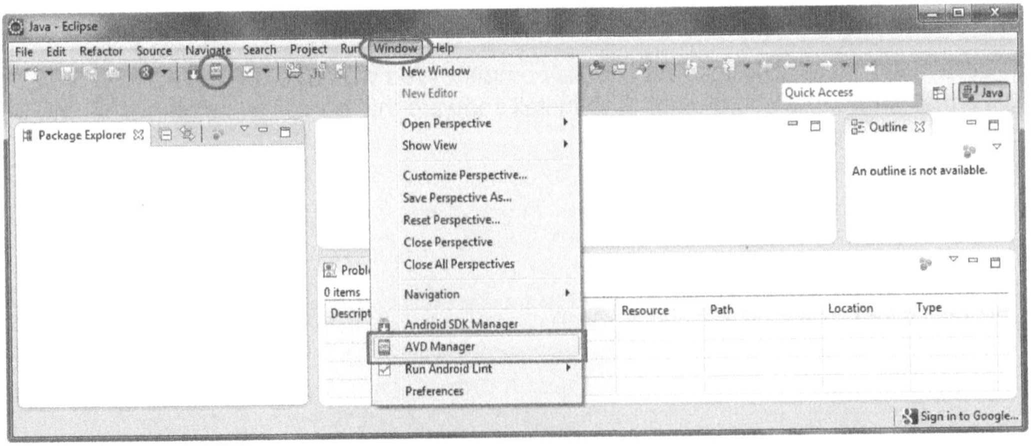

Figure 3-30. Starting the AVD Manager

2. In the Android AVD Manager window, select the New button (see Figure 3-31).

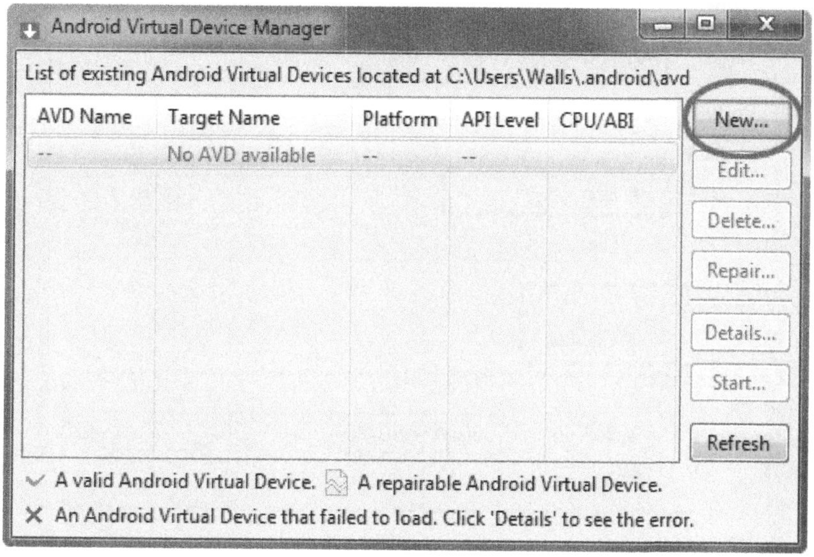

Figure 3-31. Creating a new AVD to test Android 4.1 compatibility in an Android 4.1 emulator

3. Fill in the Create new Android Virtual Device (AVD) dialog as follows:

    ▪ Enter a name for the emulator in the Name text box. I used the name
    Android_4.1_Emulator.

    ▪ From the Target drop-down menu, select an API. I chose the Android 4.1 -
    API Level 16 from the menu of all the APIs installed.

    ▪ In the SD Card section, set a memory card size for the SD card. I selected a
    size of 512MB (for the widest phone and tablet support).

    ▪ In the Skin section, choose a screen resolution for the device skin. I selected
    the default WVGA screen setting because my Android phone has an 800 ×
    480 resolution display. Most Androids smartphones and tablets out there
    use WVGA or higher resolution, so by choosing this option, you'll obtain the
    widest phone handset and tablet compatibility.

    ▪ Check the Snapshot Enabled Checkbox to allow the emulator to persist
    (remain) in memory between executions for faster emulator performance
    during development.

    Figure 3-32 shows the dialog I completed to create an Android 4.1 smartphone
    emulator. Click the Create AVD button after you've filled in the dialog.

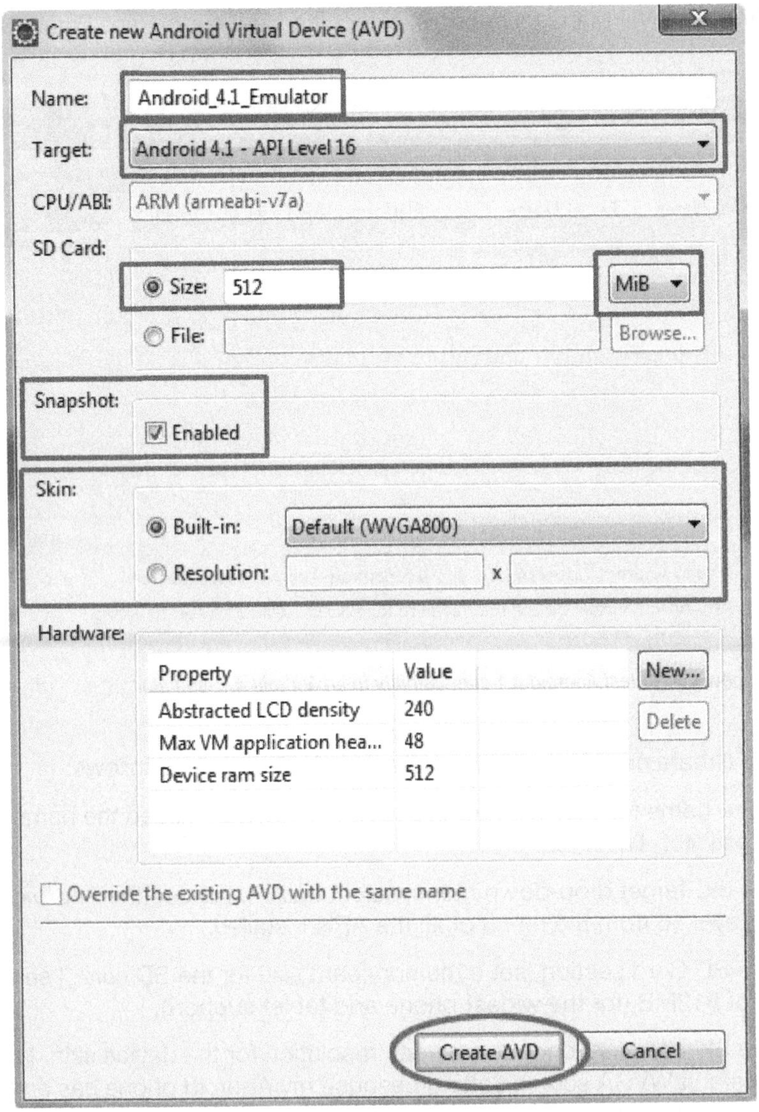

Figure 3-32. Creating the 4.1 emulator for testing our apps later on in the book

As you can see in Figure 3-33, the new virtual device is now listed in the Virtual Devices' section of the Android AVD Manager window. If you also are going to test applications on the other Android Platform versions that you have installed, go through this same process, and add these emulators as well at this time. Some more popular Android versions include 2.3.7, 3.2.6, and 4.0.4.

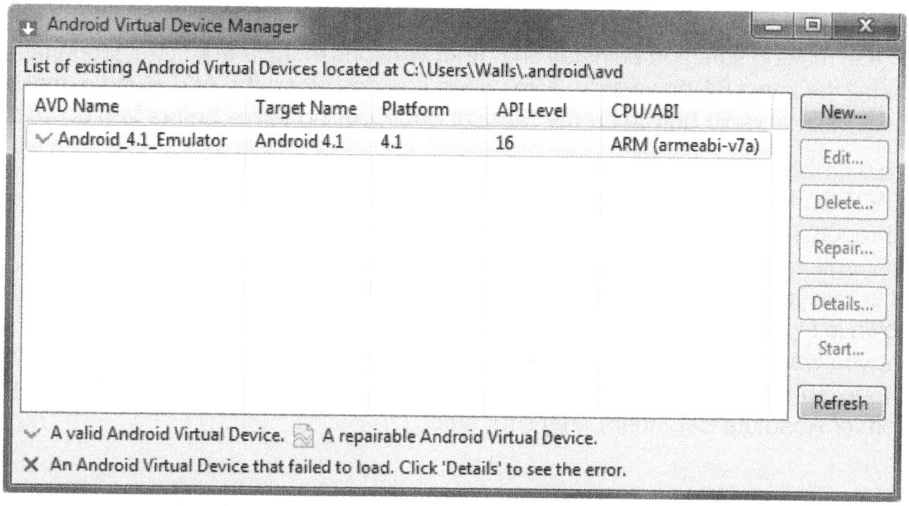

Figure 3-33. The Android 4.1 emulator once it is added to the list of installed AVDs

USB Smartphone Drivers: External Devices

Because the latest USB driver for Android was installed as part of the SDK installation process in a previous section, you've already taken care of installing the most up-to-date USB drivers to interface the Eclipse Juno 4.2 for Java EE IDE with your Android smartphone or tablet devices.

It is important to note that this driver is only for Windows. Using the external Android smartphone on Mac and Linux does not require this driver download.

The driver is not intended to make your Android phone or tablet visible to Windows. You can simply plug your Android device in via USB, and it will be visible on your Windows desktop. However, this driver is necessary to have the development interface to and from Eclipse 4.2.

Note that the USB driver that you installed earlier went into the ADT plug-in for Eclipse, *not* into the Windows driver registry. Possibly the term *driver* is misleading in this instance, as this driver provides the ability for Eclipse to talk with your Android smartphone, tablet, e-reader, or iTV set during development, so that Android packages (*.apk* files) can be transferred to the smartphone, tablet, e-reader, or iTV for testing and development purposes.

ADT Bundle and 64-bit IDE Support

Android 4.2 changed the installation process to set-up an Android IDE drastically, adding 64-bit support, and making the entire process much easier by making Android SDK, ADT, and Eclipse into one huge 400MB "Bundle" that can be downloaded and installed using fewer steps. I'll go through it briefly here, because it's much less work, and I'll refer to figures used earlier in this chapter, instead of duplicating similar screens again here.

If you go to the Android Developer web site, you will now see a 400MB ADT Bundle download button, that is all you will need to get, along with the Java 6 JDK. If you want to use 64-bit Java and Android/Eclipse IDE on your 64-bit workstation, be sure to go to the same Java 6 site download area as you did to get the 32-bit Java 6 JDK, but instead download the 64-bit JDK for Windows jdk-6u37-windows-x64.exe making sure you uninstall any other versions of Java from your workstation first, before you install the latest 64-bit version. Also, when you download the ADT Bundle, make sure to select the 64-bit version radio button on the "accept our licensing terms before you download" screen.

After the Java 6 64-bit JDK is installed, use the same work process shown in Figures 3-2 through 3-6 to install the ADT Bundle ZIP file onto your hard disk drive. You can skip the work process shown in Figures 3-7 through 3-19, but you will still get the dialog shown in Figure 3-20 at some point asking you to allow Google to see how you use their product. The work process shown in Figures 3-21 through 3-23 is always a good idea to make sure that you're current, and you will still need to set-up AVDs, as shown in Figure 3-30 through 3-33, so that you have Emulators for the Android device hardware that you want to test for and support. As you can see, the new ADT Bundle allows you to skip at least a dozen or more major steps in setting up your Android Development environment, so it's a real boon for Absolute Beginners, that's for sure!

Installing GIMP 2.8 for Image Editing for Android Apps

One last thing that we should install for use with Android Application development is the open source digital image editing and compositing software called GIMP, currently at version 2.8.2, and available for all of the same platforms (Windows, Macintosh, and Linux) that Android ADT is.

I'm not going to use any screenshots in this section, as downloading and installing GIMP 2.8.2 is relatively easy compared to what we just went through in this chapter to get an Android Development environment working on our system! Other leading open source software packages that you should Google the names of, and then download and install, for a complete Android, Business and New Media development workstation are: Audacity, Blender3D, RoseGarden, Apache OpenOffice, and EditShare Lightworks. Amazing free for commercial use software!

So, let's get started with GIMP 2.8! Go to www.GIMP.org and click the orange download button at the top-right of the homepage, and go to the GIMP.org/downloads/ page and click the orange link at the top that says: Download GIMP 2.8.2 — Installer for Windows XP SP3 or later. If you use Mac or Linux, then click on the link below that says: Show Other Downloads.

Once you click on the Download 2.8.2 for Windows link, you will get a dialog saying that you have chosen to open *gimp-2.8.2-setup-1.exe* — click on the Save button to save the 73MB file to your MyDocuments/Downloads/ Folder (unless you specify another location for the file at download time). Once the download is finished, you will have the GIMP 2.8.2 installer file. If you have more than one workstation, copy this file to a USB key, so that you can install it on all of your systems because it's one hot piece of open source digital imaging software!

Find the file in your Downloads folder, using the Windows Explorer, and double-click on it to execute it, or double-click the recent file download entry for GIMP in your browser's download manager (or right-click on the file, and select Open, Run or Install). Then select the language you want to install it in (I selected English), and you will get a colorful GIMP 2.8 Installer Screen.

Click the Install button on the right, and watch the fun begin! You will get a progress bar showing you hundreds of files, totaling hundreds of megabytes of powerful (free) digital imaging software, being installed on your system. When the install is done, select the Finish button and Voila! Done!

Once GIMP 2.8 and the other software packages that we suggested earlier are installed on your system, be sure and use the "Pin to Taskbar" work process that we showed in Figures 3-5 and 3-6 earlier in this chapter to add all of your cool new software to your LaunchBar in Windows, so that you can admire the sheer power of your Android development workstation at all times. While you are at it, drag a few of the key system utilities that you will use in app development from your Start ➤ All Programs ➤ Accessories folder to the Taskbar as well, such as the Notepad (a Plain Text Editor), Calculator, the CharacterMap Utility, and your OS MediaPlayer.

Whew! We're finally finished! Now we can get on to the business of Android development!

Summary

To set up your Android development environment, you began by installing the Oracle Java SE 6 JDK, which is required to run the Java programming language, and then the Eclipse 4.2 for Java EE IDE (Java EE is proof that Java can indeed be used to develop very large-scale, enterprise-quality applications).

Your next major step was to install the Android SDK, which contains all of the tools and utilities that you will need to develop Android applications. Once the SDK was installed on your hard drive, you went into Eclipse and pointed Eclipse to the Android SDK installation directory, so that Eclipse and Android's SDK can work seamlessly hand in hand.

With the JDK and Android SDK installed, the next logical step was to install ADT into the Eclipse IDE, which the Android development environment uses as a "host," or platform, to support its ADT plug-in.

After installation, you used the Eclipse Check for Updates features to check on the Internet for the very latest versions of the Eclipse and Android development tools. You installed the updates that were necessary (which unfortunately takes a while, even on a fast connection). Next, you added an AVD on which to test your future Android applications, which you soon will be coding like a Pro.

Finally, just to make sure that you put together a comprehensive Android Development Workstation, you stepped through the installation of GIMP 2.8 (which is used in this book for digital imaging work processes), and also you wisely downloaded and installed the five recommended leading open source packages in each genre that we do not specifically reference in this book but that you will eventually use in your Android development work process.

For digital video editing, that would be EditShare Lightworks; for 3D—Blender 3D; for digital audio editing—Audacity; for business tasks—Apache OpenOffice; and for music composition— RoseGarden. This is admittedly a bit beyond the "call of duty" of this book, but we figured, hey, if you are going to spend a day configuring your Android Development Workstation, why not go all the way, and do that for every type of new media development that Android supports, and get it over with? Besides, having all of these professional packages on your workstation makes it just that much more valuable than it was at the start of this chapter. Congratulations, you have just recovered what you paid for this book a hundred times over! In the next chapter, we'll examine the Android platform and all of its components, to prepare for writing Android applications. And speaking of prepared, after this chapter, your Android development workstation is ready to Rock!

Chapter 4

Introducing the Android Software Development Platform

The Android platform is a collection of software that includes an operating system and a number of higher-level libraries that simplify the task of communicating with the operating system. It also includes several applications that smartphone, tablet, e-reader and iTV users have come to expect, such as a phone (obviously) dialer, e-mail client, social media client, contact manager, Google Maps, Google Search, a web browser, a calendar, basic games, and so on.

Everything in the Android development environment, as well as all of the included applications, can be programmed with a combination of Java and XML thanks to the so-called *runtime* that is included with the Android SDK. The runtime translates the Java and XML code that you write into a language that the operating system and the device understand.

The foundation on which Android is built is carefully coded and painstakingly tested Linux 2.6, an operating system that rarely crashes. Linux and its core services manage the physical phone, tablet, e-book e-reader, or iTV set and give Android applications complete access to the features of each consumer electronics device, including the touchscreen, memory, data, security, various network receivers and transmitters, camera, GPS, Bluetooth, Wi-Fi, and more.

Linux doesn't do it all alone. Android has a large number of libraries that provide higher-level customized functions and services for 2D graphics, 3D graphics, and the audio and video file formats in widest use today. In other words, Android supports all of the rich media formats you could possibly want to use, including the powerful ON2 VP8 video codec, now in Android 4.x (for more information, visit: http://developer.android.com/guide/appendix/media-formats.html). ON2 was acquired by Google and rereleased as an open codec called WebM for HTML5 and Android. It's quality to file size (and thereby performance) ratio is impressive to say the least.

This chapter introduces the Android 4 software development environment, and shows you how to write your first Android application.

> **Note**   In this book, you'll build apps using a combination of XML and Java, which sit in a layer on top of the operating system (with the runtime as the component that translates Java and XML into instructions for the operating system). However, you could, if you wished, access the operating system and its services directly, using lower-level languages such as C or C++ using the Android NDK, or native development kit, rather than the higher level software development kit, or SDK, that we are using for this book. You might consider this "under the hood" approach for an application that needs the utmost speed, such as a 3D game or a real-time heart-monitoring program, but the NDK is far beyond the scope of this introductory book.

Understanding Java SE and the Dalvik Virtual Machine

The Android runtime environment provides a core set of operating system libraries that can be accessed via Java and XML. These give you access to device features and lower-level Android operating system functions so that you don't have to do any of that hard programming yourself. You simply include the appropriate components from the libraries you need in your program—something called *importing*—and then your application code can employ their built-in capabilities. You'll learn how to put a significant number of these powerful code engines to work in later chapters.

To run Java SE code, Android uses a tool called the Dalvik Virtual Machine (DVM). The DVM is an optimization mechanism and technology that allows application code and resources to be highly optimized for use in mobile and embedded environments.

Embedded environments are ones in which a computer is actually embedded inside the consumer electronics product, and this is now commonplace in smartphones, tablets, e-book e-readers, iTV sets, and iDVD players, to name a few. I've also seen phone-watches and smart appliances (refrigerators); so it's not limited to Internet 2.0 (portable or mobile) devices either!

The good news is that the DVM is *not* something that a developer needs to worry about. I describe it here only to give you a sense of what's going on under the hood with Android.

When you launch an Android application, it creates a process that allocates memory and CPU processing resources (processor time slices) to the application, so that it has the resources needed to function. Each time an application is launched and a process is spawned, an instance or copy of the DVM is launched into your Android smartphone, iTV, or tablet's memory. The DVM actually takes the Java language instructions along with the application's design guidelines (in an XML format), and combines them with any external resources (images, audio or video files, 3D, and so on), and translates them all into optimized low-level binary code that goes into the Android device's memory and eventually into the processor for processing.

So, what is the advantage of this DVM? Using DVM allows many more applications to run within the somewhat limited memory resources (1GB to 2GB) and processing power (1GHz to 2GHz) of consumer electronic devices, and it also protects all of the other spawned (active in memory) processes from interfering with each other. In this way, the crash of one application will *not* bring down the entire operating system (as happened in the olden days of DOS and Macintosh). That's a huge advantage, because other apps cannot take down your app, or heaven forbid, vice-versa.

The Directory Structure of an Android Project

Android does its best to externalize all application assets that do not absolutely need to be in your Java code. It does this by using the simpler XML markup language to define UI (user interface) designs and data structures that would otherwise need to be explicitly declared and coded in Java. This modularization is aided and implemented by having a clearly defined project hierarchy folder structure, which holds logical types of application assets together in an orderly fashion.

Because Android is very particular about where the *assets* of your project are stored within the project directory, you need to learn where each belongs early in the game. When it comes time to generate your application—a process called *compilation*—Android looks into these standardized folders to locate each type of asset it needs, and expects to find, like assets logically grouped together.

The assets of a project include its Java code, XML layouts, XML animation definitions, and the rich media files that your Java code and XML markup reference. As shown in Figure 4-1, default folders are automatically created in an Android project to hold menus, images, layouts, colors, fixed data values, raw (uncompressed) media, XML constructs, and animation. These default folders will be created by the Android Developer Toolkit (ADT) New ➤ Project ➤ Android Application Project function that we installed and tested in Eclipse 4.2.1 at the end of Chapter 3.

Figure 4-1. Android's file structure, showing the res (resources) folder and its subfolders

The Java code that drives an application is located in the */src (source code)* folder and in any subfolders that are defined by your Java code.

You'll find other assets used by your application in logical subfolders of the */res* (resources) folder as needed. It is very important that *only folders* go in the */res* folder. If the Android compiler sees any files in this folder, it will generate a compiler error.

> **Note**   The name of the game is to avoid compiler errors at all costs because if Eclipse sees compiler errors in your code, it does not even bother generating your application. And if your application is not generated, you certainly cannot test it to see how well it works.

If you don't have any resources of a certain type (say animation), you do not need to have an empty folder for it. This means that you do not need to create folders that you will not use.

Common Default Resources Folders

The most common of the default resources (/res) subfolders are shown in the Figure 4-1. The following are the eight provided when you create a project in Eclipse:

- *layout*: UI screen layouts go in the /res/layout folder, which holds XML files containing UI layout definitions written in XML.

- *drawable-hdpi:* high-resolution images in PNG format (which Google prefers) or the JPEG format (acceptable but not favored by Google) go into the /res/drawable-hdpi (high resolution screen-drawable imagery, usually 800 by 480 pixels) folder.

- *drawable-ldpi:* low-resolution images in PNG format (which Google prefers) or the JPEG format (acceptable but not favored by Google) go into the /res/drawable-ldpi (low resolution screen-drawable imagery, usually 320 by 240 pixels) folder.

- *drawable-mdpi:* medium-resolution images in PNG format (which Google prefers) or the JPEG format (acceptable but not favored by Google) go into the /res/drawable-mdpi (medium resolution screen-drawable imagery, usually 480 by 320 pixels) folder.

- *drawable-xhdpi*: extra-high-resolution images in PNG format (which Google prefers) or the JPEG format (acceptable but not favored by Google) go into the /res/drawable-xhdpi (high resolution screen-drawable imagery, usually 1,280 by 720 pixels or HD) folder

- *values:* XML files that define constant values are in the res/values folder.

- *values-v11*: honeycomb theme XML files that define new UI theme values are in the res/values-v11 (referencing API Level 11 through 13, also known as Android 3.x or 3.0, 3.1, and 3.2) folder.

- *values-v14*: Ice Cream Sandwich theme XML files that define new UI theme values are in the res/values-v14 (referencing API Level 14 through 16, also known as Android 4.x or 4.0, 4.0.3, and 4.1) folder.

- *menu*: XML files defining menu layouts are in the res/menu folder.

The Values Folder

Let's examine the *res/values* folder from one of my current projects in more detail. This is where you place predefined application values in the form of XML files that define the variable names (x or y, for instance) and their values that are later referenced in your Java code. For example, these values might be strings (collections of text characters) or constants (hard-coded values that your Java code uses in its program logic and can't change).

Think of the *values* folder as holding all of your constant values for your application in one place. This way, if you need to adjust them during application development and testing, you make the changes in a single location.

Figure 4-2 shows a few examples of files that can be placed in this folder as in the following:

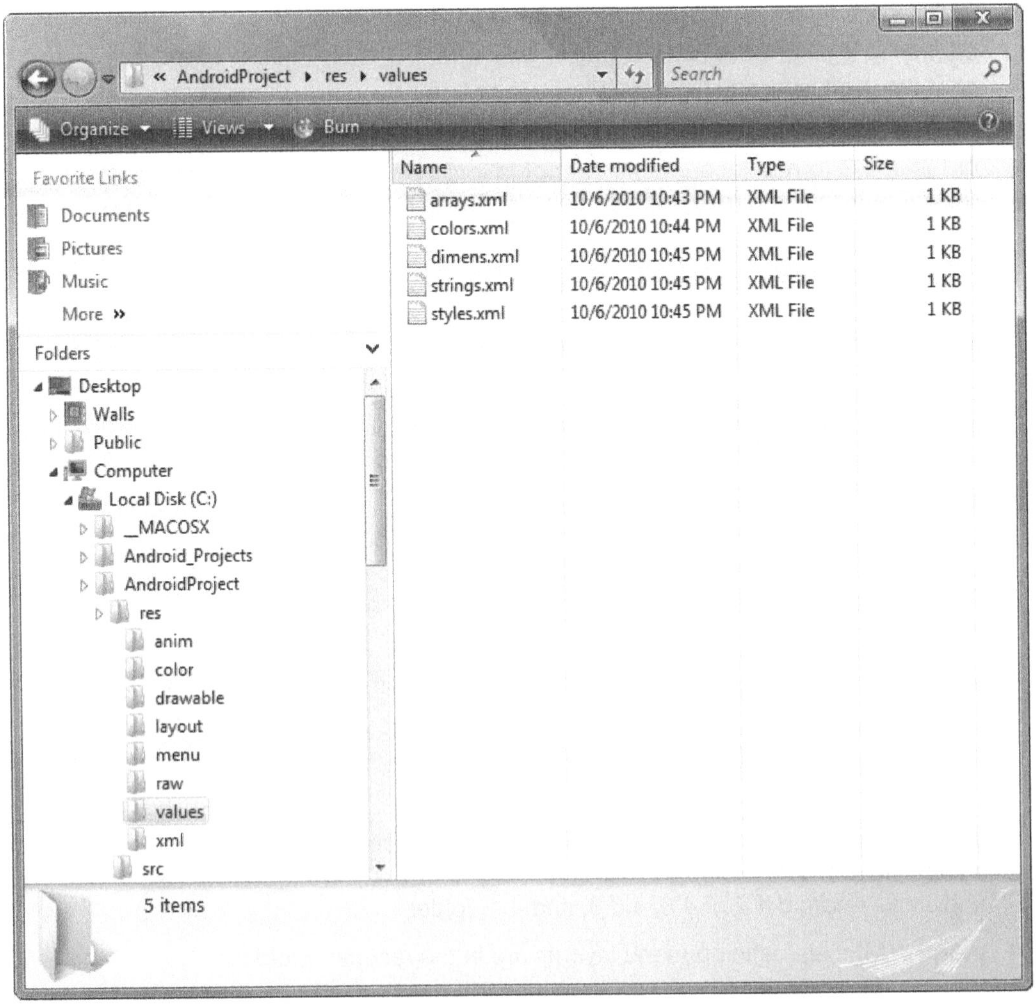

Figure 4-2. Files in the res/values folder. These files contain constants for an Android application

- **colors.xml**: An XML file that will define the color values to be used in the app. These allow you to standardize the UI. For example, you would define your background color. Then, if you decide to tweak it later, you need to do the tweaking in only one place.

- **dimens.xml**: An XML file that defines dimension values, such as standard heights and font sizes for your UI. You can then use these values across your app to ensure it is consistent.

- **arrays.xml**: An XML file that defines a series of values to be used together (known as an *array*). For example, this could be a list of icon files or a list of options to display to the user.

- **strings.xml**: An XML file that defines text strings to be used in the application. For example, you can place any screen titles or the app's name here and reference them in your code. If you need to change these items, you simply do it here rather than in your code.

- **styles.xml**: An XML file that defines styles to be used in the application. These styles are then applied to the UI elements that require them, so you separate the look of your app from the layout and functionality. This makes your app easier to maintain.

Notice the Android file name conventions for the different types of XML files in the *values* folder, adding another level of complexity.

Leveraging Android XML (Your Secret Weapon)

One of the most useful features of Android as a development environment is its use of XML to define a great number of attributes within your application's infrastructure. Because you don't need to work inside the Java programming language to handle these attributes, you save hundreds of lines of Java code. Everything within the application—from your UI layouts, to your text strings, animation, or inter-process communication with Android's operating system services (like vibrating the phone or playing a ringtone)—can be defined via XML.

What makes XML ideal for Android development, and especially for beginners, is its ease of use. It is no more complicated than HTML markup. So, if you know how to use tags to boldface text or insert an image in your website, you already understand how to use XML.

You will be learning how this works in the next chapters of the book. Suffice it to say that you will become familiar with XML in your Android development. XML brings a lot of flexibility to Android development.

Android's use of XML for application design is very similar to the way HTML, cascading style sheets (CSS), and JavaScript are used in today's popular Internet browsers. CSS is used to separate the layout and look of a web page from its content and behavior, which are specified by HTML markup and JavaScript code, respectively. This approach leads to more modular and logically structured web pages. Designers can work on the look of a website using CSS, while search engine optimization (SEO) professionals optimize its findability with HTML, leaving user interaction to programmers who know how to use JavaScript. The same approach applies to Android. Designers can create the UI for an application with XML, while programmers can call and access its elements using Java without affecting screen formatting, animation, or graphics. Genius.

XML gives us amazing flexibility to accommodate variations within our apps, such as different screen sizes, languages, themes, and UI designs. Here, we'll look at a couple of brief examples to give you an idea of XML's power.

Screen Sizes

Because UI designs can be defined precisely by an XML file, it's easy to deal with the variety of screen sizes available on Android devices today. Let's say that you want to do a custom layout for each of the four primary screen sizes used in Android phones:

- Quarter VGA (QVGA), 240 × 320 pixels also known as low DPI or LDPI
- Half VGA (HVGA), 320 × 480 pixels (the "sweet spot" for low-cost Android phones) also known as medium DPI or MDPI
- Wide VGA (WVGA), 800 × 480 pixels (found on the newer phones and now a common tablet and e-reader resolution) also known as High DPI or HDPI
- Wide SVGA (WSVGA), 1,024 × 600 pixels (found on the newest smartphones and tablets) also known as extra high DPI or XHDPI
- HDTV 1280 x 720 and 1920 x 1080 (found on HD smartphones, tablets, e-readers and iTVs) also known as TVDPI

How does XML provide a solution? Simply create a UI design in XML for each size and use Java to determine the screen resolution of the phone. We also noted in the previous section that Android provides drawable folders for the graphics file assets for each of these standard screen resolutions, so be aware that you must develop graphics for at least four different screen size targets for your Android applications. No one said that Android applications development was going to be easy!

Desktop Clocks

As another example of how XML can be leveraged, let's take a look at a few lines of code that define an important utility: Android's popular desktop clock. (In Chapter 6, you'll learn how to create your own custom desktop clocks.)

The XML tag for an Android program function usually has the same name as its Java counterpart, so you can access the power of the programming language from simple XML. For example, here is the XML tag that corresponds to Java's AnalogClock:

```
<AnalogClock />
```

Android's XML tags start with a left-angle bracket (<), followed immediately (no space) by a class name, a space, a slash mark, and a right-angle bracket (/>).

To customize an AnalogClock, you must add *attributes* to the AnalogClock tag, inserting them before the closing part of the tag (/>). Suppose you want to add an ID to reference the utility from other parts of the application. Here's how:

```
<AnalogClock android:id="@+id/AnalogClock" />
```

This adds an ID to your AnalogClock with the name AnalogClock, which you can use to reference it elsewhere in your application.

For each XML tag in Android, there are dozens of parameters that allow you to control the tag's appearance and implementation, including its positioning, naming (used in the Java code), and other options.

In real-life, for readability, programmers usually write this code with each configuration parameter indented on a separate line, like this:

```
<AnalogClock
        android:id="@+id/AnalogClock"
        android:layout_width="fill_parent"
        android:layout_height="wrap_content"
/>
```

The Android compiler considers everything inside the AnalogClock tag to be a parameter, or a customization option, until it reaches a closing tag (/>). The fill_parent parameter stretches content to fill a container, and the wrap_content parameter shrink-wraps the content. We'll cover these and other view and layout concepts later on in Chapters 6 and 7.

Using Your Android Application Resources

In addition to Java code and XML markup, the resources your application draws on consist primarily of new media elements and other file types that contribute to its functionality in one way or another. These may include XML files that contain animation parameters or text strings, bitmap image files, and even audio and video files (audio and video "streams" on the other hand are external to an app and come from a server, and thus are not a resource in this context).

One of the primary reasons for externalizing resources is that you can have sets of resources for variations, such as different screen sizes or language versions. *Language localization* localizes the application to any given country. These language localizations can be easily referenced in the Java code and switched when necessary by pointing to different external file names or folders.

Bitmap Images

Let's look at an example of a common application resource: the bitmap image. Your PNG or JPEG bitmap image goes into its proper */res/drawable* folder depending on its pixel dimensions. It can then be referenced by its file name only (*excluding* its extension) in the Java code, as well as in XML. For this important reason, be sure not to give a PNG file and a JPG file the same name, or you will have problems when it comes time to compile your code.

Also, contrary to normal file-naming conventions, image file names can contain only numbers, an underscore character, and lowercase letters, so make sure to remember this rule (one of the many anomalies of Android programming).

In summary, to set up bitmap images to be used in your application, do the following:

- Name them correctly, using only numbers, underscores, and lowercase letters.

- Use the PNG or JPG format, or WebP if you are creating apps for the Android 4 or later (4.0, 4.0.4, and 4.1) platforms only.

- Make sure they are in the proper */res/drawable* folder, based on their pixel dimensions, so that Android can find them.

Alternate Resource Folders

Another great example of resource usage is supplying different UI screen layouts for portrait and landscape orientations. Usually, we will set our default screen UI for phones to portrait mode, as most people use their phone in this way (turning it sideways only to view video).

Android provides support for alternate resources. If you set them up correctly, Android will determine the current settings and use the correct resource configurations automatically. In other words, you provide resources for each orientation, and Android uses the correct resources as the user changes from one orientation to another.

Each set of alternative resources is in its own folder, where it can be referenced and located later on in your Java code. We can provide resources for different screen orientations and resolutions in this fashion, and have Android decide which folders to look in for our application resources based on each user's smartphone, tablet, or e-reader model.

Android currently offers four screen resolutions: low resolution (320 × 240), medium resolution (480 × 320), high resolution (800 × 480) and extra high resolution (1,024 × 600 or 1,280 × 720). Look for a fifth TVDPI resolution 1,920 × 1,080 classification to be added in Android 4.2 to accommodate Google TV and HD iTVs. Note that you can always add your own alternate resources folders now, Android just creates the */drawable-ldpi* folders for you as a convenience and to remind you to provide graphics for all the common device screen sizes, but if you were doing an iTV app you could create a */drawable-tvdpi* folder yourself and reference it from your app.

To add an alternate resource folder, create a directory under */res* with the form *<resource_name>–<config-qualifier>*. For instance, android created */res/drawable-hdpi* for you in its New Project Creation Process, to hold your high DPI resolution drawables or images.

This created an alternate resource folder for high-density dots per inch (hdpi) images. The alternate folder will be used automatically if the Android smartphone screen uses a WVGA (800 × 480) screen high-end model. Otherwise, it will use the normal HVGA (320 × 480) screen images, located in the default */res/drawable-mdpi* folder, if the device screen resolution is not automatically detected.

If you want to also support low-end screens, you can use the low-density dots per inch qualifier, `ldpi`. There is a medium-density dots per inch qualifier, `mdpi`, as well as an extra high dots per inch qualifier called `xhdpi`.

So, to have images for QVGA, HVGA, WVGA, and WSVGA screens arranged into folders in a way that allows Android to automatically recognize the folder hierarchy, set up your folder structure as follows:

- */res*, with only subfolders, place NO individual files in this folder

- */res/drawable-ldpi*, with the following low-density DPI (120 DPI) screen images (QVGA):

  - *ic_launcher.png* (application icon file), 36 × 36 pixels

  - *background.png* (application background), 320 × 240 pixels

- */res/drawable-mdpi*, with the following medium-density DPI (160 DPI) screen images (HVGA):

  - *ic_launcher.png*, 48 × 48 pixels

  - *background.png*, 320 × 480 pixels

- */res/drawable-hdpi*, with the following high-density DPI (240 DPI) screen images (WVGA):

  - *ic_launcher.png*, 72 × 72 pixels

  - *background.png*, 800 × 480 pixels

- */res/drawable-xhdpi*, with the following extra-high-density DPI (320 DPI) screen images (WSVGA or HDTV):

  - *ic_launcher.png*, 96 × 96 pixels

  - *background.png*, 1,024 × 600 or 1,280 × 720 pixels

Note that there are two HDTV resolution graphics standards, HDTV 1,280 by 720 and True HD 1,920 by 1,080. You're well on your way to correctly setting up your Android application's resources. One more file we need to examine is *AndroidManifest.xml*.

Launching Your Application: The AndroidManifest.xml File

When Android launches your application, the first file it seeks out is the application *manifest* file. This file is *always* located in the root of your project folder and directory structure, and is *always* called *AndroidManifest.xml* so that it can be located easily on startup.

The Android manifest declares some very high-level definitions and settings for your application using (surprise!) the XML markup language. The following are some of the key items *AndroidManifest.xml* includes:

- References to the Java code you will write for your application, so that your code can be found and run.

- Definitions of the components of your Android application, including when they can be launched.

- Definitions of permissions for application security and for talking with other Android applications.

- Declaration of the a minimum level of Android operating system version support, which amounts to defining which version(s) of Android your application is going to support.

All of the apps to be written in this book will support Android versions 2.2, 2.3.7, 3.0, 3.1, 3.2, 4.0, 4.0.4, and 4.1.2. We call this "Android API Level 8 through 16 compatibility" because it supports every version of Android from Version 2.2 (Froyo) through the current Version 4.1.2 (Jelly Bean).

Tip   I try to develop for the 2.2 API Level 8 so that my applications run on API versions 2.2, 2.3.7, 3.0, 3.1, 3.2, 4.0, 4.0.4, and 4.1.2. Later versions are obviously backward compatible, so the further back you develop your minimum version level support, the more people will be able to use your application. If you want to make money selling Android apps, this concept translates directly into dollars, as there are millions of 2.2 and 2.3.7 devices still out there, including the original Amazon Kindle Fire which runs 2.3.7.

Creating Your First Android Application

By now, you're probably aching to fire up Eclipse Juno 4.2 for Java EE and create an Android 4.1 application to see how all of this works together. A tradition in all programming languages for new users is the crafting of the "Hello World" application, so let's create our own Hello Absolute Beginner application right here and now.

First, we'll launch Eclipse and create the application. Then we'll take a look at the files and Java and XML code that Eclipse generates to get your app up and running. Finally, we'll give the app an icon to display on the Android device's (smartphone, tablet, e-reader or iTV) main menu.

Launching Eclipse

The first step is to launch Eclipse Juno 4.2 for Java EE. From there, you'll create an Android project to house the application code, markup, and assets.

To launch Eclipse, find and click the Eclipse shortcut launch icon on your workstation. If a security warning dialog like the one shown in Figure 4-3 appears, click Run. If you don't want to see this dialog every time you start Eclipse, uncheck the box that reads "Always ask before opening this file."

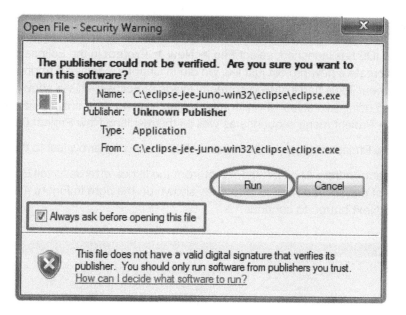

Figure 4-3. The Windows security warning dialog for Eclipse Juno 4.2 for Java EE launch

Next you will see the Eclipse Juno startup screen. Then, in a few more seconds, a dialog will appear, allowing you to tell Eclipse where your projects folder is kept on your hard disk drive. I'm going to accept the default User Directory with my nickname, so the entry is *C:\Users\Walls\workspace*, as shown in Figure 4-4. If you don't want to specify this each time you start Eclipse, you can check the "Use this as the default and do not ask again" option. Once you click the OK button, Eclipse will start, and the IDE will appear.

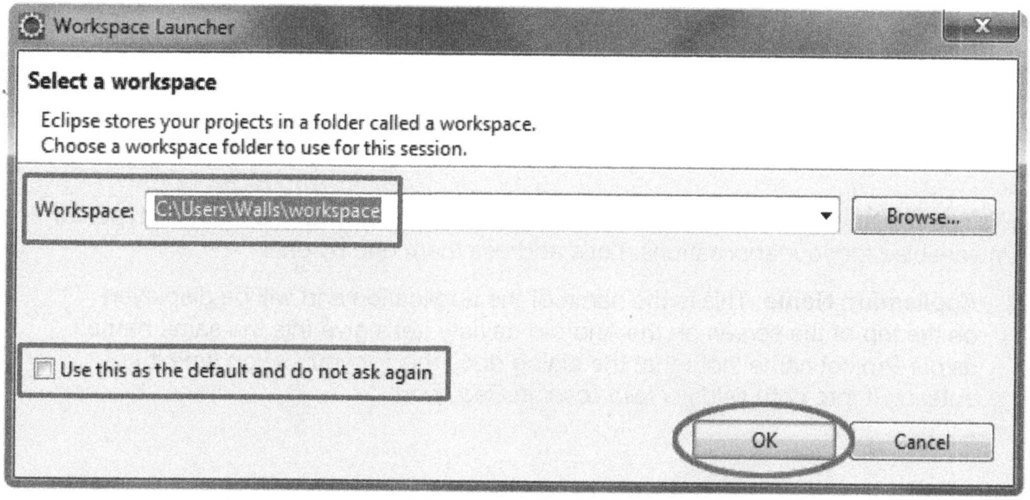

Figure 4-4. The Eclipse workspace location definition dialog

Creating an Android Project

1. Once the IDE has launched, select **File ➤ New ➤ Project** in the Eclipse main menu to create a new project just like we did in Chapter 3 to see if Android Development Tools had installed correctly inside of Eclipse. This is shown in Figure 4-5 using two screenshots combined into one (to save space) the File ➤ New ➤ Project menu sequence as well as the resulting New Project Dialog.

2. In the New Project dialog, open the Android folder using the arrow just to the left.

3. Next, select Android Application Project from the list of wizards to tell Eclipse the type of project you wish to create, as shown on the right in Figure 4-5. Click the Next button to continue.

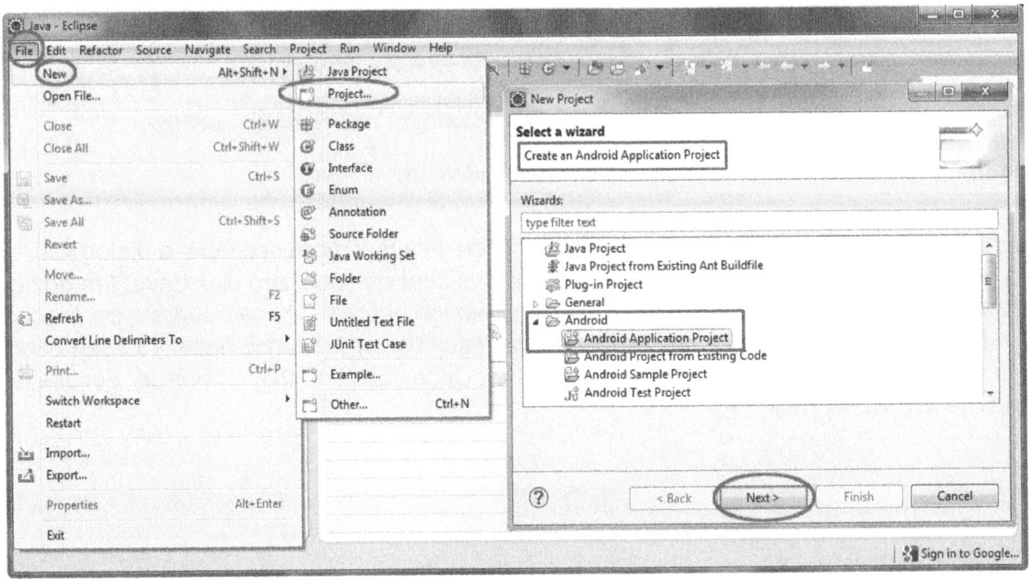

Figure 4-5. The Eclipse 4.2 New ➤ Project ➤ Android Application Project menu sequence and dialog

Next you'll see the New Android Application dialog, which allows you to specify all types of important variables for your applications. Let's address them one by one.

- **Application Name**: This is the name of the application and will be displayed on the top of the screen on the Android device. Let's give this the same name as our Project name (note that the dialog does this for you as you type it in, entering it into both fields): *HelloAbsoluteBeginner*.

Caution   We have omitted spaces from the folder name because spaces are not supported in Java names. It is not advisable to use spaces in names of folders that you use for software development.

- ▤ **Project Name:** This is the name of the folder in your C:\Users\YourName\ workspace\ folder that holds your Hello Absolute Beginner application folders and files. Let's give this folder the same name as our application: HelloAbsoluteBeginner

- ▤ **Package name**: This is the name you want to use for your Java *package*. For now, we will simply define this as the name of the container that will hold all of the Java code our application uses. Let's name this package first.example. helloabsolutebeginner. (Java package names are separated by periods, much like file pathnames are separated by back slashes.)

- ▤ **Build SDK**: This panel allows you to specify the version of Android that your application will support. The more you support, the more users will be able to use your application, so usually we would use a build target of Android 1.6. That version has everything that we will need to build most applications that work across all current Android smartphones. For now, however, let's just accept the default current API Level 16, which means we're developing this first application to run on the current Android 4.1 Jelly Bean platform and 4.1 phone and tablet emulator we just installed in Chapter 3.

- ▤ **Minimum Required SDK**: I am also going to accept the default Minimum Required SDK of API Level 8, which means your application will be compatible back to Android 2.2 smartphones and tablets, meaning users with Android 2.2, 2.3.7, 3.0, 3.1, 3.2, 4.0, 4.0.4, and 4.1 compatible hardware will be able to run the application.

- ▤ **Create Custom Launcher Icon**: Leave this box selected so that we can see the dialog (next) that helps to automate creation of an App Icon for the Launch Area on your Android smartphone or tablet. We also will see how to create these icons manually later on in this chapter as well.

- ▤ **Create Project in Workspace**: Leave this box selected as well so that Android will create the project folder structure for this application under your *C:/Users/ Name/workspace/* folder on your system's hard disk drive.

Figure 4-6 shows the completed New Android Application dialog for this example. When you are finished filling it out, click the Next button.

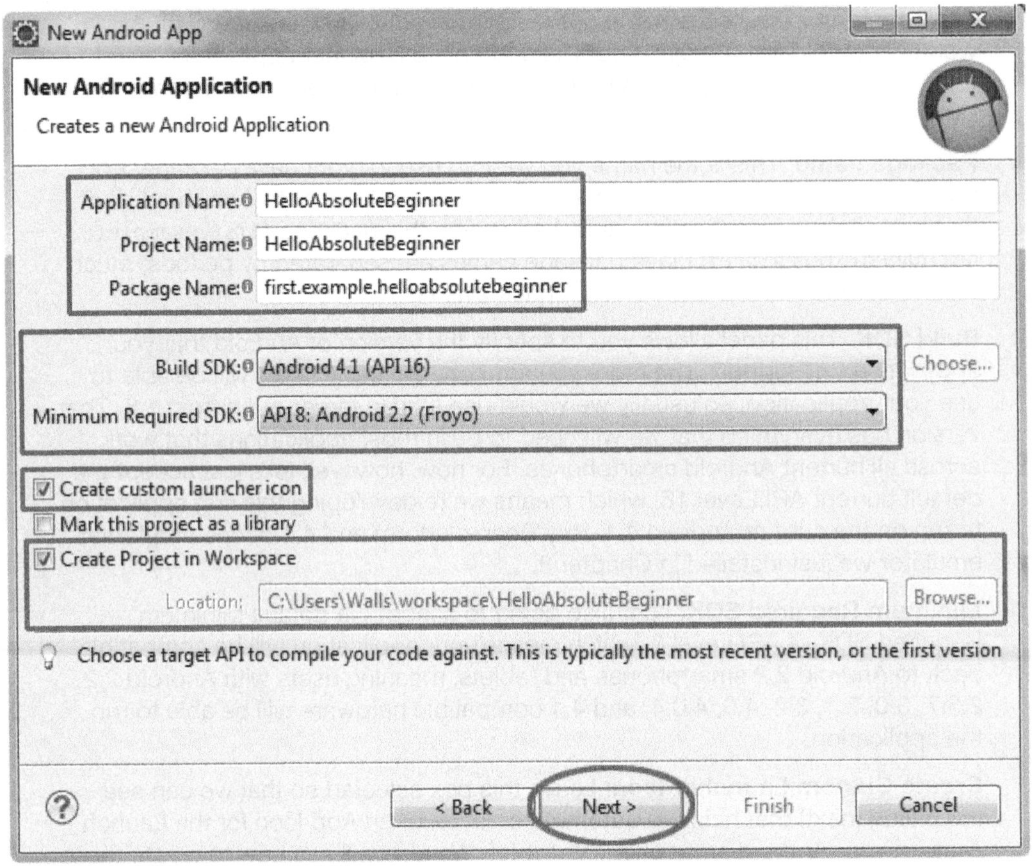

Figure 4-6. The New Android Application dialog for your HelloAbsoluteBeginner Android app

After you click the Next button in the New Android Application dialog, you will get the Configure Launcher Icon Dialog as shown in Figure 4-7. Because we haven't created our Application Launch Icons as yet, just accept the default settings and click on the Next button to advance on into the new Android App project creation process.

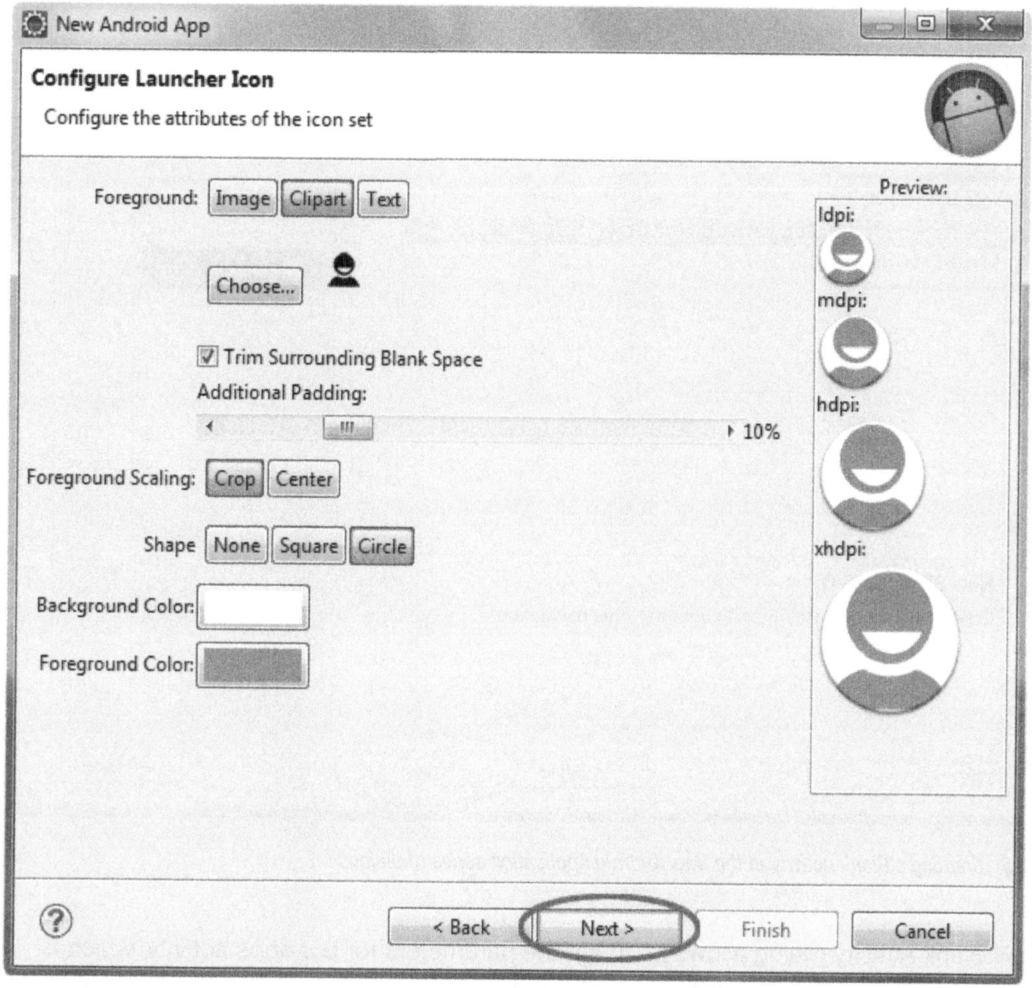

Figure 4-7. Accepting the Default Configure Launcher Icon Dialog settings

Next you will see the Create Activity Type Dialog shown in Figure 4-8 and for which we will be selecting a settings value of "Blank Activity," so that we can create a Blank (basic) Activity and see the basic (minimum) code that the New Android App functionality in Eclipse will create for us automatically. This auto-code generation is just what we need right now as an absolute beginner, and as you will see Android Development Tools in Eclipse does a great job at giving new developers a head start by writing some of the basic application bootstrapping code for them! Let's hit the Next button shown in Figure 4-8 and continue the New Android App project creation process to set the parameters for our Activity as shown in Figure 4-9.

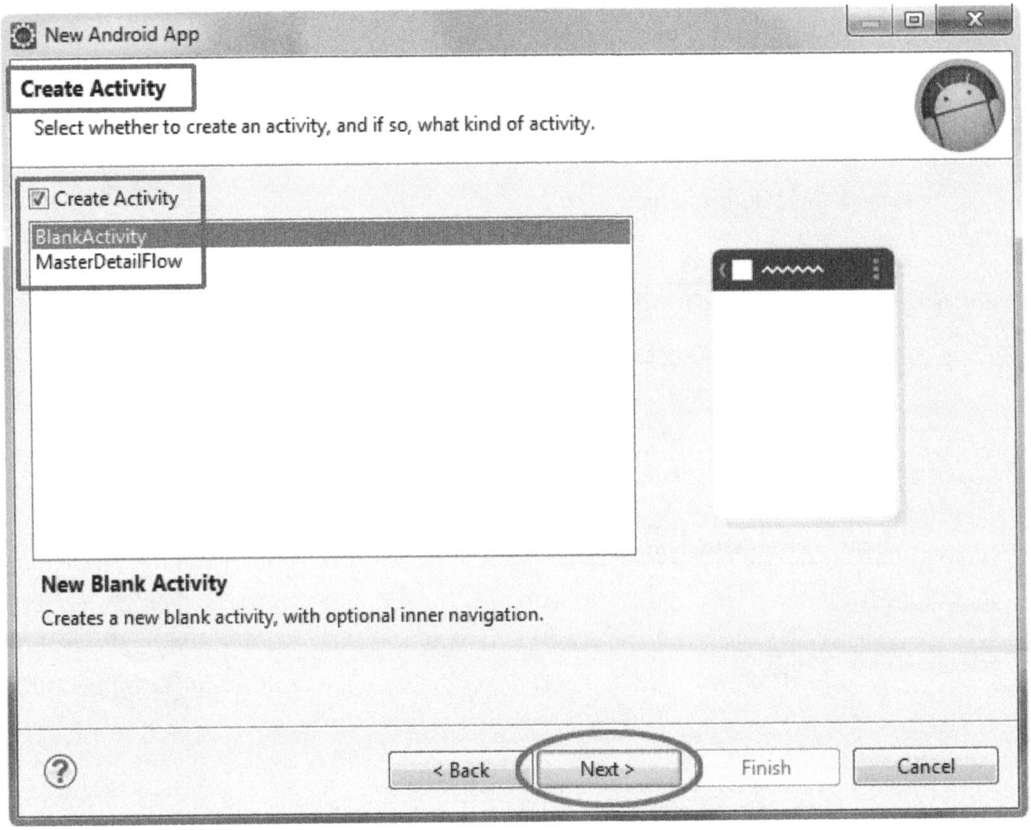

Figure 4-8. Creating a Blank Activity in the New Android Application series of dialogs

The New Blank Activity Dialog allows us to set the parameters for our apps activity, which is essentially the user interface or "front end" of our app that the users will use to control and utilize the app. Let's use "HelloActivity" for our Activity Name and Title and "activity_hello" as our layout (user interface) name as shown in Figure 4-9. Leave the Navigation Type and Hierarchical Parent settings at their defaults for now, and let's see how Android inserts our naming conventions into the Java code and XML markup for our app. Click on the Next button to continue the process.

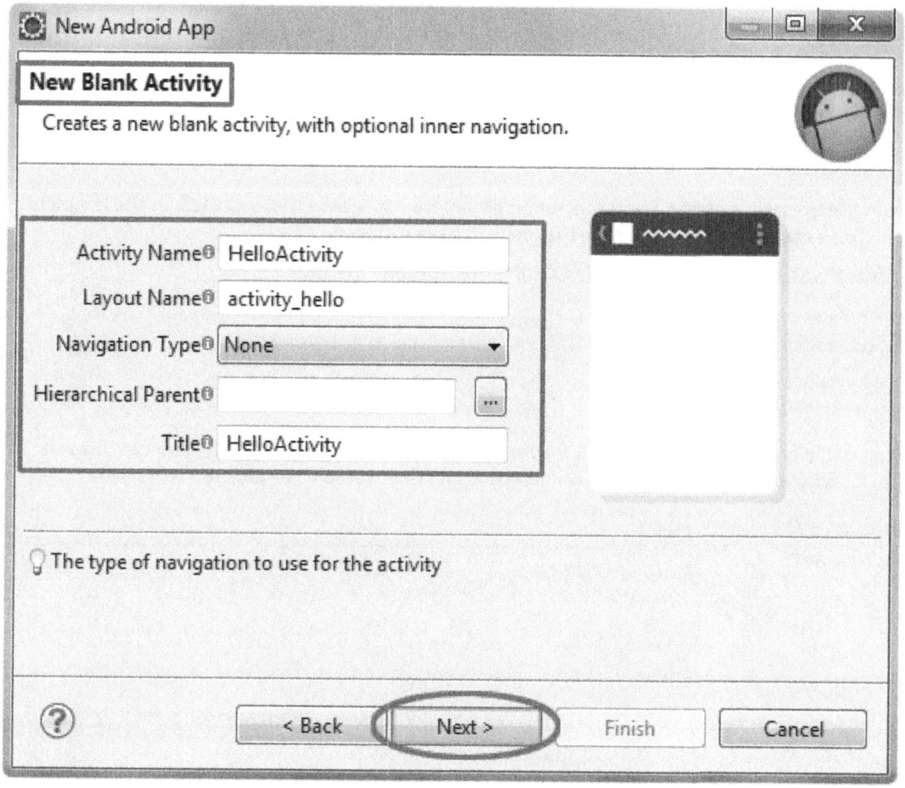

Figure 4-9. Filling out the parameters for our New Blank Activity in the New Android Application dialogs

Normally the New Android Application process would now create your New Android Project for you, but before it does so, it checks the state of your current Android Development Environment Installation (which we created in Chapter 3) to make sure that you have all of the SDKs, APIs, and so on that will be needed for the New Project you are specifying. In this case, Android found a missing API that would be needed to be installed for this Application to work (compile) properly, so it brings up the following dialog to let you know it needs something to be added to your current development environment. Again I am combining two screens into one in Figure 4-10 to show both the alert dialog and the repository search and fetch progress after you click the "Install/Update" button, to OK the addition of Android 2.2 support to your collection of SDKs and APIs. Make sure you are connected to the Internet before clicking the Install/Update button shown in Figure 4-10! Note that if your Android installation is 100% up to date that you will not get the Install Dependencies dialog and will not have to go through the process shown here in Figures 4-10 through 4-12.

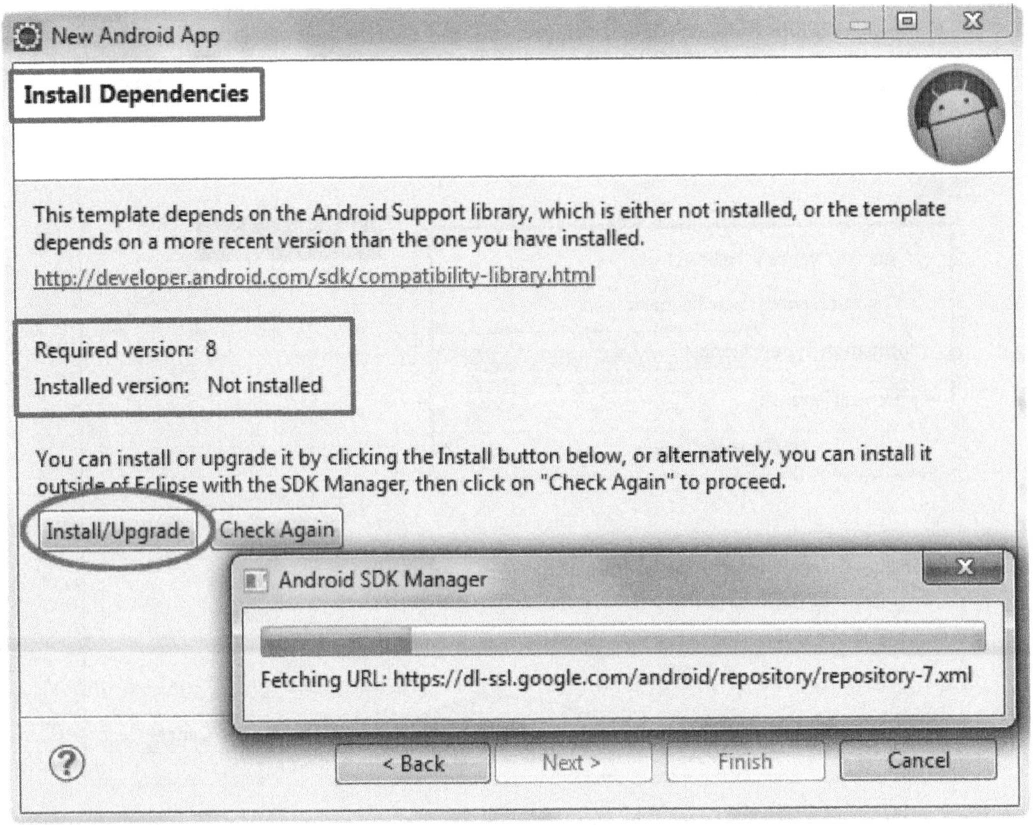

Figure 4-10. Installing/Upgrading Dependencies found to be needed by Android to support your application

After you click the Install/Upgrade button in the New Android Application dialog, and the necessary files are located and fetched from the repository, you will get the Choose Packages to Install Dialog as shown in Figure 4-11. Select the Accept All Radio Button as we have in the past and then click on the Install button to have the Froyo Android 2.2 API packages installed via your Internet connection.

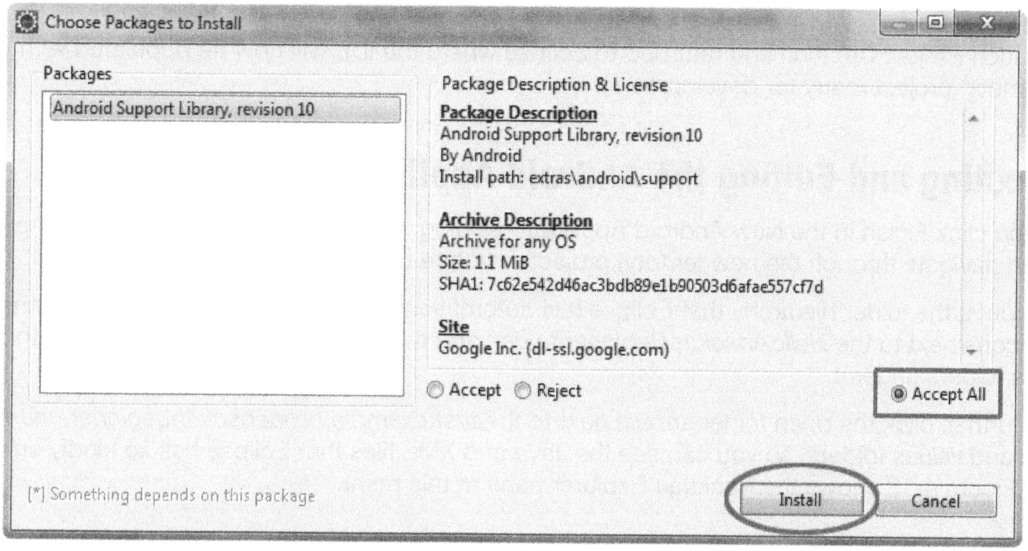

Figure 4-11. Accepting the suggested Packages to Install that are needed to support your New Android Application settings

After you click Install in the Choose Packages to Install dialog, you will get the progress bar dialog shown in Figure 4-12 showing you the speed and progress of your installation.

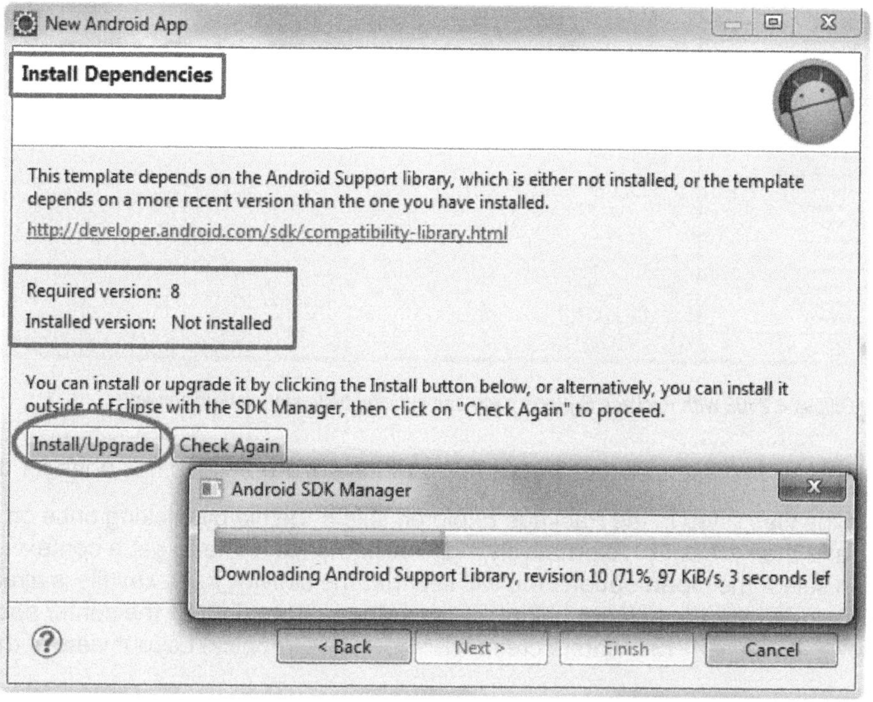

Figure 4-12. Download Progress Bar for installing the Android Support Library needed for your application

Once the Android 2.2 API installations are complete you will be finished with the New Android Application Project Creation and returned to Eclipse where the IDE will now be populated with your new (empty) project ready for development!

Inspecting and Editing the Android Application Files

After you click Finish in the New Android Application dialog, you are returned to Eclipse. In the IDE, you can navigate through the new (empty) project structure using the Package Explorer pane.

Let's look at the folder hierarchy that Eclipse has automatically created for our project. Click the arrow icons next to the *HelloAbsoluteBeginner* folder, and then click the arrow icons next to the *src* and *res* folders under it.

Going further, click the open folder arrows next to the *first.example.helloabsolutebeginner*, *menu*, *layout*, and *values* folders, so you can see the Java and XML files that Eclipse has so kindly created for us. Figure 4-13 shows the Package Explorer pane at this point.

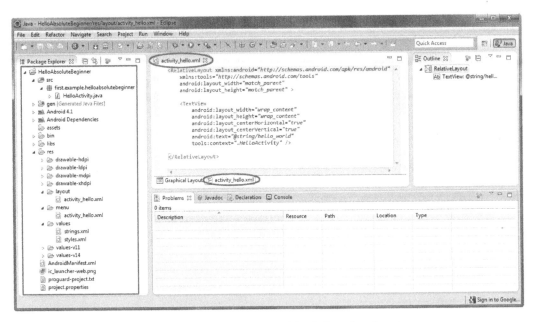

Figure 4-13. The Eclipse 4.2 IDE with Package Explorer pane and activity_hello.xml markup shown

Now let's open some of these files and see just how much coding Eclipse has done for this project.

To open any of the files listed in the Package Explorer, select the file by clicking once on it (the icon will turn blue), and then press F3. Alternatively, right-click the file name to get a context-sensitive menu, and then select the **Open** option. You will see that the *activity_hello.xml* file is already open, to see the markup code click the activity_hello.xml tab at the bottom right of the center coding area of Eclipse as shown in Figure 4-13. A later screen will show the Graphical Layout view of this XML file.

Opening the HelloActivity.java Activity

The *HelloActivity.java* file holds our activity class. Right-click it and select Open to explore it now. As shown in Figure 4-14, Eclipse has already written the code to create a UI screen for the application and set its content to the UI defined in the *activity_hello.xml* file (with the `R.layout.activity_hello` text), which we will look at next.

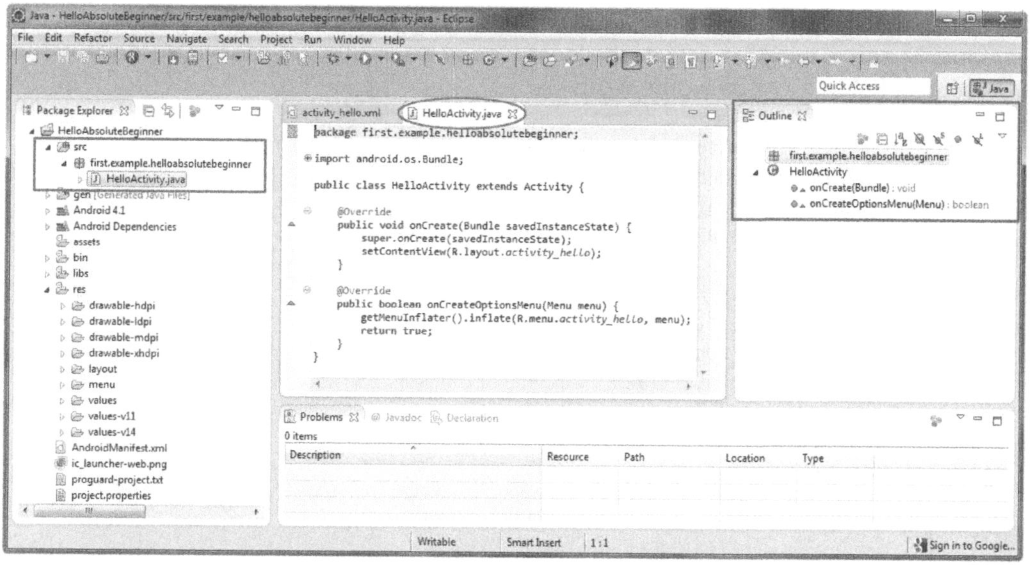

Figure 4-14. Our HelloActivity.java activity creation code shown in the Eclipse 4.2 IDE

Let's examine this in a little more detail:

```
package first.example.helloabsolutebeginner;

import android.os.Bundle;

public class HelloActivity extends Activity {
    @Override
    public void onCreate(Bundle savedInstanceState) {
        super.onCreate(savedInstanceState);
        setContentView(R.layout.activity_hello);
    }
    @Override
    public boolean onCreateOptionsMenu(Menu menu) {
        getMenuInflater().inflate(R.menu.activity_hello, menu);
        return true;
    }
}
```

As you can see, Eclipse used the information in our New Android Application Project dialog to create a usable Java file, which includes a `first.example.helloabsolutebeginner` package declaration, import statements, a `HelloActivity` activity class, and `onCreate()` methods that create a layout

(UI) and menu structure placeholder. Also notice in Figure 4-14 that on the right of the Eclipse IDE a useful "Outline Pane," which gives a bird's-eye hierarchical overview of your java code, which will become more useful as your code becomes more complicated!

Opening the UI Definition

Next, let's take a look at our UI (user interface) markup code in the *activity_hello.xml* file in the *layout* folder, as shown in Figure 4-13. The XML code in the *activity_hello.xml* file is quite a bit different from the Java code. To see it, click the activity_hello.xml tab at the bottom of the middle code editing pane or section of Eclipse, or see Figure 4-13.

```
<RelativeLayout xmlns:android="http://schemas.android.com/apk/res/android"
    xmlns:tools="http://schemas.android.com/tools"
    android:layout_width="match_parent"
    android:layout_height="match_parent"
    >
<TextView
    android:layout_width="wrap_content"
    android:layout_height="wrap_content"
    android:layout_centerHorizontal="true"
    android:layout_centerVertical="true"
    android:text="@string/hello_world"
    tools:context=".HelloActivity"
    />
</RelativeLayout>
```

XML uses tags similar to those used in HTML markup to define structures that you will be using in your applications. In this case, it is a UI structure that contains a RelativeLayout tag, which keeps our UI elements organized via relative layout positioning and a TextView tag, which allows us to put our text message on the application screen.

Note   If you don't see something such as Figure 4-13 or Figure 4-15, to view the file, right-click its icon in the *layout* folder, select **Open**, and then choose *activity_hello.xml* at the bottom of the middle pane in the Eclipse window.

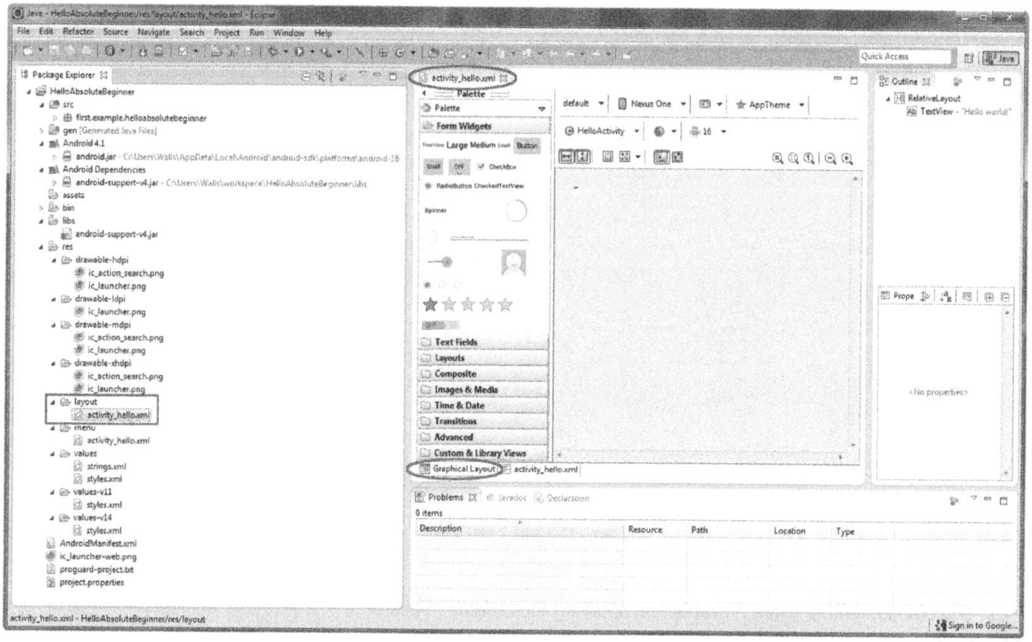

Figure 4-15. *The Graphical Layout Editor in Eclipse where our UI layout for our activity is created*

Notice that the TextView tag uses an attribute called android:text, which is set equal to @string/ hello_world. This is a reference to the *strings.xml* file, which we are going to look at next.

Opening the Strings Resource File

So far, we have looked at the Java code, which points to the *activity_hello.xml* file, which in turn points to the *strings.xml* file. Open that file now (right-click the file's icon in the Package Explorer and select **Open**) it is located in the values folder underneath the resources folder (/res/values). The file will open in a third tab within the Eclipse IDE, as shown in Figure 4-16.

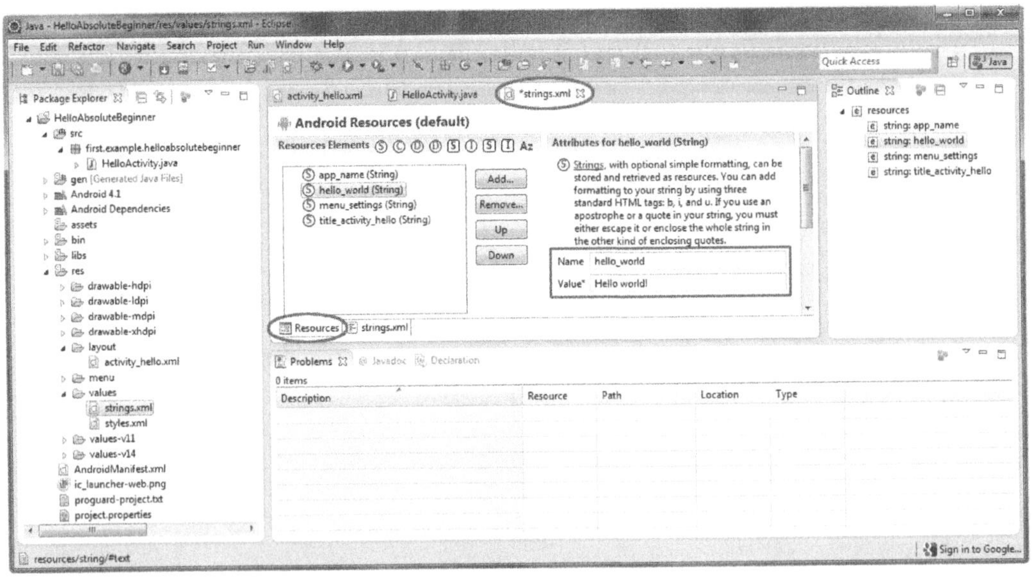

Figure 4-16. The strings.xml file when it first opens showing the default values

When you open the *strings.xml* file, you will see that Eclipse has already added four variables: app_name, hello_world, menu_settings , and title_activity_hello. The string variable named hello_world is to hold the text that we want our application to display. The app_name variable is to hold the string data that will appear in the title bar at the top of the application. We already specified it in the New Android Application dialog as HelloAbsoluteBeginner.

Notice the tabs at the bottom of the editing pane labeled Resources and strings.xml. These tabs allow you to switch between the actual XML code and the more user-friendly interface that you see in Figure 4-16, which makes editing Android resources a bit easier than coding straight XML. Because we're absolute beginners we'll utilize these features to make our development work easier, at least for now.

Because the app_name value is already specified thanks to our New Android Application dialog, let's leave it alone and set the value of hello_world to something new.

Setting a Variable Value in strings.xml

To set the value of hello_world, all you need to do is to click its name in the left pane of the Resources view and edit its text in the right pane of the Resources view. Once you click hello_world, two fields will appear. One contains the string variable name (hello_world), and the other has its value. In the Value field, type **Hello Absolute Beginner!**, as shown in Figure 4-17. This is the value (the text) that will appear on the screen of our App when we run it later on in this chapter.

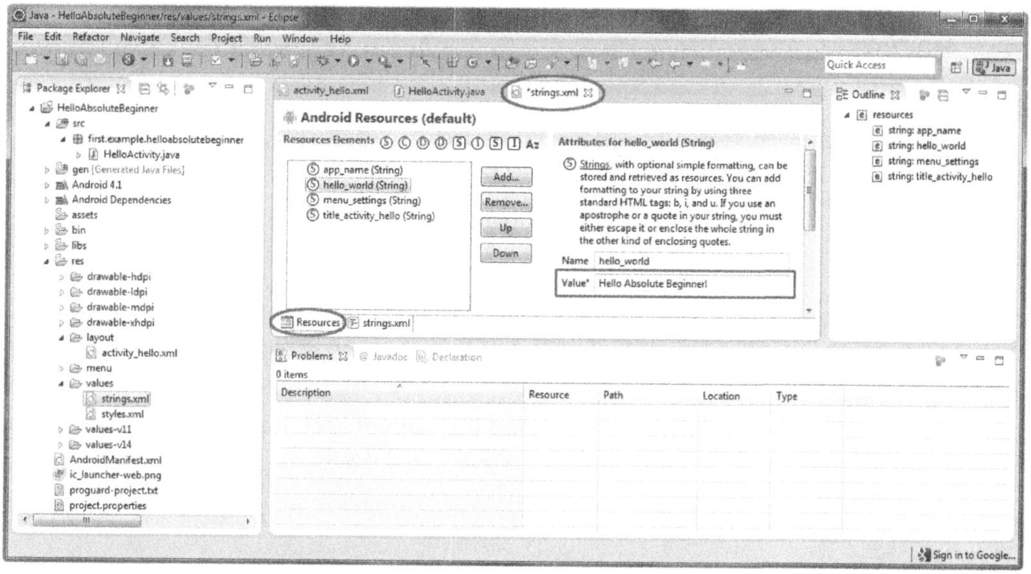

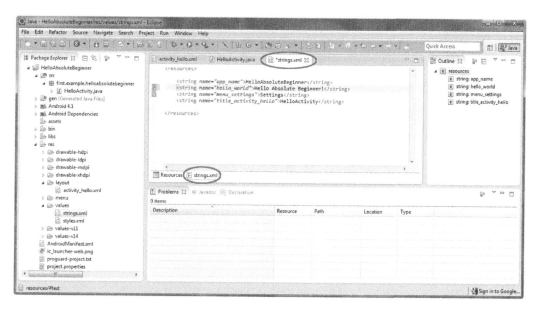

Figure 4-17. Editing the value of the hello_world String to display: Hello Absolute Beginner!

Once you have entered a new string value for the hello_world variable, click the strings.xml tab at the bottom of the editing pane, and take a look at the XML code that Eclipse has generated for you, as shown in Figure 4-18.

Figure 4-18. The updated XML code for the strings.xml resource file as shown under the strings.xml tab

In this view, you can see the actual XML code for the string tags, which are nested inside the <resources> tags that allow us to define resources for our Android application.

```
<resources>
    <string name="app_name">HelloAbsoluteBeginner</string>
    <string name="hello_world">Hello Absolute Beginner!</string>
    <string name="menu_settings">Settings</string>
    <string name="title_activity_hello">HelloActivity</string>
</resources>
```

Each <string> tag has a variable name attribute so we can refer to it by name in our Java code. Tags end with the same tag that they started with, but they have an added forward slash, like this: *<string>XXX</string>*.

As you can see in the XML code, Eclipse has created the correct XML code for us to use to write our Hello World message to the smartphone, tablet, e-reader, or iTV screen. The code reads as follows:

```
<string name="hello_world">Hello Absolute Beginner!</string>
```

Now it's time to save the *strings.xml* file you just edited using the CTRL-S shortcut (File ➤ Save) and then we can compile and run your first app, the Hello Absolute Beginner application.

Running the App

To compile and run the application, right-click the *HelloWorldAndroid* folder icon in the Eclipse Package Explorer and select **Run As ➤ Android Application** as shown in Figure 4-19.

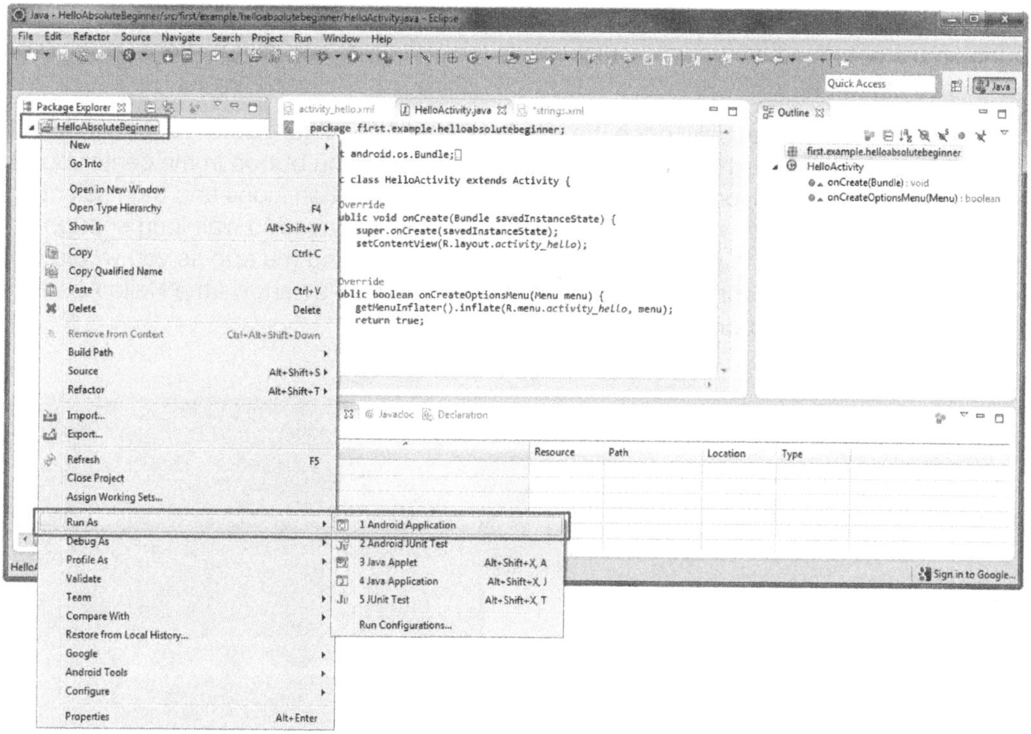

Figure 4-19. Using the right-click (on Project Folder) Run As ➤ Android Application menu sequence

The first thing Eclipse will do when you try to run your app is to make sure your files are all saved. If they are not, you will see a dialog like the one shown in Figure 4-20, which appears in this case because we modified the hello_world variable but did not hit the CTRL-S (Save) keystroke afterward that saves the file. Therefore, we'll let Android Development Tools do it for us by clicking the "Yes" option in the dialog that asks us if we want to save the file before running the app.

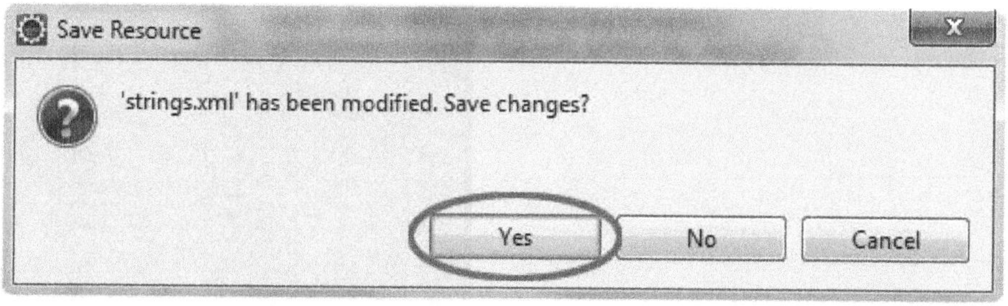

Figure 4-20. If you forgot to save your strings.xml file via CTRL-S then Eclipse will let you know about it

Eclipse will then compile your app, and will open a version 4.1 emulator window to display a virtual Android device (smartphone or tablet) representation (emulator) on which to run it. When the emulator first starts up, it will display the standard smartphone (or it could be a tablet) screen, simulating an Android OS background image and the standard Android icons for system time, signal strength, battery charge level, network type (3G, 4G, etc.) and so on. Note that it may take some time for the emulator to load into memory (especially the first time) and to load your app and run it once it is in memory.

The app should launch automatically once the emulator starts, but if for some reason it doesn't, to actually run the app in the emulator, you may need to click the Menu button in the center-bottom area of the screen, or use the Home button to display your application icons and then select an icon to run. Usually your application will just run automatically, you just need to wait long enough for this to happen. You can also use the phone interface, finding and running the app as you would in real life because this is a test environment. Give it a shot now. Figure 4-21 shows the Hello Absolute Beginner App running in the Android 4.1 emulator.

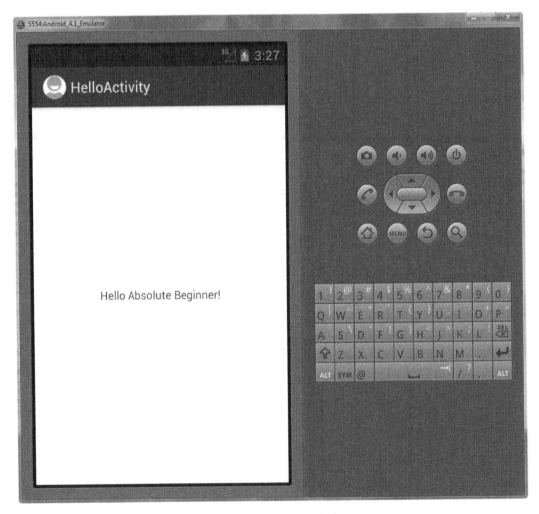

Figure 4-21. Running the Hello Absolute Beginner's app in the Android 4.1 device emulator

After you exit the 4.1 Emulator for the first time by clicking the Red X at the top right of the window, you will probably get an "Auto Monitor Logcat" error dialog as shown in Figure 4-22, which suggests that you enable ADT to automatically monitor the Logcat output for messages (usually error messages) from the Android Applications run in the Emulator. Select the "Yes, Monitor Logcat" option, and click on the OK button to continue.

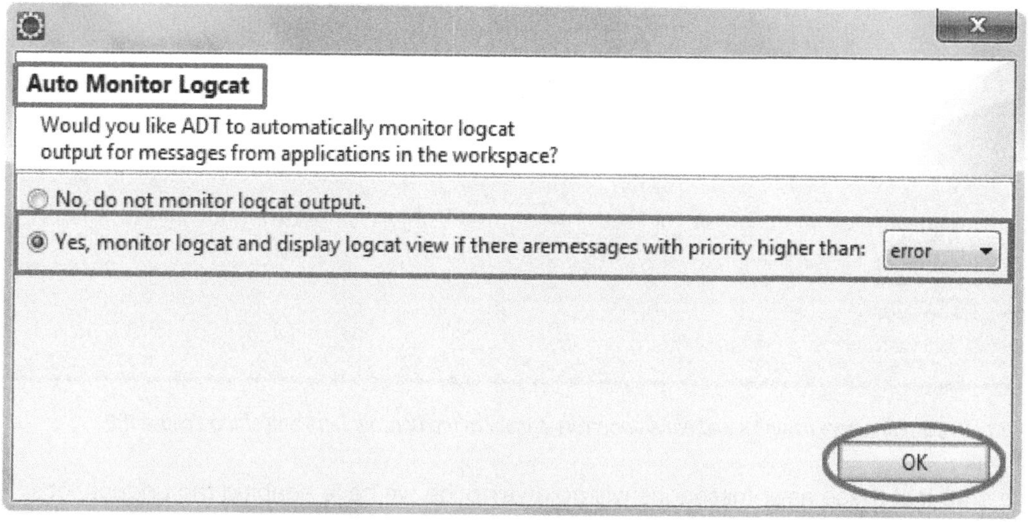

Auto Monitor Logcat

Would you like ADT to automatically monitor logcat output for messages from applications in the workspace?

◯ No, do not monitor logcat output.

◉ Yes, monitor logcat and display logcat view if there are messages with priority higher than: error ▼

OK

Figure 4-22. Setting Android to monitor LogCat and display LogCat view in the Eclipse IDE

After you click OK you will be returned to Eclipse where you will see what no programmer or developer wants to see in his or her IDE—Red Ink! The red text at the bottom of the IDE In the Console tab will show feedback on the compile and run process, and in this case it related not to problems in our code but to the fact that the Logcat was not set up, which we rectified in our previous step by telling the ADT to set it up for us. You can see the Logcat error messages in Figure 4-23.

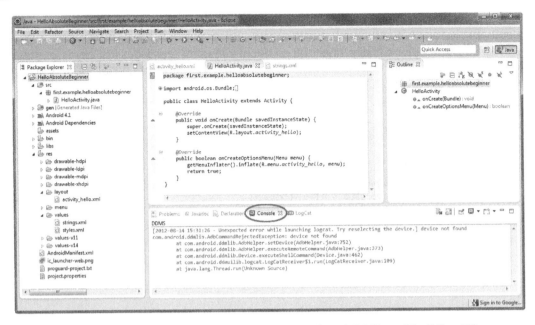

Figure 4-23. Displaying where compiler and emulator errors appear in the Console Tab/Pane of the Eclipse IDE

To make sure that these error messages will go away once we have enabled the Logcat, let's practice our right-click (on the project name) Run As ➤ Android Application menu sequence again, and see if we can get some black text in the console window this time, which is what we want to see and represents feedback on what ADT is doing to compile and run your app each time you invoke this Run As Android App menu sequence. The results are shown in Figure 4-24.

Figure 4-24.   Displaying what a clean compile and emulator console feedback output should look like

Congratulations, you have created your first error-free Android 4.1 application. Next, we'll customize its Android icon.

Adding an Application Icon

The final item that we are going to do in this chapter is give our application an icon that will show up on users' Android devices and can be used by them to launch the application. We'll use what you have learned about defining alternate resources by creating an icon that works on small, medium, large, and extra large screens. We'll add the appropriate ic_launcher.png files into the correct alternate dpi resolution folders provided by our Android Application project we just created, so that

Android automatically finds and uses the correct application launcher icon for each type of Android device screen size and density:

- *res/drawable-ldpi* for small low density dot per inch (LDPI) screens

- *res/drawable-mdpi* for average medium density dot per inch (MDPI) screens

- *res/drawable-hdpi* for large high density dot per inch (HDPI) screens

- /res/drawable-xhdpi for extra large extra-high density dot per inch (XHDPI) screens

Not surprisingly, this is done by giving your icon an exact name and file format, and putting it into an exact directory. When Android finds an icon file there, it automatically puts it into play as your application's icon. The files must follow these rules precisely:

- Be placed in the correct */res/drawable-dpi* folder, which holds all of the drawable resources for that screen resolution

- Be named *ic_launcher.png*

- Be a 24-bit PNG file with an alpha channel (transparency), also known as a 32-bit PNG, so that the icon overlays on any system background wallpaper seamlessly

Here, I'll use my 3D company logo in an Android Green hue, but you can use any image that you like. Also, I will use open source GIMP 2.8 for this image editing example, because all readers will have it installed, but you can use any image-editing program you prefer, such as Photoshop CS6 or Corel Painter. So let's fire up the GIMP 2.8 software package that we installed earlier in the book and prepare a 24-bit PNG file with transparency (alpha channel).

Adding Transparency

The first thing we need to do is to put the logo onto a transparency. Here are the steps to remove the white background from the logo

1. Open the MindTaffyLogoAndroidGreen.gif logo file using the GIMP File ➤ Open menu sequence. It is 200 × 200 pixels and the first frame of an Animated GIF file that is from my WallaceJackson.com website.

2. Select the "Select By Color" tool (fifth in the toolbar) and set the tolerance at 15 (bottom middle tool tab for Select by Color tool settings) and the Select By setting to Composite. Make sure the Antialiasing option is checked as well and then click the white area to select it as shown in Figure 4-25.

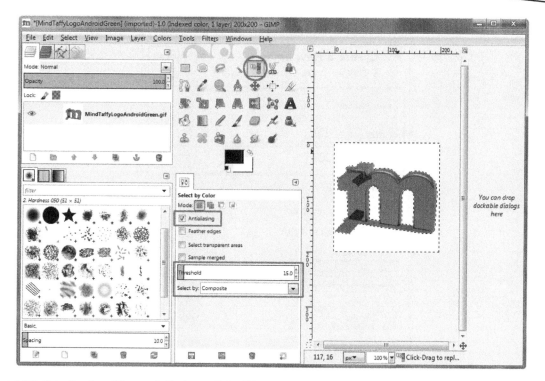

Figure 4-25. *Selecting the white area in the image that will be our transparent icon to remove white values*

3. Right-click in the white area in the layers tab (upper-left in Figure 4-25), which is directly underneath the layer showing the MindTaffyLogoAndroidGreen. gif image that we opened in Step 1, and select the "New Layer" option to open the New Layer Dialog as shown in Figure 4-26. Name the new layer "Transparency," and accept the other defaults as provided, and click OK.

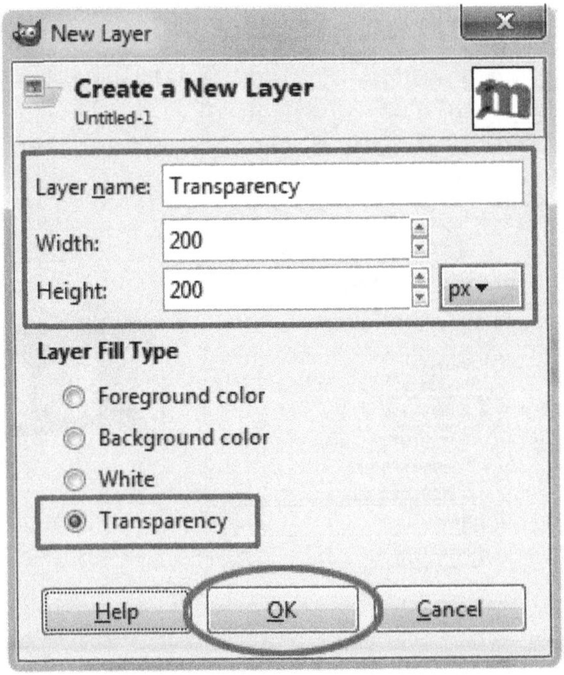

Figure 4-26. *Naming the layer "Transparency" and setting its width, height, and fill type options*

4. Choose the Select Menu and then the **Invert menu option** shown in Figure 4-27 to invert the selected white areas. This will grab only the logo because before only the white (nonlogo) areas were selected and therefore after the Invert operation only the logo pixels (nonwhite area) will be selected. Pretty cool.

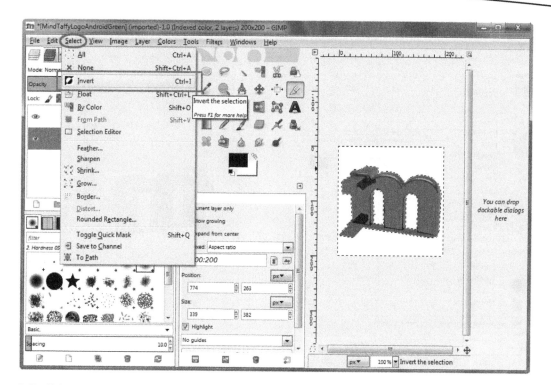

Figure 4-27. Using a Select ➤ Invert menu sequence to select the logo portion of the image rather than the white

5. Next select the **Edit Menu ➤ Copy Option** shown in Figure 4-28 to copy this selected logo image data to the clipboard. Note that in GIMP when you have your mouse over a menu or option it tells you exactly what it will do, and I have included these in the screens in this chapter to make it even easier to follow along.

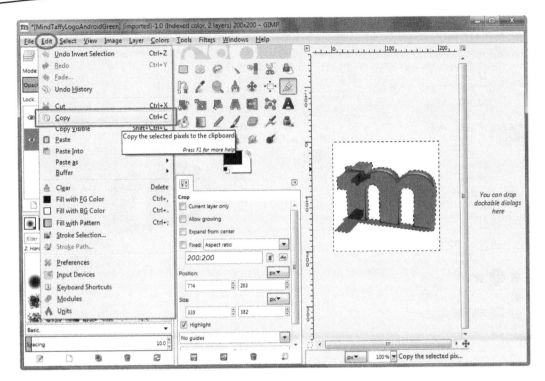

Figure 4-28. Using the Edit ➤ Copy menu sequence to copy the selected logo data to the clipboard (memory)

6. Click on your Transparency Layer on the left to select it (the layer will turn blue) if it isn't selected already, and then hit the CTRL-V keystroke combination to paste the pixel data from the clipboard, or you can use the Edit Menu ➤ Paste Option if you want a more visual work process. Next, click on the Eye Icon (turns layer visibility on or off) next to the original MindTaffyLogoAndroidGreen.gif layer at the bottom of the layer stack, so all that is showing in your preview on the right is the transparency layer and the floating selection (the logo only pixels), which you just pasted. The result of this work process are shown in Figure 4-29. Transparency in GIMP (and Photoshop for that matter) is represented by a checkerboard pattern, in case you are wondering!

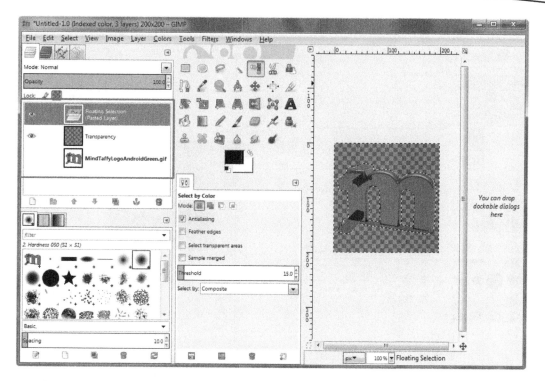

Figure 4-29. Pasting the Logo (icon) data onto the transparency layer and turning off visibility of original art

7. Now that we have the Launcher Icon image in the transparent format needed to "composite" it (blend it seamlessly) with any Android desktop out there, we will use the Image Menu's Scale Image Option, shown in Figure 4-30, to turn this 200 by 200 pixel image into the target icon image sizes (96, 72, 48, and 36 pixels) that we will need for our four Drawable Resources Folders.

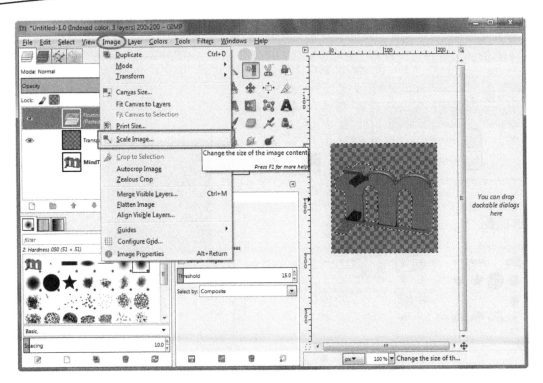

Figure 4-30. *Using the Image ➤ Scale Image… menu sequence to scale the image to target icon resolutions*

The Scale Image dialog shown in Figure 4-31 allows us to specify what image size we wish to scale our image down to, in this case 96 pixels for our */drawable-xhdpi/* folder location, and to also choose an Interpolation Algorithm, in this case "Cubic" (known as "Bi-Cubic" in Photoshop) interpolation, which yields the highest quality level, as you will see. Once you set your scaling parameters, click the "Scale" button to commit the scaling operation, and scale your 200 pixel image into a 96 pixel extra high density Android device icon!

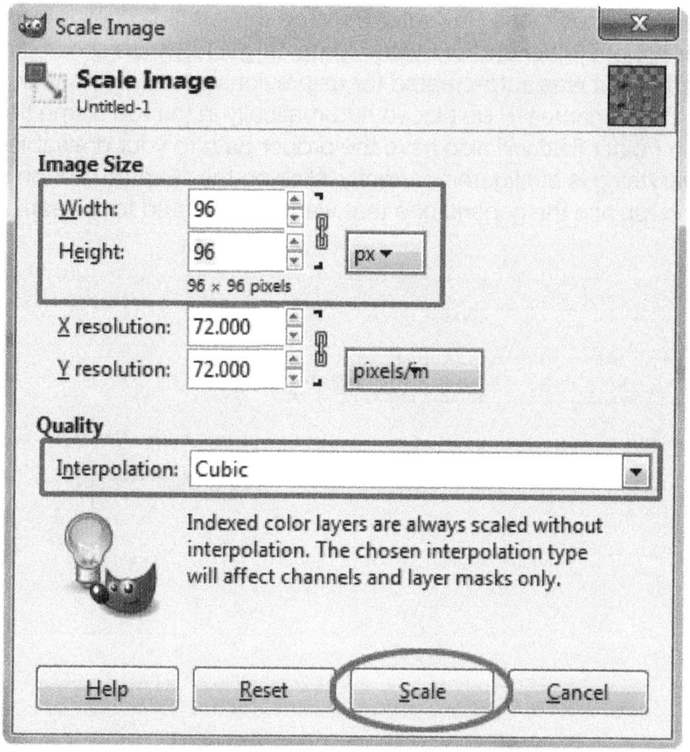

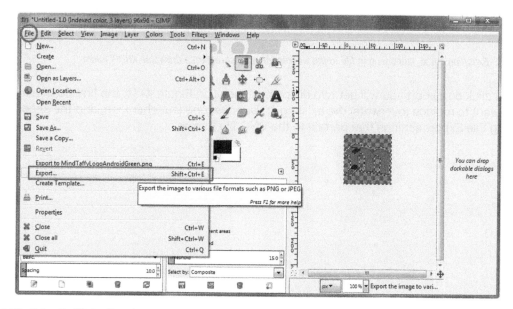

Figure 4-31. Setting the Scale Image parameters to 96 by 96 pixel for XHDPI icon requirements

Next we will select the File Menu ➤ Export Option shown in Figure 4-32. Also note that our transparent icon is now at the required 96 by 96 pixel size.

Figure 4-32. Using the File ➤ Export menu sequence to export our 96 pixel XHDPI icon

In the File Export dialog, use the Places Navigator Pane on the left to find your workspace folder and the HelloAbsoluteBeginner project folder and drawable-xhdpi target folder as shown in Figure 4-33. Click on the *ic_launcher.png* file that was auto-created for us previously to select that file for replacement with our new custom icon. The filename will be placed automatically in the top Name field for you when you do this, and the Save in Folder field will also have the proper path to your drawable-xhdpi folder from your C: drive! Once everything is configured correctly, click on the "Export" button to over write your custom XHDPI icon and replace the generic one that was auto-created for us earlier.

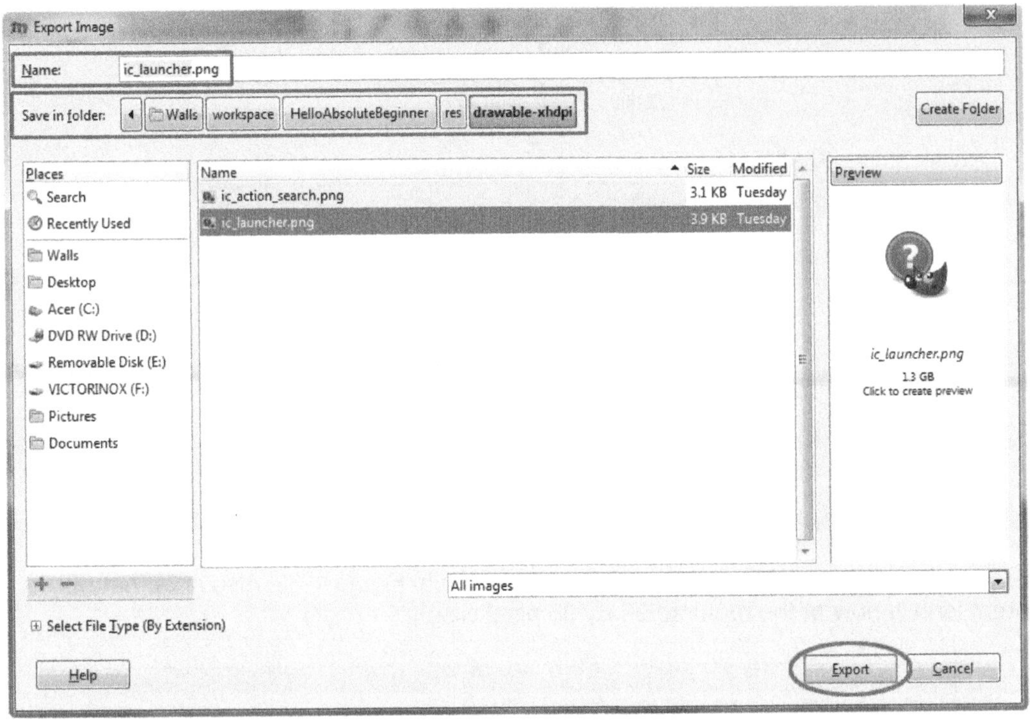

Figure 4-33. Exporting our ic_launcher.png *file to the workspace project resource drawable XHDPI folder*

Once you click on Export you will get two dialogs as shown in Figure 4-34, the first confirming that you want to replace (overwrite) the existing *ic_launcher.png* launcher icon, and the second requesting File Export settings that pertain to the PNG file format.

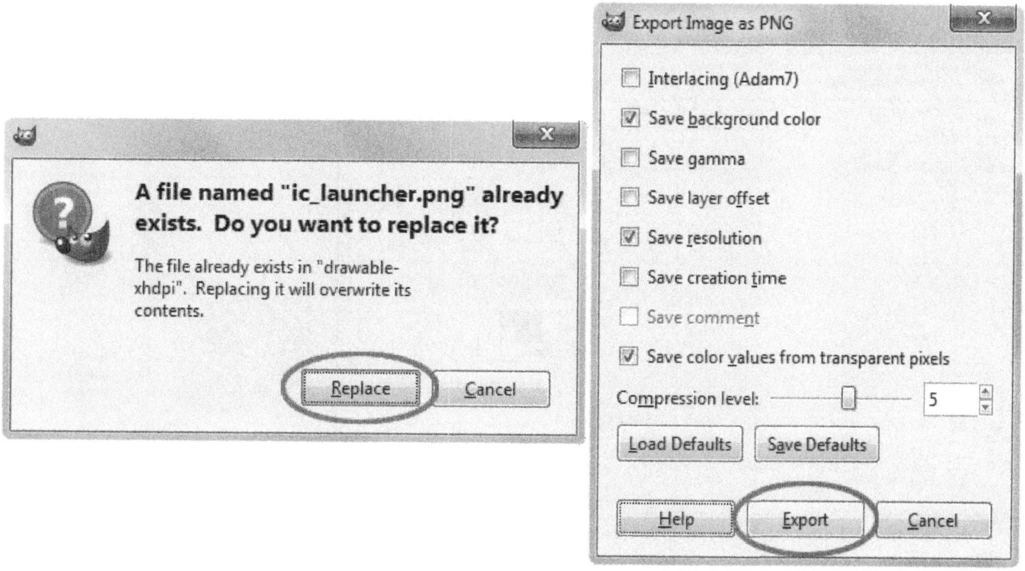

Figure 4-34. Confirming the replacement of the original icon and settings for the PNG32 file format

To create the other three resolution icons, rather than going through the entire work process outlined earlier, let's take a clever shortcut that involves the Edit Menu ➤ Undo Option shown in Figure 4-35 to save a dozen steps of work! All we need to do is use the Edit ➤ Undo Scale and redo the last couple of steps (Image Scale and File Export) and then do the same work process to scale the 200 pixel transparent image to 72, 48, and 36 pixels and then File ➤ Export to the HDPI, MDPI, and LDPI drawable folders under your project file, replacing the *ic_launcher.png* file in each folder with its required resolution equivalent. Make sure to scale from the 200 pixel image each time (i.e., 200 pixels scale to 72 pixels, 200 pixels scale to 48 pixels, and 200 pixels scaled to 36 pixels) as the quality result will be significantly better than if you used a work process in which you scaled from 200 to 96 and then 96 to 72, 72 to 48, and 48 to 36. This is because the more data you give the original Image Scaling Algorithm the better job it will do (the more it will have to work with) giving you a great result, so if you want to design your Launcher Icons at 864 pixels (which is what Google recommends in their graphics design guidelines) then by all means go for it!

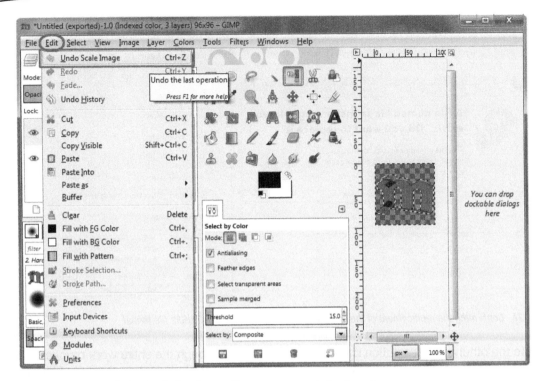

Figure 4-35. Undo the 200 pixel to 96 pixel scale operation so we can scale to other sizes

Summary

Android is very particular about which types of files you use and where you put them in your project folder. We will be looking at the particulars of how things need to be set up to work properly in Android throughout the rest of this book.

In this chapter, you created and compiled your first project for Android inside Eclipse using the Android application development environment you installed in Chapter 3. You saw that the Android Development Environment in Eclipse gives you a lot of development assistance, and as a beginner, you'll want to take advantage of every bit of help you can get. The proof is in the pudding, as they say.

You just developed your first Android Hello Absolute Beginner application and needed to change only a single line of code in the Eclipse for Java EE IDE. You saw how Android sets up a basic application file and directory structure, and which Java and XML files are needed to create a UI, a menu, and a basic application. You saw how to Compile and Run your app in the Android 4.1 Device Emulator using the Run as Android Application command.

Your Android application icon is very important to the branding of your application, as it represents your application on the users' desktop, which is usually crowded with all of the other installed application icons. Customizing your own app icon is as simple as creating the PNG32 graphics and then putting the icon files into their correct target resolution (DPI) folders. You just must make sure that the icon is saved in the correct file type, is the correct resolution, uses an alpha channel, and has the correct file name: *ic_launcher.png*.

The next chapter provides an overview of Java and how Android compartmentalizes things having to do with an application. In the remaining chapters, we will get down to actually coding in Java and creating XML markup that delivers your application's UI and functionality in more advanced ways and with more advanced features.

Chapter 5

Android Framework Overview

The primary programming language used in developing your Android applications is Java SE, from Oracle (formerly Sun Microsystems). As noted in Chapter 1, Java SE stands for Java Standard Edition, and many people shorten this to just Java when referring to the programming language. Two other editions of the Java programming language are called Java EE, short for Java Enterprise Edition, and Java ME, for Java Micro Edition.

Java EE was designed for use on potentially massive computer networks, such as vast collections of blade computers that are used to run large enterprises or corporations with thousands of active users, although Java EE also can be run on smaller installations as well as long as they have enough system memory and a couple of processing cores. Its differentiating features beyond Java SE are that Java EE features more multiuser scalable functionality than Java SE, which is designed more for a single user on a single computer system, say a home PC or a laptop, or better yet, an Android device such as an iTV set, e-book e-reader, tablet, or smartphone.

Java ME is designed for embedded systems to create highly portable computers such as mobile phones. It has fewer features than Java SE, so that it can fit onto a standard mobile phone (usually termed a "feature phone" today) without using too much memory and resources to run it. Most entry-level mobile phones (flip-phones) run Java ME, but Android smartphones run the more powerful Java SE. Android phones can run Java SE because they have a full gigabyte of memory and a 1GHz or faster CPU, so essentially today's Android touchscreen smartphones are tiny Linux computers.

Java is an object-oriented programming (OOP) language. It is based on the concepts of developing modular, self-contained constructs called *objects*, which contain their own attributes and characteristics. In this chapter, you will learn about the OOP characteristics of Java, and the logic behind using these modular programming techniques which are used to build applications that are easier to share and debug due to implementing this OOP approach.

After you've had a taste of the power of Java, we'll quickly cover XML because it's the way you define UIs and configurations in your Android apps, as you saw firsthand in Chapter 4 when you built your first Android application. Without XML, you would need to rely solely on Java code to define everything, which would make developing apps a lot more complicated, especially for the design department.

Finally, we'll cover the main parts of the Android framework, and you will be able to see the object-oriented programming (OOP) underpinnings that Android supports. We'll briefly cover each component and explain which chapter covers it in more detail.

The Foundation of OOP: The Object

The foundation of OOP is the object itself. Objects in OOP languages are similar to objects that you see around you every day, except they are virtual and not tangible. As with tangible real-world objects, Java objects have characteristics, called *states*, and things that they can do, called *behaviors*. One way to think about this is that objects are nouns, or things that exist in and of themselves, and behaviors are like verbs, or things that nouns do.

As an example, consider a very popular object in all of our lives: the automobile. Some characteristics, or states, of a car might be as follows:

- Color (red)
- Direction (N, S, E, or W)
- Speed (15 miles per hour)
- Engine type (gas, diesel, hydrogen, propane, or electric)
- Gear setting (1, 2, 3, 4, or 5)
- Drivetrain type (2WD or 4WD)

The following are some things that a car can do, or behaviors:

- Accelerate
- Shift gears
- Apply the brake
- Turn the wheels
- Turn on the stereo
- Use the headlights
- Use the turn signals

You get the idea.

Figure 5-1 is a simple diagram of the object structure using the car example. It shows the characteristics, or attributes, of the car that are central to defining the car object, and the behaviors that can be used. These attributes and behaviors define the car to the outside world.

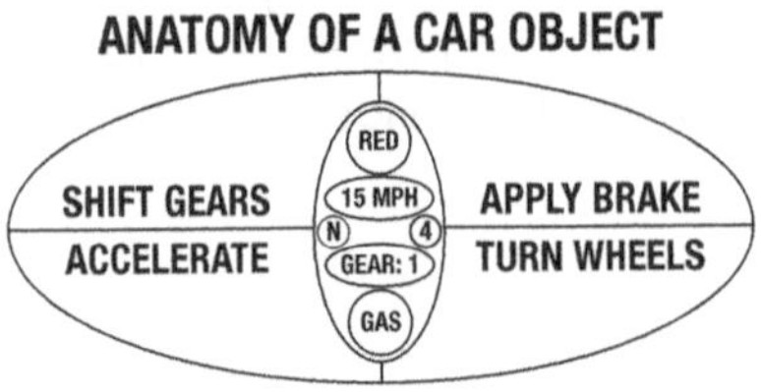

ANATOMY OF A CAR OBJECT

Figure 5-1. Car object showing car characteristics (inner oval) and car behaviors (outer oval)

Objects can be as complicated as you want them to be, and can nest or contain other objects within their structure, or *object hierarchy*. A hierarchy is like a tree structure, with a main trunk and branches and subbranches as you move up (or down) its structure. A good example of a hierarchy that you use every day is the multilevel directory or folder structure on your computer's hard disk drive.

Directories or folders on your hard disk drive can contain other directories or folders, which can in turn contain yet other directories and folders, allowing complex hierarchies of organization to be created. We saw a great example of this in Chapter 4, where our Eclipse Workspace folder was in our Users folder, our HelloAbsoluteBeginner project folder was in our Workspace folder, and our Launch Icons were in Resource (Drawable) folders within that HelloAbsoluteBeginner project folder!

You can do this same hierarchical construction with objects that can contain subobjects, which can themselves contain further subobjects, as needed to create your structure. You'll see plenty of nested objects when working with Android because nested objects are useful for grouping objects that are used in only one place. In other words, some types of objects are useful only to one other type of object in an Android app, so they are provided in a nested hierarchy underneath that object type.

You should practice identifying objects in the room around you, and then break their definition down into states (characteristics) and behaviors (things that they can do), as this is how you will need to think to become more successful in your OOP endeavors with the Java programming language and the XML markup language. It is important to note that both Java and XML can be used to define objects for Android applications. We already defined a TextView resource object having six characteristics in Chapter 4 using XML (see lucky Figure 4-13 for that object definition).

You'll notice that in real life, objects can be made up of other objects. For example, a car engine object is made up of hundreds of discrete objects that function together to make the engine object work as a whole. This same construction of more complicated objects out of simpler objects can be done in OOP languages, where complex hierarchies of objects can contain other objects that have been created in previous Java code.

Some OOP Terminology

Now let's cover some of the technical terminology used for Java objects. First, objects have fields and methods, as follows:

- *Fields*, called *variables*, hold the object's states.

- *Methods* are programming routines that operate on the object's internal states. If object characteristics can be thought of as nouns, then methods can be thought of as verbs, using this analogy. Methods also allow other objects external to the object itself to communicate with the object.

One of the key concepts of OOP is *data encapsulation*, where the object's fields are allowed to be modified directly only through that same object's methods. This allows the object to be self-sufficient. For example, to turn the car, you use the steering method, which positions the wheels in the desired direction.

With data encapsulation, each object that is part of a larger object construct can be built and tested individually, without requiring accessing data from other objects or modules of the application (which can translate into bugs). Without data encapsulation, people could simply access any part of your object's data and use it however they pleased. This could introduce bugs, affecting the methods you have perfected to manipulate your object and provide your solution.

Data encapsulation promotes the core concept in OOP of *modularity*. Once an object is created and tested, it can be used by other objects without worrying about its integrity. Data encapsulation thus allows code reuse, so programmers can develop libraries of useful objects that do not need to be rewritten or retested by other programmers. You can see how this can save developers time and money by structuring only the work that needs to be done and avoiding redundant work processes.

Data encapsulation also allows developers to hide the data and the internal workings of the object if desired.

Finally, objects make debugging easier because they can be added or removed modularly during testing to ascertain where bugs are located within the overall code. In our car object example, the attributes of our car are encapsulated inside of the car object, and can thus be changed only via the methods that surround them in each diagram. For instance, one would use the Shift Gears method to change the Gears=1 field variable to Gears=2.

The Blueprint for an Object: The Class

In real life, there is seldom just a single type of object. Usually, there are a number of different types and variations. For instance, for a car object, there are many different manufacturers, sizes, shapes, seating capacity, engine types, fuel types, transmission types, and so on.

In Java SE, we write something called a *class* to define what an object can do (its methods) and the fields it has. Once this class has been coded in Java, we can then create an *instance* of each object that we wish to use by referencing the class definition. In architectural terms, the class is a type of blueprint as to what the object is, what states it contains, and what it can do (what methods it has).

> **Note**   An instance is a concrete object created from the blueprint of the class, with its own states or unique data attributes. For example, you might have a (second) blue car instance that is traveling south in third gear. (In the example, our first car instance is red and traveling north in first gear.)

To illustrate this further, let's construct a basic class for our car object example. To create a car class, you use the Java keyword class, followed by your name for the new class that you are writing, and then curly brackets to hold your code definition, like so:

```
class Car {Code definition for a car class goes in here. We will do this next.}
```

The first thing that we usually put inside our class (inside the curly {} brackets) is the data fields (*variables*) that will hold the states, or attributes, of our car. In this case, we have six fields that define the car's gear, speed, direction, fuel type, color, and drivetrain (two- or four-wheel drive), as specified in the basic diagram shown earlier in Figure 5-1.

To define a variable in Java, you first declare its data type (int means a whole number, and String means text), followed by your variable name. You can also (optionally) set a default, or starting, value by using an equal sign and a data value. The variable definition ends with a semicolon.

> **Note**   Semicolons are used in programming languages to separate each code construct or definition from the other ones within the same body of code.

So, with our six variables from our anatomy of an object diagram in place, our class definition looks like this:

```
class Car {
    int speed = 15;
    int gear = 1;
    int drivetrain = 4;
    String direction = "N";
    String color = "Red";
    String fuel = "Gas";
}
```

Remember that these are all the default values—the ones each object instance will have when we create it.

Notice how the example spaces out the curly braces ({}) on their own lines and indents lines, so that you can see what is contained within those braces more easily.

The next part of the class file will contain the methods that define how the car object will operate on the variables that define its current state of operation. Methods also can return a value to the calling entity, such as values that have been successfully changed or even answers to an equation. For instance, there could be a method to calculate distance that multiplies speed by time and returns a distance value.

To declare a method that does not return any value to the calling entity, you use the void keyword. A good example of using void is a method that triggers something—the method is used to invoke a change in the object, but does not need to send a value back to the calling function.

If your method or function returns a value, instead of using the void keyword, you use the data type of the data that is to be returned, say int or string. For example, an addition method would return a number after finishing its calculation, so you would use int.

After the void keyword comes a name for the method (say, shiftGears). This is followed by the type of data (in this case, an int) and variable name (newGear) in parentheses.

```
void shiftGears (int newGear) {
```

The variable contains a data parameter that will be passed to the method, so the method now has this variable with which to work.

> **Note**   The normal method-naming convention is to start a method name with a lowercase
> letter, and to use uppercase letters to begin words embedded within the method name, like this:
> `methodNameExample()`. Read more about naming conventions for Java at:
> `http://www.oracle.com/technetwork/java/codeconv-138413.html`

Some methods are called without variables, as follows:

```
methodSample();
```

To call the `shiftGears()` method, you would use the following format:

```
shiftGears(4);
```

This passes 4 into the `shiftGears()` method's newGear variable, which sets its value. This value is
then passed into the interior of the `shiftGears()` method logic (the part inside the curly braces),
where it is finally used to set the object's gear (internal) field to the new gear shift value of 4, or
fourth gear.

A common reason to use a method without any parameters is to trigger a change in an object that
does not depend on any data being passed in. So, we could code an `upShift()` method and a
`downShift()` method that would upshift and downshift by one gear level each time they were called,
rather than change to a gear selected by the driver. We then would not need a parameter to shift
gears on our car; we would just call `upShift()` or `downShift()` whenever gear shifting was needed.

> **Note**   Notice the empty parentheses after the method names in the text. These are used when writing
> about the method, so that the reader knows that the author is talking about a method. You will see this
> convention used throughout the rest of this book.

After the method declaration, the method's code procedures are contained inside the curly braces.
In this example, we have four methods:

- The `shiftGears()` method sets the car's gear to the gear that was passed into
  the `shiftGears()` method.

  ```
  void shiftGears (int newGear) {
      gear = newGear;
  }
  ```

- The `accelerateSpeed()` method takes the object's speed state variable and adds
  an acceleration factor to the speed, which causes the object to accelerate. This
  is done by taking the object's current speed setting, or state, and adding an
  acceleration factor to it, and then setting the result of the addition back to the
  original speed variable, so that the object's speed state now contains the new
  (accelerated) speed value.

```
void accelerateSpeed (int acceleration) {
    speed = speed + acceleration;
}
```

- The applyBrake() method takes the object's speed state variable and subtracts a braking factor from the current speed, which causes the object to decelerate, or to brake. This is done by taking the object's current speed setting and subtracting a braking factor from it, and then setting the result of the subtraction back to the original speed variable, so that the object's speed state now contains the updated (decelerated) braking value.

```
void applyBrake (int brakingFactor) {
    speed = speed - brakingFactor;
}
```

- The turnWheel() method is straightforward, much like the shiftGears() method, except that it uses a string value of N, S, E, or W to control the direction that the car turns. When turnWheel("W") is used, the car will turn left.

```
void turnWheel (String newDirection) {
    direction = newDirection;
}
```

The methods go inside the class and after the variable declarations, as follows:

```
class Car {
    int speed = 15;
    int gear = 1;
    int drivetrain = 4;
    String direction = "N";
    String color = "Red";
    String fuel = "Gas";

    void shiftGears (int newGear) {
        gear = newGear;
    }

    void accelerateSpeed (int acceleration) {
        speed = speed + acceleration;
    }

    void applyBrake (int brakingFactor) {
        speed = speed - brakingFactor;
    }

    void turnWheel (String newDirection) {
        direction = newDirection;
    }
}
```

This Car class allows us to define a car object, but it can't do anything until we use it to instantiate an object. In other words, it does not do anything until it is called.

For us to create an instance of an object, we must instantiate it. Here's the onCreate() method of an Android application, where we instantiate two cars and use them (refer to the example in Chapter 4 to see how to create an onCreate() method in an Android app):

```
public void onCreate(Bundle savedInstanceState) {
    super.onCreate(savedInstanceState);
    setContentView(R.layout.activity_car);

    Car carOne = new Car();            // Create Car Objects
    Car carTwo = new Car();

    carOne.shiftGears(3);
    carOne.accelerateSpeed(15);        // Invoke Methods on Car 1
    carOne.turnWheel("E");

    carTwo.shiftGears(2);              // Invoke Methods on Car 2
    carTwo.applyBrake(10);
    carTwo.turnWheel("W");
}
```

On launch or creation of our Android application, we now have two empty car objects. We have done this using the Car() *class constructor*, along with the new keyword, which creates a new object for us, like so:

```
Car carOne = new Car();
```

The syntax for doing this is very similar to what we used to declare our variables:

- ▪ Define the object type Car.

- ▪ Give a name to our object (carOne).

- ▪ Set the carOne object equal to a new Car object definition, which has all the default variable values set.

To invoke our methods using our new car objects requires the use of something called *dot notation*. Once an object has been created and named, you can call methods by using the following code construct:

```
objectName.methodName(variable);
```

So, to shift into third gear on car object number one, we would use this:

```
carOne.shiftGears(3);
```

So, as you can see in the final six lines of code in the onCreate() method, we set carOne to third gear, accelerate it from 15 to 30 mph by accelerating by a value of 15, and turn east by using the turnWheel() method with a value of "E" (the default direction is north, or "N"). Car two we shift into second, `applyBrake()` to slow it down from 15 to 5 mph, and turn the car west by using the `turnWheel("W")` method via our dot notation. Also note that you can place comments in your code by preceding them with two forward slashes. When the compiler sees this it ignores anything after the two slashes until the end of that line.

Providing Structure for Your Classes: Inheritance

There is also support in Java for developing different types of car objects by using a technique called *inheritance*, where more specific car classes (and thus more uniquely defined objects) can be *subclassed* from a more generic car class. Once a class is used for inheritance by a subclass, it becomes the *superclass*. There can be only one superclass, but there can be an unlimited number of subclasses. All of the subclasses inherit the methods and fields from the superclass.

For instance, from our `Car` class, we could subclass an `Suv` class that extended the `Car` class to include those attributes that would apply only to an SUV type of car, in addition to the methods and states that apply to all types of cars. An SUV car class could have `onStarCall()` and `turnTowLightOn()` methods, in addition to the usual car operation methods. Similarly, we could generate a subclass for sports cars that includes an `activateOverdrive()` method to provide faster gearing and an `openTop()` method to put down the convertible roof. You can see these subclasses in the extension of our car object diagram shown in Figure 5-2.

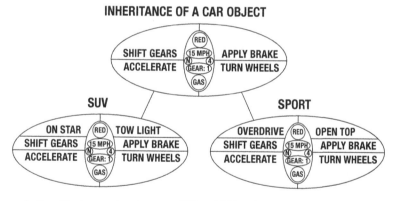

Figure 5-2. *Inheritance of a Car object superclass to create SUV and SPORT Car subclasses*

To create a subclass from a superclass, you extend the subclass from the superclass using the extends keyword in the class declaration, as in the following:

```
class Suv extends Car { New Fields and Methods Go Here }
```

This extends to `Suv` all of the fields and methods that `Car` features, so that the developer can focus on just the new or different fields and methods that relate to the differentiation of the SUV from the regular car definition. Because the original core fields and methods come from the `Car` class, it becomes the superclass, and the `Suv` class becomes the subclass. `Suv` is said to be *subclassed* from the `Car` superclass.

To refer to one of the superclass methods from within the subclass you are writing, you can use the super keyword. For example, in the Suv class, we may want to use a generic car's applyBrake() method, and then apply some other factor to the brakes that is specific to SUVs. The following code does this:

```
class Suv extends Car {
    void applyBrake (int brakingFactor) {
        super.applyBrake(brakingFactor);
        speed = speed - brakingFactor;
    }
}
```

This means the SUV's brakes are twice as powerful as a generic car's brakes because the SUV applyBrake() method first calls the applyBrake() of the superclass via the super.applyBrake(brakingFactor); line of the method and then again decrements the speed variable by the brakingFactor a second time, making the brakes twice as powerful or effective.

Be sure to use good programming practices and refer to Javadoc documentation for the superclass fields and methods within each subclass. This documentation lets the users know that the superclass's fields and methods are available because they do not explicitly appear in the code for the subclass.

Defining an Interface

In many Java applications, the classes conform to a certain pattern, so that the rest of the application knows what to expect of those classes when they are instantiated as objects. This is especially common when using a framework like Android.

The *public interface* that the classes present to the rest of the application makes using them more predictable and allows you to use them in places where any class of that pattern is suitable. In other words, the public interface is a label that tells the application what this class can do, without the application needing to test its capabilities.

In Java terms, making a class conform to a pattern is done by implementing an interface. The following is an ICar interface that forces all cars to have the methods defined in the interface. This also means that the rest of the application knows that each car can do all of these actions because the ICar interface defines the public interface of all cars.

```
public interface ICar {
    void shiftGears (int newGear);
    void accelerateSpeed (int acceleration);
    void applyBrake (int brakingFactor);
    void turnWheel (String newDirection);
}
```

So, a car is not a car unless it contains these particular methods.

To implement an interface, use the implements keyword as follows, and then define all the methods as before, except they must be public.

```
class Car implements ICar {
    int speed = 15;
    int gear = 1;
    int drivetrain = 4;
    String direction = "N";
    String color = "Red";
    String fuel = "Gas  ";

    public void shiftGears (int newGear) {
        gear = newGear;
    }

    public void accelerateSpeed (int acceleration) {
        speed = speed + acceleration;
    }

    public void applyBrake (int brakingFactor) {
        speed = speed - brakingFactor;
    }

    public void turnWheel (String newDirection) {
        direction = newDirection;
    }
}
```

Adding the public keyword before the void keyword allows other classes to call these methods, even if those classes are in a different package (packages are discussed in the next section). After all, this is a public interface, and anyone (more accurately any class) should be able to use it.

Bundling Classes in a Logical Way: The Package

Each time you start a new project in Android, the Eclipse IDE will create a package to contain your own custom classes that you will define to implement your application's functionality. In the Hello Absolute Beginner application that we created in the previous chapter, our package was named first.example.helloabsolutebeginner. In fact, the New ➤ Project ➤ Android Application Project dialog asked us for this package name.

The package declaration is the first line of code in any Android application, or in any Java application for that matter. The package declaration tells Java how to package your application. Recall the first line of code in our Hello Absolute Beginner application:

```
package first.example.helloabsolutebeginner;
```

After the package keyword and declaration come import statements, which import existing Java classes and packages into your declared package. So, a package is not only for your own code that you write yourself, but also for all code that your application uses, even if it is open source code written by another programmer or company, or in the case of Android applications, API code that serves up functionality available within the Android operating system (OS).

Basically, the package concept is similar to the folder hierarchy on your computer. A package is just a way of organizing your code by its functionality. Android organizes its classes into logical packages, which we will routinely import and use throughout this book. Each Android API Level (Level 16 for the current Android Jelly Bean OS version 4.1) contains a collection of functional packages that are used by developers to access its feature set.

In our Hello Absolute Beginner application in the previous chapter, we needed the following `import` statements in our *HelloActivity.java* file to support class functions in our application:

```
import android.os.Bundle;
import android.app.Activity;
import android.view.Menu;
```

This is basically to address where the code for each `import` statement is located. Here is a generalization of how an `import` statement follows a path to the class:

```
import platform.functionality.classname;
```

This applies to our statement as follows:

- `android` says this is an Android package.

- `os` refers to the broad operating systems functionality of the package in question.

- `Bundle` refers to the class we are importing and subclassing.

Thus, the `Activity` class, which is the super class for any activity that you create, is found within the `android.app` package. This `app` part says that this package logically contains classes that are necessary for the creation of Android OS applications, and one of these is the `Activity` class, which allows us to define UIs, and the other is the Bundle class from the android.os package that allows us to bundle up application variables. Both of these can be seen in our Chapter 4 Java code in the Eclipse IDE by clicking the plus (+) symbol next to the import statements.

You may be wondering if the package is the highest level of organization in Java. The answer is no, there is one higher level. This level is sometimes called a *platform* or *application programming interface* (API) level. This is a collection of all the core packages for a given language, such as Java SE or Java ME, or all the packages of a specialized product, such as Android. Android 4.1 Jelly Bean API Level 16 is the sixteenth Android Platform to be released so far and it contains a great many packages with which to define it's total functionality.

An Overview of XML

There are actually two types of languages used in Android development: Java and XML. XML stands for eXtensible Markup Language. Developed in 1996, XML is similar to HTML (which stands for Hyper-Text Markup Language), which is used for website design.

The primary use of XML is to structure data for items that require a predefined data structure, such as address books or computer-aided design (CAD). Like Java, XML is very modular, which allows complicated data definition constructs to be created.

XML uses structures called *tags*, just as HTML does. And as in HTML, these tags use tag keywords bracketed by the ‹ and › characters. For example, in Android, the ‹resources› tag contains resource definitions, and the ‹string› tag contains string resource definitions. The ‹string› tag also features *attributes* (which I think of more as parameters of sorts); for instance, a ‹string› tag has a name attribute that allows it to be named. Remember that the values must be inside quotation marks to be validated (passed over to) the XML processor (parser). Like this:

‹string name="string_name_here"›This is the Value of the String Here‹/string›

> **Note**   A *parameter* is a choice of data options that can be set, telling some code what you want it to do—sort of a way that you can configure it exactly to your liking. So, you could set a background color of red by specifying a red parameter to a method or as an attribute to an XML color element or parameter.

In our Hello Absolute Beginners application in Chapter 4, we defined four string resources with the following XML in the *strings.xml* file:

```
<resources>
        <string name="app_name">HelloAbsoluteBeginner</string>
        <string name="hello_world">Hello Absolute Beginner!</string>
        <string name="menu_settings">Settings</string>
        <string name="title_activity_hello">HelloActivity</string>
</resources>
```

You can readily see the modularity via the nesting of tags. The ‹resources› tag contains the four ‹string› tags and their attributes, putting them into one resources group. Nesting can be as many levels deep as required for more complicated data definition constructs.

XML is used in Android to define constructs so that you do not need to create them in the more complicated Java code environment. It is easier to write definitions in XML than it is to write them in Java. This is because XML has the simpler markup format used in HTML, rather than the more complicated block code structure used in Java. This makes it easier for nonprogrammers to help write applications.

XML constructs can be turned into Java constructs by a process called "inflating," which we actually got a taste of in the Java code in our HelloAbsoluteBeginner application that created (inflated) the Options Menu using our *activity_hello.xml* menu definition via the line of code that reads:

getMenuInflater().inflate(R.menu.activity_hello, menu);

Because XML is easier to use than Java, and because this is a book for absolute beginners, we will do everything that we can using XML instead of Java. Android allows this, and the XML works as well as Java code to achieve exactly the same results.

The Anatomy of an Android Application: The APK File

The cornerstone of Android application development is the application package file format, or the APK file format. When you compile and output an application for distribution to your Android users, the Eclipse IDE and Android SDK output your application file name with an *.apk* extension. There is only one *.apk* file, and it includes all of your application code (in the form of a DVM executable *.dex* file format), as well as any new media resources or assets and the *AndroidManifest.xml* file (which we'll discuss in detail in the final section of this chapter).

Interestingly, the Android Market, now branded as "Google Play" increased APK file size limits for *.apk* files from 25MB to 50MB, which is great news for developers. Using something called "expansion files" as of May 2012 an application can now support up to 4GB (4,000 Megabytes) of data beyond the 50MB APK file that holds your application and its primary assets. Two additional expansion files of up to 2GB each can be accessed from your application's APK file, but that said, the smaller you can get your application, the faster it will download, and the smoother it will function across consumer electronics devices. Also, if you have 4GB of extra application data, be aware that your users will have to use the space on their Android device's SD card to store this data, which may well use up valuable space that they may want or need for other purposes.

So, back to learning about APK. If your application is called Zoomerza, for instance, the file that you will get on final publishing will be called *Zoomerza.apk*, and it will run on any Android phone, iTV, e-reader, or tablet. This file format is closely related to the standard Java *.jar* format, and uses the familiar ZIP type of data compression. The *.apk* file is specifically set up so that it can be run in place (as is) without going through any data unpacking processing.

You can look at the *.apk* file using the familiar file packing and unpacking software packages, such as PKZIP, WinZip, WinRAR, Ark, and 7-Zip. If you are interested in looking inside your application's *.apk* file to see its folders, it will not hurt the *.apk* file to do so because you are using a nondestructive "Read" operation and not writing or rewriting (overwriting) the APK file.

If you have Windows Vista, Windows 7, or Windows 8, the ZIP functionality is built into the operating system. An easy way to see your *.apk* file is to rename it as a *.zip* extension and open it inside the Windows Explorer file management utility. By now you should know how to find your Workspace Folder and HelloAbsoluteBeginner Project Folder. The HelloAbsoluteBeginner.apk file will be in the /bin subfolder under the main project folder. Bin stands for "Binary" an early term for "Executable" files, and as expected in this folder we have the Android executable APK file and the "classes.dex" Dalvik executable class files needed for the App. The Windows 7 Explorer and the folders (path) to the file, as well as the /bin folder contents and the right-click menu (right-click on the APK file) and rename option are all shown in Figure 5-3.

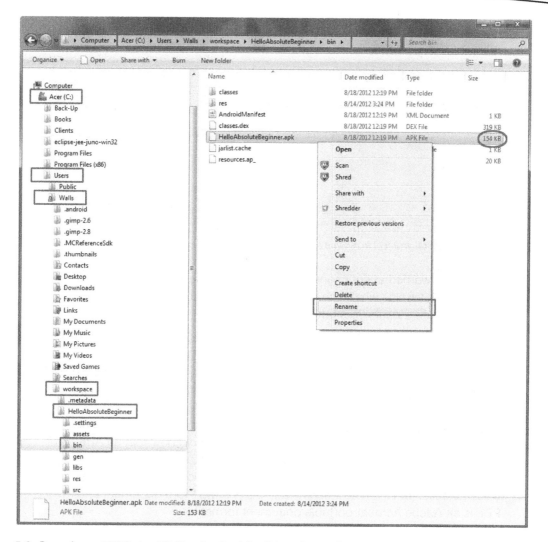

Figure 5-3. *Renaming an APK file to a ZIP file using the right-click on filename ➤ Rename option in Windows 7*

Another clever way to do this without renaming the file is to right-click the *.apk* file and use the **Open with** option to select a ZIP extraction utility. Let's do it the easy way here using just the Windows 7 Explorer utility, so you can see what I'm talking about.

1. Rename *HelloAbsoluteBeginner.apk* to *HelloAbsoluteBeginner.zip*. This is shown In Figure 5-4.

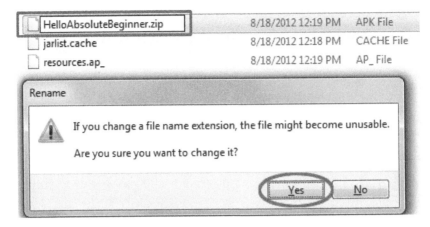

Figure 5-4. *Confirm an intent to rename a APK file to a ZIP file so we can look inside it*

2. When you're warned about changing the file name extension, which the OS uses to determine what type of file it is working with, choose to do the rename operation via the Yes button.

3. Click to select the renamed *HelloWorldAndroid.zip*. You will now be able to see the internal file structure, as shown in Figure 5-5. This is because by renaming the APK file extension to a ZIP file extension, the Windows OS now knows to use its ZIP File Viewing Code to see the APK File Contents! If we could somehow teach the Windows OS that an APK file extension is the same as a ZIP file extension, then we would not have to do the rename operation to get around the fact that Windows does not know that an APK file is essentially a ZIP file, only using a different file extension delimiter. File extensions are usually three letters preceded by a period, so an .EXE is an executable file, for instance, whereas a .DOC is a MS Word document and a .PDF is an Adobe Acrobat portable document format file.

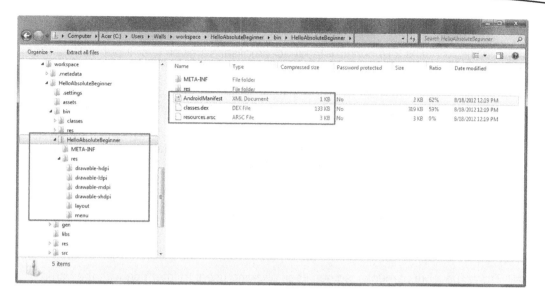

Figure 5-5. *Viewing the internal file structure of our recently renamed* HelloWorldAndroid.zip

As shown in Figure 5-5, the application includes an *AndroidManifest.xml* file and a *classes.dex* file. It also contains the */res* folder with all of the */drawable* subfolders as well as the */menu* and */layout* subfolders, which hold and organize the various application assets we used to develop the HelloAbsoluteBeginner Android 4.1 application.

Android Application Components

Android is designed to afford developers with the maximum amount of modularity possible. This modularity makes it easy for developers to exchange functionality between their applications, which is a central concept of the open source paradigm on which Android is based. For instance, if you have coded a cool animated UI element, and you make this available to other applications, they can implement your class and use that element in their own apps. You do not even need to have that code located inside those other applications. As long as the application that contains the element's code is running (or can be launched) on the Android smartphone, you can call the method via the Android operating system.

There are four main types of components that can be (but do not need to be) used within an Android application:

- **Activities**—These handle the UI that is displayed on the smartphone screen.
- **Services**—These handle any background processing needed for the application.
- **Broadcast receivers**—These handle communication within and between your apps.
- **Content providers**—These handle data and database management operations.

Let's take a closer at each of these components, to prepare for their hands-on use during the rest of this book. Here, you'll get an overview of what Android is made of, before we get into the details about class creation and more advanced topics in later chapters.

Android Activities: Defining the UI

An Android *activity* contains a UI construct that accomplishes a given user-input task via the smartphone, tablet, e-reader, or iTV display screen.

Android applications can have more than one activity. In fact, more complex applications usually have one activity for each UI screen implementation. For example, if you are programming a game, you might have the following activities:

- The introductory splash screen with the Continue to Play Game button OR Press Button to Play Game button and an Exit Game Now button

- The instructions screen, with a scrolling text UI outlining the Game Rules

- The high-score screen, with UI elements that allow the user to manage their high-score entries

- A player groups screen, where users choose who will play the game with them

- The actual core gameplay screen itself allowing users to interface with the game

If an application has more than one activity, one is marked as the activity that is presented when the application is launched. In our game example, that is the splash screen (although it could be the instructions screen). This activity has an onCreate() method that calls the *activity_hello.xml* file, as you saw in the Hello Absolute Beginner application we created in the previous chapter. For a game, this might be named *activity_splash.xml*.

Here is the code for the onCreate() method from the Activity base, or super, class (note the super keyword) and sets the content View to the *activity_hello.xml* UI definition:

```
public class HelloAbsoluteBeginner extends Activity {
    /** Called when the activity is first created. */
    @Override
    public void onCreate(Bundle savedInstanceState) {
        super.onCreate(savedInstanceState);
        setContentView(R.layout.activity_hello);
    }
}
```

An activity can be full screen, or it can be part of a screen, allowing for floating windows on top of other windows. An activity can also make use of other windows. For instance, an activity might show a pop-up dialog requesting that the user enter information, or it could display a product information window when a user clicks a product name or SKU. We will learn how to code each of these Activity scenarios, and much more, throughout the remainder of this book.

We will get into Activity class creation in all of the following chapters, and cover it specifically in Chapters 6, 7, and 8 next.

Android Services: Processing in the Background

Unlike activities, services do not have any visual UI (that's what an activity is for). Services handle the processing or heavy lifting for your application. They are often used for doing things that need to be done in the background or back end of the application, while the user works with your UI in the foreground or front end of your application.

Here are some examples of what service components can do:

- Calculate complex numeric values
- Process game logic in real time
- Play new media elements such as video or audio files (local) or streams (remote)
- Pull data from remote network locations (servers)
- Transfer data between devices via Bluetooth

Services handle calculations or processing that needs to be done in the background while the user is busy looking at the results of this processing on the activity-generated UI screen elements.

Not surprisingly, you create your own services in Android by subclassing the Android Service class. Services can run in the background, even after an activity UI screen is no longer visible, such as when a user picks an MP3 audio file to play, and then does something else with the phone while listening to the music. We will take a closer look at using services in Chapter 11. There, you'll learn how to use a MediaPlayer to play audio and video streams in the background of your applications.

Broadcast Receivers: Announcements and Notifications

Broadcast receivers are communication components that receive messages that are sent between the Android operating system and other application components, or between Android application components themselves.

The Android operating system often sends out messages regarding the status of what is going on in real time with the Android phone itself. These are statuses that any Android application may want or even need to know about to protect the application integrity, such as if the phone is about to lose power and your app needs to save files.

The following are some examples of Android operating system-initiated broadcast messages:

- A low battery life warning
- A time zone change notice
- A language preference change notice
- A message that the camera has been used to snap a picture

And here are a couple examples of application-to-application broadcast messages:

- An alert that data has finished downloading.
- A message that streaming video media has arrived, is cached, and is ready for the start of playback.

Your application can implement as many broadcast receivers as you like to intercept any of the types of messages that need to be monitored for your application's operation.

Like Android services, broadcast receivers operate in the background and thus, do not have any associated UI elements. However, this does not mean that the broadcast receivers cannot trigger or invoke a UI activity in response to the messages that they carry. In fact, it is common practice to have broadcast receivers trigger UI elements that alert the user as to what is going on within the application.

Broadcast receivers can also use the Android NotificationManager class to alert the user via built-in phone notification methods, such as flashing the screen backlight, playing a sound, triggering phone vibrations, and placing a persistent alert icon on the smartphone status bar.

Broadcast receivers are created by extending the Android BroadcastReceiver class. We will look at using them in Chapter 11.

Content Providers: Data Management

Content providers in Android provide a way to make data available to your application and to other applications, if that is desired. This can be data that is created in and for your own application, or it can be data that can be accessed by your application, but that is created by other applications, or even by the Android operating system utilities themselves to provide useful services to smartphone, tablet, e-reader, and iTV users. It can also be data that is created by your application and is then made accessible to other Android applications. The content provider component is both powerful and flexible in its ability to create, control, and manage data assets.

For example, an Android phone utility uses a content provider to access the Contacts database that is kept within your smartphone, tablet, e-reader, or iTV set. Android comes with a number of built-in content provider databases, including contacts, images, audio, and video, among others. These can be accessed via Android operating system utilities, as well as by your applications through your custom Java coding.

Content data can be stored in a file system on your SD card in your smartphone, tablet, e-reader, or iTV, off-device in a remote HTTP server, or in a proper SQLite database. The latter is the preferred method for storing and accessing data within Android, and you'll see that in action in Chapter 10, which covers using content providers via Android's built-in SQLite functionality.

To create your own content provider, you extend the ContentProvider base class, which implements a standard set of methods that are used to store and retrieve data. Applications access the methods defined by your ContentProvider class with a ContentResolver object, which is used to talk to any content provider, to navigate through the data in the database that is needed by the application.

A content provider is activated when it receives a request for data from a content resolver, which you will see in detail as we cover Content Providers in Chapter 10. The other three components—activities, services, and broadcast receivers—are activated via asynchronous messages called *intents*, which we'll look at next, and again in greater detail in Chapter 11.

Android Intent Objects: Messaging for Components

An `Intent` object in Android holds the contents of a message that is sent between modules, typically to launch them or to send them new task instructions. For activities and services, an `Intent` object provides an action to be taken, the data that the action needs to operate on, and optionally, some details or additional information that may be required for more complicated operations.

You communicate with each type of Android component (activity, service, and broadcast receiver) using a different set of methods to receive the `Intent` object that is passed to it. For this reason, `Intent` objects are easy to keep separate and well-defined, as they will be different for each type of Android component.

The components use the `Intent` object methods as follows:

- An activity is started up, or if it's already started, given a new task, by passing an `Intent` object to the `Context.startActivity()` method. The `Activity` class can look at the contents of the `Intent` object via the `getIntent()` method, and at subsequent intent objects via the `onNewIntent()` method.

- An Android service component is started by passing an `Intent` object to the `Context.startService()` method, which then calls the service class `onStart()` method, and passes it the `Intent` object that contains the actions for the service to perform and the data on which to perform them.

- If the service is already running and the `Intent` object contains new instructions, then the intent is passed to the `Context.bindService()` method to establish an open connection between the calling component and the service that is being used. This always open, real-time connection between code modules is commonly called *binding* in programming.

- An Android broadcast receiver component is started by passing an `Intent` object to the `Context.sendBroadcast()` method, or optionally to the `Context. sendOrderedBroadcast()` method or `Context.sendStickyBroadcast()` method. The `Intent` object in this case contains the message action to be taken and the data (the message) on which that action needs to be taken.

We will look very closely at using `Intent` objects with activities later on in Chapter 11.

Android Manifest XML: Declaring Your Components

You have seen that Android needs to have a single XML file in your root project folder: *AndroidManifest.xml*, which is the file that Android uses to launch your application. The only other file in your project root folder is *default.properties*, which is generated by Eclipse and should never be modified. So, the only file in your project root folder that you ever need to worry about is *AndroidManifest.xml*. As you saw in Figure 5-5 earlier in this chapter, the *AndroidManifest.xml* is also in the resulting APK file that holds your application code and resources, so it is obviously a very important file.

The Android manifest uses XML for several good reasons:

- It is easy to code as it uses easy to understand markup programming structure.

- It allows you to define a logical data structure that is easy for Android to parse (break down into logical data definition components) and understand.

- It can exist outside your Java code, so that Android can access it (inflate it) before it starts looking at your Java code and asset resources.

The Android manifest XML file is essentially a road map for the Android operating system, telling it what your application is going to do, which components will be needed, and which Android assets it needs permission to use within the Android operating system environment.

When your application is launched initially, the *AndroidManifest.xml* data definitions are used by Android to set up areas of system resources and memory needed for application components that will need to be supported. *AndroidManifest.xml* also is used to define secure access permissions for the more sensitive areas of the Android operating system (such as private, internal operating system databases) that you will need to access with your application.

Let's take a look at the *AndroidManifest.xml* file for our Hello Absolute Beginner app.

```
<manifest          xmlns:android="http://schemas.android.com/apk/res/android"
        package="first.example.helloabsolutebeginner"
        android:versionCode="1"
        android:versionName="1.0">
    <uses-sdk android:minSdkVersion="8" />
    <uses-sdk android:targetSdkVersion="16" />

    <application  android:icon="@drawable/ic_launcher"
                  android:label="@string/app_name"
                  android:theme="@style/AppTheme" >
        <activity android:name=".HelloActivity"
                  android:label="@string/title_activity_hello">
            <intent-filter>
              <action android:name="android.intent.action.MAIN" />
              <category android:name="android.intent.category.LAUNCHER" />
            </intent-filter>
        </activity>
    </application>

</manifest>
```

The opening parameter of the manifest tag is the XML schema version and encoding declaration—standard fare inserted for us by Eclipse (as are the other manifest entries). This is followed by the following tags:

- **<manifest>**: This tag has four standard attributes, including the first.example. helloabsolutebeginner package name that we entered in our New Android Application Project dialog. The xmlns:android attribute points to the online definition of the Android XML schema and is also standard fare in all XML files. The other two attributes are the Android XML version code and name, which are version 1 and 1.0, respectively.

> **Note**   An XML schema definition is a road map as to what is allowed in a given XML file—that is—the structure that it must follow and the tags or attributes it may contain. Think of it as defining all of the rules that you need to follow for any given class of XML file in which the Android manifest is a certain class of XML for use with Android development that needs to conform to a set format and rules.

- **<application>**: This tag's android:icon attribute points to our *ic_launcher. png* files in our */drawable* folders. The android:label attribute points to our application name (the name that goes in the application title bar at the top of the smartphone screen) in the *strings.xml* file. The android:theme attribute points to our application themes in the *styles.xml* files. Note that the <application> tag is nested inside the <manifest> tag. You can see this nesting by looking at the order of the closing tags at the end of the manifest file structure as well as the amount of indentation.

- **<activity>**: Here, we declare our application's activity class by specifying its name via the android:name attribute as .HelloActivity, which we also specified in our New Android Application Project dialog. We also declare our activity label via the android:label attribute as title_activity_hello found in the strings. xml file. Note that if we had a service class or broadcast receiver class, we also would declare them in this area of the manifest, along with their related <service> and <receiver> tags, as you will see in Chapter 11.

- **<intent-filter>**: This tag specifies the action and category of the Intent object that launches our application. The action is android.intent.action.MAIN, which launches the activity on the main screen of the Android device. The category is android.intent.category.LAUNCHER, which specifies that HelloActivity is the activity that launches the application (because it is the activity that contains this <intent-filter> tag).

- **<uses-sdk>**: This tag specifies our minimum SDK support level of Android 2.2 SDK 8 via the attribute named android:minSdkVersion, which we also specified in our New Android Application Project dialog. This tag also specifies our target SDK support level of Android 4.1 SDK 16 via the attribute named android:targetSdkVersion, which we also specified in our New Android Application Project dialog. This comes before the opening (and thus closing) tags for the <application>, <activity>, and <intent-filter> tags.

After closing the <application>, <activity>, and <intent-filter> tags (in reverse order, of course, so they are nested properly, we close our <manifest> tag, and we are finished declaring our Hello Absolute Beginner application manifest XML file.

We will look at Android manifest files in later chapters that cover more advanced Android features, so you will be learning more about these tags before you are finished with this book.

Summary

This chapter gave you an overview of the Java and XML languages as well as the various components of the Android operating system. We also looked at the *AndroidManifest.xml* file, which ties everything together and is utilized when Android initially launches your application.

The main component of Java is the object, which contains fields, or states, and methods that operate on those object states to change the attributes of the object, just as in real life.

This object-oriented programming, or OOP, approach allows objects to mimic real-world objects, and also allows data encapsulation, which helps us to develop and code objects that are more secure and self-contained. This modularization helps in testing and debugging, especially with more complex programming projects because problems can be localized more precisely.

Objects can be created using classes, which are programming code constructs that are used to define the object fields and methods and thus the object architecture. These classes define the initial, or default, fields for the objects that are created from them, as well as the programming code that defines methods for changing these default states as the program executes. We used a car example to demonstrate the different attributes and methods that would define a car object, such as acceleration, braking, steering, and gear shifting.

Classes can be used to create more detailed classes through a process called *inheritance*. Through inheritance, the original base class becomes a superclass, and new, more finely detailed classes are subclassed from the base class to form different types of class definitions. In our car example, we created SUV and sports car classes, which allowed us to create SUV and sports car objects.

Once you have finished coding all of your classes, you can bundle them logically together in a *package*, which allows you to group your classes, and even your application, together as one logical, well, package. You use the `import` statement to load Android packages and classes. The format `import platform.package.classname` allows you to precisely specify which packages and classes you wish to include and use in your own Java applications.

We also took a look at XML, which uses tags to allow users to structure data. Tags can be nested to become subsets of other tags, and thus complicated and precise data structures can be created. Android uses XML so that some of the programming can be done in an easier language than Java. This allows nonprogrammers to become involved in the application design process.

The Android APK (*.apk*) file holds our application code binaries and resources in a compressed *.zip* file format. This includes the *classes.dex* Dalvik executable classes file and the Android manifest XML file and the application resources. Renaming the *.apk* file to *.zip* allows you to look inside the file and see its assets. Recently, file size limits for *.apk* files were increased from 25MB to 50MB, and by using two external 2GB *expansion files* Android applications can now be as large as 4GB!

Next we looked at Android application components. Android *activity* components hold your application's UI elements, and are the front-end of your application to your end users; let's call them your application's "eyes," as they let users "see" your application's content. Android *services* define your processing routines, and are the back end of your applications; let's call them your application's "brain," as they do the thinking (processing) for your app. Android broadcast receivers send messages between your application components and are your intercomponent application messengers; let's call them your application's "mouth and ears" because they do the communicating for your app. Android content providers store and distribute your application data within your application to other applications and to the Android operating system itself; let's call them your application's "memory" because they store things away long-term for your app.

We next looked at Android Intent objects. These are our task managers. They send instructions between our application components as to which actions to perform and on which data to perform them. Using our analogy from the previous paragraph, think of these as the neurons that fire in your app's "brain" and carry thoughts (intents) and impulses from one part of your app's "brain" to another.

Finally, we covered the all-important Android manifest XML file, *AndroidManifest.xml*. This file defines for the Android operating system exactly how to start up your application, including which components will be used, and which permissions and SDK levels your application will support on various model smartphones, tablets, e-readers, and iTV sets.

All of the concepts in this chapter will be covered again in greater detail in the remaining chapters of this book, so by the end of the book, you will have gone from Absolute Beginner to Android Applications Programmer!

Chapter 6

Screen Layout Design: Views and Layouts

One of the most important parts of any application's design and development is the graphical user interface (GUI) and screen layout design. Many of the most widely circulated Android applications are popular because of their visual design, animated graphics, and easy- or fun-to-use interfaces. We will explore the Java classes that provide the core foundation for all of these front-end capabilities in this chapter.

Android View Hierarchies

In Google Android, to interface with the smartphone, tablet, or iTV screen, you use two core Java classes. These are two of the most important and often used classes in Android development:

- The View class (Hierarchy: java.lang.Object ➤ android.view.View)

- The ViewGroup class (java.lang.Object ➤ android.view.View ➤ android.view.ViewGroup)

View and ViewGroup are core, high-level classes, created or subclassed from the Java Object class, as are all Java classes. As can be seen, the View class is taken from (subclassed from) the Java language Object class and the ViewGroup is then subclassed from the View superclass. So Views are the highest level view objects in Android and ViewGroups are more specialized view objects because they are farther down in the hierarchy. Remember, farther down in the class hierarchy means more specialized in what they do (just like in real life).

View objects are created using the View class. The View class also can be used to create many lower-level, or more customized, Java classes. Those classes that are subclassed from the View class, such as the ViewGroup class, inherit the characteristics of their superclass.

So, the basic screen layout in Android is controlled by the View class, which contains a complex data structure that represents the content and layout parameters for a given rectangular section of the device's display screen, whether that is a smartphone, tablet, e-reader, or iTV.

Using the View Class

There may be one or more View objects that make up the entire display screen, depending on how you use the View and ViewGroup classes to create the UI structure for your Android application's screen.

Each View object controls and references its own rectangular view parameters, allowing you to control many attributes. Here are just some examples of the many attributes controlled by the View class parameters that are available to Android application programmers:

- Bounds (measurements)
- Layout on the screen (position)
- Order in which its layers are drawn (compositing)
- Scrolling (directional movement)
- Focus (which screen elements are currently active)
- Keystroke interactions
- Gesture interactions

Finally, Views have the ability to receive events—interaction events between your application's end user and the View object itself. For this reason, the View class is the logical Java construct to subclass to build more detailed and specific UI elements, such as buttons, check boxes, radio buttons, and text fields.

> **Note** The View class serves as the foundation for UI elements that are subclasses of the View class. Recall that in Java, a *subclass* is a more specific or detailed implementation of the class from which it is subclassed. For instance, the Button class is subclassed from the TextView class, which is subclassed from the View class, which is subclassed from the Object class. The Button class is subclassed from the TextView class because the Button has a TextView label and is thus a more specialized version of a TextView; that is, it is a clickable TextView with a button background and appearance.

So many UI classes have been subclassed from the View class that there is a name for them: *widgets*. All of these widgets are contained in a package (a collection of classes) called android. widget. For example, you can access a Button class via this package using android.widget.Button.

Nesting Views: Using the ViewGroup Class

One of the most useful classes subclassed from the View class is the ViewGroup class. The ViewGroup class is used to subclass layout container classes, which allow groups of View objects to be logically grouped, arranged, and cascaded onto the screen.

ViewGroups are layout containers, usually collections of UI elements. In the diagram in Figure 6-1, View could mean a button, a text field, a check box, and so on. This applies to any other type of UI element.

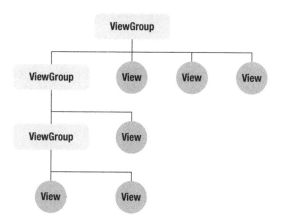

Figure 6-1. ViewGroups and nested Views and ViewGroups

The remainder of this chapter explores the different types of ViewGroup subclasses. These are the foundation that Android developers use to organize and group their View objects (UI elements) on the Android device display screen, whether that is a smartphone, tablet, e-reader, or iTV set.

Direct subclasses of the ViewGroup class include AbsoluteLayout, RelativeLayout, FrameLayout, GridLayout, LinearLayout, ViewPager, PagerTitleStrip, AdapterView, FragmentBreadCrumbs, and SlidingDrawer. We'll look at the two most often used ViewGroup subclasses: LinearLayout and RelativeLayout. We'll also explore one of the coolest ViewGroup subclasses: SlidingDrawer. This layout class can be used to greatly expand your Android screen real estate by 100% by adding another screen that can be pulled in from offscreen.

In the diagram in Figure 6-1, the top level ViewGroup object is the *parent* of the View objects and ViewGroup objects underneath it, which are called its *children*. The ViewGroup object in the second row is both a child as well as a parent, and the same goes for the ViewGroup object in the third row. The View objects in the fourth row of the diagram are children only (joke: but not only children because there are two of them).

As you can see, ViewGroup objects can contain other ViewGroup objects (a concept called *nesting*; it's all so familial, isn't it?), but View objects cannot contain other objects. They are the end object, so to speak, and are simply UI components for which you can set properties via a plethora of configuration parameters, as you will soon see.

Defining Screen Layouts: Using XML

The primary way of defining screen layouts (I will stop calling them ViewGroup objects now, assuming that you are now classifying them as such when you see the term) is via XML. This screen definition XML goes inside a file you define in your Android Application Project creation process, in our case, in Chapter 4, it was called *activity_hello.xml*, placed inside a folder called */res/layout* within your project folder. Layouts are important to your Android applications, which is why Layouts have their very own layout folder in the standard project resource folder architecture for Android.

Once this *activity_hello.xml* file was in place, with your XML screen layout (UI) definition inside it, you then used the Java onCreate() method to push it onto your screen on the startup of your application activity, as you experienced first hand in your Hello Absolute Beginner app that you created back in Chapter 4.

We'll first take a look at the onCreate() code and how it works, and then we'll use it for real in the following sections, where we will create three vastly different types of user interface screen layouts.

Setting Up for Your Screen Layout

Back in Chapter 4, three simple lines of Java code inside an onCreate() method set your content view to the *activity_hello.xml* screen layout XML definition:

```
public void onCreate(Bundle savedInstanceState) {
        super.onCreate(savedInstanceState);
        setContentView(R.layout.activity_hello);
}
```

As we then learned in Chapter 5, the words before the method name determine who can access its methods and data as well as which type of values it returns. A public method is one that is open (accessible) to any part of your Android application. A void method is one that completes a task without returning any value or data.

The words that follow the method name (always enclosed in parentheses) are the data parameters that an application can pass to the method for its use. *Parameters* are chunks of data that the method needs to complete its processing tasks.

The savedInstanceState object is a Bundle object, which is a collection of all of the states for your activity screen UI elements. It exists so that the screen UI elements can be restored to their previous positions if the screen is replaced by navigation to other screens during the use of your application. As you learned in Chapter 5, the state of a UI screen consists of its attributes and their values, including the UI element user settings, which UI element has the focus, and similar attributes that define the current user (usage) settings or state of use of your screen user interface elements.

> **Note**   The Activity class saves your state for you, so you don't need to worry. Simply extend it, pass it the savedInstanceState Bundle, and it does the rest for you.

The super keyword calls the superclass (the class containing the onCreate() method that was subclassed from android.app.Activity), so it is basically referencing the onCreate() method of the android.app.Activity class from which our activity class was subclassed. Thus, the keyword "super" is really just a shortcut (shorthand) for android.app.Activity.onCreate(savedInstanceState).

Because it is called locally from this activity class via super, it affects this activity locally, and applies to this activity only, even though it accesses the parent code by using the super keyword to jump up one level to get the original code routine. This local savedInstanceState object is the one Android kindly saves for us when it deals with saving state for the Activity in which it was declared.

The onCreate() method will always be called by the Android operating system when any activity (remember that all activities for your app are defined in the *AndroidManifest.xml* file) is started. This part of your code is where all of your initializations and UI definitions will be performed, so it must be present—at least if you need your users to interact with the Android device's screen area.

The way that layouts contain other nested layouts in XML code (as shown previously in Figure 6-1) is by nesting them inside each other's tags. The closing tags are nested at the bottom of these structures, and they must be nested in the correct order, to show Android which layouts are nested inside of which other layouts. Layouts inside of another layout tag structure conform to, and are controlled by, their parent layout container. The code examples in this chapter indent the nested code structures to more clearly show the nested layout hierarchy.

You are about to see all of this in action in the next few sections, where we'll start with the most basic layout container in Android: the linear layout, and progress to more complex layout configurations. First we'll talk about the LinearLayout class, which has been subclassed from the ViewGroup class, which is subclassed from the View class, which is subclassed from the Java language Object class like this: java.lang.Object ➤ android.view.View ➤ android.view.ViewGroup.

> **Note**   Java implements subclasses so that there is no redundancy within the construction of your code. Once a method has been written, it is then available to every subclass (and their subclasses) that inherit from its base class. The one exception to this is a method or class that is declared using the "private" keyword, such as: **private void doNotComeIn()** and with this declaration keyword the other classes or methods cannot see the data or variables inside of that class or method.

Using Linear Layouts

In a standard screen user interface (UI) layout, buttons are usually placed across the top of the screen, or sometimes down the side of the screen, in a straight line. This is exactly what the LinearLayout class does for you. It is designed to contain and automatically arrange UI elements placed inside of it across the screen (using the horizontal orientation parameter) or up and down the screen (using the vertical orientation parameter).

> **Note**   The LinearLayout container should not contain any scrolling views (I think that's common sense, but some folks will try anything once) as there are other containers specifically designed (subclassed) for precisely that purpose.

In Java code, to set the LinearLayout object's orientation, use the .setOrientation(integer) method, with either the constant HORIZONTAL for horizontal or VERTICAL for vertical:

```
myLinearLayout.setOrientation(HORIZONTAL);
```

HORIZONTAL is a Android OS predefined constant that represents the integer value of zero (0) and VERTICAL is an Android OS predefined constant that represents the integer value of one (1) just in case you are wondering what the actual integer values are that are used internal to the class.

We mention this just to let you know that after the `LinearLayout` has been set up in your XML markup, it's possible to change its orientation on the fly inside your Java code if you need to. In most cases however a LinearLayout is declared once in XML and then used as-is in the app.

> **Note**   Recall that *constants* are hard-coded values that your Java code uses in its program logic and can't change. In this case, Android provides easy-to-remember names so that you don't need to remember numeric values. You use the name HORIZONTAL, rather than the value it is set to, which is 0. This also helps if the value of HORIZONTAL ever changes. You're protected because the name does not change, even if the value inside Android does.

Here's the attribute for orientation in the `LinearLayout` tag for XML:

```
android:orientation="vertical"
```

Thus, the entire `LinearLayout` opening tag for a Vertical UI layout looks like this:

```
<LinearLayout android:orientation="vertical">
```

However, we should really have a few more key parameters in the `LinearLayout` tag to make it more useful and standardized, so here's how a Horizontal UI layout would normally be coded:

```
<LinearLayout xmlns:android="http://schemas.android.com/apk/res/android"
        android:layout_width="match_parent"
        android:layout_height="match_parent"
        android:orientation="horizontal">
        <The Items To Be Arranged Horizontally Would Be Inside This Container>
</LinearLayout>
```

The first parameter of the `LinearLayout` XML tag is the path to the Android XML naming schema definition (xmlns:android stands for: eXtensible Markup Language Naming Schema for Android, just in case you may be wondering). This parameter sets the variable android used in the rest of the tag to: `http://schemas.android.com/apk/res/android`, so that you don't need to write all of the other XML parameters like this:

```
http://schemas.android.com/apk/res/android:layout_width="match_parent"
```

The value for the layout width and height parameters, `match_parent`, simply tells the `LinearLayout` to expand to match its parent container size. Because this is the top level `LinearLayout` container, the android:layout_width="match_parent" would mean to fill the Android device (smartphone, tablet, e-reader, or iTV) display screen width from one side to the other side. We already know what the orientation does, so now we have our `LinearLayout` defined. Anything we place inside this container will display horizontally across the screen, from left to right.

As discussed earlier in the chapter, the Java onCreate() method is used to load the *activity_main.xml* layout parameters for an application.

Well, it's time to fire up Eclipse again, and create a new application to see how all of this cool stuff works together.

Creating the LinearLayouts Project in Eclipse

We'll build a simple UI that stacks some TextView elements along the left side of the screen, just to see how LinearLayout works. Let's fire up Eclipse and get started!

After you launch Eclipse, you will be presented with a Workspace Launcher dialog, where Eclipse will present you with a suggested workspace folder. Because this was demonstrated in Chapter 4, let's not re-create the wheel here, if you need a visual refresher, please refer to the screenshot as shown in Chapter 4 in Figure 4-4.

The first item that we need to do is to CLOSE the open HelloAbsoluteBeginner project that we have been working on so far in Eclipse because Eclipse always saves your current open project on each EXIT of its application. To do this, simply right-click on the top-level HelloAbsoluteBeginner project folder name, and bring up the context-sensitive menu that shows everything that you can do with that object (right-clicks are really helpful once you master them).

Near the bottom of the lengthy menu (there are lots of things that can be done with a top-level project, familiarize yourself with this menu as a means of learning Eclipse) you will find the "Close Project" option, which once selected, will close the HelloAbsoluteBeginner project folder (but will still keep it's closed folder icon on the screen, as you will see in future screen shots in this chapter and throughout the book). This is shown below in Figure 6-2.

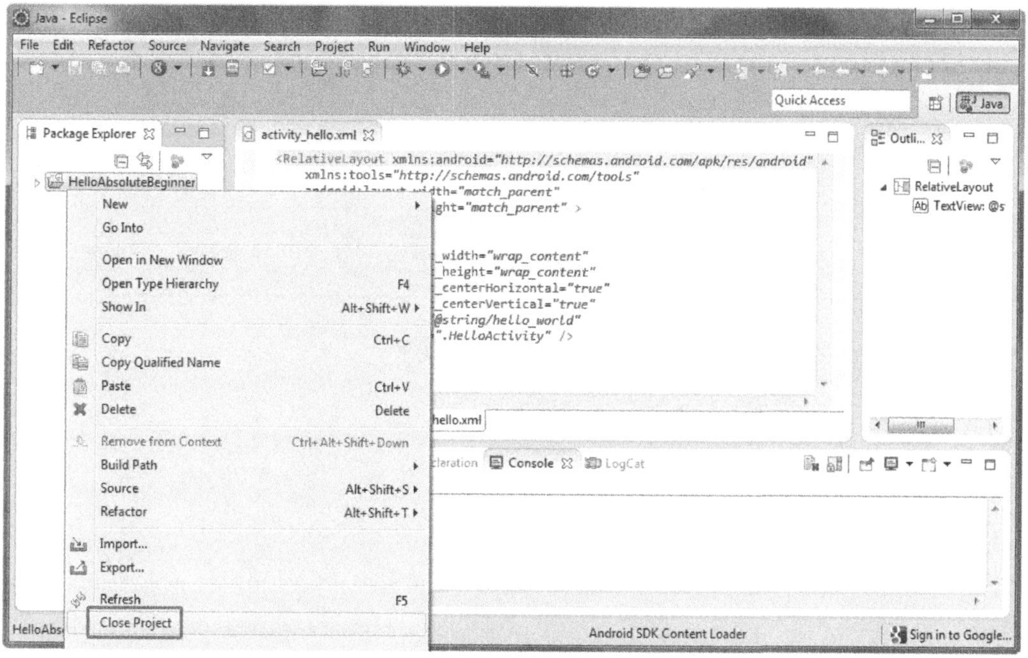

Figure 6-2. Closing the HelloAbsoluteBeginner project workspace inside of Eclipse

After you have closed your HelloAbsoluteBeginner project folder, select **File ➤ New ➤ Project**, as shown in Chapter 4, Figure 4-5. Then select the Android Application project wizard from the *Android* folder, as shown in Figures 6-3 and 6-4.

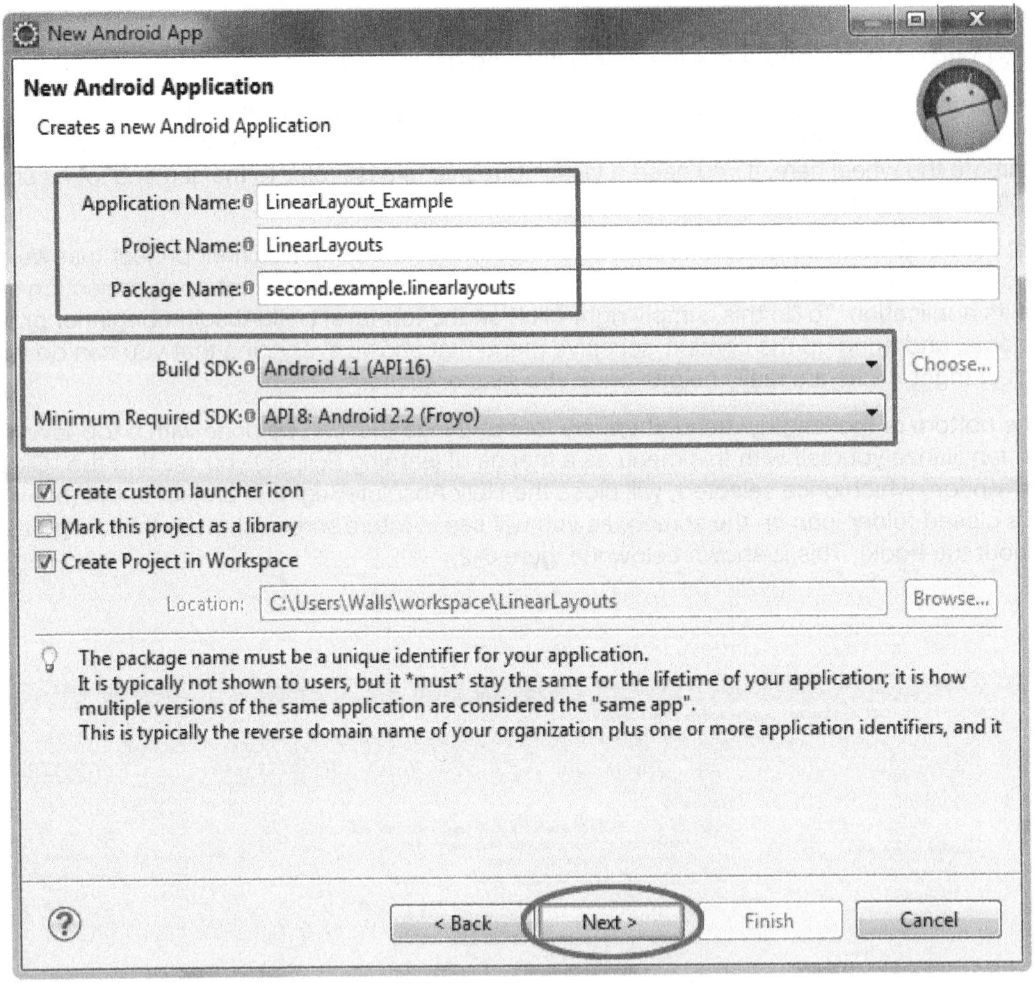

Figure 6-3. Defining a new LinearLayout Android application project in Eclipse

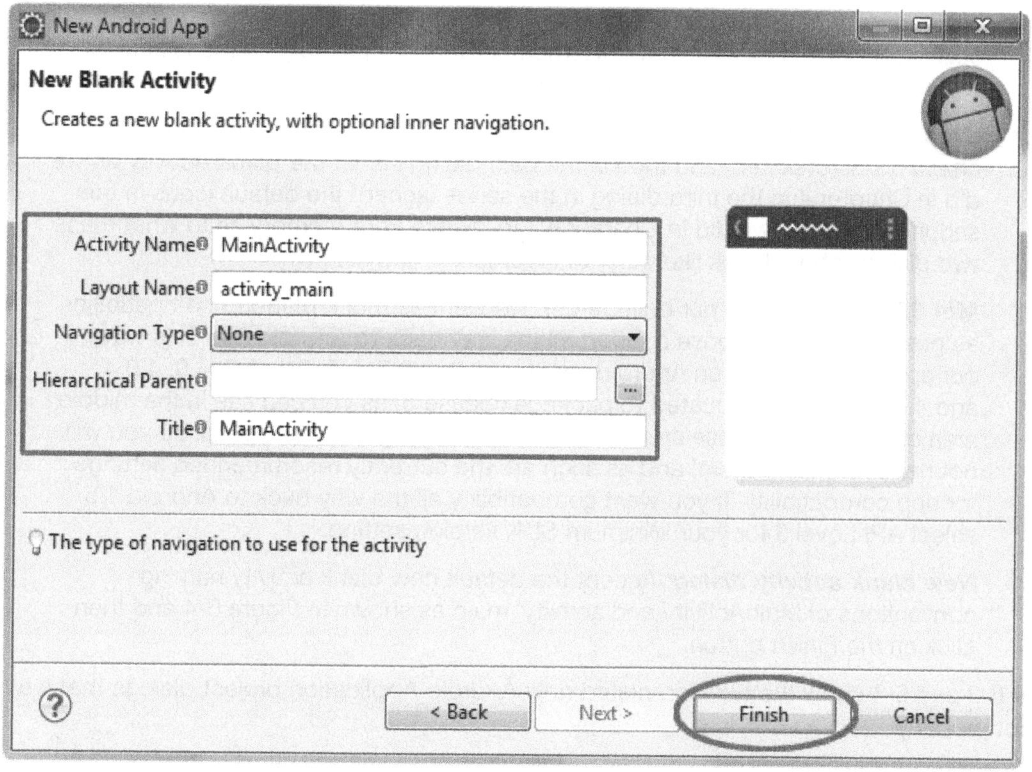

Figure 6-4. *Creating a new Android Blank Activity in Eclipse using the default (Android suggested) values*

Once we hit the Next button shown in Figure 6-3 and accept our default icon dialog settings, we get to the New Blank Activity dialog shown in Figure 6-4 and accept its default values as well. Default values in Eclipse ADT (Android Development Tools Plug-In Environment) give us an indication of how Android wants to see things named, numbered, and referenced, showing Android Best Development Practices, if you will.

Now we need to create our new project resources, as shown in Figure 6-3. This involves the same important project elements that we defined for our project in Chapter 4:

- **Application name**: In the Application name field in the New Android Application Dialog, enter: **LinearLayout_Example**. This is the name that will appear under our icon and in the title bar of our application.

- **Project name**: In this field, enter LinearLayouts. This is the Eclipse project name. Because this dialog "dual types" the App and Project names together, do this by backspacing over the "_Example" part and then add an "s". This will be the name of the top-level folder in Eclipse that will hold all of this project's files.

- **Build target**: For our build target, we want to use the current Android Jelly Bean 4.1 OS, which is signified by API Level 16.

- **Package name**: In the package name field in the Properties section, enter `second.example.linearlayouts`. (Remember that the package name is at least two names separated by a period, and preferably three names.)

- **Create custom launcher icon**: Make sure the Create custom launcher icon check box is checked, and then in the next dialog select the Blank Activity as we did in Chapter 4 in the third dialog in the series (accept the default icons in the second dialog, as we did In Chapter 4). To refresh your memory as to what these two dialogs should look like, refer to Figures 4-7 and 4-8.

- **Min SDK version**: For our build target, we want as much platform compatibility as possible, so we choose support all the way back to Android 2.2. This way, our app also will work on Android versions 2.2, 2.3.7, 3.0, 3.1, 3.2, 4.0, 4.0.4, and 4.1. Version 2.2 equated to package release 8, as you can see in the middle area of this dialog. These are also the default settings for this dialog, so you will not need to modify them, and as such are the currently recommended settings for app compatibility. If you want compatibility all the way back to Android 1.5 select API Level 3 for your Minimum SDK version setting.

- **New blank activity dialog**: Accept the default new blank activity naming conventions of MainActivity and activity_main as shown in Figure 6-4 and then click on the Finish button.

Figures 6-3 and 6-4 show the two completed new Android Application project dialogs that we need to fill out properly.

Editing the activity_main.xml File

Now it's time to work on the activity_main.xml file that was generated for us by the New ➤ Project ➤ Android Application project sequence of dialogs. Right-click *activity_main.xml* (if it is not open in a tab already, which it should be) and select Open. Click on the *activity_main.xml* tab at the bottom of the central coding pane, and you will see some default XML code setting up a RelativeLayout with a TextView. Let's rename the TextView object's text parameter from hello to textareaone because we need more than one object to align vertically.

Next let's change the word *Relative* to *Linear* in the top (opening) tag and the bottom (closing) tag, and notice how the information in the Outline Pane on the right changes to reflect that you are now using a LinearLayout container instead of a RelativeLayout container.

Next let's add the android:orientation="vertical" attribute above the layout default attributes. Notice that after you type in the android and hit the colon, a helper window pops up (shown in Figure 6-5) and gives you all of the LinearLayout parameter options that are possible.

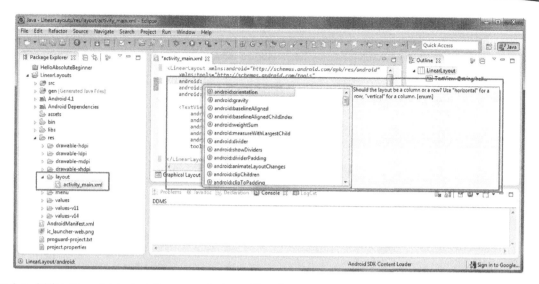

Figure 6-5. *Adding the android:orientation parameter to our LinearLayout container in Eclipse*

Double-click on the orientation option and Eclipse will insert the code for you, then just type in "vertical" between the quotes and you're finished adding the parameter that will orient your LinearLayout UI vertically.

Finally, let's remove the android:layout_centerHorizontal="true" and the android:layout_centerVertical="true" parameters because these are parameters that are used with RelativeLayout, and because we don't want to center our UI. If you forget to remove these, Eclipse will flag these two lines with a yellow triangle on the left side of each line of code, and if you mouse over the tiny yellow triangles on each line, Eclipse will advise you via the ToolTip pop-up that android:layout_center is not a valid parameter for a LinearLayout. Pretty sleek IDE feature!

Here is how the final code should look, which also appears in the activity_main.xml tab shown in Figure 6-6:

```
<LinearLayout xmlns:android="http://schemas.android.com/apk/res/android"
    xmlns:tools="http://schemas.android.com/tools"
    android:orientation="vertical"
    android:layout_width="match_parent"
    android:layout_height="match_parent" >
<TextView
    android:layout_width="wrap_content"
    android:layout_height="wrap_content"
    android:text="@string/hello"
    tools:context=".MainActivity" />
</LinearLayout>
```

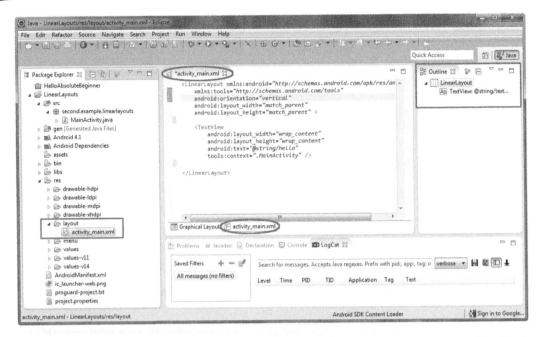

Figure 6-6. View of the Eclipse activity_main.xml once all of the editing is finished

In this file, add another TextView object, by copy and pasting the <TextView> element like this:

```
<LinearLayout xmlns:android="http://schemas.android.com/apk/res/android"
    xmlns:tools="http://schemas.android.com/tools"
    android:orientation="vertical"
    android:layout_width="match_parent"
    android:layout_height="match_parent" >
<TextView
    android:layout_width="wrap_content"
    android:layout_height="wrap_content"
    android:text="@string/hello"
    tools:context=".MainActivity" />
<TextView
    android:layout_width="wrap_content"
    android:layout_height="wrap_content"
    android:text="@string/hello"
    tools:context=".MainActivity" />
</LinearLayout>
```

Next we will edit the text strings in the *strings.xml* file to say: "Text Area One!" and "Text Area Two!"

Editing the strings.xml File

The text strings are edited in the *strings.xml* file, found in your project's */res/values* folder (shown in the Package Explorer). Right-click on the *strings.xml* file and select **Open**, so it opens in its own tab in the editing area, or simply select the file and press the F3 key to open it.

Change the `hello` text to `Text Area One!` Also add another string variable `textareatwo` and set it to `Text Area Two!` Here's the code:

```
<resources>
    <string name="app_name">LinearLayout_Example</string>
    <string name="textareaone">Text Area One!</string>
    <string name="textareatwo">Text Area Two!</string>
    <string name="menu_settings">Settings</string>
    <string name="title_activity_main">MainActivity</string>
</resources>
```

Figure 6-7 shows the strings added to the file.

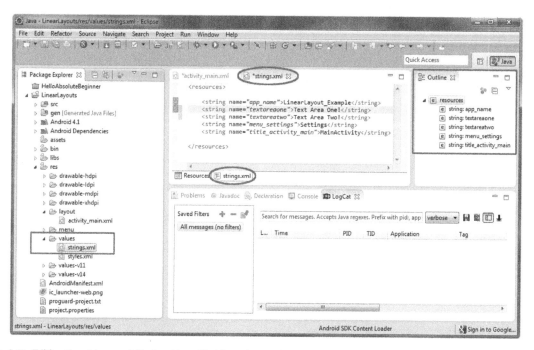

Figure 6-7. *Editing the strings.xml file to add our Text Area One and Text Area Two string values*

Notice that the `app_name`, `menu_settings`, and `title_activity_main` strings were added from the information you gave in the new Android Application project creation dialogs, so you don't need to code this (but this is where you change the `app_name` later on, if you want to be meticulous, when we do our RelativeLayout and SlidingDrawer examples).

Updating activity_main.xml File

Next, change *activity_main.xml* to reference the `textareaone` and `textareatwo` string variables, which we set in the *strings.xml* file in the previous step, as shown in the TextView tag XML markup and in Figure 6-8.

```
<LinearLayout xmlns:android="http://schemas.android.com/apk/res/android"
    xmlns:tools="http://schemas.android.com/tools"
    android:orientation="vertical"
    android:layout_width="match_parent"
    android:layout_height="match_parent" >
<TextView
    android:layout_width="wrap_content"
    android:layout_height="wrap_content"
    android:text="@string/textareaone"
    tools:context=".MainActivity" />
<TextView
    android:layout_width="wrap_content"
    android:layout_height="wrap_content"
    android:text="@string/textareatwo"
    tools:context=".MainActivity" />
</LinearLayout>
```

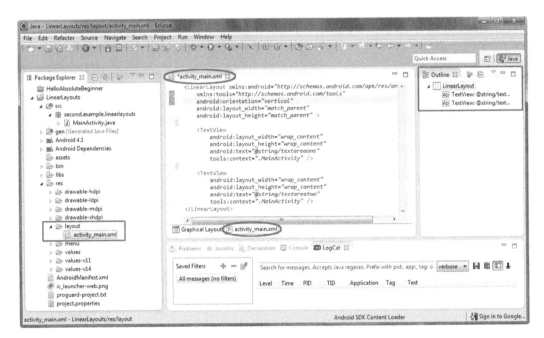

Figure 6-8. Final LinearLayout XML code in activity_main.xml Eclipse XML editor tab and pane

Viewing MainActivity.java

Now it is time to take a look at what our Java code is doing. Right-click the *MainActivity.java* file on the left in the Package Explorer and select **Open**.

> **Tip** REMEMBER there is another way to open a file for editing in its own tab: just select the *.java* or XML file and press the F3 key. A tab will open showing the contents of that file.

The file opens in its own tab next to the activity_main.xml and strings.xml tabs in Eclipse. Here is the code (Figure 6-9 shows what it looks like in Eclipse):

```
package second.example.linearlayouts;

import android.os.Bundle;
import android.app.Activity;
import android.view.Menu;

public class MainActivity extends Activity {

    @Override
    public void onCreate(Bundle savedInstanceState) {
        super.onCreate(savedInstanceState);
        setContentView(R.layout.activity_main);
    }
    @Override
    public boolean onCreateOptionsMenu(Menu menu) {
        getMenuInflater().inflate(savedInstanceState);
        setContentView(R.menu.activity_main, menu);
        return true;
    }
}
```

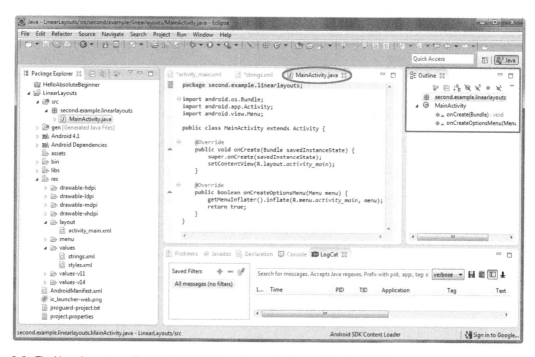

Figure 6-9. The LinearLayouts application MainActivity.java Java code view and the Code Outline pane

As you can see, the package name that we defined in the New Android Application project dialog is declared at the top of the Java code, as well as three `import` statements that reference the Java classes that are needed (accessed or used) in the Java code: the `Activity` class, `View` class and the `Bundle` class. Below this is the Java code that loads the XML layout that we created earlier in the other two tabs and another routine that loads the Menu (currently not used) that is added as part of the default create a new blank activity routine that we have now encountered twice.

Running the LinearLayout App

Now we are ready to compile and run our Android application. Make sure you have saved all of your changes in each of the three tabs in Eclipse by clicking on each tab and then hitting CTRL-S on your keyboard (the File ➤ Save shortcut), and notice that before you Save, there is an asterisk on the top tab, and that after you Save, that asterisk is gone; this is how Eclipse tells you when one of your coding tabs has changes in it, and needs to be saved.

Because we have already set up our Android 4.1 smartphone and tablet device emulator in Chapter 3, all we need to do to compile and run our app is right-click the top-level *LinearLayouts* project folder in the Package Explorer on the left and select **Run As ➤ Android Application**. Also make sure to click on the Console tab at the bottom of Eclipse so that you can see what is happening during the compilation process.

In Figure 6-10, you can see the process that the Android compiler goes through to compile and launch your app in the 4.1 emulator. After at least 30 seconds or so (if not longer) of loading, the emulation environment will launch your app (it will load faster on subsequent compiles, as it has already been established in your computer's memory). Note the name of the project and the name of our activity as they are loaded into the emulator. The only line of red code is the last line that tells us that we have closed the emulator.

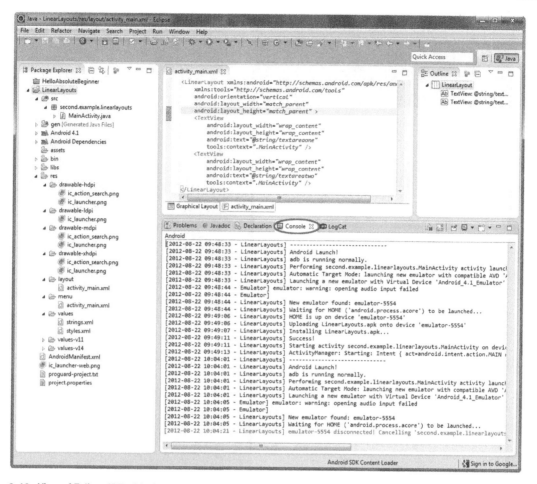

Figure 6-10. View of Eclipse IDE with LinearLayout XML code and Console Tab compiler progress output

You'll see that the LinearLayout vertically stacks our text fields as expected, as shown in Figure 6-11.

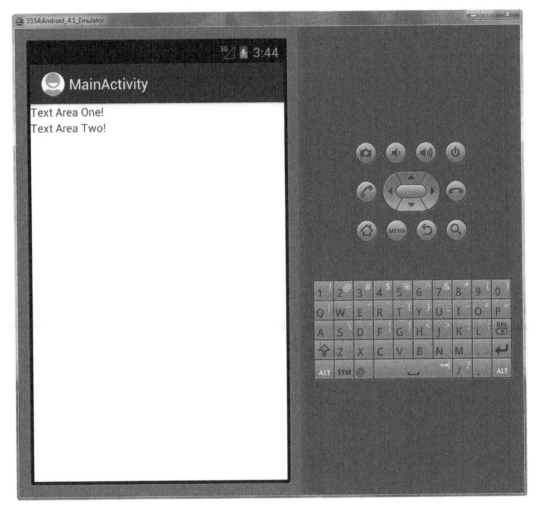

Figure 6-11. Running the LinearLayouts application in the Android 4.1 emulator

Using Relative Layouts

Relative layouts are for the more complicated UI layouts where you need to define the UI elements in not quite a linear fashion. In fact, the RelativeLayout tag is the default tag used in the standard blank activity code bootstrap provided by the New ➤ Project ➤ Android Application project sequence of dialogs, as we have seen twice already, so it's clearly a recommended default layout container as far as Google Android is concerned.

The RelativeLayout class allows you to define how the UI elements (the View objects) are to be placed on the screen *relative* to each other, rather than just laid out linearly. For this reason, the XML definition for a RelativeLayout may contain more screen layout variables and parameters, so this example will be a number of lines of markup code longer (eight additional lines of code, or 50% more code, to be exact) than the LinearLayout example.

If you start to get into the habit of nesting several LinearLayout containers to achieve a more complex UI layout result, you may want to consider using a single RelativeLayout container to achieve the same results with better control, fewer nested levels, and more efficient XML code.

Simpler is always better, so if you can write a UI layout using fewer nested ViewGroup containers, it will always use less memory, and will function more quickly (smoothly). The RelativeLayout container allows you to arrange all sorts of UI elements together in a single ViewGroup to achieve a more complex layout using only a single layout container.

RelativeLayouts are also the optimal type of layout container for using sliding drawers, another direct subclass of the ViewGroup class. Sliding drawers extend the screen real estate of the smartphone, tablet, or iTV by allowing drawers to slide out onto the screen from any of the four sides (top, left, bottom, or right). This is very cool layout container functionality (class) that is built into the Android SDK, as you'll see in the last part of this chapter.

Because we already have our linear layout application open in Eclipse, let's change it to a relative layout configuration. That way, we won't need to type in all the same code, or go through the Project Close and New Project sequence of dialogs yet again. To change a layout, all you need to do is to change the XML code in your *activity_main.xml* file.

Because our Java code references *activity_main.xml*, we do not need to change anything in the MainActivity.java tab to make these changes work, a testimony to the power of modularity via XML in Android. We also do not need to change (or even remove) the content in *strings.xml*, even though the second text area string setting will not be used in the application anymore. If you are meticulous, which is a good thing for a programmer to be, you can always remove it because you know that it is not referenced any more.

> **Note**   If the unused code were lines of code in Java, Eclipse would notice that these variables were not used (referenced by other code, more accurately) and Eclipse would warn you about it much as it warns you about unsupported XML parameters via the little yellow caution signs.

We'll edit *activity_main.xml* now. And while we are at it, we'll also add some other UI elements—an editable text field and a couple of buttons—so that you can see how easy it is to create (or in this case, change and refine) a UI layout scheme inside of the Android Development Environment.

In the first tag of *activity_main.xml*, change LinearLayout and its closing tag back to RelativeLayout and remove the android:orientation="vertical" parameter. We will add some UI elements to the inside of the RelativeLayout tag (before the closing tag </RelativeLayout> line of markup code).

Let's leave in one <TextView> tag and delete the other. Give the remaining tag an ID and a default, or starting, text value. So, this can be specified not only via a reference to a data declaration in *strings.xml* (as in our previous example), but also directly, right here in the *activity_main.xml* file (just to show you two ways to do it) without referencing *strings.xml*, as follows:

```
<TextView
        android:id="@+id/label"
        android:layout_width="wrap_content"
        android:layout_height="wrap_content"
        android:text="Type here:"
        tools:context=".MainActivity"/>
```

> **Note**   If you choose to "hard code" text into the *activity_main.xml* file without using the proper work process of referencing the string variables in the *strings.xml* file, Eclipse will flag that line of markup with a yellow hazard sign with an exclamation point in it. So that we can generate clean screens in Eclipse for the rest of this book, we will use the *strings.xml* file to hold our string values because that is clearly the way Android wishes things to be done relative to our use of strings!

The TextView is the first UI element, so we don't have any relative layout attributes—there is nothing for this UI element to be relative to yet, other than to be relative to the upper-left corner of the screen, which by the way, is the default alignment, and can be referenced by pixel X,Y coordinates of 0,0, because screen layout coordinates originate from the left and top of the screen, much like a spreadsheet is numbered from it's upper-left corner.

Next, let's add an `<EditText>` element. This can be done either by typing in the code shown in the next section, or by dragging from the visual layout editor in Eclipse, which is accessed via the "Graphical Layout" tab shown on the screenshot in Figure 6-12. Because this is an Absolute Beginners book, we'll show you how to "Drag-N-Drop" your UI Designs in the Graphical Layout Editor in Eclipse, which will write all the XML markup for you, so that all you have to do is check it and modify it, if needed. Under Palette, click the Text Fields "drawer" to open it, and drag the abc (tooltip will say: Plain Text) UI element onto the screen at the right, under the Type Here: text as shown in Figure 6-12.

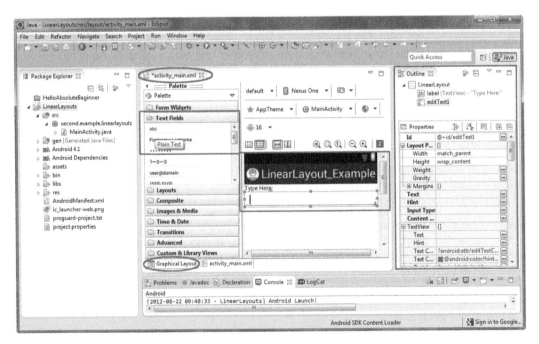

***Figure 6-12.** Adding the EditText UI widget using drag-and-drop in the Eclipse Graphical Layout Editor*

Next, click on the activity_main.xml tab next to the Graphical Layout tab to see the XML markup that was just written for us! The resulting XML markup should read as follows (if it does not, edit it directly so that it does):

```
<EditText
        android:id="@+id/editText1"
        android:layout_width="match_parent"
        android:layout_height="wrap_content"
        android:layout_below="@+id/label"
        android:layout_marginTop="10dip" (add this tag to the code the GLE has written for you)
        android:ems="10" >
        <requestFocus />
</EditText>
```

It will be laid out relative to (below) the TextView as shown because that is where you drag-N-dropped it in the visual layout editor. The key line of XML is the fourth parameter, called layout_below, which references the ID of the TextView, telling Android to position the EditText object below the TextView object that has an ID value of "label." This is pretty straightforward logic, and is also very powerful.

You'll soon see that Eclipse (Android ADT more accurately) wants you to use the *strings.xml* file to hold text constants, as you will see a little triangular yellow "warning" icon next to your android:text parameter. When you mouse-over this, it will say: "Hard-Coded String: Should Use @string Resource" and you will also see another one of these next to the <EditText> tag that reads: "Text Field does not specify an Input Type or a Hint." Both of these warnings are not important now (that is, they will not prevent your app from compiling and running in the 4.1 emulator), but these warnings are generally helpful to the programmer, and also let us know how Android thinks things should be done (optimally) within their development environment, and within your app code structure.

Because the text label and the text field are a little cramped together, lets add an android:layout_marginTop="10dip" to space things out a little bit. This adds 10 device independent pixels (DIP; you can also use the abbreviation DP if you like) to the top of the EditText field, which spaces (pushes) it down and away from the text label that we already had in place in the upper-left 0.0 corner location on the screen.

Finally, we observe that Eclipse GLE added a nested <requestFocus /> tag inside (before) the end of the </EditText> closing tag. This is so that this UI element will have "focus" on application launch and will be ready to receive text data. What this does is to get the text entry area ready for use and is the equivalent of the user manually clicking on the text field to tell it to accept text data entry. What having this <requestFocus/> tag inside of the <EditText> tag does for you is that now your user does not have to touch the screen to show Android where they want to start working (i.e., entering text), and your end user can simply begin entering text immediately on launching the app, because the focus has been set for them where it logically should be set—within the first text entry field on the user interface screen.

Note that to set the focus on the button (which we will add next) would be wrong UI design because you can't click the OK button until you have entered the text in the first place! Figure 6-13 shows what the XML should look like in Eclipse; notice that selecting the EditText tag (shown in light blue highlighting) shows the span (medium blue spanning the left margin) of the code contained within that tag.

Figure 6-13. EditText widget XML code generated by the Graphical Layout Editor plus our 10 DIP margin

Next, let's click on the Graphical Layout Editor tab again, and add an OK button UI element, by dragging a button UI element out of the Form Widgets section (on the left, under Palette) of the Graphical Layout Editor Tab (in the center code editing area of Eclipse) as shown in Figure 6-14. Note that as you drag and position the UI element (in this case, a button), that the Eclipse Graphical Layout Editor actually shows you in real time what the XML markup parameters it will code for that positioning location are via a light-yellow tool-tip. Super cool stuff, so play around with it for a while!

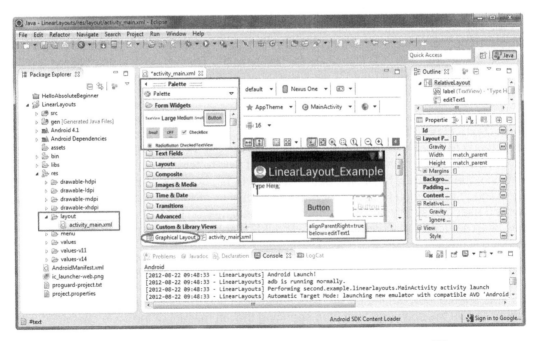

Figure 6-14. Dragging the OK button widget out of the Form Widgets drawer in the Graphical Layout Editor

You can also hand code this OK button via the `<Button>` XML tag, as in the following example, if you prefer not to use the Drag-N-Drop GUI Editor in Eclipse. Note that the helper tooltip in the screenshot in Figure 6-14 shows what XML parameters will be placed in the following code based on the orange dashed line representation of where your mouse is holding the button for eventual placement via mouse button release (drop).

Here's the code that Eclipse GLE generates for you:

```
<Button
        android:id="@+id/button1"
        android:layout_width="wrap_content"
        android:layout_height="wrap_content"
        android:layout_alignParentRight="true"
        android:layout_below="@+id/editText1"
        android:text="OK" />
```

This `<Button>` tag shows some of the power of relative positioning. The button is below the `EditText` (using the parent's ID parameter), aligned right relative to the parent container, which means aligned to the right side of the screen because the parent container is the <RelativeLayout> tag, which has parameters telling it to fill the screen (this is what match_parent means for this tag), thus in this case the RelativeLayout container (tag) IS the screen.

Let's add a Cancel button to the left of the OK button, over on the left side of the screen, and let's align it below the EditText UI element, using this code (or you can try using the Graphical Layout Editor in Eclipse, as shown in Figure 6-15, again to get some more practice doing it the easy way).

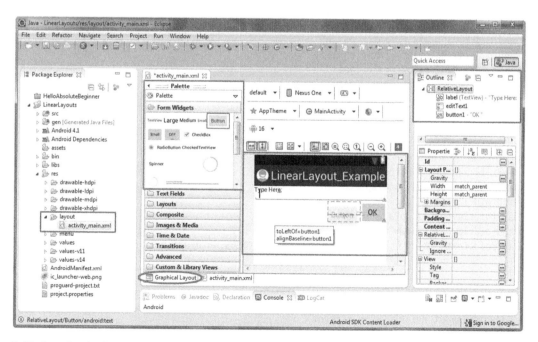

Figure 6-15. Dragging the Cancel Button onto the user interface in the Graphical Layout Editor

Here's the XML markup that should be generated

```
<Button
        android:id="@+id/button2"
        android:layout_width="wrap_content"
        android:layout_height="wrap_content"
        android:layout_below="@+id/editText1"
        android:text="Cancel" />
```

Notice that because the default button alignment is to the left of the screen that the only relative positioning definition tag that we need is one that specifies android:layout_below of the EditText UI widget named editText1. Here is all of the new RelativeLayout code in the *activity_main.xml* file (Figure 6-16 shows it in Eclipse):

```
<RelativeLayout xmlns:android="http://schemas.android.com/apk/res/android"
    xmlns:tools="http://schemas.android.com/tools"
    android:layout_width="match_parent"
    android:layout_height="match_parent" >

<TextView
    android:id="@+id/label"
    android:layout_width="wrap_content"
    android:layout_height="wrap_content"
    android:text="Type here:"                      (Generates Warning: Hard Coded Text)
    tools:context=".MainActivity" />

<EditText                              (Generates Warning: No Hint Parameter Included)
        android:id="@+id/editText1"
        android:layout_width="match_parent"
        android:layout_height="wrap_content"
        android:layout_below="@+id/label"
        android:layout_marginTop="10dip"
        android:ems="10" >
        <requestFocus />
</EditText>

<Button
        android:id="@+id/button1"
        android:layout_width="wrap_content"
        android:layout_height="wrap_content"
        android:layout_alignParentRight="true"
        android:layout_below="@+id/editText1"
        android:text="OK"/>                        (Generates Warning: hard Coded Text)

<Button
        android:id="@+id/button2"
        android:layout_width="wrap_content"
        android:layout_height="wrap_content"
        android:layout_below="@+id/editText1"
        android:text="Cancel"/>                    (Generates Warning: Hard Coded Text)

</RelativeLayout>
```

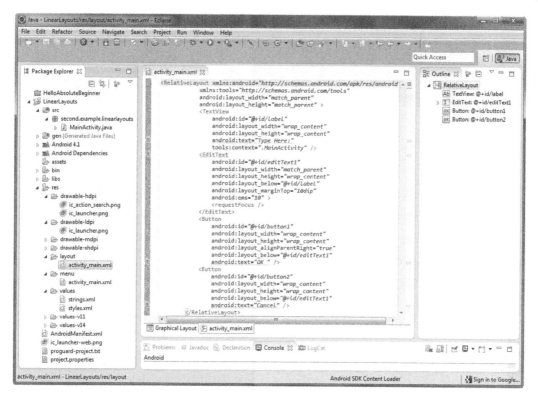

Figure 6-16. *Final XML markup for the RelativeLayout in the activity_main.xml file with warnings*

Now let's compile the project and run it in the Android 4.1 emulator. Right-click the *LinearLayouts* project folder at the top of the Package Explorer pane and select **Run As ➤ Android Application**. Figure 6-17 shows our app running in the Android 4.1 device emulator. As you can see, the RelativeLayout code works great and formats our UI perfectly.

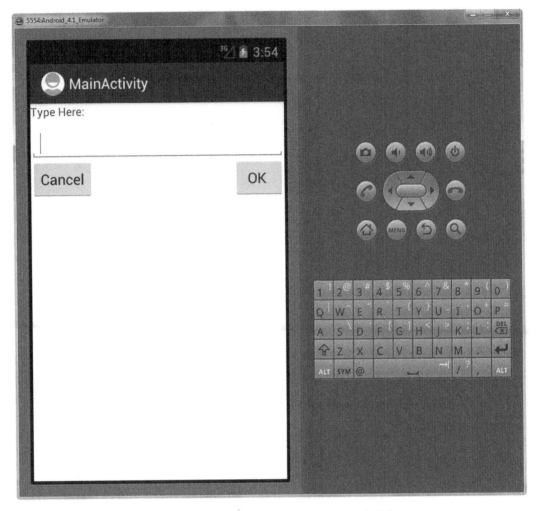

Figure 6-17. Running the RelativeLayout example in the Android 4.1 device emulator in Eclipse

Now let's add some animation to our UI by creating a sliding drawer layout container for our UI elements.

Sliding Drawer: Expanding Your UI

One of the more advanced layout containers in Android is SlidingDrawer, another direct subclass of the ever so useful ViewGroup class. This layout is not used quite as often as the others, but it's extremely handy and a lot of fun as well.

A sliding drawer is useful because it gives us a way to expand the screen area that can be used by UI components, or even for application content, for that matter.

A SlidingDrawer container should be used inside either the RelativeLayout container or the FrameLayout container, according to the developer documentation, which you should always review on developer.android.com before using any Android Class, just to see what it can do and how it should be coded. Android Developer documents in this case recommend using the RelativeLayout container, if possible, instead of the FrameLayout container. You cannot use SlidingDrawer as its own container because it needs to slide out of (and over) something. Logical enough when you think about it.

> **Note**   FrameLayout is not as useful as LinearLayout or RelativeLayout, and as such, is not as frequently used as a standard Android layout container type. It can be used to hold a single UI element inside of a frame, and for that reason it is useful in certain scenarios and thus is still supported.

How does sliding drawer expand your screen area? By sliding a drawer (vertically or horizontally) onto the display from off the screen, you have another virtual (hidden) screen available for use. This can be useful if you need the entire screen for your content because you can keep your UI controls in a drawer that slides on or off the screen whenever those UI elements are needed.

Now let's add a sliding drawer to our RelativeLayout of the previous section, and see just how cool an application user interface (UI) we can create using only two dozen lines of XML code. We'll create an app with an analog clock that slides out inside of its own drawer whenever we need to see what time it is.

Leave our existing project's RelativeLayout XML tag intact, but delete the text and button elements inside. Then add the SlidingDrawer tag inside of the RelativeLayout container because a drawer always needs to slide out of something (and over the top of the other content in the RelativeLayout container). Let's practice doing this the easy way, with the Eclipse Graphical Layout Editor, and then we'll take a look at the XML code once it's been auto-generated for us and "tweak" it with our own customized parameters to fine-tune our desired end result.

After you delete the TextView, EditText, and Button tags inside of the RelativeLayout container tag using the activity_main.xml tab in Eclipse, switch over to the Graphical Layout Editor by clicking on the Graphical Layout tab at the bottom of the central editing pane in Eclipse. Click on the Composite (stands for Composite Layouts) section (notice that the UI works as a type of sliding drawer that we are implementing here) and drag the SlidingDrawer icon onto the now blank App UI screen on the right, and once the green lines fill the app screen, drop it into place as shown in Figure 6-18.

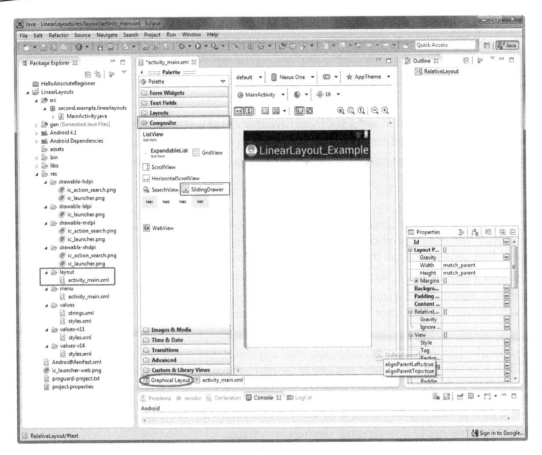

Figure 6-18. Dragging the SlidingDrawer UI widget onto the blank RelativeLayout container to fill screen

Now click on the activity_main.xml tab and take a look at the code that Eclipse (more accurately, the ADT plug-in) wrote for us. You'll see a SlidingDrawer container inside of the RelativeLayout container, and inside of the sliding drawer you will see a Button UI element used for the SlidingDrawer "handle" (a SlidingDrawer UI element must always have a handle defined) and a LinearLayout container ready to hold your content that will be inside of the SlidingDrawer. Figure 6-19 shows the XML code that was auto-generated.

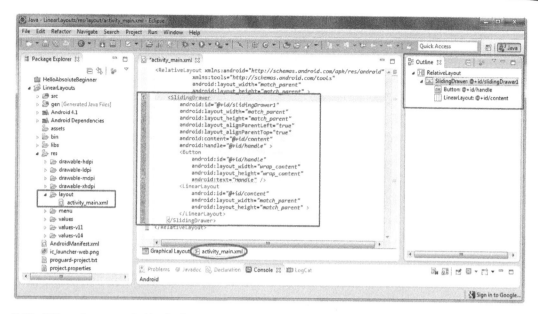

Figure 6-19. XML markup generated by the Graphical Layout Editor for the SlidingDrawer tag

If you like, you can right-click on the project name and do a Run As ➤ Android Application and see the handle at the bottom of the screen, click it, watch it animate to the top of the screen (opening the drawer), and then click it again, and watch it animate back down to its original position (i.e., drawer closed). Then close the emulator and go back to the Eclipse Graphical Layout Editor tab, so that we can add an AnalogClock object (widget) inside of the drawer to give our app some useful functionality.

Find the AnalogClock icon under the Time and Date section at the left side of the Graphical Layout Editor and drag the AnalogClock widget icon onto the UI area on the right. Once you drop it, you will have a square resizable area at the upper-left of the container (default position of 0,0 as we learned about previously). Shown below in Figure 6-20 is the drag operation we went through to place the AnalogClock UI widget into our SlidingDrawer; notice that Eclipse ADT gives you guidelines for positioning as you are dragging the UI elements into place; again, be sure to play around a bit with this functionality to get used to it, and then to leverage it completely to your development advantage.

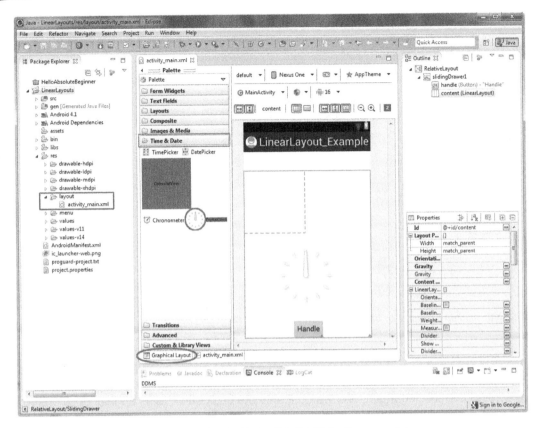

Figure 6-20. *Dragging and positioning the AnalogClock widget within the SlidingDrawer container*

Grab the bottom-right handle of the AnalogClock widget box and drag it down and to the right until it fills the container (screen). This will center the AnalogClock widget on the screen (the AnalogClock widget does not scale as some of the other UI widgets do). You might think that you can click and drag in the middle of this square area to move and position it, but once you try that, you will see that it does not work that way, so position it with the lower-right handle instead. ADT will show you the original size (green square) and the new size (orange square) as you drag the handle, as shown on Figure 6-21.

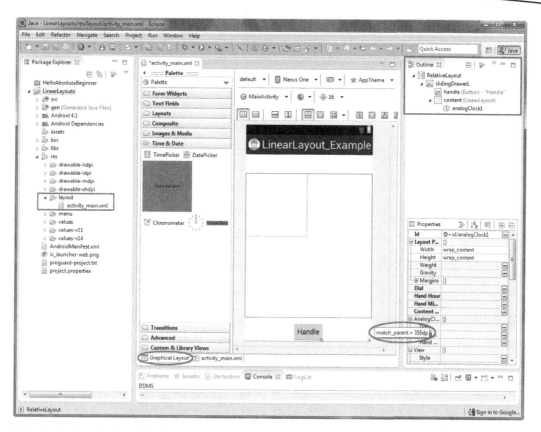

Figure 6-21. *Positioning the AnalogClock size boundaries in the SlidingDrawer via the Graphical Layout tab*

Now let's take a look at the XML markup that was generated for us, by simply clicking on the activity_main.xml tab. There should now be an AnalogClock tag inside of the LinearLayout tag, which there is, as shown in Figure 6-22. We now can see a really good example of tags that are nested deeply inside of each other.

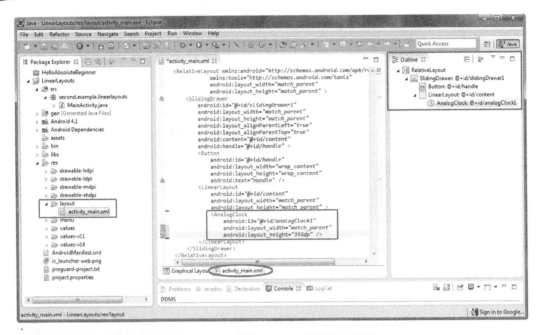

Figure 6-22. XML markup generated by Graphical Layout Editor for AnalogClock widget

Let's right-click on the project name and Run As ➤ Android Application to see our SlidingDrawer open up and give us a nicely centered analog clock. Figure 6-23 shows the before and after of the SlidingDrawer closed and open in the display portion of the Android 4.1 emulator.

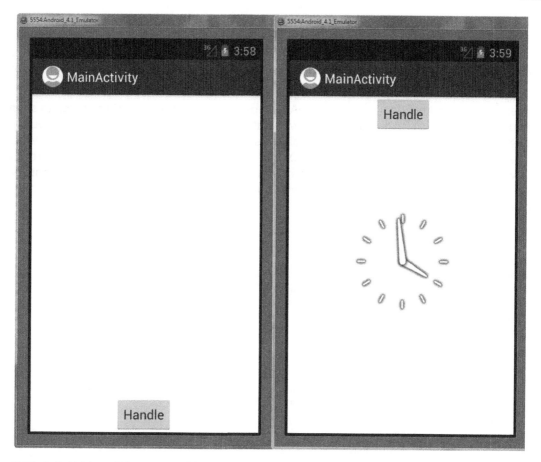

Figure 6-23. Android 4.1 emulation screens of SlidingDrawer container in an open/close position

Now let's make a couple of minor modifications to the XML code to make the app a little bit more colorful, user friendly, use fewer lines of code, and work across all screen sizes automatically. Notice that our AnalogClock parameters are different, one uses "match_parent" and the other uses "355dp," which would work fine on a 320 by 480 smartphone, but not as well on a 800 by 480 tablet or 1,280 by 720 iTV. So, first, to make our app work across different screen sizes, lets change the android:layout_ height to have the same match_parent setting as the android:layout_width parameter does.

Next let's make the app more user friendly and change the Button text parameter to read "Open Drawer" instead of "Handle," so the user sees what is going on with the app. Now you can Run As ➤ Android Application (again) if you wish to see that the app still works the same with the new parameters and settings.

Next you may be wondering: is the LinearLayout container that the Graphical Layout Editor coded for us unused (or redundant) in this example? Couldn't the AnalogClock be directly inside of the SlidingDrawer container, along with the Button Handle? Let's remove the LinearLayout tag, its parameters, and closing tag, and find out!

Be sure to rename the AnalogClock ID parameter to "content" so that the SlidingDrawer android:content parameter points to something (the ID of the LinearLayout container that we deleted had been set to "content" and so we need to change the ID AnalogClock1 to "content"). Now Run As ➤ Android Application again and see that the new code indeed works the same, saving several lines of code, and more important, memory space that would have been used to define a redundant container that was not really needed. This also puts us into the two dozen lines of code realm that we were shooting for.

Finally, let's add an android:background="#D0A0A0" parameter to the SlidingDrawer tag to set a background color to differentiate the open drawer state from the closed drawer state, so you can really see the edges of the SlidingDrawer container itself. Although we are doing this with XML code, shown next, it is also doable by entering #D0A0A0 in the background field under the Properties pane to the lower-right of the Graphical Layout Editor pane when you have the SlidingDrawer container selected in the Graphical Layout Editor (click just above the AnalogClock selection to select the SlidingDrawer container above it).

Here's the final code:

```
<RelativeLayout
    xmlns:android="http://schemas.android.com/apk/res/android"
    xmlns:tools="http://schemas.android.com/tools"
    android:layout_width="match_parent"
    android:layout_height="match_parent">
    <SlidingDrawer
        android:id="@+id/slidingDrawer1"
        android:layout_width="match_parent"
        android:layout_height="match_parent"
        android:layout_alignParentLeft="true"
        android:layout_alignParentTop="true"
        android:background="#D0A0A0"
        android:content="@+id/content"
        android:handle="@+id/handle" >
    <Button
        android:id="@+id/handle"
        android:layout_width="wrap_content"
        android:layout_height="wrap_content"
        android:text="Open Drawer"  />
    <AnalogClock
        android:id="@+id/content"
        android:layout_width="match_parent"
        android:layout_height="match_parent" />
    </SlidingDrawer>
</RelativeLayout>
```

As you can see from the code indenting, the SlidingDrawer tag goes inside the RelativeLayout tag. It has two other XML tags that go inside of it: one that defines the button that will be used as the handle for opening and closing the sliding drawer (the Button tag), and another that defines the content inside of the drawer (the AnalogClock tag).

There are two required tags that must be in a SlidingDrawer layout container, the android:handle and the android:content. The android:handle can point to anything that can be used as a handle, the most common would be a button (default) or a drawable asset such as a custom 3D handle that you might create just for this purpose.

The other XML tag that must be inside any `SlidingDrawer` layout container is android:content. Whatever XML tag you want to use for your content must have an ID specified that matches the name that is specified in the `SlidingDrawer` android:content parameter. In this case, we are using `content` as the content container's ID, but it could be anything you like, for instance we could have specified android:content="@+id/analogClock1" instead of changing the AnalogClock's ID to "content."

We used the Android's `AnalogClock` XML tag to give us some impressive working content for this exercise with very little coding effort. Note that we are accomplishing this in only three lines of XML code. In fact, this entire "clock in a drawer" Android application is using primarily XML, and essentially no Java logic, other than to display the UI design on the Android smartphone, tablet, e-reader, or iTV screen.

So that we can see the boundaries of the `SlidingDrawer`, which we have set in the `SlidingDrawer` tag layout_width and layout_height parameters, we have placed an android:background parameter in the `SlidingDrawer` tag. The content is given a teaberry color value background that matches our Android RAZR phone. This android:background parameter will work in virtually any XML tag relating to the screen, and uses a standard hexadecimal color value representation (#D0A0A0) inside of quotes just as it is used in HTML and CSS. If you are entering the value into the Properties Editor pane on the right side of Eclipse, then you don't need to include the quotes around the hexadecimal color value.

Finally, just to be super precise and exacting, you can click the strings.xml tab and change `LinearLayout_Example` to `SlidingDrawers_Example` and delete any unused TextView values.

Figure 6-23 shows the sliding drawer example running in the emulator. Some cool things to change so that you can see what this layout container can do are to change the orientation (to horizontal) and the layout width and height parameters of the `SlidingDrawer` tag itself. I suggest that you practice compiling and testing Android applications by changing these XML parameters and then choosing **Run As ➤ Android Application** a bunch of times. This will help you to get used to the development work process and more comfortable with Eclipse, and how easy it is to use.

Using Padding and Margins with Views and Layouts

Padding adds spacing to a View (or a widget subclassed therefrom), so that that View's content is offset by a certain number of pixels on each of the four sides. This way, the content doesn't touch the edges of the View and look unprofessional. In other words, padding adds space around the outside of a View's content, and you can choose to do so on any of the four sides of the View object. When using padding, the padding is considered to be part of the View, which may affect the way Android lays out the View. Remember, we are talking here about a View Class or Object, that is, a user interface widget, not the view on your Android device's screen!

Padding values are only available to `Views`, not to `ViewGroups` (and thus not available in screen layout containers). This is logical because View objects (usually widgets) are contained inside something (ViewGroups) but contain nothing inside of them, that is, they are what they are (Button, Clock, Radio Button, Text Field, etc.).

`ViewGroups` instead support margins, which allow the same results as padding to be obtained, except that the margins are not considered part of the `ViewGroup`. For me, this makes UI design more organized and easy to remember: `Views` use padding values and `ViewGroups` use margin values and also can use padding values.

Setting Padding in Views

Padding can be set for your View objects (usually widgets) in three ways, two of which we have seen so far in this book. The first and easiest way to set a padding value for a UI element widget is to use the Properties Editor pane in Eclipse, where all of the properties of a selected UI element in the Graphical Layout Editor will be displayed on the right side (or wherever you place that pane) of the Eclipse IDE.

The second way to set properties of a UI widget is in the XML editor pane, where when you type android: a window containing all of the parameter options (including padding settings) will pop-up as soon as you type the colon symbol after you type in android (in lower case). Then you can double-click on the parameter that you want and type in its value or even type in the entire parameter from memory without using the helper that works in the XML editing pane. Most of the time you will use one of these two methods to set padding; using Java for setting padding values is not a "Best Practice," unless you are doing something really vanguard and need to have real-time control over padding values.

That said, padding can also be set via your Java code, using the .setPadding() method with four values, for left, top, right, and bottom. Think of going around a clock, starting at 9:00, separated by commas. So, to put a four-pixel border inside your view, you would use the following (remember that the order of parameters is left, top, right, bottom):

```
objectName.setPadding(4,4,4,4);
```

You can also separate each side in the Java methods, just like you can with the XML tag parameters. So, to get the padding for the left side of the view, use .getPaddingLeft(). To set just the padding on the top to eight pixels, you would write something like this:

```
ObjectName.setPaddingTop(8);
```

Setting Margins in ViewGroups

For ViewGroups, including layout containers (the subject of this chapter), the easiest way to set margins during development is via the XML parameters for any ViewGroup object.

Four layout margin values are available in XML:

- android:layout_marginBottom
- android:layout_marginLeft
- android:layout_marginRight
- android:layout_marginTop

We used the android:layout_marginTop in our RelativeLayout example earlier in this chapter to space the text entry UI element down and away from the text label UI element. In fact, we will be using this throughout the book to space out our centered UI objects evenly.

Be sure to experiment with using these four parameters on your UI elements. You'll see that you can control exactly how your UI elements are spaced around on the screen as you become familiar with what margins can do.

Summary

Android allows us to easily design screen layouts via XML, which makes it much simpler than it would be via Java code. Nonprogrammers, such as designers, can get involved with the UI design process without needing to know any Java coding.

We also saw that we can use the Graphical Layout Editor tab/pane in Eclipse to visually drag-N-drop UI elements (widgets) onto our screen design, and have the ADT plug-in in Eclipse write the bulk of our XML UI markup code for us, which is really great for absolute beginners!

In this chapter, we started to take a look at the foundation for laying out our UI areas on the Android smartphone, tablet, e-reader, or iTV screen using the View and ViewGroup classes. We use the View class, its subclasses (widgets) and the ViewGroup class and its subclasses (layout containers) to lay out our UI screen and its component UI elements. Android provides several of these ViewGroup subclasses, including the LinearLayout, SlidingDrawer, and RelativeLayout classes that we looked at (and used) specifically in this chapter.

LinearLayout is one of the most used layout containers in Android programming, and the one used in many of the basic Android apps that come with the operating system. It arranges UI elements from right to left or top to bottom. It is possible to nest LinearLayout containers within each other to achieve more complicated UIs, but often it is better to use a RelativeLayout container for more complex UI designs.

RelativeLayout is another often used layout container in Android programming. It allows you to arrange UI elements by specifying their placement on the screen relative to each other. This allows for more complicated UI layouts than just the rows or columns supported by the LinearLayout class. We also have seen that the RelativeLayout is the layout container that Android will use if you have Android Development Tools (the ADT Eclipse Plug-In) create a blank activity for you in the New ➤ Project ➤ Android Application Project sequence of dialogs.

We also took a look at one of the more innovative (and animated) ViewGroup layout containers called SlidingDrawer. This allows you to slide UI elements on and off the screen, in and out of view of the user. This layout container can be used to greatly increase screen real estate by allowing UI elements to exist offscreen in a "drawer" that slides out only when the user needs it.

In the next chapter, we will look at adding more complex UI elements into RelativeLayout ViewGroup layout containers using even more View objects (called *widgets*). The android.widget package gives us all sorts of precoded UI elements that are derived from the android.view.View superclass. Let's move on to Chapter 7 now as you understand layouts and are ready to create (code) full-blown UI designs!

UI Design: Buttons, Menus, and Dialogs

The UI design determines the usability of your application, which will ultimately determine its success and even its profitability if you are selling it. We'll build on what we learned in Chapter 6 as UI elements in Android are View classes (widgets) and are grouped together using ViewGroup classes (layout containers).

A standard UI is composed of a number of familiar components that can be used by your application's users to control their user experience (often called the UX). These UI elements include items such as buttons, check boxes, radio buttons, menus, text fields, dialog boxes, progress bars, system alerts, and similar screen-based elements that are available to us under Android as widgets as we learned in Chapter 6.

This chapter covers how to use several of the most important Android widgets for UI design. First, we'll cover adding image buttons, text, and images to your UI. Then you'll learn about the different types of menus available. Finally, we'll cover displaying dialogs, including alerts, which carry messages to your application user. There's a lot of cool stuff to cover, so let's get started.

Using Android UI Elements (Widgets)

One of the foundational areas of user interface (UI) design is creating and placing the functional elements of the design that allow your user to seamlessly interface with your application. These elements include buttons, text fields, check boxes, radio buttons, scrollable lists, and the like. We can't cover all of these in one chapter, but we can cover some of the more useful and visually impressive UI elements, just in case you need to make your apps stand apart from the crowd!

One of the most impressive types of user interface elements is the image button, which is an image that is a button itself or an icon on a button that visually represents what that button will do. In this next section we will learn how to combine an Android ImageButton widget along with a TextView widget and an ImageView widget to show how these Android View Classes can be implemented to add some graphics-intensive UI elements to your layout containers that we learned about in Chapter 6. This will provide a good foundation for then learning more about using graphics in Android in Chapter 8 which covers graphics design in Android.

Android has all of the standard UI elements already coded and ready to use in a single package called `android.widget`. Here, we'll explore how to add an image button, text area, and image to your app's UI.

> **Note**   Recall that a *package* in Java is a collection of ready-to-use classes that you can leverage within your application. You just need to tell Java that you are going to use them by importing them via the Java `import` command.

Adding an Image Button to Your Layout

In Chapter 6, we crafted a UI that included the `Button` class, which is used to create the standard Android system format buttons, and lets you do so with the greatest of ease. Now, we'll look at the more complex `ImageButton` class. For professional, customized, high-end graphical UIs, this is the class that you will need to use to gain the most visual control over the user experience as well as increased wow factor.

The `android.widget` package's `ImageButton` class allows you to use your own imagery to create custom multistate buttons that are cooler looking than the standard buttons that come standard with the Android operating environment.

There is a distinct work process to creating a successful multistate 24-bit or 32-bit PNG image button; one that will composite perfectly over background imagery if the button is using an 8-bit alpha channel. We'll get into much more detail about PNGs and alpha channels in the next couple of chapters.

Android supports 24 bits of PNG image data, with another 8 bits of anti-aliased image transparency channel (requiring another 8-bit alpha channel). Let's do the math: 24 + 8 = 32. So, what we really have is a 32-bit PNG image, with 8 bits of data for each of the red, green, and blue image channels, and another 8 bits of data for the alpha (transparency) channel. Therefore, 24-bit images are usually called RGB images, and 24-bit images with 8-bit alpha channels are usually called 32-bit images or RGBA (Red Green Blue Alpha) images.

In case you're not familiar with some of the terms I used in the previous description, here are some brief definitions:

- *Compositing:* The process of using (partially) transparent layers (like vellum on an overhead projector) to form a single new image out of more than one component parts or layers.

- *Alpha channel:* That portion of each layer which is transparent, and thus does not hold any image data, thereby passing through visible image data from other layers underneath it.

■ *Anti-aliasing:* The edge treatment that is used to make the edges of images within these transparency layers perfectly smooth when these edges are not perfectly square, which they rarely are. Anti-aliasing can be seen by zooming into an image and looking at the edges between different colors. Pixels at the edges are averaged between the two colors to creating a slight fade effect that makes the edges look smoother when the image is zoomed out.

Defining Multi-state Image Button Graphics in XML

The XML markup is significantly more complex for multistate image buttons than it is for regular buttons. Your XML file needs to tell Android which image to use for each state of the button:

■ Pressed (for touchscreens, the pressed image will be shown when the finger is actually touching the button image on the screen)

■ Released or normal (untouched); this is the "default" image state

■ Focused (in use currently and/or was last touched and thus is currently holding the UI Focus until another UI widget is utilized [touched or used] by the user)

Let's look at the code for our *button1.xml* file, which we will reference later when we create our ImageButton XML entry in the *activity_main.xml* file that goes in the */res/layout* folder. You don't need to create this file now.

```
<selector xmlns:android="http://schemas.android.com/apk/res/android">
    <item android:state_pressed="true"
          android:drawable="@drawable/button1_pressed" />
    <item android:state_focused="true"
          android:drawable="@drawable/button1_focused" />
    <item android:drawable="@drawable/button1_normal" />
</selector>
```

The first line defines a selector tag and points to the Android XML naming schema, as you have seen in previous chapters. A selector tag allows selection between several <item> options contained inside (nested within) it, as you may have guessed already. Inside the selector tag, we nest three item tags to show which drawable (bitmap) images to use (to select) for state_pressed=true, state_focused=true, and finally the default or normal button state. These item tags must be in the exact order outlined above, as they are evaluated by Android in that order (Is it Pressed? Does it have Focus? Is it not Pressed or does not have Focus?).

For this XML code to work we must have three 32-bit bitmap PNG images in each of our project's */res/drawable-dpi* folders named *button1_pressed.png*, *button1_focused.png*, and *button1_normal.png*.

Just like we did with our icons, we will have to go through the digital imaging work process that yields buttons optimized for LDPI, MDPI, HDPI, and XHDPI pixel density screens because Android devices now span smartphones to tablets to e-readers to iTV sets. So we will really be creating a dozen image assets for each ImageButton UI element that we utilize in our screen design. We'll do this after we create our new UI design project (next), and before we create and code our UI design project, so that our app's image assets are ready for use before we actually write the code that tries to access them.

> **Note**   Recall that each of the PNG image file names must use only lowercase letters and numbers and also can use the underscore character. These are Android's file naming rules. If you stray from this file naming rule at all, you will generate errors, warnings, and debugging headaches! So memorize this rule now to minimize future wasted debugging time!

The first `item` tag has an `android:state_pressed` attribute, which is set equal to `true`, and a second `android:drawable` attribute, which is set equal to the location of the file and its name (*sans* the *.png* extension, as we learned about previously) and will automatically point to the correct /drawable-dpi/ folder based on what screen density Android detects that your app is running on.

The @ equates to your project's resources folder, */project/res/*, so in this case, a low DPI resolution image for @drawable/button1_pressed will equate to *C:/Users/YourName/workspace/UI_Design/res/drawable-ldpi/button1_pressed.png* in the Android compiler (as well as the folders for the MDPI, HDPI, and XHDPI image assets, depending on what resolution device Android detects that you are using). The other `item` tags follow the same format as the first one.

Creating the UI Design Image Button Project in Eclipse

Now that we've reviewed the concepts, let's create the project for real. As you've done in previous chapters, fire up Eclipse and use the right-click Close Project command on your LinearLayouts project folder and then select **File ➤ New ➤ Project ➤ Android Application Project** to create a new Android application project.

We'll create the UI_Design Project first, so that Eclipse will create a nice graphic for us that we can modify with GIMP and then use for our ImageButton for this example. Let's get started!

In the New Android Application Project dialog sequence, set the project configuration options as follows:

- ▓ *Application name:* We'll call this application **UI_Designs**.
- ▓ *Project name:* Name the folder UI_Design.
- ▓ *Package name:* Using the proper package name format, enter third.example. userinterfacedesign as the name.
- ▓ *Build target:* So our application runs on the current Android operating system version 4.1, choose Android 4.1 API Level 16.
- ▓ *Min SDK version:* So our application runs on all of the popular Android operating system versions from 2.2 through 4.1, choose Android 2.2 or API Level 8 (the default setting) for our minimum or lowest level API support.
- ▓ *Configure launcher icon:* Accept the Default (Checked) Value for this dialog option.
- ▓ *Create blank activity:* Accept the MainActivity and activity_main defaults for this sequence of dialogs as we have done before.

If you need to refresh your memory on how to fill out all of the New Project Dialogs, please revisit the screenshots in Chapters 4 and 6 now. I'll include the main (initial) dialog in Figure 7-1 to show our primary project naming settings.

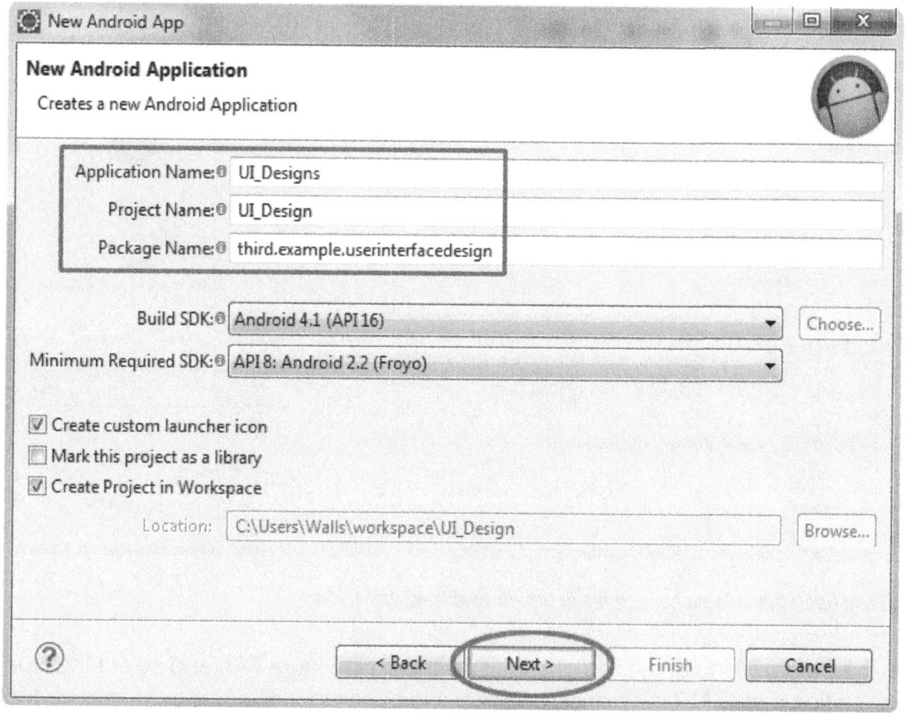

Figure 7-1. Naming our UI_Design project, application, and package in Eclipse

Creating Our Three UI Design Image Buttons in GIMP 2.8

The first thing that we need to do is to create the three button graphics that we will use to show you how to create multistate image buttons in Android using the ImageButton widget. Because Android has provided us a cool graphic with an alpha channel (transparency) called *ic_launcher.png* in our new project creation process, let's use that for our ImageButton graphic, as it's already in our /res/ drawable/ folders, now that we have created our UI_Design Project.

You will need to go through the work process shown below (we'll use the XHDPI image asset for our example) on each of the *ic_launcher.png* files in each of the four /drawable-dpi/ folders. Remember that they all need to be named the same way, because Android will differentiate between which file is which using the folder name and not the file name.

Fire up GIMP from your OS TaskBar and go into the File ➤ Open Image menu sequence to access the Open Image Dialog shown in Figure 7-2. Navigate using the left file navigation pane of the dialog to your C:/Users/YourName/workspace/UI_Design/res/drawable-xhdpi/ folder and select the *ic_launcher.png* file as shown in Figure 7-2 and then click on the Open button.

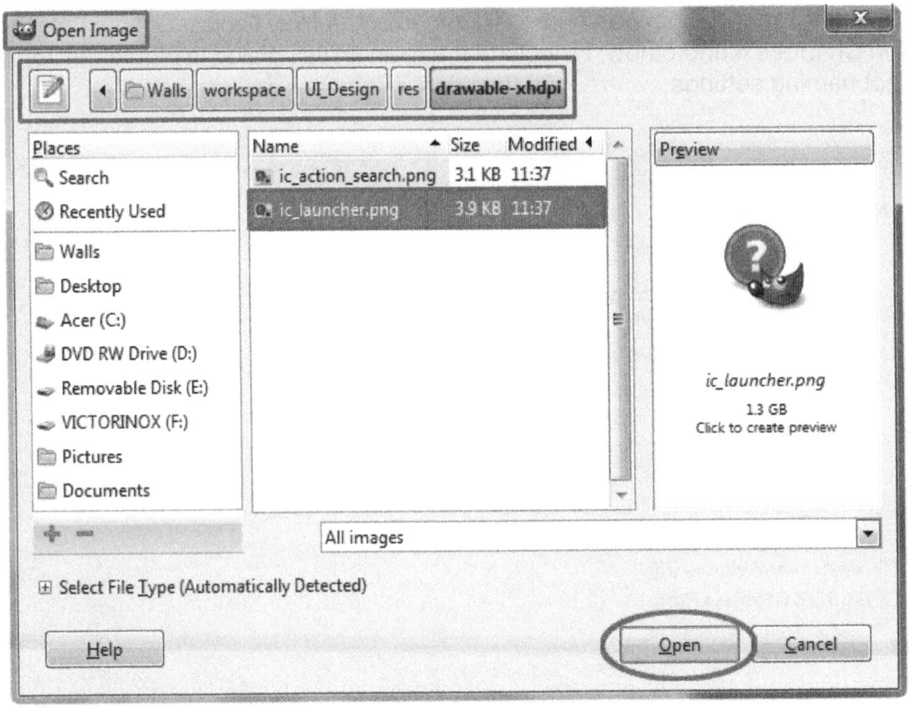

Figure 7-2. *Find and Open the ic-launcher.png file in the /drawable-xhdpi/ folder*

Next, click on the Colors Menu at the top of GIMP, as shown in Figure 7-3, and select the Hue-Saturation submenu item. Notice that GIMP is as good as Eclipse is at giving you a context-sensitive tooltip telling you what that menu selection will do before you select it. In this case, it tells us we are about to adjust the color (hue) value of the graphic that we have just opened.

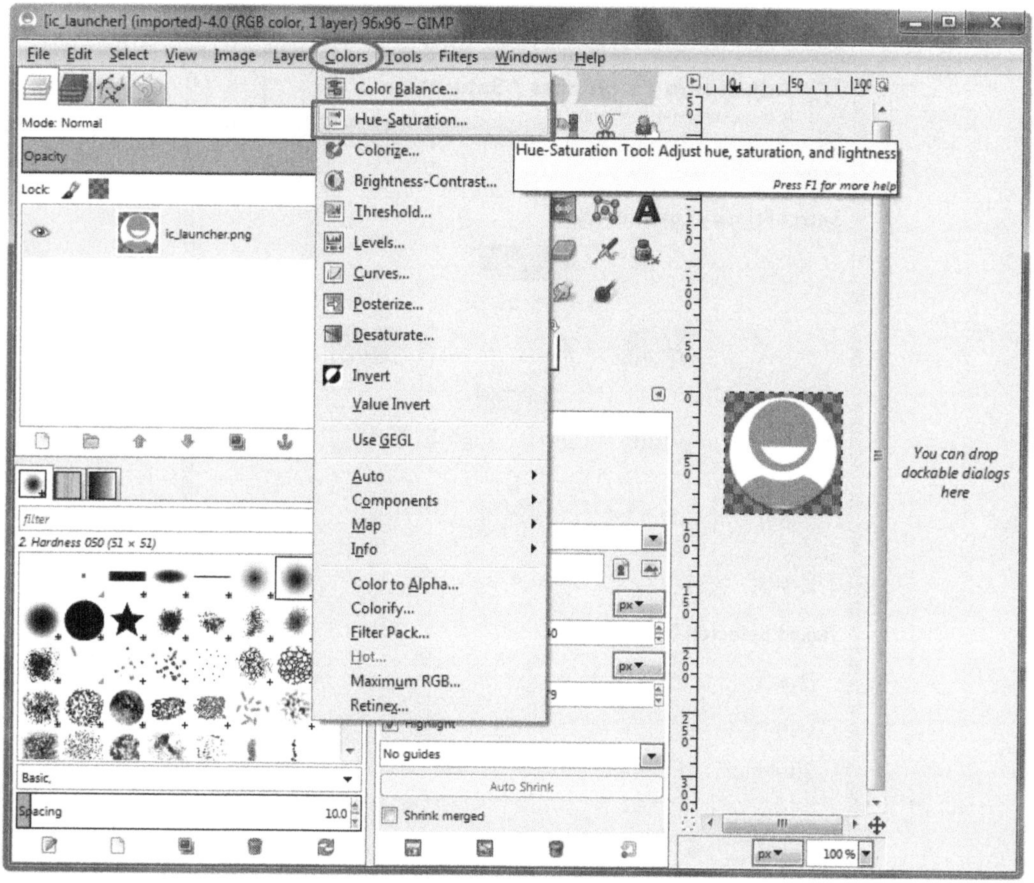

Figure 7-3. Selecting the Hue-Saturation tool from the Color Menu in GIMP 2.8

Once we have the Hue-Saturation color adjustment tool dialog on the screen, use the HUE slider or the Hue value numeric entry box on the right to shift our Hue (color) value backwards in the color wheel by 90 degrees, or a value entry of –90 if you wish to type it in. Make sure that the Preview Checkbox has a check in it (is selected for use) as shown in Figure 7-4, so that you can see the color change in the ic_launcher graphic go from blue to green. This will make our ImageButton graphic turn green when our users touch it. When everything is set, and you have a nice green color, select the OK button to make the color change permanent.

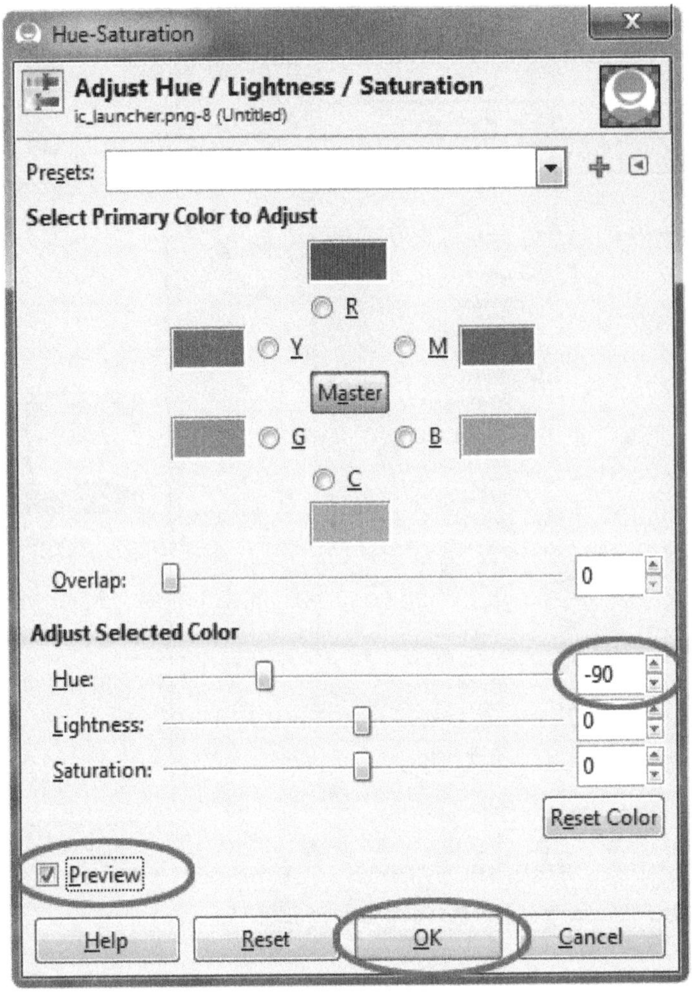

Figure 7-4. Changing the ic_launcher color value from blue to green

Because the "Pressed" button state is more effective when it animates when the user touches it on the screen, let's also rotate it 90 degrees so the little guy (or gal) depicted in the image turns their head to the side. To do this, we click on the Image Menu at the top of GIMP and select the Transform submenu and then the Transform 90 degrees counter-clockwise sub-submenu as shown in Figure 7-5.

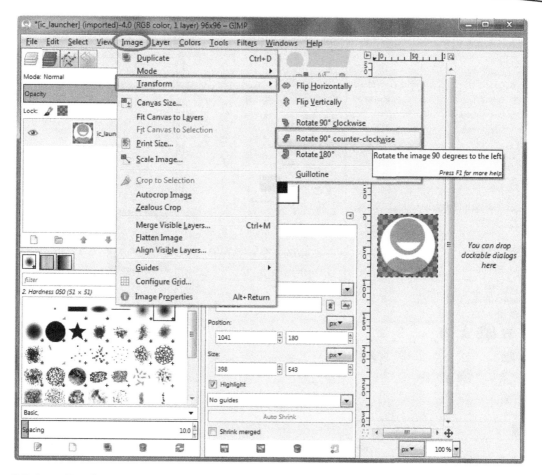

Figure 7-5. Image Transform Menu path for rotating our Pressed State graphic 90 degrees counter-clockwise

Now we are ready to use the GIMP File ➤ Export dialog to save our *button1_pressed.png* graphic file to it's new name and target location in the /drawable-xhdpi/ folder in our resource folder. Select the File ➤ Export menu as shown in Figure 7-6 to bring up the File ➤ Export Dialog so we can save our first of three ImageButton state files.

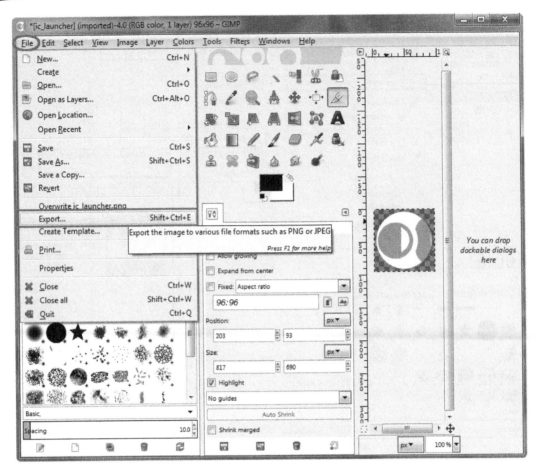

Figure 7-6. *Using the File ➤ Export utility to save the new Pressed State graphic PNG*

Name the button graphic *button1_pressed.png* in the Export Image dialog's name field as shown in Figure 7-7 using the Places Pane on the left to show GIMP where you want to save the file. Note the path to the File will also be shown graphically at the top of the dialog underneath the file name, next to the "Save in folder:" specifier. Once everything is set correctly, use the Export button to save the first of your three ImageButton image graphics to the /res/drawable-xhdpi/ folder.

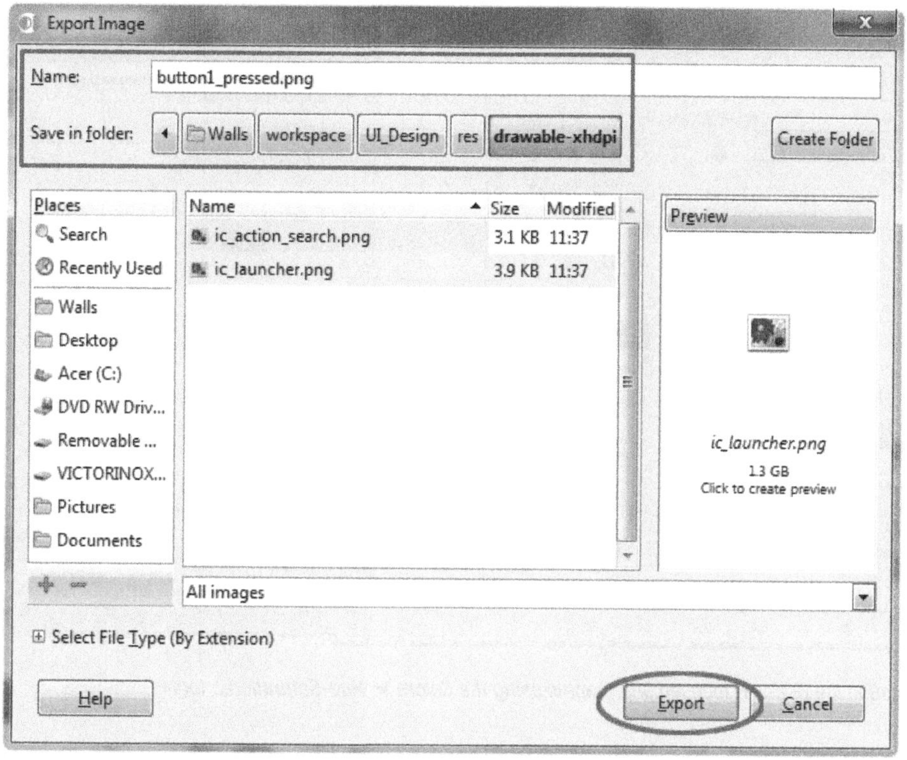

Figure 7-7. Saving the button1_pressed PNG file to the /drawable-xhdpi/ folder

When the PNG format settings dialog comes up make sure to use the same PNG settings that we used back in Chapter 4 in Figure 4-34 (just in case you have forgotten which of these options need to be selected).

Next, let's create the *button1_focused.png* button graphic by using the GIMP Edit ➤ Undo feature (or the CTRL-Z keystroke sequence) twice, to undo the rotation and the color changes, taking us back to the original blue image. Another way to do this would be to use the File ➤ Revert function, or to use the File ➤ Close function (without saving, of course), and then to use the File ➤ Open on the ic_launcher.png file again, as we did at the beginning of this work process back in Figure 7-2.

Next we are going to apply the same Color ➤ Hue-Saturation menu sequence that we used (shown previously in Figure 7-3) to turn our ImageButton graphic from blue to green, but this time we are going to turn it red to indicate that it has the focus, and is in use or is the one last (currently) used.

To do this we will use a color rotation value of 150 degrees clockwise (positive) around the color wheel from blue, which as you can see in Figure 7-8 gives us a nice bright red color result in our button image. Make sure that you have the Preview Option checked so that you can see what the dialog is doing to your image as you play around with the color adjustment options.

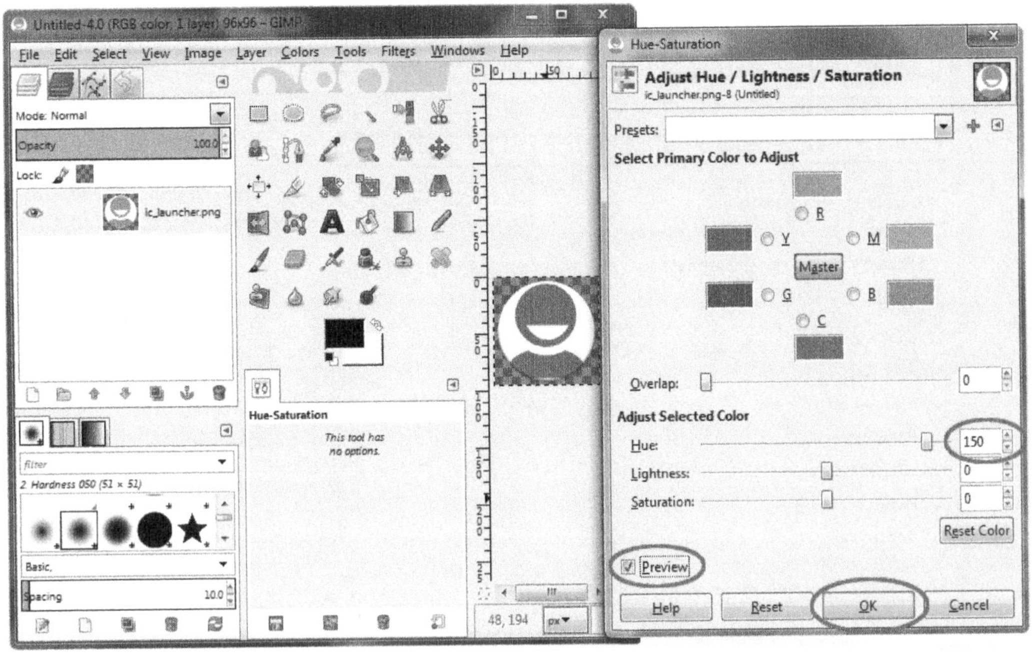

Figure 7-8. Creating the button1_focused.png graphic using the Colors ➤ Hue-Saturation... tool

Once you have a nice red color, go through the steps shown in Figure 7-6 and 7-7, except that you will want to use the file name: *button1_focused.png* for this red version that will turn your ImageButton red when it is in use! Pretty cool! Now finally let's create our *button1_normal.png* ImageButton state graphic so that it is different from our application launcher icon, and we'll be ready to code!

Finally we are going to apply yet again the same Colors ➤ Hue-Saturation menu sequence that we used (shown previously in Figure 7-3) to turn our ImageButton graphic from blue to green, but this time we are going to turn it Amber to indicate our Normal (default) Image Button state. Don't forget the two Undo steps that will bring your button back to it's original blue state, just like we did before.

To do this we will use a color rotation value of 160 degrees counter-clockwise (negative) around the color wheel from blue, which as you can see in Figure 7-9 gives us a rich amber color result in our button image. Make sure that you have the Preview Option checked so that you can see what the dialog is doing to your image as you play around with the color adjustment options.

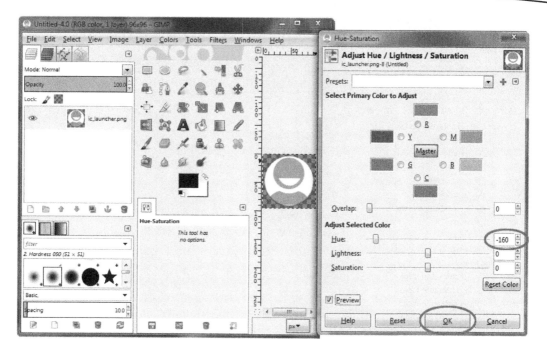

Figure 7-9. Creating the button1_normal.png graphic again using the Colors ➤ Hue-Saturation... tool

Once you have an acceptable amber color, again go through the steps shown in Figure 7-6 and 7-7 except that this time you will want to use the file name: *button1_normal.png* for this amber version that will be the default image (state) used for your button.

Next we need to create the XML file that will show Android which of the button states to select for each of the user actions that will be involved with animated buttons: Normal (no action), Pressed (touched), and Focused (last touched). Let's get into that now! Open up Eclipse and take a look in your UI_Design Project resource folder under the /res/drawable-xhdpi/ folder to make sure that all of your new ImageButton states (assets) are ready for use. This is shown in Figure 7-10.

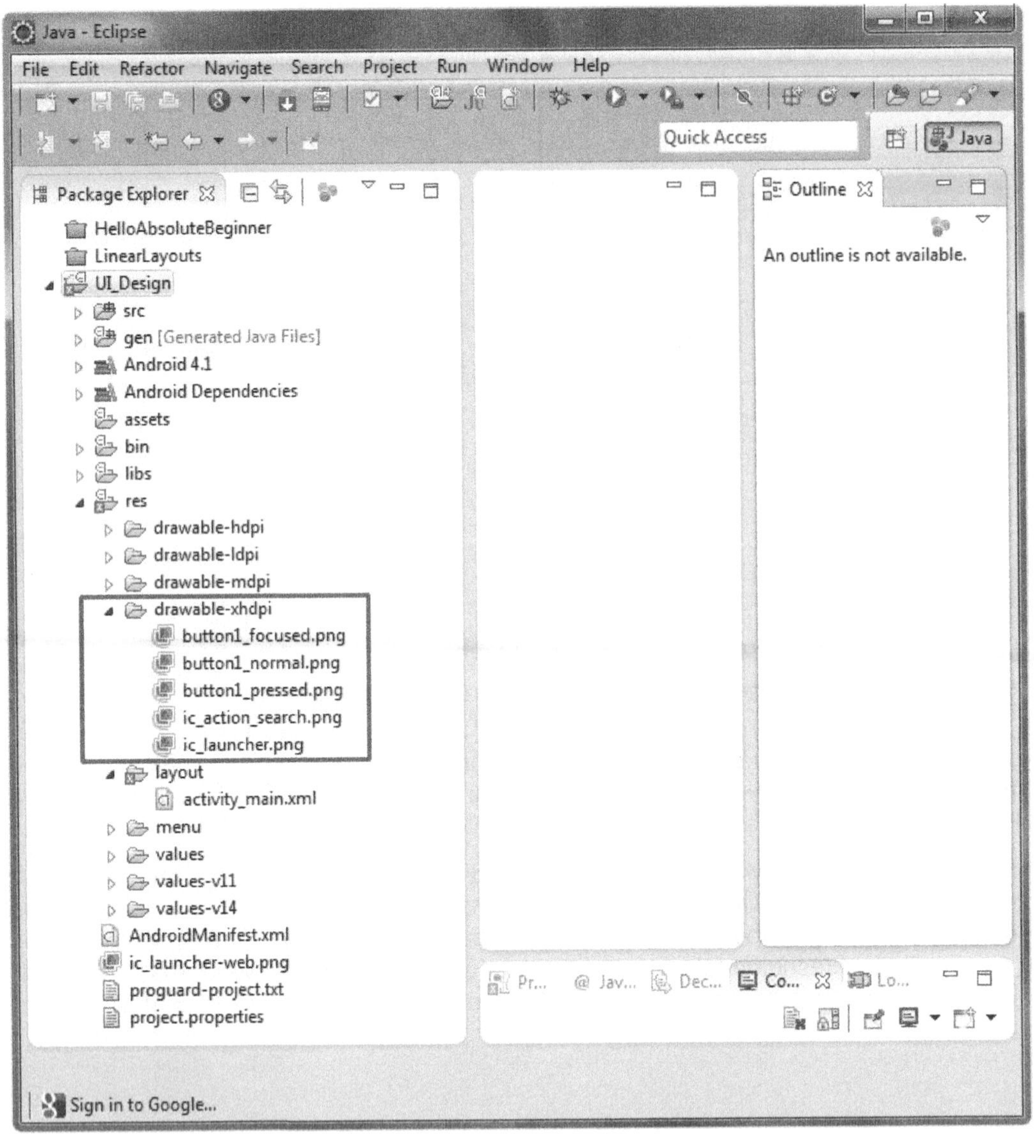

Figure 7-10. UI_Design Project resource folder and drawable-xhdpi sub-folder with ImageButton assets

Creating the button1.xml File

You now have an empty Eclipse project loaded with image assets. Next, we'll create the *button1.xml* file so that we can add the button state definition XML, which we looked at earlier in the chapter.

Open the project tree on the left in the Package Explorer tab, and expand the */res* folder by clicking the arrow. Then right-click the *drawable-xhdpi* folder and select **New ➤ File**, as shown in Figure 7-11.

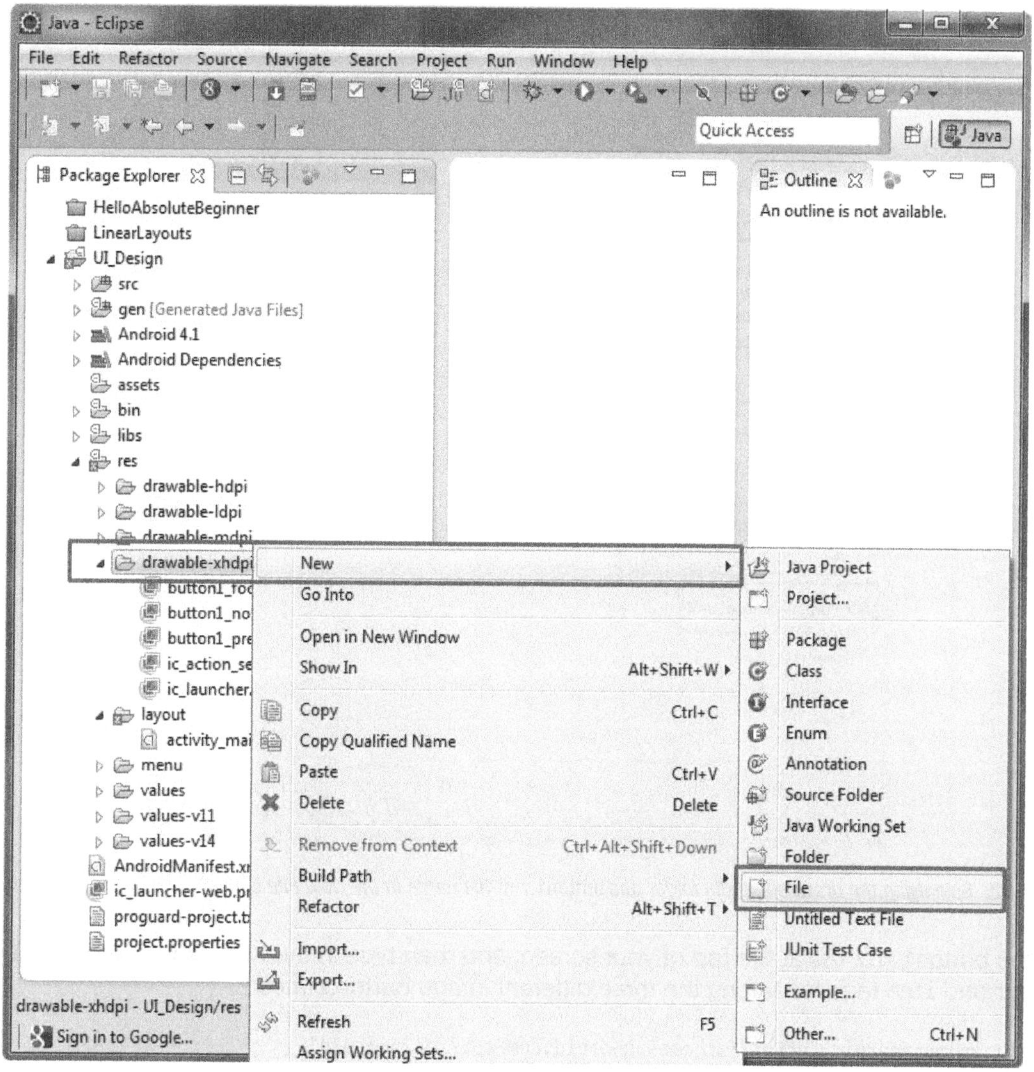

Figure 7-11. Creating a new file in the /res/drawable-xhdpi/ folder to hold our button1.xml XML markup

In the New File dialog, ask Eclipse to create the file *button1.xml* in the *UI_Design/res/drawable-xhdpi* folder, as shown in Figure 7-12. Then click Finish to create an empty text file. This is one of the most basic ways that you can have Eclipse create a new, empty text file for you. We will cover other ways of creating new XML files in later chapters.

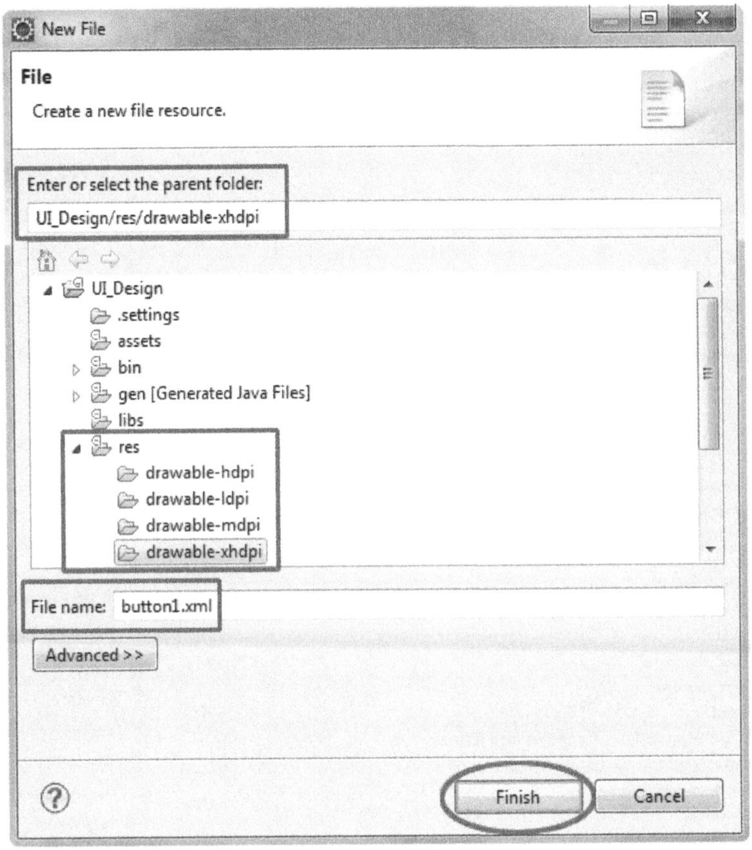

Figure 7-12. Specifying the drawable-xhdpi folder and button1.xml *file name in the New File dialog*

Click the button1.xml tab at the top of your screen, and then type in the XML code that defines the selector and item tags for setting the three different image button states:

```
<selector xmlns:android="http://schemas.android.com/apk/res/android">
        <item android:state_pressed="true"
                android:drawable="@drawable/button1_pressed" />
        <item android:state_focused="true"
                android:drawable="@drawable/button1_focused" />
        <item android:drawable="@drawable/button1_normal" />
</selector>
```

If you enter this XML markup before you create your three image file assets, you'll notice that Eclipse will show you that there are three errors in the markup relating to the missing image file assets. Place your mouse over the red X on the left margin by the markup code. This pops up a diagnostic message regarding why Eclipse thinks this code needs your attention, and you will be informed that your code references image assets that do not yet exist or Eclipse cannot locate.

If you have added them but Eclipse cannot "see" them, then right-click on your UI_Design project folder and select the "Refresh" option, and the error flags will disappear as Eclipse will "refresh" it's view of your project assets and find the unrecognized (missing) file references.

Once everything matches up then Eclipse will show your code in a clean (unwarning laden) environment, as shown in Figure 7-13.

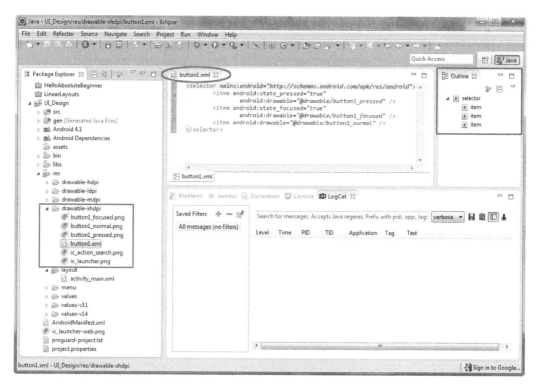

Figure 7-13. *The* button1.xml *code and matching button1 state PNG files in Eclipse*

Note   Once we have valid XML specifiers and code in place, the Eclipse error messages will disappear. But this does show us how Eclipse is watching out for you in real time, and offering warnings about what might be missing, what might generate compiler errors, and other common problems. You will observe this throughout your use of the Eclipse IDE.

Editing the activity_main.xml File

Next, open the /res/layout/ folder and right-click the *activity_main.xml* file to open it for editing. Notice that our image button source files now appear inside of the Package Explorer pane.

We need to replace the default text tag in the *activity_main.xml* file with an ImageButton tag, as follows:

```
<ImageButton android:id="@+id/button_one"
          android:layout_width="wrap_content"
          android:layout_height="wrap_content"
```

```
                android:src="@drawable/button1"
                android:contentDescription="@string/app_name">
</ImageButton>
```

Figure 7-14 shows the IDE at this point.

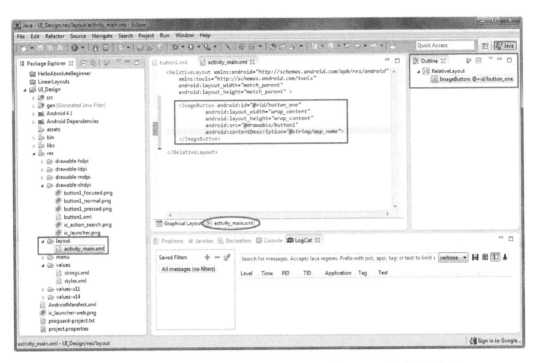

Figure 7-14. *Eclipse with a default RelativeLayout container and a new ImageButton tag added on the inside*

The first attribute adds an ID of button_one to the ImageButton so we can access it inside our Java code. The next two lines define the width and height of the image button via the wrap_content attribute—all very standard Android programming fare.

The next line accesses the *button1.xml* file that we created to reference the various image button states. Notice that you do not need to add the *.xml* extension here, just as you don't need to add the *.png* for your graphic files. Finally, we have the android:contentDescription tag set to our app_name variable that we already defined in our *strings.xml* file as UI Design.

The Content Description tag is a relatively new tag for ImageView and ImageButton objects that is there for accessibility purposes, primarily for the sight and hearing impaired. If you do not include an android:contentDescription tag in your ImageView or ImageButton UI element widgets, Eclipse will place a warning (yellow triangle) symbol next to the (in this case) ImageButton tag in the left margin. This warns you that you will need to add this tag for accessibility reasons, at least if you want to get rid of this warning icon. Note that your code will still compile and run without it.

To provide this accessibility for your UI elements, you would need to define a text variable in your *strings.xml* file that describes each of your visual UI elements in a way that if someone who is impaired was navigating your UI, they will know what element functions they are dealing with (have pressed or focus status).

In this case because the ImageButton is a UI design element, I am simply using an existing variable in *strings.xml* so that we do not have to go into the strings.xml and create a new variable, as we have already learned how to do that in previous chapters, and don't really need the extra practice here.

Figure 7-15 shows how our UI Examples app looks when run in the Android 4.1 emulator (right-click *UI_Design folder* and select **Run As ➤ Android Application**).

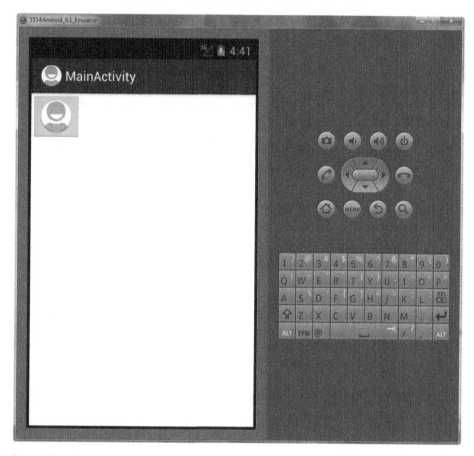

Figure 7-15. Our multistate image button running in the Android 4.1 emulator

When you click the image button, it rotates left and changes color from amber to green and uses the standard blue background to highlight the button being clicked.

Because we want just the nontransparent part of the image to be the button, which is why we use transparency and an alpha channel in GIMP 2.8, we will need to also set a background color, or transparency, for the ImageButton widget itself next. This will pass the transparency in the Image through the ImageButton transparency to whatever is behind both of these design elements. In this case, it will remove the gray background color setting of the ImageButton widget (replacing it with transparency) and let the white background color setting of the RelativeLayout container through.

Replacing the Default Background

We usually do not want to use the default Android ImageButton solid grey color background for a graphic image button, as we normally want the button image to seamlessly overlay the background content, usually a background image. We want the ImageButton background to be transparent, so we can use this ImageButton to put an image on top of a button and its text, or in this case, allow us to make the image (the nontransparent portion, anyway) itself into a button.

In this example, we are changing the color of the button, rather than changing the size or shape of the button, so the transparent area remains exactly the same, pixel for pixel, between the different image state graphics. Thus, we can either set the background image to our normal button state (which has transparency exactly where we need it to be), or we can set the background color using a 32-bit color value setting that features a 100% transparent 8-bit alpha channel by using the #00000000 setting (which means zero red, zero green, zero blue, zero alpha). This is similar to setting HTML color with the pattern #RRGGBBAA. This is the most elegant solution because it uses eight characters of code (in the form of a parameter) instead of an image asset to accomplish what we want, and more importantly because it accommodates image states that may have differently shaped alpha channel regions. Let's implement background transparency now.

We'll do this using the Graphical Layout Editor, so that you get additional practice using this cool Eclipse design tool that helps you design your UI widgets and layouts interactively without having to write lots of XML code.

Click the activity_main.xml tab at the top of your screen, and then click the Graphical Layout Editor tab at the bottom of the pane, which will then render your XML for the ImageButton (see Figure 7-16) so that you can see what the XML code will look (render) like when it is run in the Android 4.1 emulator. As you have seen in previous chapters, Eclipse will render your XML markup exactly as it would look in the emulator. Eclipse also provides (on the left) drag-and-drop widgets and layouts, so you can visually design your UI. The normal work process is to switch back and forth between the XML markup coding tab and the Graphical Layout Editor tab, so you can make sure your XML code is nested properly. This is also a great way to learn XML layout and UI coding in Android.

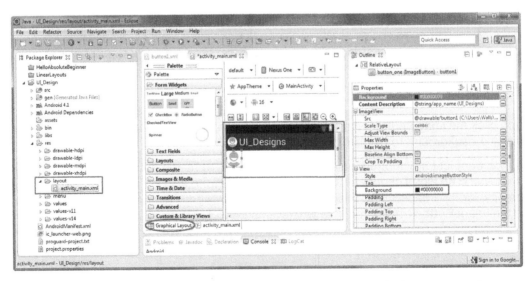

Figure 7-16. Using Graphical Layout Editor and Properties tabs to set an image background value to transparent

An even more useful tab is the Properties tab at the right side of the screen. This tab shows all of the properties assigned or available to the UI element tag that you have selected in the Graphical Layout Editor. Click the ImageButton element, and a blue line with resizing handles will surround the ImageButton, showing you what is currently actively selected. In the Properties tab, you will see all of the properties and variables that you can set and customize for the ImageButton class.

Click the Background property in the Properties tab to highlight it. Notice that for many of the parameter option fields in the Properties Pane that Eclipse provides a button with three dots (called an "ellipse" in coding terms) on it; this is used to search for a file to use as a background image.

Because we are just going to set the background value to transparent, we do not need to use this file locator button for this particular example. Instead, let's type the transparency value of **#00000000** into the field next to Background in the Properties tab, as shown in Figure 7-16. Then click somewhere else in the IDE, or hit the return key to accept the value. The value will then be accepted and the results displayed in the Graphical Layout Editor tab.

That finishes up our custom image button. If you want to confirm that our ImageButton has no background, and changes color and rotates as its own button now, right-click on the UI_Design folder, and Run As ➤ Android Application to view your success! I'll include a partial view of the emulator in Figure 7-17 to show the button without any background coloring. It looks much more professional because you can't see the boundaries of its UI container (in this case the ImageButton Tag/Widget). Click it and it turns green and rotates—but now, just the circular part!

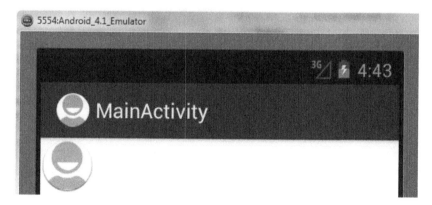

Figure 7-17. *Running the ImageButton in the 4.1 emulator to see transparent background*

Next, let's take a closer look at how to add text to your application's UI, as text is such an important element of any application.

Adding a TextView Widget to Your Layout

Besides buttons, another very common UI element is text. Android provides the TextView class to implement text in a UI. We have already seen this UI element briefly in our Hello Absolute Beginner App in Chapter 4 and our LinearLayout App in Chapter 6, so let's get a little bit more practice with it here, and explore some of it's other setting parameters.

Because we have been leveraging the Graphical Layout Editor in Eclipse, let's continue to explore its functionality because it's a great learning tool for an absolute beginner. Click the left header bar called Form Widgets to open the form widgets selection view. Clicking these headers will toggle them open, and shut others that are open at any time (as we have seen in Chapters 4 and 6).

Next, click the scrollbar (gray, with a tiny arrow) if you don't see the TextView widget, which should be at the top left of the widgets listed. Select and drag (and drop) it into the Layout view window under the ImageButton. Our TextView is now in the UI graphical layout view and is ready to customize by using the Properties tab at the right side of the Eclipse IDE. Let's do that now.

Scroll down to the Text properties and set up some custom values, such as **Sample Text**, and a text color of dark gold to match the ImageButton default image (an RGB value of #777722 will work well; this is a hexadecimal numeric representation of a 24-bit value). Figure 7-18 shows the Eclipse IDE at this point.

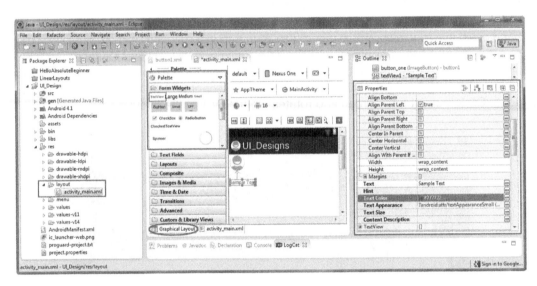

Figure 7-18. Using the Eclipse Graphical Layout Editor to add and configure a TextView widget

Finally, we'll set a DIP (device independent pixel) value for padding, so there is some space around our TextView. Scroll to the Padding properties in the Properties tab at the right side of your Eclipse IDE, and type in **12dip**, as shown in Figure 7-19, with no spaces between the 12 and the dip. Then click another field, and you will see the text space itself out. If you can't find the Padding parameter field, notice that there are little plus and minus sign UI widgets inside of the Properties Pane. Click the minus sign next to the Layout Parameters that will close that grouping of parameters and then click on the plus sign next to the View (parameters) that will open up the parameters for items like Padding and Focus. Leave the TextView parameters widget closed (which will show a plus sign, whereas open will show a minus sign) as shown in Figure 7-19.

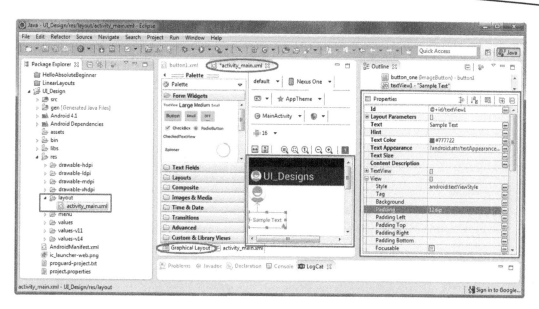

Figure 7-19. Setting the padding value for our TextView via the Properties tab in the Eclipse IDE

Adding an Image

Finally, let's add another popular type of UI element used for design: the image. Go to the code bundle for this book and copy the two 32-bit PNG image files named *image1.png* and *image2.png* into your UI_Design/res/drawable-xhdpi folder.

Right-click the UI_Design folder in the Package Explorer pane, and select the Refresh command to update the project inside of Eclipse, or select the folder and then hit the F5 function key at the top of your keyboard. Both work processes will achieve the same result and Eclipse will "see" the new image files.

Now, let's add an ImageView tag to our XML. To do this, drag the ImageView from the Images & Media drawer on the left, and then drop it under the TextView as shown in Figure 7-20. As you can see in the screenshot, the Graphical Layout Editor gives us a real-time code view (using the tooltip, which changes it's tag parameter data display in real time as you drag the UI element to determine your UI widget placement) of what our XML parameters are going to be if we drop the widget at exactly that location. Kudos to the Eclipse/ADT UI designers for an amazing GLE feature. This now gives us a RelativeLayout ViewGroup containing our ImageButton, TextView, and ImageView tags (remember that these are all Views or widgets).

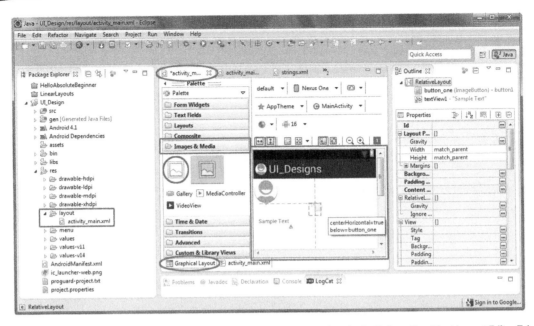

Figure 7-20. *Dragging an ImageView widget onto our RelativeLayout UI container in the Eclipse Graphical Layout Editor Tab*

Once you drop the ImageView into place, Eclipse automatically opens the Reference Chooser dialog, showing all of the image assets it has found (in the /res/drawable-xhdpi folder, in this case). Select *image1* for our ImageView source imagery, as shown in Figure 7-21. Click the OK button to select *image1.png* and close the dialog.

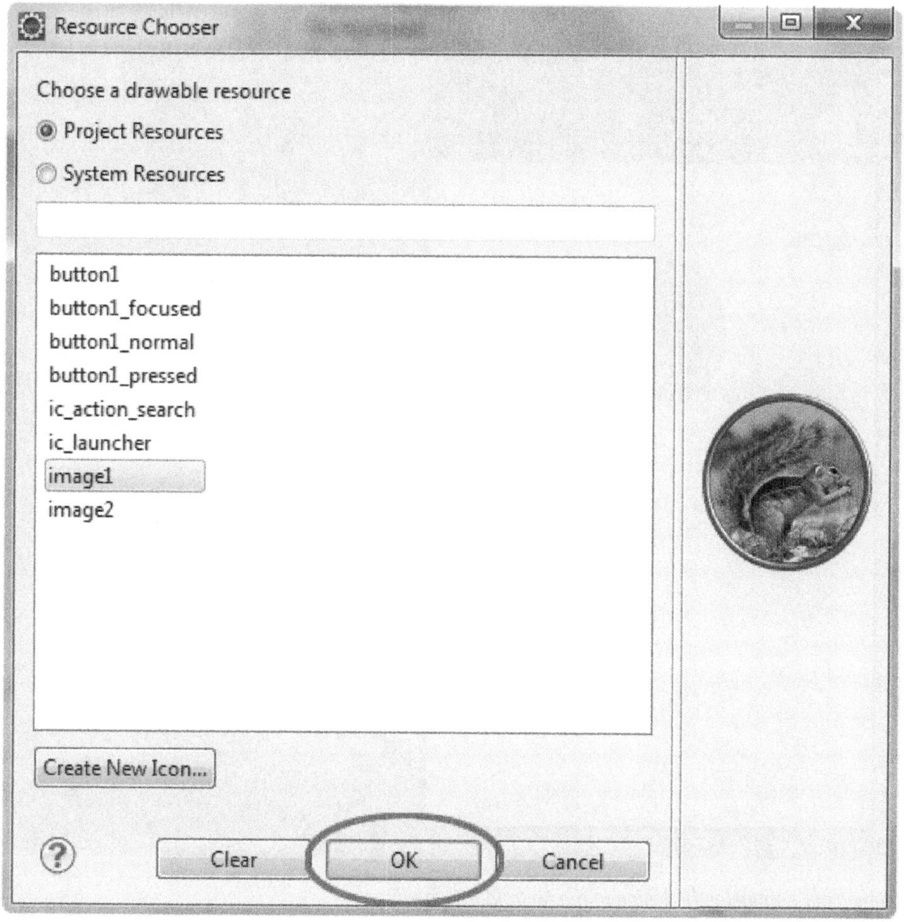

Figure 7-21. Choosing our image1 resource via the Reference Chooser dialog, accessed by dropping the ImageView in our RelativeLayout container

In your Graphical Layout Editor tab, you will now see the image and how its transparency area composites smoothly with the white background color.

Later, when we add a menu to our app, we will change the background color to black to show how this image transparency can help with UI compositing over different background colors or imagery.

So now in the next 4.1 emulator screen, you will see our ImageButton, TextView, and ImageView with enough screen area to hold a bottom menu with five menu items. Right-click on the UI_Design project folder, and select Run As ➤ Android Application to see the results of your work, as shown in Figure 7-22. We'll add the bottom menu in the next section, so that you can learn about how to add useful menus to your Android applications.

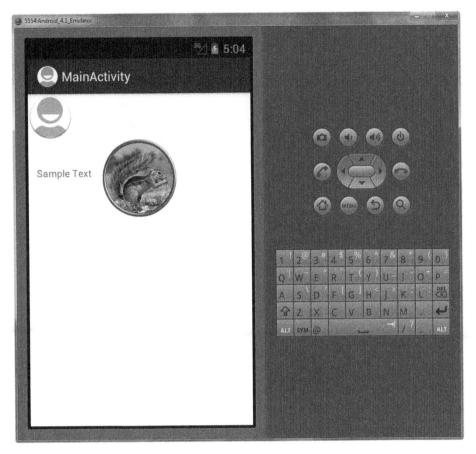

Figure 7-22. Running our completed UI design in the Android 4.1 emulator

Using Menus in Android

Menus in Android are quite different from the top-mounted text menus found directly beneath the title bar in PC applications. The menu function on a smartphone or tablet is a bit different for ease of use, and is sometimes an actual physical button called Menu on some Android smartphones and tablets. Other Android devices may have a soft button or touchscreen button area for menu access, or even a Menu button on a remote control for GoogleTV. Nevertheless, the menu function is an important one in Android, as well as in application development in general, so we're covering it in detail in our UI Design chapter.

Pressing the Menu button calls up a menu, which is—you guessed it—at the bottom of the screen, instead of at the top. To make it even more user-friendly, it is composed of five large rectangular icons stacked on top of each other that can be easily touched to control your application features.

For our application, we will have our menus do things with our ImageView object, background color, and alert dialog (which we'll add later on in this chapter), so that everything we cover in this chapter ties together nicely in one single UI_Design application.

Creating the Menu Structure with XML

As you might have guessed, you set up your entire menu structure in an XML file. In fact, you encountered menu inflater code in the Java that your New ➤ Project ➤ Android Application ➤ Blank Activity generated for you! Once you learn how to code menus in this section, you will be able to modify that bootstrap menu inflating code and turn it into your own application's menu system.

The menu XML file goes in a /res subfolder named /menu, as required by Android. This folder is created for you by the New Android Application Project functionality, so it's all ready for us to use. In fact, it has a default activity_main.xml file with the single menu item XML already in it for us, ready to open and edit.

You are probably wondering why Android (via the File ➤ New ➤ Project ➤ Android Application project creation helper) named both our Menu and Layout folder XML names with the activity_main name that Android specified as a default in the new project creation sequence of screens. It may seem confusing now, but there is a very good reason for it, and you are already used to files with exactly the same name in different folders being completely different assets, as that is how multiresolution image assets are handled in the /res/drawable-dpi/ folders. Same concept here.

The reason why this is done becomes clearer as you develop more complex apps with multiple activities (screen layouts containing UI elements and menus), because each set of Layout and Menu folders has their own XML definition with exactly the same name, thereby grouping them logically together by name. Android figures that developers are smart enough to know (remember) that Menu-related XML is in the /res/menu/ folder and that Layout (UI) XML is in the /res/layout/ folder. So if you had an activity_alternate.xml file for a second UI screen (which we actually will, in a later chapter) the widget UI layout activity_alternate.xml file would live in /res/layout/ and the activity_alternate.xml for the second screen's menuing system would live in /res/menu/. Got it?!

Let's open up the activity_main.xml file in our /res/menu/ subfolder and type in the XML shown below to create our five button menu. The easiest way to do this is to edit the first item text to match what we want, and then to copy and paste it four times underneath it, and edit a few minor parameters to differentiate each button.

```xml
<menu xmlns:android="http://schemas.android.com/apk/res/android">

    <item android:id="@+id/buttonone"
        android:title="@string/showimage1"
        android:orderInCategory="100"
        android:showAsAction="never" />

    <item android:id="@+id/buttontwo"
        android:title="@string/showimage2"
        android:orderInCategory="200"
        android:showAsAction="never" />

    <item android:id="@+id/buttonthree"
        android:title="@string/showwhite"
        android:orderInCategory="300"
        android:showAsAction="never" />
```

```
    <item android:id="@+id/buttonfour"
          android:title="@string/showblack"
          android:orderInCategory="400"
          android:showAsAction="never" />

    <item android:id="@+id/buttonfive"
          android:title="@string/showalert"
          android:orderInCategory="500"
          android:showAsAction="never" />
</menu>
```

The menu XML tag is fairly straightforward. It simply declares the location of its XML schema definition and inside (before the </menu> specifier) it contains nested item tags that specify attributes for each menu item to be added. The Android menu holds five items comfortably as you will see here. Most Android applications use five or fewer menu items per activity or UI screen.

Each of the item tags has the following five attributes:

- The android:id attribute allows the item tag to be given a name and referenced within your Java code.

- The android:title attribute is the title or label for the menu button. The title is in the *strings.xml* file, where text constants are defined (we'll do that next).

- The android:orderInCategory attribute is the order of importance of the menu item within its group of menu items.

- The android:showAsAction="never" attribute makes sure that the menu items only appear in your bottom menu area, and not in the top action bar items in the Android OS. The android:showAsAction is only supported on Android 3.x and Android 4.x devices, and because we are coding in this book to support 2.x devices, we are leaving it set to the "never" setting for this reason. If you are coding to Android 3.x or Android 4.x devices and you wish to have your menu items displayed on the top action bar in the OS, then you set this parameter to "ifRoom" instead.

Figure 7-23 shows the completed *UI_Design/res/menu/activity_main.xml* file.

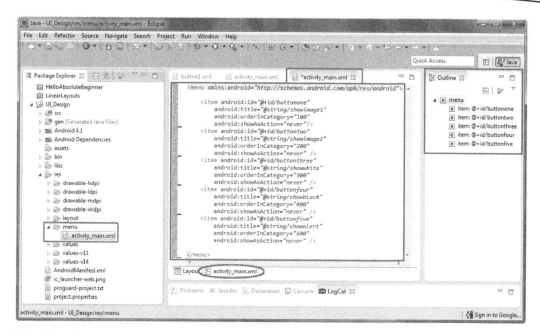

Figure 7-23. *View of the /res/menu/ folder and the activity_main.xml menu file showing menu and item tags*

Defining Menu Item Strings

Next, we'll go into the *strings.xml* file in the /res/values folder (located below the menu folder in the Package Explorer pane in Figure 7-23) to edit our application's string constants. We'll add the text for our five menu items. Follow these steps to add the five /res/values/ folder's *strings.xml* file data values that are referenced inside of our /res/menu/ folder's *activity_main.xml* file:

1. Right-click the *strings.xml* file and select Open to open it in a tab for editing in the Eclipse IDE, as shown in Figure 7-24.

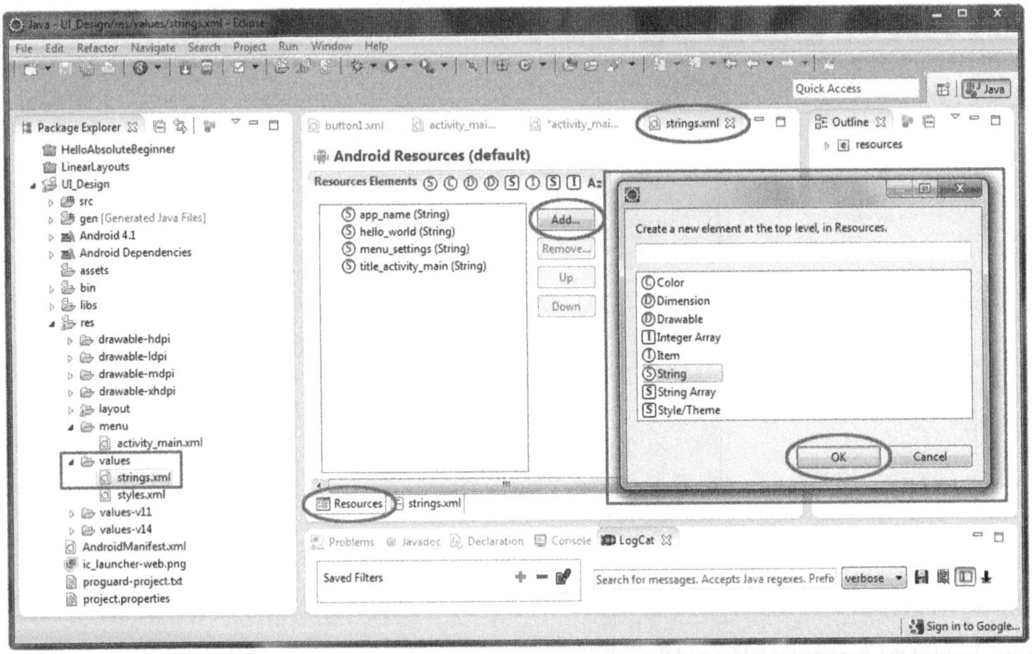

Figure 7-24. Adding string values for our five menu items in the Resources Editor in Eclipse

2. Click the Resources tab at the bottom of the pane to see a visual representation of the string data resource values in the *strings.xml* file. Notice that besides string (text value) resources there are also color, dimension, and other kinds of resources that can be represented as string values in the *strings.xml* file in the /res/values/ folder.

Tip Remember that if you want to see the XML, click the strings.xml tab next to the Resources tab. You can switch back and forth between the code view and the helper view, which is a great way to learn how to code XML UI elements!

---

3. Click the Add button to bring up the dialog shown on the right in Figure 7-24. We have again combined two screens in one here to save space and time. Select String and click OK to add a string value to our *strings.xml* file.

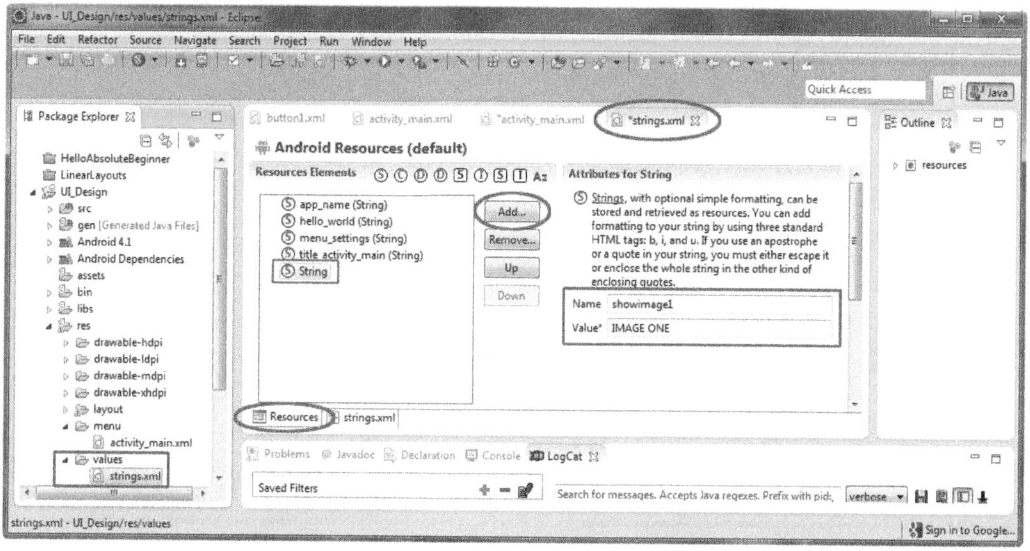

Figure 7-25. Entering String Value Parameters in the resource dialog as part of the Add String Resource work process

4. In the area on the right, in the Name field, enter **showimage1**. In the Value field, enter **IMAGE ONE**. Click on the Add button to add this string value to the *strings.xml* file and simultaneously request the string value for your next string data entry.

5. Repeat step 4 to add four more string values with the following names and values:

    ■ showimage2, IMAGE TWO

    ■ showwhite, USE WHITE

    ■ showblack, USE BLACK

    ■ showalert, SHOW ALERT

6. Set our default white background color of #FFFFFF as a Color object, as shown in Figure 7-26, by selecting a Color Data Object (rather than a String Data Object) on the last two Add Data Value sequences.

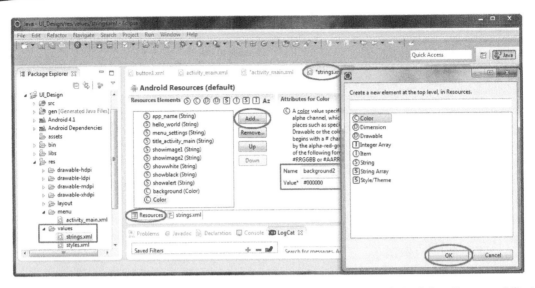

Figure 7-26. *Adding the two background color string data resources in the* strings.xml *file via the Eclipse Resources Editor tab*

7. Add a black background called background2, using a value of #000000. To add this to the list on the left, click the Add button as if you were going to add another value, and simply leave the data fields blank and exit the Resources Editor.

If you want some practice using the Remove Button, and want to be meticulous in your programming and make sure that there are no unused string variables in your strings.xml file, you can select (and Remove) the menu_settings variable that ADT created for us in the New ➤ Project sequence, as we have replaced that needed variable with five of our own, and it will thus be unreferenced in any code, and can therefore be deleted (but does not absolutely have to be). Figure 7-27 shows the strings.xml Resource Editor Pane after we have added our five menu title and two background color string variables.

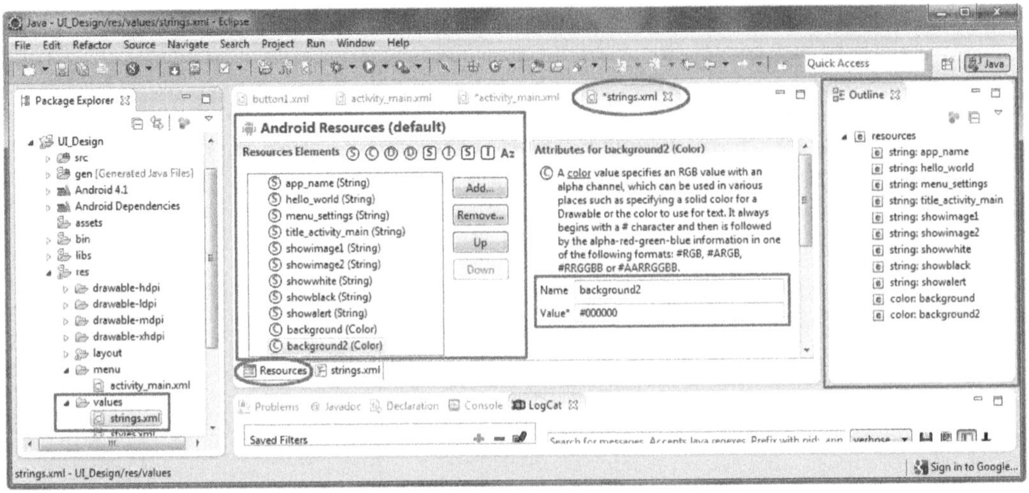

Figure 7-27. *Android Resources Editor and Outline tabs showing the seven added resources*

Inflating the Menu Structure via Java

Now it is time to add in our Java code, which inflates our menu from the XML file into our application's memory. The term *inflating* a resource describes the process of the Android operating system taking the data definition described in an XML file and populating a Java object that can be accessed and used in Java with that data. In this case, it is our `activity_main.xml` object from the /res/menu/ folder, which contains five menu selection buttons, their settings, and their text captions.

Here are the three lines of Java code that Eclipse so generously added to our *MainActivity.java* file for us during the File ➤ New ➤ Project ➤ Android Application Project creation operation:

```
public boolean onCreateOptionsMenu(Menu menu) {
        getMenuInflater().inflate(R.menu.activity_main, menu);
        return true;
}
```

Android has a dedicated Java object for inflating XML code constructs into a Java object-based format for use with Java. This is precisely what you are seeing here inside of the `onCreateOptionsMenu()` method, which uses the `.inflate()` method and the *R.menu.activity_main* path to our *activity_main.xml* file. This method creates a `MenuInflater` object, which contains our inflated menu objects. The OS then "gets" the MenuInflater object and puts into memory via the getMenuInflater() method. Later on in the book we'll learn about the Java construct that allows us to "chain" Java commands together into a single line of code, as we see here as the method() attaches itself to the .method call.

As you learned previously, the *R* equates to the /res/ folder of our project, so *R.menu.activity_main* in this case is equivalent to (inflates to, if you will) the following complete file path reference: *C:/Users/Walls/workspace/UI_Design/res/menu/activity_main.xml*.

ADT also added a menu-related `import` statement at the top of our code to tell Android which UI code we would be using. We should specify `android.view.Menu` that forms the Menu Class foundation for our menu and `android.app.Activity` for the inflation methods that access the data structures defined in the /res/menu/activity_main.xml file containing our menu UI design coded in the XML format. In this case Eclipse added the import statement for us.

```
import android.view.Menu;
```

Figure 7-28 shows the code our New ➤ Project ➤ Android Application helper added to *MainActivity.java.*

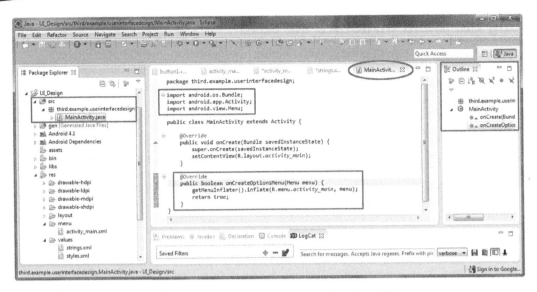

Figure 7-28. *Creating our menu using the getMenuInflater() method in the Eclipse Java editing pane*

Note that we have implemented our application's UI and options menu using only a half-dozen lines of Java code. We have offloaded about 80% of the menu implementation coding to XML (30 lines of XML markup relative to 6 lines of Java code, or one-fifth Java, which is 20%), and we can continue to add features and fine-tune menu options inside the XML markup as well.

Running the Application in the Android Emulator

Let's run our code and see our menu in action. Right-click on the UI_Design folder in the Package Explorer pane, and select: **Run As ➤ Android Application**. After the emulator loads, and you start up your application, the emulator should look like Figure 7-29.

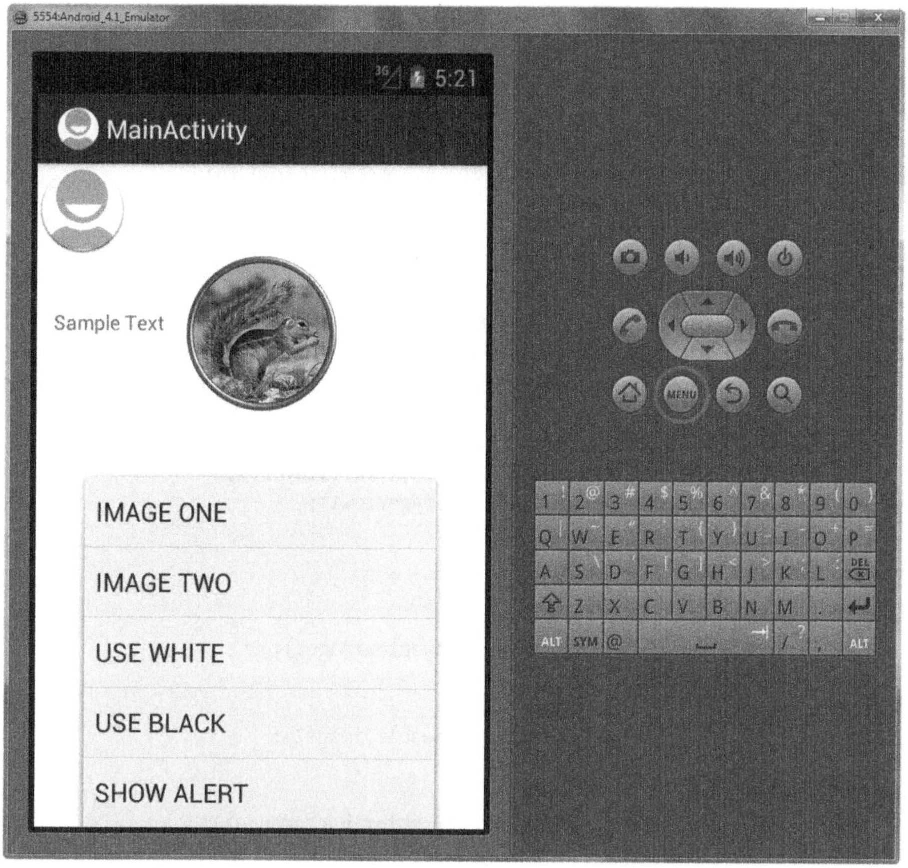

Figure 7-29. Running our UI Design application in the Android 4.1 emulator

As you can see, the Android phone has a prominent Menu button, second from the left (bottom row) in the emulator, which we can press to display our menu at the bottom of the screen. If you click the various buttons, they will highlight in blue and close the menu, which you can re-open again with the Menu button.

So, the default way an empty menu (no code yet completing its function) works is harmless to the application. This allows us to develop and test the way our menu looks via XML before we add in the Java logic to implement the actions that will be called when each button is pressed. This allows our UI designers to work separately from our programmers without breaking the application! Next we'll code some basic programming logic to make our menu items functional.

Making the Menu Work

Let's add our menu item implementations now. First, we need to give our RelativeLayout an ID, so that we can find it in our Java code.

```
<RelativeLayout xmlns:android="http://schemas.android.com/apk/res/android"
    android:id="@+id/uilayout"
    android:layout_width="match_parent"
    android:layout_height="match_parent" >
```

Now, we need to implement the onOptionsItemSelected() method, where we code the choices between our different menu item selections, and write the code that defines what they do in our application, if and when they are selected. Here is the Java code for the method we will write:

```
public boolean onOptionsItemSelected(MenuItem item) {
    RelativeLayout bkgr = (RelativeLayout)findViewById(R.id.uilayout);
    ImageView image = (ImageView)findViewById(R.id.imageView1);

    switch (item.getItemId()) {

    case R.id.buttonone:
                image.setImageResource(R.drawable.image1);
                return true;
    case R.id.buttontwo:
                image.setImageResource(R.drawable.image2);
                return true;
    case R.id.buttonthree:
                bkgr.setBackgroundResource(R.color.background2);
                return true;
    case R.id.buttonfour:
                bkgr.setBackgroundResource(R.color.background);
                return true;
    case R.id.buttonfive:
                // The Alert Code For Next Section Goes Here!
                return true;
    default:
            return super.onOptionsItemSelected(item);
    }

  }
```

This code is a bit more complex than our MenuInflater() code. At its core, it implements a switch structure. The switch is a Java iteration construct that says, "In the case of *this*, do *that*, and in the case of *this*, do *that*; otherwise, as a default, do *this*." This type of code construct is perfect for the main Android menu, as it usually has only five or six items. Let's type this code block into our MainActivity.java editing pane after the routine that inflates our new menu.

Once you are finished typing the new method into your MainActivity.java class, you will notice that there are three little red X icons in the left of the Java editing pane that signify that our code has a problem. Click on the first one as shown in Figure 7-30 to get Eclipse and ADT to tell you what is wrong and to give you some solutions to the problem.

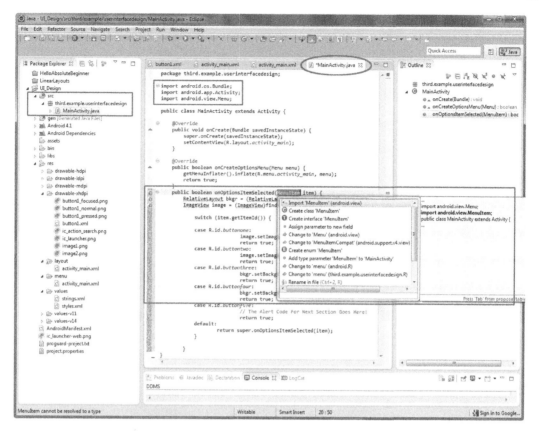

Figure 7-30. Debugging error flags inside Eclipse and adding Import statements needed

As you can see, Eclipse is telling us that we do not have the import statement that is required to run the method referenced in that line of code. Pretty Nifty! Double-click on the Import MenuItem (android.view) selection listed at the top of the pop-up, and Eclipse and ADT will write the import statement code for you. Do this for the next two warning flags as well to import the other packages (libraries) that are needed for RelativeLayouts and ImageView widget usage.

Figure 7-31 shows the *MainActivity.java* code in the Eclipse editor in context with our previous two code blocks once our Import statements are added and the editing area is "clean" with no errors or warnings showing. In the figure, the new code is boxed. We will cover the top import statements, then the outer onOptionsItemSelected() method, and then its inner switch statement and programming logic for each button inside of the case statement, and what it needs to do regarding the UI (switch images, set background colors, and so on).

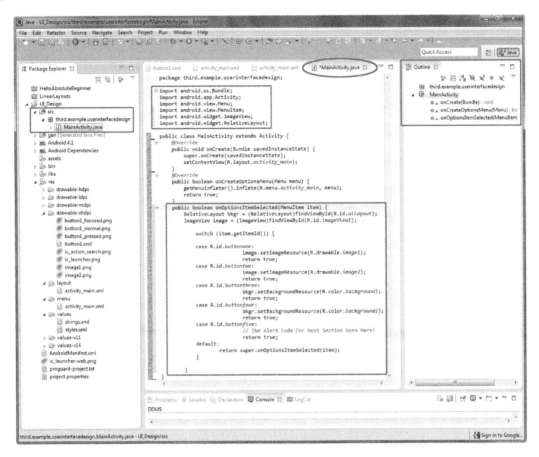

Figure 7-31. Java code to implement our menu functionality shown in the Eclipse IDE

First are the import statements for the Android classes that we are going to use in our onOptionsItemSelected() method (see the top box in Figure 7-31):

- Because we reference MenuItem in our onOptionsItemSelected() method, we need to import android.view.MenuItem.

- Because we are going to switch image resources in our ImageView UI object, we also need to import android.widget.ImageView.

- Because we are going to change our RelativeLayout background color from black to white, we need to import android.widget.RelativeLayout as well.

Remember that importing the class libraries that we are going to use in our Java code makes sure that these classes are in memory when Eclipse needs to use them during the compilation of our Java code.

Next, let's examine our onOptionsItemSelected() code. First, we need to create references to our RelativeLayout and ImageView objects, so that we can operate on these objects. This way, we can adjust their resource values to change the image used in the UI and the background color used when the user selects our menu buttons' image and background color change menu options.

The first line creates a RelativeLayout object called bkgr and sets it to the RelativeLayout that is assigned the ID uilayout via the findViewById() method. The second line creates an ImageView object called image and sets it to the ImageView that is assigned the ID imageView1 in the same way. These IDs can be seen in the /res/layout/ folder's *activity_main.xml* file and corresponding tab, so you can check that everything matches.

Finally, we have the Java switch statement. It starts with switch(item.getItemId, which means "Decide between the following options (each case statement) based on the ID of the MenuObject that we named item. If nothing matches, just use the default action at the bottom of the statement decision tree list." The case statements work as follows:

- The first case statement says, "In the case of the item MenuItem with an ID of buttonone being passed into this case statement, set the image ImageView object's image resource to the 32-bit PNG image called *image1* in the /res/drawable folder, using the setImageResource() method."

- The second case statement says, "In the case of the item MenuItem with an ID of buttontwo being passed over, set the image ImageView object's image resource to the 32-bit PNG image called *image2* in the /res/drawable folder, using the setImageResource() method."

- The third case statement says, "In the case of the item MenuItem with an ID of buttonthree being passed over, set the bkgr RelativeLayout object's background resource to the color resource called *background* in the /res/values/ *strings.xml* resource, using the setBackgroundResource() method."

- The fourth case statement says, "In the case of the item MenuItem with an ID of buttonfour being passed over, set the bkgr RelativeLayout object's background resource to the color resource called *background2* in the /values/ *strings.xml* resource using the setBackgroundResource() method."

- The fifth case is left open for our next section, and thus the button does nothing at this point.

If none of the case statements match IDs passed over to them to operate on, then the default action is called (executed), which is to pass over to the onOptionsItemSelected() method of the superclass (in this case, to do nothing).

Now let's Run As ➤ Android Application, and make sure that our code works! Shown below is a screen shot of the Android 4.1 emulator after the menu is brought up (twice) via the Menu Button (see right side of emulator), and the Image Two option and then the black background option were selected.

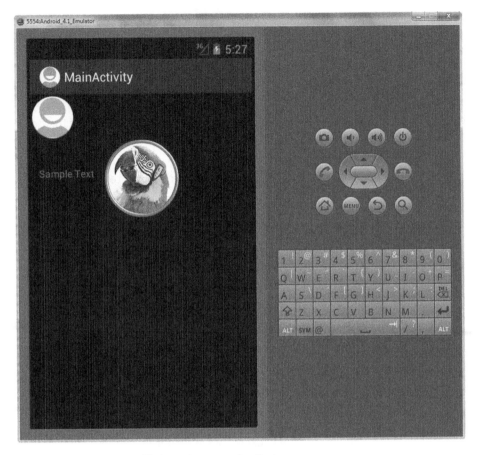

Figure 7-32. Running our UI Design App with the option menus functioning

Adding Dialogs

An Android dialog can be created as part of an activity, and is presented in the form of a small, gray and white pop-up window that appears on top of the current activity's UI. Android dims that UI so that it does not compete with the dialog box.

The Dialog class is used to create an interruption of your current activity to collect or relay information to your application's end user. Examples of uses for dialogs include alert notifications, end-user option selection, information data collection, date selection, time selection, task or processing progress bar monitoring, and so on.

Using Custom Dialog Subclasses

Five custom subclasses of the android.app.Dialog class are provided as part of the Android API:

- AlertDialog

- CharacterPickerDialog

- ProgressDialog

- DatePickerDialog

- TimePickerDialog

You can also subclass your own custom Dialog class (say, CustomDialog), so that it does exactly what you need it to do.

The general way to create a basic dialog within any given activity is via the onCreateDialog(int) method. Android uses this method to track the dialog created, which activity it belongs to, and its current state.

To display a dialog once it is created, you use the showDialog(int) method, specifying the number of the dialog you wish to display. To hide or dismiss a Dialog object, use the dismissDialog(int) method, and the Dialog object will be removed from memory and the application.

Here, we'll take a closer look at the most often used (and the recommended) Dialog class: AlertDialog. Android provides an easy and powerful way to construct alert dialogs with many features.

Displaying an Alert Dialog

The AlertDialog class provides a lot of built-in dialog features, such as a title, user message, up to three buttons, and a list of selectable items. You can even use check boxes and radio buttons in your dialog.

The AlertDialog works its magic via a dialog builder that provides a ready-made dialog code structure for you to easily create complicated dialogs via the android.app.AlertDialog class.

As shown in the boxed areas of Figure 7-33, there are four main parts to adding our AlertDialog to our existing Android application.

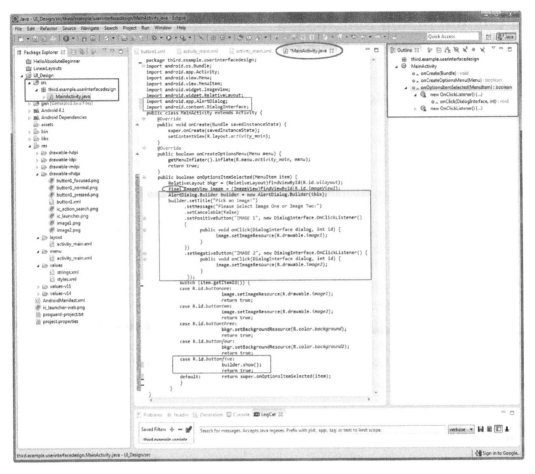

Figure 7-33. *Java code for implementing our alert dialog builder in the Eclipse IDE*

First, we add the `import` statements for the Android utilities we are going to leverage to provide our `AlertDialog` object:

```
import android.app.AlertDialog;
import android.content.DialogInterface;
```

Next, we create our `AlertDialog.Builder` object, which we name `builder`. This is a new (empty and initialized) `AlertDialog.Builder` object.

```
public boolean onOptionsItemSelected(MenuItem item) {
    RelativeLayout bkgr = (RelativeLayout)findViewById(R.id.uilayout);
    final ImageView image = (ImageView)findViewById(R.id.imageView1);
    AlertDialog.Builder builder = new AlertDialog.Builder(this);
```

To work with the `image` object inside the `builder` dialog object that we are constructing, we need to add the keyword `final` to our declaration of this object variable (you'll see why in the next step). The `final` keyword is used for variables, methods, and classes. A `final` variable cannot be given a new value after it has been assigned one (although we can alter the variable object like any other object). A final method cannot be overridden. Also, a final class cannot be extended, and is thus, in a sense, protected from further programming modifications.

The preceding code basically says, "I want to declare an object named builder that is of the type AlertDialog.Builder, and I wish to set it equal to this new AlertDialog.Builder object that I am creating here. Therefore, please instantiate an empty AlertDialog.Builder object for me to define and fill with my own custom parameters."

After this has been declared, builder exists as an empty AlertDialog ready to fill with our own custom parameters. OK, on to the fun part, and to the third and major part of our AlertDialog definition.

Here is the code to customize our dialog:

```
builder.setTitle("Pick an Image!")
      .setMessage("Please Select Image One or Image Two:")
      .setCancelable(false)
      .setPositiveButton("IMAGE 1", new DialogInterface.OnClickListener()
      {
            public void onClick(DialogInterface dialog, int id) {
                  image.setImageResource(R.drawable.image1);
            }
      })

      .setNegativeButton("IMAGE 2", new DialogInterface.OnClickListener() {
            public void onClick(DialogInterface dialog, int id) {
                  image.setImageResource(R.drawable.image2);
            }
      });
```

We work with the image object, which we know can't be reassigned a value because it is final. This is to deal with situations where the event listener is used after the onOptionsItemSelected() method has terminated. In this case, a non final image variable would not be around to take a new assignment, whereas a final variable is frozen in memory for access at all times (of course, this may never happen, but Java was built this way just to be sure).

Notice in this block of code that sets our AlertDialog parameters (I am amazed that they did not offload AlertDialog parameters to an *alert_dialog.xml* file) that a new concept called *method chaining* is used. This allows a large number of parameters to be set without the builder object being explicitly typed before each dot-notation construct.

In method chaining, the first method is attached to its object with dot notation. In our example, it looks like this:

```
builder.setTitle("Pick an Image!")
```

The follow-up methods that set the other parameters are simply .setMessage(), .setCancelable(false), and so on.

I've formatted the preceding code for ease of reading. But to give you a little more grip on method chaining, the first three method calls could be rewritten as follows, illustrating the method chain:

```
builder.setTitle("Pick an Image!").setMessage("Please Select...").setCancelable(false)
```

Also note that between contiguous methods, there is no semicolon at the end of these parameter setting lines of code. Semicolons are required on only the last and final method call—in this case, after `.setNegativeButton()` to end the `builder` definition. This chaining allows programmers to write denser code, or to use fewer lines of code to accomplish more tasks. Pretty cool stuff.

> **Note** In this case, the order of the chained methods doesn't matter because each one returns an `AlertDialog.Builder` object with the new parameter set, alongside all the other parameters that have been set so far. In other cases, the order of chaining may matter. Android has been well designed to make chaining easy and convenient.

The code for setting the title, the message, and whether the Back button on the phone is able to cancel the dialog (in this case, it is not cancelable) is pretty straightforward here, so let's go over what is happening inside each button.

You can have up to three buttons in an `AlertDialog` object. These buttons are hard coded into the Android operating system as follows:

- `PositiveButton`
- `NeutralButton`
- `NegativeButton`

This explains the `setPositiveButton()` and `setNegativeButton()` methods shown in the preceding code.

The convention in Android AlertDialogs is to use `PositiveButton` for one-button dialogs, `PositiveButton` and `NegativeButton` for two-button dialogs, and all three for three-button dialogs. The code inside the two buttons in our dialog is nearly identical, so let's go over what is happening inside the first button, `IMAGE 1`.

```
.setPositiveButton("IMAGE 1", new DialogInterface.OnClickListener()
{
        public void onClick(DialogInterface dialog, int id) {
                image.setImageResource(R.drawable.image1);
        }
})
```

The setPositiveButton() method allows us to name the button IMAGE 1 and creates a new OnClickListener() implementation for the DialogInterface. Note that we declared android.content.DialogInterface in an import statement initially, and it is being used here to create a PositiveButton.

Inside the OnClickListener, we have a public method onClick(), which defines what will be done when the button is clicked. We pass onClick a dialog object of type DialogInterface and an integer ID value that represents which of the buttons was clicked or the numerical order of the button that was clicked—both of which are what OnClickListener wants to evaluate in the event the user clicks that button. Note that we will be getting into event listeners in much greater detail in Chapter 9.

Inside this onClick container is where our code goes to change our ImageView object to the appropriate image resource. Because we have already done that in the menu code, we can simply copy the image.setImageResource(R.drawable.image1) code from down in our switch construct for ButtonOne.

Finally, down inside of our switch statement, where before we had a placeholder comment, we can now display the dialog by calling the show() method of the builder object that we created earlier. This line of code could not be much simpler:

```
builder.show();
```

Whenever the fifth menu button is clicked, our dialog will be shown. We can select between the two images, which will then be set on our screen appropriately.

Now, right-click on your UI_Design folder, and select **Run As ➤ Android Application** to see your work. Figure 7-34 shows the dialog as it appears in the emulator after you click the SHOW ALERT button in the menu.

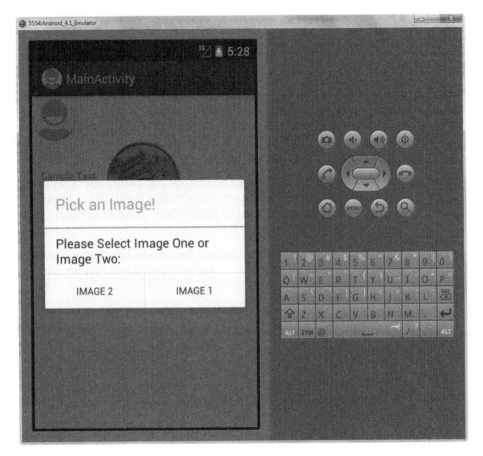

Figure 7-34. Viewing our Pick an Image! alert dialog in the Android 4.1 emulator

Summary

With the exception of dialogs, Android allows us to put together our user interface, or UI, designs using XML markup instead of Java code, and to implement them using just a few dozen lines of code in many instances, such as when creating a system options menu. Allowing user interface design via XML markup allows applications designers to get one step closer to the application coding process.

In this chapter, we created an application that has all of the primary UI objects that can be used to construct an application:

- ImageButtons allow us to create custom, highly visual UI elements.
- TextView and ImageView objects allow us to put relevant information on the screen.
- Menu items allow us to use the Android Menu button to control our application.
- Alert dialogs interface with our users to gather information or inform about decisions.

In the next chapter, you will learn how to add graphics design elements, to provide even more visual new media user experiences within your Android applications. Right after that in Chapter 9 we'll revisit in detail the OnClick() event handler that you learned about briefly in the last section on AlertDialogs.

Chapter 8

An Introduction to Graphics Resources in Android

This chapter will serve as an introduction to how to best integrate and optimize graphical elements within your Android apps. These include static graphics such as bitmap images, as well as motion graphics, such as tween animation (transform-based or procedural animation), bitmap animation (frame-based or flipbook animation) as well as image transitions (crossfades, or blended image fades from one image into another image).

You will learn how to best use imaging techniques available to your application's View objects that make up your UI, and how to support all four levels of Android screens (QVGA, HVGA, WVGA, and WSVGA) via custom resource assets.

> **Note**   Because VGA is 640 × 480 pixels, quarter VGA (QVGA) is 320 × 240 pixels, or one-quarter of a VGA screen or LDPI; half VGA (HVGA) is 480 × 320, or one-half of a VGA screen (MDPI); wide VGA (WVGA) is 800 × 480, or a widescreen version of a VGA screen (HDPI), wide SVGA (WSVGA) is 1,024 × 600; and the latest Android devices on the market are now supporting HD resolution, which is 1,280 × 720 and these would currently be termed XHDPI. Android 4.2 added the TVDPI specification, which supports GoogleTV iTV sets running 1920 x 1080 and Mega-Tablets running 1920 x 1200 resolutions.

We'll cover the use of graphics objects in both the areas of user interface (UI) design (custom buttons, for instance) and user experience (UX) design (the content itself, say music videos or an interactive children's storybook). If the graphic is used to control the operation of the app, it is classified as UI design, if the graphic is used as eye-candy, or is part of the content (the storyline for instance), it is classified as UX design. Both are vitally important to the success of your application.

We'll look at two primary graphics related packages: the android.graphics.drawable package (I knew there was a reason that resource folder was called *drawable*) and the android.view.animation package. These are collections of useful classes for maximizing bitmap imagery and for working with images that support the fourth dimension (time) via motion, commonly called animation.

In a later chapter, once we know how to control events (which connect our UI elements to functions such as video playback), we'll take a look at digital video. Using the VideoView class makes playing digital video a snap. Android 4.0 and later added one of the most impressive video codecs available today to Android. VP8 was acquired by Google from ON2 who developed it. It was originally called VP8 and is sometimes called WebM, as it was released for HTML5 by Google, who generously released this technology into open source. There is also a technology (supported in Android 4.0 and later) called WebP, which is the static image version of WebM. Both WebM and WebP use an advanced compression technology to get better quality with a smaller data footprint (better file compression, or a smaller file size). If you are developing for Android 4.x exclusively, you can use WebP instead of PNG24 and PNG32, otherwise, stick with PNG24 and it's slightly larger (25% larger than WebP on average) file size.

Introducing the Drawables

The central set of classes used to control the graphics-related content within your Android application is called the drawable package. This package handles classes and methods related to drawing the following types of visual assets onto the Android display screen:

- **Bitmaps**: In a bitmap, a collection of pixels make up an image—it's a map of image bits, if you will. This is the most commonly used drawable asset.

- **Shapes**: Shapes are line drawings. They also are known as *vectors*, like the lines architects use in CAD drawings. Common vector formats are EPS, AI, or SVG.

- **Gradients**: Gradients are smooth transitions from one color to another color. They can be shaped in a straight line or occupy a circular area.

- **Transitions**: Shape transitions are smooth vector changes between one shape and another shape. This process is sometimes referred to as *morphing or tweening*.

- **Animation**: Animation involves an image, shape, or object that moves in some way.

- **Image transitions**: These are smooth cross-fades between one image and another image. They are usually used to smoothly transition from one image to another image.

In Android development, graphics-related items such as gradients, image transitions, animated transformations, and frame-based animation can all be termed *drawables*. With the exceptions of transformational (tween or procedural) animation, all of these center their resource assets in the */res/drawable* folder. (And you thought tweens were 12-year-olds, right?)

The */res/drawable* folder is also where you should put XML files that define things like frame-based image animations and crossfading image transitions (which we will look at throughout this chapter). So get used to seeing *drawable* everywhere you look because it will be one of the most used folders in your resources (*/res*) folder.

Implementing Images

The way that Android is set up to automatically implement your images via the project folder hierarchy is a bit hard to understand at first. But once you get used to it, you'll find that it is actually amazingly simple to use graphic resources, as extensive asset reference coding is all but eliminated. You will see this in action in this chapter, as we will implement powerful graphics features using as few as five or six lines of Java programming logic.

I'm not sure what could be much simpler than this: put your imagery into the appropriate project/res/drawable folder, and then reference it by file name in your Java or XML code. Yes, all that you need to do is reference it in your XML and Java code, and you are finished, and with perfect results (assuming that your imagery is optimized correctly, which we are also teaching in this book).

In this chapter, we will look at which image formats to use, which techniques to implement, and which work processes to follow as much as (or more than) we will be dealing with XML attributes and Java code snippets (although these are fun to play with as well).

Core Drawable Subclasses

Android offers more than a dozen types of customized drawable objects. In this chapter, we'll look at the following core subclasses of `android.graphics.drawable`:

- **BitmapDrawable object**: Used to create, tile, stretch, and align bitmaps.
- **ColorDrawable object**: Used to fill certain other objects with color.
- **GradientDrawable object**: Used to create and draw custom gradients.
- **AnimationDrawable object**: Used to create frame-based animations.
- **TransitionDrawable object**: Used to create crossfade transitions.
- **LayerDrawable object**: Used to create composited PNG32 bitmaps or WebP bitmaps via multiple image layers.

> **Note**   If you want to review all of the drawable objects, look at the `android.graphics.drawable` package document on the Android Developers website (`http://developer.android.com/reference/android/graphics/drawable/Drawable.html`). You'll find that there is a plethora of graphics power in Android's 2D engine.

The most pervasive and often used type of drawable is the bitmap. A *bitmap* is an image composed of a collection of dots called *pixels,* where "pix" stands for "pictures" and "els" stands for "elements." Yes, a bitmap is, quite literally, a map of bits. So, let's get started with adding bitmaps to your Android apps.

Using Bitmap Images in Android

How do we best optimize our *static* (motionless or fixed-in-place) bitmap imagery for use within our Android applications? That's what this section is all about. We have already worked with bitmap images in the previous chapters, in the context of our ImageButton and ImageView objects, so you already have a decent amount of experience with using truecolor 32-bit PNG (PNG32) files to obtain an excellent graphic result. Remember that a 32-bit PNG is a portable network graphic format with 8-bits of red, green, blue, and alpha (ARGB or RGBA) and that 4 × 8 = 32, thus: PNG32.

Besides the WebP format that is supported in Android 4.0 and later, Android supports three mainstream bitmap image file formats: PNG, JPEG, and GIF. We'll talk about how Android truly feels about each one, so you can choose the right formats to meet your graphics-related design and user experience objectives.

PNG Images

The most powerful file format that Android supports, and the one that it recommends using over all others, is the portable network graphics, or PNG (pronounced "ping") format. There are two primary types of PNG:

- **Indexed-color** PNG8, which uses a limited 256-color (8-bits of color allows 256 color values) image palette, which is an index of up to 256 colors that an image uses to make up its pixel colors

- **Truecolor** PNG32, which uses a 32-bit color image that includes a full 8-bit alpha channel (used for image compositing) and 8-bits each of red, green, and blue image channels, or PNG24 for a truecolor PNG image with no alpha channel included

PNG is known as a *lossless* image file format because it loses zero image data during the compression processing. This means that the image quality is always 100% maintained. If designers know what they are doing, they can get very high-quality graphics into a reasonably small data footprint by using either the indexed-color PNG8 or the truecolor PNG32 or PNG24 image file formats, depending upon how many colors are using in that image.

Indexed-color PNG8 files use approximately one-fourth of the amount of data (bits) that a truecolor 32-bit RGBA PNG32 image does. Remember the math we did in the previous chapter: 8 × 4 = 32. A smaller data footprint is achieved by using only 8 bits, or a 256-color "palette" of 256 of the most optimal (the most frequently used in the image) colors that are best suited to represent a particular image, but with much the same visual result as if 24-bits (16,777,216 colors) worth of color values were used. This is done primarily to save data file size, thereby decreasing the image's data footprint (file size) considerably.

Each 8-bit "indexed" color image (PNG8 or GIF) will have its own custom index or palette of colors to use to represent the pixels in that image. More colors can be simulated in 8-bit images by "dithering," which is a process where fine dot patterns are used between two different colors to simulate an intermediate color (similar to the concept of anti-aliasing that we discussed earlier in the book). This is done to minimize "color banding" in 8-bit images, and dithering is an option in the 8-bit image compression process that can be turned on or off as needed. Dithering adds a small amount of data overhead to the file size, or increases the data footprint slightly, within the resulting file, as more data (the resulting dot patterns) is added to the compressed file, but the visual results are usually well worth the few extra kilobytes.

Truecolor PNG32 images use a full 32 bits of data for each of the image pixels to represent the four image data channels that are found in most bitmap images: alpha channel, red channel, green channel, and blue channel (RGBA or ARGB). If an alpha channel is not used to define image transparency for compositing purposes, then the RGB PNG image would be called a 24-bit PNG24 image, as it uses 24-bits (3 × 8) of data, rather than 32-bits.

The alpha channel determines where the image is going to be transparent and is used for image compositing. As you learned in Chapter 7, compositing is the process of using more than one image in a series of layers to create a final image out of several component layers or parts. Image compositing is so important that Android even has a LayerDrawable, which you learned at the beginning of this chapter, and which you can research farther at: http://developer.android.com/reference/android/graphics/drawable/LayerDrawable.html if you are going to be doing a lot of compositing in your application. We already looked at using layers in GIMP earlier in the book, and this drawable class gives your Android applications this same capability.

Another benefit of image compositing is that in your programming code, you can access different image elements of a composited or layered image independently of other image elements because they are all on their own layer. For example, you might do this for more advanced game engine programming, where what seems to be one image to the game player is actually in fact a series of image layers that composite seamlessly together at run time, via code and clever GIMP or Photoshop compositing work. This allows your Java (and XML) code to grab onto individual image elements without having to use 3D (OpenGL ES) rendering, which is beyond the scope of an introductory book such as this but which we look at in Chapter 12 just so that you know about it.

It is important to note that at compile time, Android looks at your PNG32 (or PNG24) graphics, and if they use less than 256 colors within the image, Android automatically remaps them to be an indexed PNG8 image, just as you would want it to do to save space (app data footprint). This means that you don't need to worry about analyzing your images to see if they should be in truecolor or indexed-color PNG format. You can simply do everything in truecolor, and if it can be optimized into indexed-color with no loss of data, Android will do that for you—making your data footprint three to four times smaller, depending on if you have used an alpha channel (PNG32 RGBA) or are using only the RGB image channels (PNG24 RGB).

If for some reason you don't want your images optimized at compile time, you can put them into the project /res/raw folder, which is for data that is accessed directly from your Java code. A good example of this is video files that have been perfectly optimized for size and quality, and just need to be played. This concept will come up in a media player example in Chapter 11, so stay tuned, as we will be using the /raw folder soon enough, I just wanted to point it out here, as it relates to circumventing the mandatory PNG image optimization that Android has implemented into it's compile-time processing.

JPEG and GIF Images

The next most desirable format to use is the JPEG image file type. This type does not have an alpha channel. It uses *lossy* compression, which means that it throws away some data to get a much better compression result, but at the expense of your image quality. JPEG stands for joint photographic experts group.

If you look closely at (zoom into, using GIMP) JPEG images, you will see a lot of *artifacts*, such as areas of strange color variations or what looks like dirt on the image (dirt that was not on the camera lens). JPEG is useful for much higher-resolution (print resolution) images, where artifacts are too small to be seen. So, it is not really as suitable for lower-resolution smartphone screens. JPEG is supported, but is not recommended for Android apps because Google wants their product to look as pristine as possible, and PNG or WebP formats are the sure-fire way to accomplish this.

Finally, we have GIF, the CompuServe graphic information format, a much older 8-bit file format. The use of this file format is discouraged because it has the poorest quality to file size ratio. Stay away from using GIFs for your Android apps if possible. Use PNG8 instead, as it has a superior image compression algorithm that results in a smaller data footprint (file size).

Creating Animation in Android

You've already learned how to implement static bitmap images in previous chapters via the *activity_main.xml* file in the /res/layout/ folder. So, let's get right into the fun stuff with animation and add some motion to your Android app screen.

Frame-Based or Cel-Based 2D Animation

Traditional 2D animation involves moving quickly among a number of what originally in the cartoon industry were called *cels*, or hand-drawn images, creating the illusion of motion. To steal a more modern term from the movie industry, each image, which is a little bit different from the next, is called a *frame*. This term refers back to the original days of film, where actual film stock would be run through a projector, displaying 24 frames per second (known in the industry as fps).

In Android, frame-based animation is the easiest to implement via XML and gives us great results. You just need to define some basic XML animation attributes—what and where the frames are—in the correct place for Android to find them. Then you can control your animation via your Java code if you need to.

In our example, we are going to animate a solid gold 3D logo. It will circle around smoothly, casting a T-shaped shadow onto the ground. Let's fire up a new project in Eclipse, and we'll see how animation works in Android.

1. If you still have the *UI_Design* project folder open from the previous chapter examples, right-click on that folder, and select **Close Project**. This closes the project folder in Eclipse (of course, it can be reopened later; as you can see, it's still there).

2. Select Eclipse **File ➤ New ➤ Project** and choose Android Application Project to open the New Android Application Project dialog sequence. Fill it out as follows (and shown in Figure 8-1).

   ■ *Project name*: Name this project GraphicDesign.

   ■ *Application name*: Let's call this application **GraphicDesign**.

   ■ *Package name*: Name the package fourth.example.graphicdesign.

■ **Build SDK target**: Choose Android 4.1 SDK Level 16 (Jelly Bean).

■ **Min required SDK version**: Enter API Level **8**, which matches with the recommended Android 2.2 compatibility build target setting.

■ **Create custom launcher icon**: Check this box.

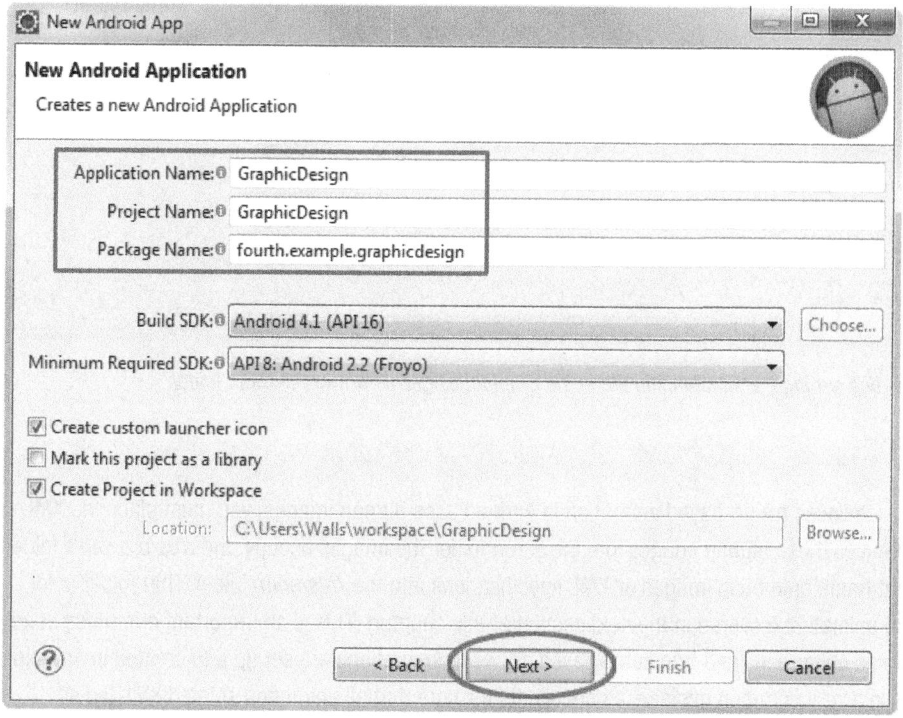

Figure 8-1. Creating our GraphicDesign Android 4.1 project

3. Now we need to define our animation's frames in an XML file, which we'll call *logo_animation*. Right-click your *GraphicDesign* folder and select **New ➤ File**. At the bottom of the dialog, enter *logo_animation.xml*. In the GraphicDesign navigation pane in the middle of the dialog, expose your directory structure (via the arrows next to the folders), and select the /res/drawable folder, so that the parent folder field above shows *GraphicDesign/res/drawable-xhdpi*. This places our *logo_animation* XML file in the correct folder. Figure 8-2 shows the completed New File dialog as well as the drop-down menu sequence, together in a single screenshot.

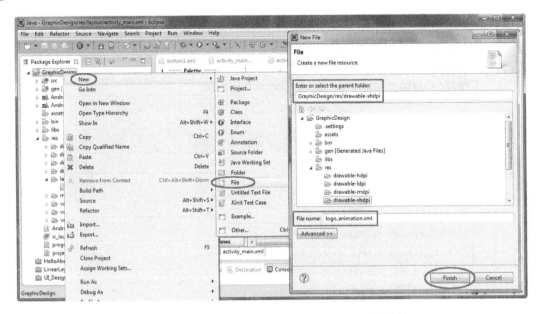

Figure 8-2. Creating our logo_animation.xml file in the GraphicDesign/res/drawable-xhdpi folder

Caution   Because frame-based animation in Android uses bitmap images, you must place the XML file that references these bitmap images into the same folder the images occupy: the */res/drawable* folder. Do *not* put frame animation images or XML specifications into the */res/anim* folder. That folder is for transform animation (covered in the next section of this chapter). This is an important difference in how frame-based animations and transform-based or tween animations are set up and created in Android. This is also a very common mistake, as one would assume that all animation-related XML would logically go into the /res/anim/ folder, but this is not in fact the case. Bitmap (frame) animation goes into the /res/drawable/ folders alongside the image assets that it uses, and procedural (vector) animation goes into /res/anim. Memorize this now to avoid hours of frustrating debugging later on!

4.   Next, click the logo_animation.xml tab in Eclipse, and type in the following XML markup to define our frame-based animation for Android (Figure 8-3 shows the new file in Eclipse):

```
<animation-list xmlns:android="http://schemas.android.com/apk/res/android"
  android:oneshot="false">
    <item android:drawable="@drawable/logoanim0" android:duration="200" />
    <item android:drawable="@drawable/logoanim1" android:duration="200" />
    <item android:drawable="@drawable/logoanim2" android:duration="200" />
    <item android:drawable="@drawable/logoanim3" android:duration="200" />
    <item android:drawable="@drawable/logoanim4" android:duration="200" />
    <item android:drawable="@drawable/logoanim5" android:duration="200" />
    <item android:drawable="@drawable/logoanim6" android:duration="200" />
```

```
    <item android:drawable="@drawable/logoanim7" android:duration="200" />
    <item android:drawable="@drawable/logoanim8" android:duration="200" />
    <item android:drawable="@drawable/logoanim9" android:duration="200" />
</animation-list>
```

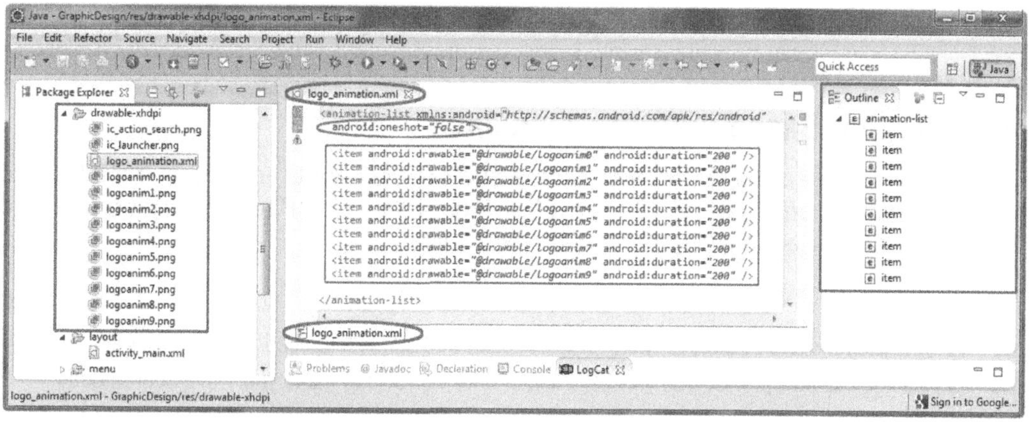

Figure 8-3. Creating the XML mark-up for the logo_animation.xml file

This is pretty straightforward XML tag markup logic here. We add an `animation-list` tag to hold our frame-based animation image (`item`) listings. This tag has its `android:oneshot` attribute set to `false`, which will allow our seamless animation to loop continuously. Setting `oneshot` equal to `true` will stop the animation after one full iteration through the ten files. We'll try both settings later, so that you can get used to using this important parameter.

Inside of the `animation-list` tag, we have ten nested `item` tags (nested because the `animation-list` closing tag comes after these ten `item` tags). These specify the location of each image in our /res/ drawable-xhdpi folder, where each image is a frame in the animation.

Using each `item` tag entry, we specify the name and location of each of our ten animation frames `logoanim0` through `logoanim9`, as well as the duration of the frame display time in milliseconds (ms). In this case, we start off using 200 ms, or one-fifth of a second, for each frame, so that the entire animation plays over 2 seconds, and at 5 fps, just barely fast enough to fake movement. We can adjust frame times later, to fine-tune the visual result and to make the animation loop more smoothly and more rapidly.

We need to put our animation frame images into the /res/drawable-xhdpi folder, so that the XML code can reference them successfully. As you know by now, in Android, everything needs to be in the correct place for things to work properly (or at all, for that matter).

1. Copy the ten animation frames into the /res/drawable-xhdpi folder from the code download.

2. Right-click the *GraphicDesign* folder in the Package Explorer and select **Refresh**, so that the IDE can see the new animation frame image assets that you have added.

3. If there are still errors on your XML editing pane, right-click your
    GraphicDesign folder and select **Validate** to clear these as well. Validate
    checks and validates your project and all of its code, so it looks one level
    deeper than Refresh, which just looks at folders to make sure that Eclipse
    sees all of your resource assets.

At this point, you should see a screen that looks similar to Figure 8-3.

Controlling Frame-Based Animation via Java

Now we are going to write our Java code to access and control our 2D animation. If the MainActivity.
java tab is not already open, right-click the *MainActivity.java* file in the Package Explorer pane, and
select **Open**, or simply select the file and then hit the F3 key.

> **Note** To right-click the *MainActivity.java* file, the */src* folder and subfolders need to be showing in the
> expanded Package Explorer project-tree view, so click on those arrows to make your Java Source Code
> hierarchy visible.

Here is the code for our *MainActivity.java* file, which holds our MainActivity class from our fourth.
example.graphicdesign package:

```
package fourth.example.graphicdesign;

import android.os.Bundle;
import android.app.Activity;
import android.view.Menu;
import android.widget.ImageView;
import android.graphics.drawable.AnimationDrawable;

public class MainActivity extends Activity {

    AnimationDrawable logoAnimation;

    @Override
    public void onCreate(Bundle savedInstanceState) {
        super.onCreate(savedInstanceState);
        setContentView(R.layout.activity_main);

        final ImageView logoAnimHolder = (ImageView) findViewById(R.id.imageView1);
        logoAnimHolder.setBackgroundResource(R.drawable.logo_animation);
        logoAnimHolder.post(new Runnable() {
        public void run() {
            logoAnimation = (AnimationDrawable) logoAnimHolder.getBackground();
            }
        } );
    }
```

```
    @Override
    public void onWindowFocusedChanged(boolean hasFocus) {
        logoAnimation.start();
    }
    @Override
    Public boolean onCreateOptionsMenu(Menu menu) {
        getMenuInflater().inflate(R.menu.activity_main, menu);
        return true;
    }
}
```

In Android Java code, AnimationDrawable is the class we need to use to implement our frame-based animation sequences. We import the android.graphics.drawable.AnimationDrawable class. Then we import the android.widget.ImageView class, which we will use as a view container to display the animation. We add the two new import statements to the ones that Android starts us out with (the first three).

Next, we add the object declaration for our AnimationDrawable object, which we are calling logoAnimation. This is as simple as writing the following:

```
AnimationDrawable logoAnimation;
```

Next, we create a final ImageView object called logoAnimHolder, which we assign to ImageView imageView1, which we will declare in the *activity_main.xml* file and access via the findViewById() method.

After that, we set the background resource for this newly created ImageView to our *logo_animation* XML file, which specifies our animation sequence and timing. This is the bridge between display (ImageView) and animation data definition (*logo_animation.xml*) that we set up via the .setBackgroundResource() method so that our animation will display through the background image setting for the ImageView.

If you are wondering why we are using the ImageView widget's Background Image parameter rather than the Source Image, this leaves it open for us to have a source image in our ImageView that uses transparency (an alpha channel) to create cool effects on top of the animated background. This essentially gives us two layers in the ImageView UI Object, as we can set source and background images for any ImageView object, and both of these could be animated if we like. If you need to, you can get some more practice by changing this source code from using getBackground() and setBackgroundResource() to instead using setImageResource() and getImageResource().

To run the animation we use the .post() method on the logoAnimHolder ImageView to implement (post to the OS) a runnable() method that will contain our run() method that runs (cycles through the animation frames, in this case) our core animation drawable object logoAnimation that we declared at the top of our MainActivity Class.

Inside of the run() method, we define the logoAnimation object that we want to run() and which we declared in the very first line of code in our MainActivity class. The logoAnimation is an AnimationDrawable object that gets its data from the logoAnimHolder object via its getBackground() method, which grabs the ImageView background image. As you can see from the logoAnimHolder .setBackgroundResource() declaration a few lines earlier, that image has been obtained from the *logo_animation.xml* file, where we define our animation frame sequence.

Thus, to get our animation to play, we use a new method called post(). This method uses a new Runnable method to invoke a run() method that runs the getBackground() method that gets the animation frames from our logoAnimHolder ImageView object. This is the code that handles the real-time nature of getting the frames every 200 ms and putting them into the ImageView object background for display on the screen.

To finally get our animation to play on the screen when the app launches, we use a onWindowFocusChanged() method to initially detect when the window (app UI screen) has Focus, in this case, to detect when the app has started, or more precisely, when the onCreate() and run() methods have finished loading (preparing themselves for execution). If we don't do this, then our app tries to run our animation before the screen is ready to accept it, and the gold logo does not animate.

Inside of the onWindowFocusChanged() method, we have our call to start() the logoAnimation object via, you guessed it, a logoAnimation.start(); line of code, instructing the logoAnimation object to start animating now that the app window has the focus and is ready to display animation!

Notice that we have not touched our standard (automatically generated) onCreate() method of our activity, we are still using our default *activity_main.xml* UI layout specification and our onCreateOptionsMenu() method of our activity is using our *activity_main.xml* UI menu specification, which in this app is not utilized. Figure 8-4 shows the four logical sections of code that we need to add to the default MainActivity class and onCreate() and onWindowFocusChanged() code:

- Import the Android Java classes that we are leveraging in our code.

- Create and name an AnimationDrawable object that is accessible to every code construct in our MainActivity class.

- Create an ImageView object tied to our *activity_main.xml* screen layout, set the background image resource of that ImageView to reflect our *logo_animation.xml* attributes, and then have our logoAnimation AnimationDrawable object take that frame data from the ImageView via getBackground().

- Run the animation with a run()method inside of an Android Runnable thread created by our logoAnimHolder.post() method.

- Start the animation using logoAnimation.start() method inside of our onWindowFocusChanged() method used to detect app initialization completion.

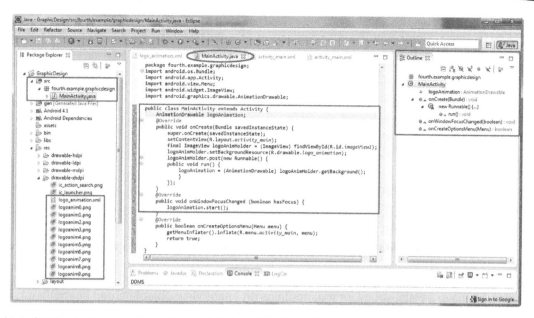

Figure 8-4. Creating the Java code that sets up and starts our XML defined frame-based animation

Finally, we need to remember put in place the ImageView named imageView1, which ties the ImageView in our Java code to the ImageView defined in our XML document (*activity_main.xml*) that defines our screen layout UI. To set-up our UI Layout *activity_menu.xml* markup in /res/layout/, we're using a default RelativeLayout container with an ImageView called imageView1 inside of it to hold our frame animation.

Here is the code, which is also shown in Figure 8-5:

```
<RelativeLayout xmlns:android="http://schemas.android.com/apk/res/android"
    xmlns:tools="http://schemas.android.com/tools"
    android:id="@+id/relativelayout1"
    android:layout_width="match_parent"
    android:layout_height="match_parent" >

    <ImageView
    android:id="@+id/imageView1"
    android:layout_width="wrap_content"
    android:layout_height="wrap_content"
    android:layout_alignParentTop="true"
    android:layout_centerHorizontal="true"
    android:layout_marginTop="=24dp"
    android:contentDescription="@+string/content_desc" />

</RelativeLayout>
```

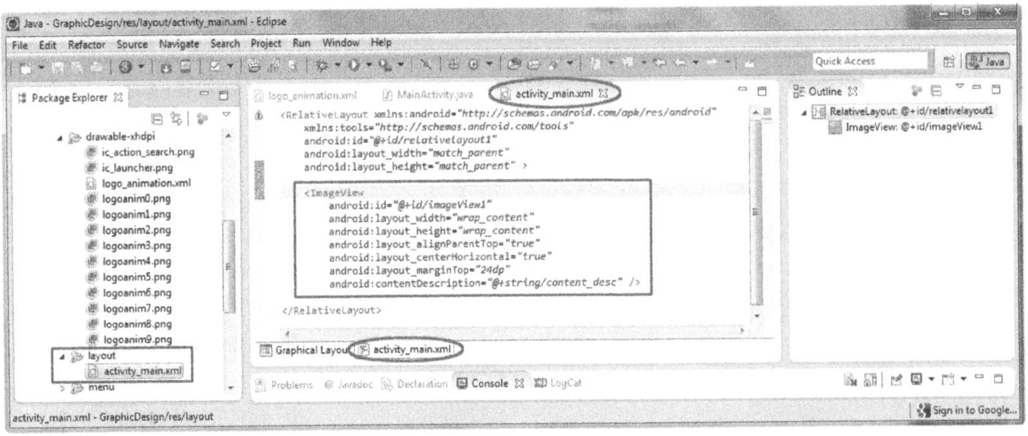

Figure 8-5. Naming our ImageView UI element in the activity_main.xml file so it matches the imageView1 name used in our Java code

In this case, we have a RelativeLayout that contains an ImageView object named imageView1, the default name that Android assigns to the first ImageView object declared or created by the Graphical Layout Editor (just in case you used that work process to create your UI).

We set our ImageView to wrap_content (basically to conform the ImageView boundaries to the 240 × 180 pixel dimension of our animation's imagery, and thus to "shrink-wrap" our animation sequence inside of our ImageView widget).

The next three parameters were automatically written for us based on our placement in the Graphical Layout Editor, and the final android:contentDescription parameter points to a short line of XML markup that we need to add to our */res/values/strings.xml* file that reads (place here whatever content you want the physically impaired to hear):

```
<string name="content_desc">Frame Animation Example</string>
```

Running the Frame-Based Animation App in the Emulator

Now let's see our animation in action. Right-click your *GraphicDesign* folder and choose **Run As ➤ Android Application**. When the 4.1 emulator comes up with a white screen, watch the 3D gold logo animation playing on it—simply amazing. But a tad too slow as the animation is not smooth enough. You'll fix that next with a little parameter "tweaking!"

Because a screenshot cannot display an animation, we'll forego the screenshot of the 4.1 emulator here to save space. Now, here's a simple exercise to try after you run this version. Make the following changes, and then save the modified *logo_animation.xml* file:

1. Change the logo_animation time values from 200 to 100 for all of the image parameters. This will play the animation faster, with a 1 second duration, at 10fps or ten frames per second, yielding a smoother animation result.

2. Change the animation-list tag's android:oneshot attribute to true.

To run our nonlooping smoother animation version, right-click the GraphicDesign folder and select **Run As ➤ Android Application**. Now when you launch the app in the 4.1 emulator, the animation will play one time and then stop. Note that by increasing the frame-rate that we obtained a much smoother visual appearance.

Next, let's add a transformational animation directly underneath our frame-based animation.

Tween Animation in Android

Tween animation is used for shape-based animation, where shapes are animated from one state to another without specifying the intermediate states. In other words, you define the start and end positions of the shape, and Android fills in the gaps to make the animation work. This shape based animation is sometimes called "Vector Animation" whereas frame based animation would be called "Raster Animation."

This contrasts with frame-based animation, which uses a sequence of cels, or bitmap images, as the flipbook animations of days gone by. So, frame animation does its work via pixels, while tween animation does its work via *transforms* that move, rotate, or scale a shape, image, or even text. Thus, tween animation is more powerful than frame-based animation. It can also be used in conjunction with frame-based animation to achieve even more spectacular results.

Tween animation in Android is completely different than frame animation. It is implemented with the set of classes found in the android.view.animation package. These classes represent the true power of tween animation in Android. They include things such as advanced motion interpolators, which define how animation transformations accelerate (or decelerate) over time; and animation utilities, which are needed to rotate, scale (resize), translate (move), and fade (effect transparency) View objects over time.

"Wait a minute," you must be musing, "does 'View objects' mean that I can apply all of this animation class power to, say, TextViews, for instance? Or even VideoViews?" Indeed it does. If you transform a TextView (rotate it, for instance), and it has a background image, that image is transformed correctly, right along with the text elements of the TextView and all of its settings.

> **Note**   Here, the word *transformation* refers to the process of rotation (spinning something around a pivot point), scaling (resizing in x and y dimensions relative to a pivot point or reference point), and x or y movement, which is called *translation* in animation. Don't get *Translation* and *Transformation* confused!

As you might imagine, tween animation definitions can get very complex. This is where the power of using XML to define complicated things, such as transformational animation constructs, becomes very apparent. Again, we thank Android for off-loading work like this from Java coding to XML constructs, so our designers can take care of it for the programmers.

In XML, the tween animation transforms are simply lists of nested tags; they are not usually set up via classes and methods. It is certainly far easier to fine-tune and refine these types of detailed animations via XML line-entry tweaks, rather than inside of the Java code, although you could probably do it that way if you wanted to, once you are an expert Java programmer.

The XML for tween animations goes in an entirely different directory (folder) than frame animation (which goes in */res/drawable*). Transform animation XML definitions (files) go in the */res/anim* folder.

Creating the text_animation.xml File

We will use a different XML file-creation method to create our transform animation XML file and its folder, so let's get into that right now.

1. Open the Eclipse File Menu at the top left of the IDE and select **New ➤ Other**... ➤ **Android ➤ Android XML File**, as shown in Figure 8-6. Then click Next.

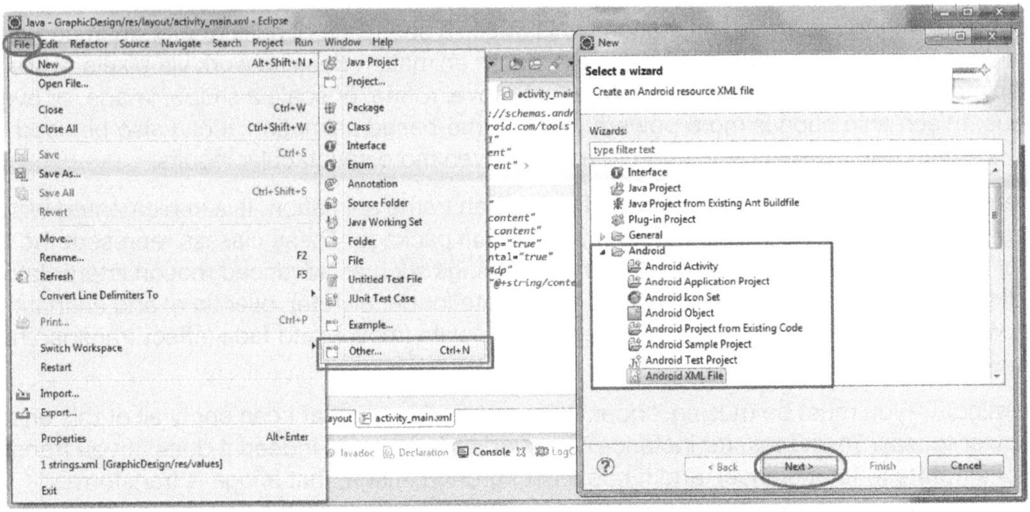

Figure 8-6. *Selecting to create a new XML file via the Eclipse File ➤ New ➤ Other menu selection route and dialog*

2. As you can see by the options in the New Android XML dialog, Android in Eclipse has a powerful XML file-creator utility that supports ten different genres of XML files via a drop-down menu, including animation. Fill out the dialog as follows (and as shown in Figure 8-7):

    ▓ *File:* The first field we want to fill out is the name of the animation XML file, which is: *text_animation.xml*.

    ▓ *Which type of resource would you like to create?:* Select Tween Animation as the XML file type, which automatically puts the XML file created into the /res/anim Folder.

    ▓ *Select the root element for the XML file:* Make sure that set is selected as the root element for the file. (The root element is the outermost tag in an XML file and contains all of the other tags.) A <set> is used to group and nest transforms into a Set of Transforms to achieve more powerful and flexible results, as you will see in our transform XML mark-up.

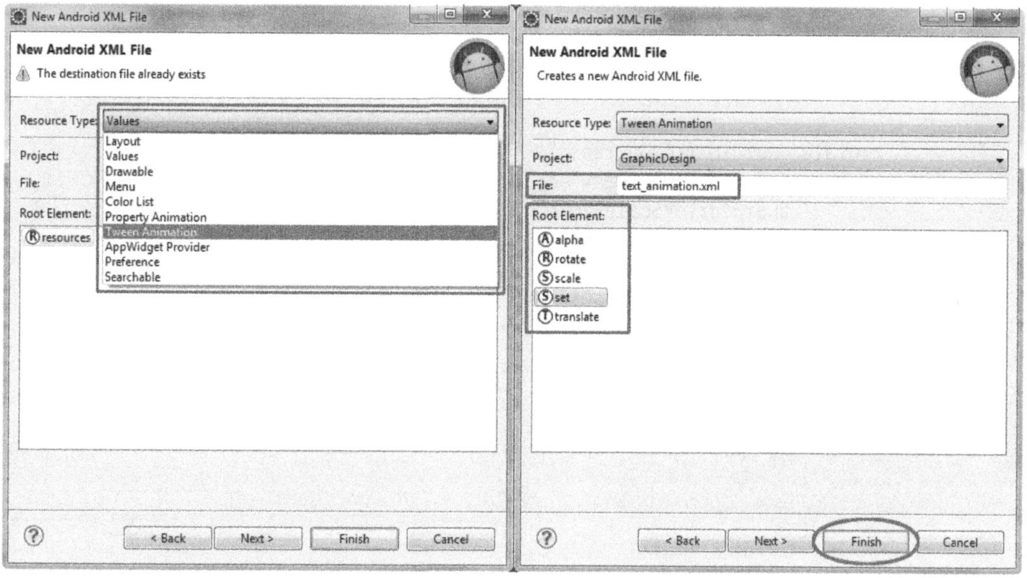

Figure 8-7. Filling out the New Android XML File dialog to specify the Tween Animation XML file

3. Now click Finish. You will see the /res/anim folder appear in your project hierarchy tree in the Package Explorer pane, with the *text_animation.xml* file inside it.

4. Now let's add in our XML tags to define our scale and rotation transforms, as shown in Figure 8-8. (Click the Source tab at the bottom of the main window to open the XML code editing window if it does not appear automatically.)

```
<set xmlns:android="http://schemas.android.com/apk/res/android"
    android:shareInterpolator="false">

    <scale android:interpolator="@android:anim/accelerate_decelerate_interpolator"
        android:fromXScale="1.0"
        android:toXScale="1.4"
        android:fromYScale="1.0"
        android:toYScale="0.6"
        android:pivotX="50%"
        android:pivotY="50%"
        android:fillAfter="false"
        android:duration="700" />

    <set android:interpolator="@android:anim/decelerate_interpolator">
        <scale android:fromXScale="1.4"
            android:toXScale="0.0"
```

```
                            android:fromYScale="0.6"
                            android:toYScale="0.0"
                            android:pivotX="50%"
                            android:pivotY="50%"
                            android:startOffset="700"
                            android:duration="400"
                            android:fillBefore="false" />

            <rotate android:fromDegrees="0"
                    android:toDegrees="-45"
                    android:toYScale="0.0"
                    android:pivotX="50%"
                    android:pivotY="50%"
                    android:startOffset="700"
                    android:duration="400" />
        </set>
    </set>
```

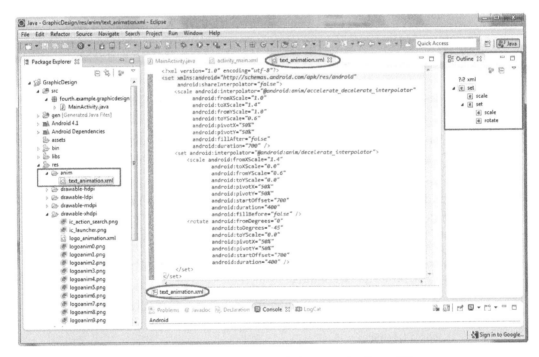

Figure 8-8. Coding our tween animation tags and their parameters in the text_animation.xml file

Notice that there are quite a few attributes for the tags that allow transformational animation over time. For instance, our scale tags allow us to specify to and from values for both the x and y dimensions, pivot points (where the scale emanates from, or from which location on the object the scale is to be performed), scale offsets for nonuniform scaling, time duration, and whether to fill before or after the transformation.

For rotation tags, we have rotation to and from degree specifications, as well as x and y pivot point settings. We also have both an offset for skewed rotations and a duration attribute that controls the speed of the rotational transformation. The pivot point defines the center point of the rotation, and an offset defines how to skew the rotation from that point, much like the old Spirograph sets that created cool, flower-like graphics.

Controlling Tween Animation via Java

Now that our TextView transform animation XML data is in place inside of our newly created /res/anim/text_animation.xml file, we can insert a half dozen lines of Java code into our MainActivity.java file, to implement the transform animation within our application, directly underneath our frame-based animation.

1. As shown in Figure 8-9, the first thing we must do is to import the Android classes that are going to be used in the text animation transformation: android.widget.TextView and the android.view.animation classes called Animation and AnimationUtils.

```
import android.widget.TextView;
import android.view.animation.Animation;
import android.view.animation.AnimationUtils;
```

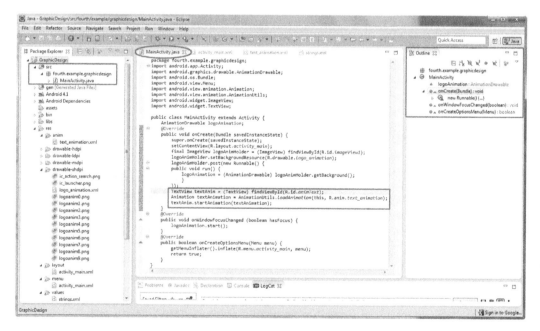

Figure 8-9. Setting up our text tween animation in our GraphicDesign project's Java code

2. Then down in our onCreate() method, we specify the TextView object textAnim and the Animation object textAnimation.

```
TextView textAnim = (TextView) findViewById(R.id.animText);
Animation textAnimation = AnimationUtils.loadAnimation(this,
                          R.anim.text_animation);
```

3. We then call the `startAnimation()` method on the `TextView` object, specifying that we want to use the `textAnimation` `Animation` object.

```
textAnim.startAnimation(textAnimation);
```

4. Finally, we need to add a `TextView` object named `animText` to our `RelativeLayout` tag and UI container in our *activity_main.xml* file, as shown in Figure 8-10.

Figure 8-10. *Adding a TextView UI object to our activity_main.xml file with an ID of animText*

5. Now we can try out the tween animation. Right-click the *GraphicDesign* folder in the Package Explorer pane and select **Run As ➤ Android Application**. It only runs once (it is not looped), so keep an eye on the emulator as it starts up!

6. It runs pretty fast. Let's add a zero on the time values in our *text_animation. xml* file, changing 400 to 4,000 and 700 to 7,000.

7. Compile and run the app again. You'll see that the animation runs ten times slower, so you can actually see what the transforms are doing to the text object. If you want it to run another order of magnitude (10×) slower still, simply add another zero as we did in Step 6 above.

Using Transitions

Transitions are preprogrammed custom special effects, like crossfades (also called dissolves) and things such as directional wipes, which we can code ourselves. By using these effects, especially in combination with each other, you can increase the perceived professionalism of your application.

You can (and should) use XML to set up such graphics transition transformations.

Android provides the `TransitionDrawable` class. Here, we will use it in conjunction with an XML file in the /res/drawables directory, just as we did in the frame-based animation example because transitions are designed to work with bitmap images just like frame-based animation.

So, let's get started.

1. Right-click the *GraphicDesign* folder and select **New ➤ File** to create a standard text file for our XML in the /res/drawable-xhdpi folder (because we are working with bitmap images).

Name the file *image_transition.xml*, found at the bottom of the New File dialog. We'll forego the screen shot because you've seen it before. Open the GraphicDesign folder, then open the /res folder, then select the /drawable-xhdpi folder, where the new file will be created.

2. Next, add the `<transition>` tag as follows. The `<transition>` tag has the usual `xmlns` reference (to make our file valid Android XML). Inside the tag, we specify two `<item>` tags referencing the images that we need to transition from and transition to. We are using the two images that we used in Chapter 7 here to show that the transitions will accommodate the alpha channel and more complicated masking of images, which is important for advanced animation design:

```
<transition xmlns:android="http://schemas.android.com/apk/res/android">

    <item android:drawable="@drawable/image1"/>
    <item android:drawable="@drawable/image2"/>

</transition>
```

3. Add these two images to the /res/drawable-xhdpi folder. Figure 8-11 shows what your screen should look like once you have added the two images, refreshed the IDE, and typed in your tags.

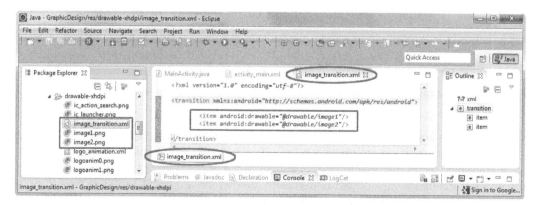

Figure 8-11. Writing our XML markup to transition between two images in our image_transition.xml file

4. Now we need to add an `ImageView` in our `RelativeLayout` to hold our image transition source imagery. Put the following in the *activity_main.xml* file underneath our animated `TextView`, as shown in Figure 8-12.

```
<ImageView
            android:id="@+id/imageTrans"
            android:layout_width="wrap_content"
            android:layout_height="wrap_content"
            android:layout_below="@+id/animText"
            android:layout_centerHorizontal="true"
            android:layout_marginTop="48dp"
            android:src="@drawable/image1"
            android:contentDescription="@+string/content_desc2" />
```

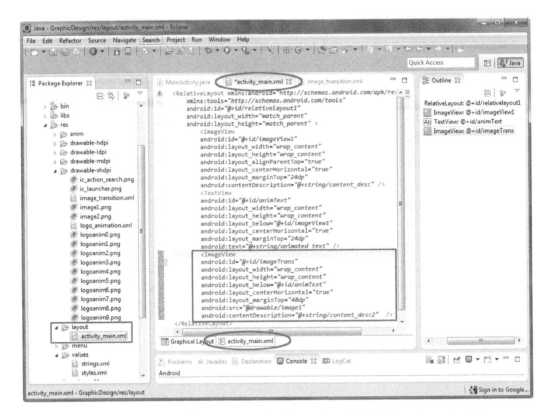

Figure 8-12. Adding an ImageView UI object to our /res/layout/activity_main.xml file to hold our image transition

We are specifying the first image (the "from" image) of our transition as the source image to use in the ImageView object, and we are naming it `imageTrans` via the now familiar `@+id/imageTrans` notation. We are also using the now familiar RelativeLayout android:layout_ below parameter to place the imageTrans ImageView object underneath (below) the animText TextView object, and using the layout margin and centering parameters as we did with the other two objects declared in the *activity_main.xml* found in the /res/layout/ folder.

Finally, let's not forget the sight impaired, and let's add an android:contentDescription parameter, which should, via our */res/values/strings.xml* file, reference the text "Image Animation Example." Be sure to right-click and open the *strings.xml* file and copy and paste the content_desc string tag, and then change the name to be content_desc2 and value to be Image Animation Example because we are referencing this in our *activity_main.xml* file here.

Now we are ready to drop a few lines of Java code (a whopping five this time) into *MainActivity.java* to add the ability to do a fade transition from one image slowly into another.

First we need to add the import statement for the class library that we are going to use in the Image Transition example, namely the android.graphics.drawable.TransitionDrawable class:

```
import android.graphics.drawable.TransitionDrawable;
```

Here is the code to set up the TransitionDrawable implementation that we will use to create the trans object that is used to access the image_transition XML file in our /res/drawable-xhdpi folder:

```
TransitionDrawable trans = (TransitionDrawable)
  getResources().getDrawable(R.drawable.image_transition);
```

This is all on one line, as shown in Figure 8-13.

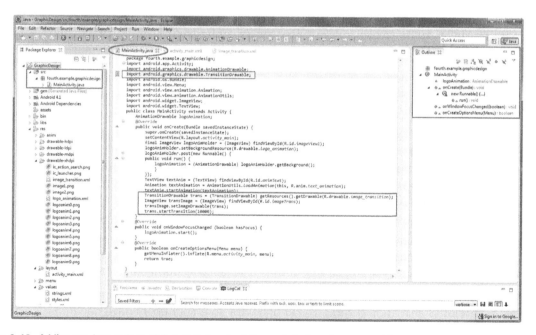

Figure 8-13. Adding our Java code to MainActivity.java to define and start our image transition

> **Tip**   We have one new import statement to add, so we need to open up the import statements
> block of code as shown in in Figure 8-13. This can be done by clicking on the plus sign (+) next to the
> import block of code. The plus sign indicates that this code block can be expanded (just click the +).
> You can click any of the minus signs (–) in your Java code window to close classes you are finished
> editing, if you want to see a higher-level view of your code, similar to the Outline Pane view on the right
> side of the Eclipse IDE. Once your code becomes long and involved, you will find that you will use this
> simple but powerful code organization feature regularly. Try it, and get used to making it a part of your
> work process inside of the Eclipse IDE.

This line of code declares our TransitionDrawable object, which we name trans. It sets trans to the
results of the call to the getDrawable() method of the object (which retrieves our image_transition
XML image transition definition) that is returned to the getResources() method that calls it to get the
image resources that will be used by the TransitionDrawable class.

This single line of code essentially declares our trans object for use and also loads the *image_
transition.xml* transition drawable specification into the TransitionDrawable trans object all in one
compact line of Java code! Remember that the image_transition drawable resource obtained
pointers to our two circular images that we are going to transition between.

Setting up that TransitionDrawable object and loading it with our XML file is the most difficult line of
code in this quartet. The next three lines of code are more familiar and a bit more straightforward:

```
ImageView transImage = (ImageView) findViewById(R.id.imageTrans);
transImage.setImageDrawable(trans);
trans.startTransition(10000);
```

We create an ImageView object in Java called transImage and, via the findViewById() method, we
link it to the imageTrans ID, referenced from the second ImageView XML tag we added earlier to
the *activity_main.xml* file in our /res/layout/ folder. We then use the setImageDrawable() method to
set the transImage ImageView object to the trans TransitionDrawable object that we just created
above it, linking or "wiring" the two objects to each other, in essence. This is the bridge between the
two main objects that allows things to work properly in this image transition section of code.

Finally, we can now talk to the trans TransitionDrawable object via its
startTransition(milliseconds) method. We will use that method to tell the transition (once it begins)
that we want it to take place over 10,000 ms, or over a 10-second duration (a slow cross-fade).

Select **Run As ➤ Android Application** and watch all the fun animation begin immediately on App
start-up. That's a lot of animation going on all at once! Be sure your users have decent processing
power (dual-core Intel processor is the best, or soon, quad-core processor Android devices) if you
choose to place a lot of animation in a single Activity UI screen in your Android application.

Summary

In this chapter, we took a look at the more advanced graphics and animation capabilities that Android offers, including what Android wants to see you using as far as graphic formats are concerned, as well as two different types of animation, and how to code image transitions.

You also learned a little more about the Eclipse IDE, the Android Runnable interface and run() method, and the high-quality WebP, PNG24, and PNG32 image file formats that are optimal for use in Android apps.

Here are some important points to remember:

- Always use PNG24 format (which is really PNG32 format, if you are using the alpha channel) or you can use WebP, but only if you are supporting Android 4 or later (4.04, 4.1, 5.0).

- Bitmap animation and tween animation are two completely different things as far as Android is concerned. Bitmap-related animation and transitions are handled through the **/res/drawable** folder. Tween animation is handled via XML files defined in the **/res/anim** folder, and can affect other objects besides just bitmap images, such as TextViews.

- Don't limit yourself when using tween animation. Use it on any type of View container you like—text, image, video, button, layout, or whatever; wax creative, and be sure to experiment.

In Chapter 9, we'll start looking at how to make all of what we have been learning about so far become interactive! This is done by setting up our applications to handle events and to listen for those events via event listeners.

We'll also cover new media assets such as audio and video using the Android MediaPlayer class over the last couple chapters of the book, so your capabilities are going to get more and more powerful! Let's get interactive with our end-users next, and get right into Chapter 9.

Adding Interactivity: Handling UI Events

In this chapter, we will explore how to wire those super-cool UI designs that you have seen in the previous chapters, so that your UI design becomes highly functional within your Android application. You worked briefly with event handling in the last section on Dialogs in Chapter Seven, so we'll give you the foundation in this chapter to be able to handle all types of events within the Android OS.

With Android's convenient *event listeners*, you can easily add in your own custom programming logic. Using the *event handling* described in this chapter, you'll be able to have your UI and graphical elements actually do something productive or impressive after they are tapped on (touchscreen), navigated to (navigation keypad), or typed into (keyboard).

We'll begin with an overview of how Android *listens* to its touchscreen and keyboard, and how to harness the power of input devices.

An Overview of UI Events in Android

The way that we talk to all of the input devices in Java, and thus in Android, is via *events* for each type of input device (touchscreen, keyboard, and navigation keys). Events are actually system-generated messages that are sent to the View object whenever a UI element is accessed in some fashion by a user. *Event* refers to something that you attend or otherwise recognize as being significant, and thus is the perfect term for these UI occurrences via Android input devices.

Listening for and Handling Events

Handling and *handlers* are two other terms used in conjunction with events in Java and Android. Once these events are triggered by a user's touch, keystroke, or navigation key, they must be *handled* within your application. This is accomplished inside a method (such as onClick() or onKeyDown()) that specifies exactly what you want to happen when one of these input events is detected by Android and is sent over to your appropriate event handler for processing.

This concept of handling events is termed *listening* in Android. You will see the terms *event listeners* and *event handlers* throughout this chapter. That's because they are what the chapter is all about: how to put into place the proper event listeners and event handlers to cover your app users' interaction via touchscreen, navigation keys, and keyboard input devices that are part of an Android device's hardware, whether it be a smartphone handset, an iTV set remote control, or a tablet or e-reader touchscreen.

Handling UI Events via the View Class

Each of the UI elements in your application is a View object widget of one incarnation or another, and each has events that are unique to that element. This is how user interaction with specific UI elements is kept separate and well organized. Each of these View objects keeps track of its own user-input events via event handlers.

The way that a View object within your layout talks with the rest of your application program logic is via a public callback method that is invoked by Android when a given action occurs in that UI View object. For instance, if a Button widget is touched, an onClick() method is *called* on that object because Android knows to call a method of that name when that event occurs. In other words, Android calls back to the object that received an event so that the object can handle it via custom Java code that you write depending on what you want that object to do.

For this callback message to be intercepted by your Java code and program logic, you need to extend your View class and override the method from the View class that your UI widget was spawned (subclassed) from. To *override* a method means to declare and define that exact method name specifically within your class, and have it do something via your own custom program logic.

Because your UI design is made of a collection of View objects (UI widgets) laid out in one or more ViewGroup layout containers, you can see how this might represent a gaggle of coding just to make sure all of your UI elements are properly listening to the keyboard, touchscreen, and navigation keys. Has Android done anything here to make things easier on us, as it has in other areas of application development?

Yes, Android has provided a way to facilitate event handling. The View class from which all of our UI widgets are subclassed contains a collection of nested interfaces featuring callbacks that are far easier to define, as they are part of the system that makes up the View class and all of its methods.

These nested interfaces that are already a part of all of your View class-based widgets are called *event listeners*. They provide the easiest way to quickly set in place code that will capture user-input events and allow them to be processed right there within your application program logic.

Event Callback Methods

In the most simple of terms, an *event listener* is a Java interface in the View class that contains a single callback method to handle that type of user-input event. When you implement a specific event listener interface, you are telling Android that your View class will handle that specific event on that specific View object (widget).

These callback methods are called by Android when the View object that the callback method is *registered* to is triggered by the user-input device used to access that UI interface element.

(I like to say the method is *wired up* to the View object, but then again, I am a programmer and drink far too much exotic coffee.)

The callback methods that we are going to cover in this chapter are the most common ones used in Android application development. They are listed in Table 9-1.

Table 9-1. Common Android Callback Methods

Method	From	Triggered by
onClick()	View.OnClickListener	Touch of screen or click of navigation keys
onLongClick()	View.OnLongClickListener	Touch or Enter held for 1 second or longer
onKey()	View.OnKeyListener	Press/release of key on phone or iTV remote
onTouch()	View.OnTouchListener	Touch, release, or gesture events
onFocusChange()	View.OnFocusChange	Focus change
onCreateContextMenu()	View.OnCreateContextMenuListener	Context menu

In the table, two of the methods are not directly triggered by user input, but they are related to input events. These are onFocusChange() and onCreateContextMenu(). The onFocusChange() method tracks how the user moves from one UI element to the next. The term *focus* refers to which UI element the user is using or accessing currently. When a user goes from one UI element to another one, the first UI element is said to have "lost focus," and the next element is said to now "have the focus." The onCreateContextMenu() method is related to the onLongClick() callback method, in the sense that context menus in Android are generated via a long-click user action. This is the touchscreen equivalent of a right-click on most computers, and is used for context-sensitive menus such as those right-click menus that we have been using frequently in the Eclipse Project Explorer pane.

To define one of these callback methods to handle certain types of events for one of your View objects, simply implement the nested interface in your activity or define it as an anonymous class within your application. If you define it as an anonymous class, you pass an instance of your implementation of the listener to the respective setListener() method, as you'll see in the next section.

In the rest of this chapter, you'll learn how to leverage the primary event listeners in Android, so that you can make your application interactive and useful.

Handling onClick Events

The onClick() method is triggered when the user touches a UI element. As you might guess, it's the most commonly used event handler out there. So, it only makes sense to start with handling onClick events.

Implementing an onClick Listener for a UI Element

First, let's create an anonymous OnClickListener:

```
final OnClickListener exampleListener = new OnClickListener()
{
    public void onClick(View arg0) {
        //Code here that does something upon click event.
    }
};
```

This is an example of an anonymous class. This line of code sets up a variable called exampleListener as a new OnClickListener object, which listens for onClick events.

> **Note**   Recall from Chapter 7 that a final variable cannot be reassigned a value once it has been set.
> This ensures that another listener does not get assigned.

It is logical, then, that inside this class definition there would be a public onClick(View arg0) handler to handle the onClick event. The public onClick handler is passed an ID reference to the View object that was clicked on, so that it knows which View object to handle. Note that the View that has been clicked is named arg0, so if you want to reference the View object in the code inside this method, it is ready to go and must be referenced via a variable "arg0." The first argument used in coding terminology would be called argument zero (arg0) as in computers we start counting from zero and not from one like we learned in school. The second argument used would be arg1 and so on.

How any given onClick handler handles a click event is up to the code inside of the onClick handler. That code basically explains what to do if that UI element was clicked on or touched, or typed with a keystroke.

If you want to come off as really cool right now, simply look up casually from the book and exclaim to your family, "I'm coding an onClick event handler in Java right now," and then look back down and continue reading.

We have defined an OnClickListener, but we need to wire it to a UI element (attach it to a UI View object) before that code can be triggered. Usually, this will go inside the onCreate() method (which you have become familiar with in the first two-thirds of this book).

It takes only two lines of code to connect a button to the exampleListener object. The first is simply our XML declaration of the Button UI object in our *activity_main.xml* UI layout definition:

```
<Button android:text="First Button"
        android:id="@+id/firstButton"
        android:layout_gravity="center"
        android:layout_width="wrap_content"
        android:layout_height="wrap_content"/>
```

The second line is where we connect the button construct with the event listener construct, by using the `Button` widget's `setOnClickListener()` method, like so:

```
Button exampleButton = (Button)this.findViewById(R.id.firstButton);
exampleButton.setOnClickListener(exampleListener);
```

Adding an onClick Listener to an Activity in Android

You will probably not be surprised when I tell you that there is an even sleeker way to define your event listeners for your activities, using even fewer object references and fewer lines of code. This is normally how you will want to do things in your Android applications programming activities, so this is how we are going to do them in all of the examples in this chapter.

You can implement an event listener directly inside the declaration of your activity, within the actual class declaration. Wow. Event listeners must be *muy importante*.

Here is a class declaration that uses the `implements` keyword to embed an `OnClickListener` directly into the class via its declaration:

```
public class MainActivity extends Activity implements OnClickListener() {...}
```

The previous two lines of code declaring the `Button` and wiring via `setOnClickListener()` would still exist inside the `onCreate()` code block, but the declaration of the `exampleListener` object and class would not be necessary.

Now it's time to create our *EventHandling* project folder and implement a button and an `onClick()` listener so that you can see event handling in action.

Creating the Event Handling Examples Project in Eclipse

For our first example, we'll set up a top-level button so that when it is clicked, the text in a `TextView` below it changes.

In Eclipse, close the *GraphicDesign* project folder (right-click on it in Package Explorer and select **Close Project**) if it's still open. Also, close all the empty tabs at the top of the Eclipse IDE, using the x icons in the top-right side of each tab. Now we're ready to create our new Android Application Project.

1. Select **File ➤ New ➤ Project** and choose **Android Application Project** to open the New Android Application Project series of dialogs as we have done before.

2. Fill it out as follows (and shown in Figure 9-1):

   ▩ *Project name*: Name the project *EventHandling*.

   ▩ *Build target*: Choose Android 4.1.

   ▩ *Application name*: Name the application **EventHandling**.

   ▩ *Package name*: The package name should be fifth.example.eventhandling.

- ***Create custom launcher icon***: Check this box.

- ***Min SDK version***: Set this to 8, which matches the Android 2.2 recommended build target and is the default setting.

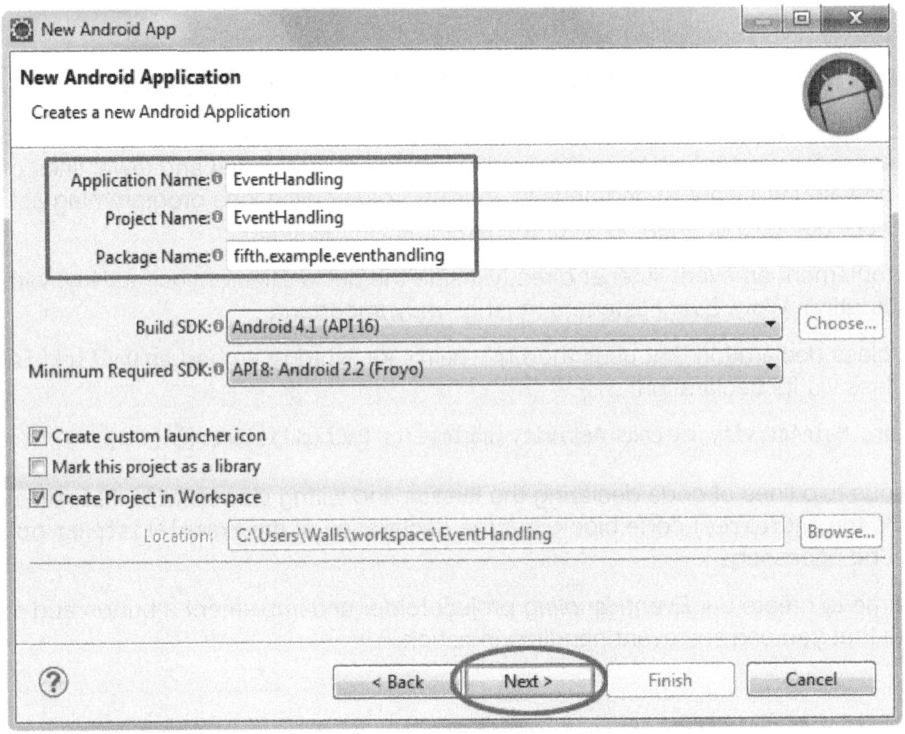

Figure 9-1. Creating the EventHandling Android project using the New Android Application series of dialogs

3. Accept the default settings in the remaining three dialogs as we did in Chapters 4 through 8.

Editing the MainActivity.java File

Now let's edit the java code:

1. In the Package Explorer, open your project tree hierarchy by clicking the arrows next to the */src* and */res* folders, so that you can see their contents. Select the *MainActivity.java* file under the */src/fifth.example.eventhandling* folder by clicking once on it (it will turn blue), and then hit the F3 key on your keyboard. This is the keyboard shortcut for the **Open** option.

2. Notice that some code has been written for us. The first thing we need to do is to implement an OnClickListener. Add implements OnClickListener to the end of the class declaration, as shown in Figure 9-2, like this: public class MainActivity extends Activity implements OnClickListener {...}

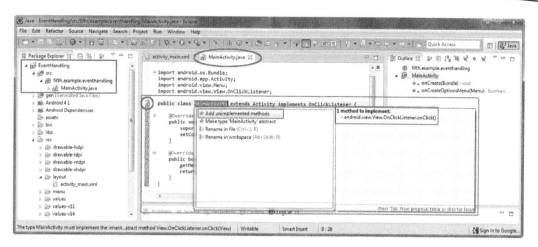

Figure 9-2. Editing MainActivity.java to implement the onClickListener functionality

3.   As you can see in Figure 9-2, after we type in the "Implements
     onClickListener" and Eclipse adds our import statement for the
     onClickListener Class, Android Developer Tools (ADT) and Eclipse alerted
     us that something is amiss. If you hold the mouse over the red X on the left
     margin of the coding pane, Eclipse will tell you what it thinks is wrong. Click
     on the red X and the MainActivity class is highlighted in blue. When you
     mouse-over the MainActivity keyword highlighted in the class definition,
     up pops a helper box (shown in Figure 9-2) saying that Eclipse wants to
     see the unimplemented onClick() method. To fix this, double-click the Add
     unimplemented methods link (the first one), and Eclipse will add the method
     and its @override for you (see Figure 9-3), as follows:

```
@Override
public void onClick(View arg0) {
        // TODO Auto-generated method stub

}
```

Figure 9-3. Implementing an OnClickListener in our class definition via the implements keyword

> **Note** Because the onClick code uses a View object, Eclipse imports android.view.View, which is shown at the top of the file.

4. There is nothing better than having our IDE write code for us. Notice that when we had Eclipse write our onClick() method that it also imported the android.view.View Class, so both of the classes we will need for Event Handling for Clicks have been added. This is all highlighted at the top of Figure 9-3.

> **Note** You need to get used to looking at what Eclipse is telling you as you code. This awareness is especially useful while you are learning the programming language and are inside the development environment. That is why I am showing you some of these automatic coding functions here in this book, rather than writing perfect lines of code every time in exactly the correct order. One of the things you need to master is your process of working within the Eclipse IDE and paying close attention to what it is telling you. If you mouse-over or click on the things it flags or highlights, you will get pop-up windows as well as tool-tips containing additional helpful information.

5. Now let's define our Button and attach our setOnClickListener() to it as we did earlier in Figure 9-4. We talked about this earlier in the chapter, but this time, the containing activity is the event listener, so we use this to refer to the containing object.

```
Button button = (Button)findViewById(R.id.button1);
button.setOnClickListener(this);
```

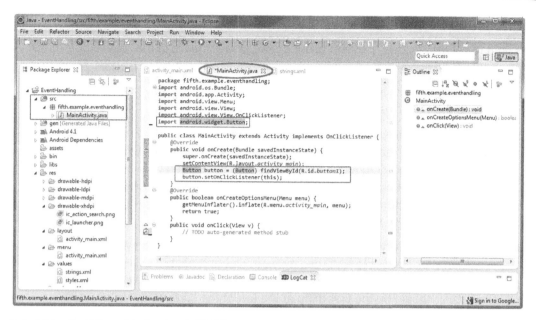

Figure 9-4. Adding the Button widget and setOnClickListener() method in Eclipse

This is all shown in Figure 9-4, along with the `import android.widget.Button;` statement that we need to use the `Button` in our code. Next, we will add the Button UI element to our RelativeLayout, using the Eclipse Graphical Layout Editor (GLE), and then hand modify the XML code to place it above our text, so that it's more intuitive for the end-users. This will remove any flags in our Java code editing pane that tell us that a button1 XML object definition does not yet exist! The first step in this process is shown in Figure 9-5.

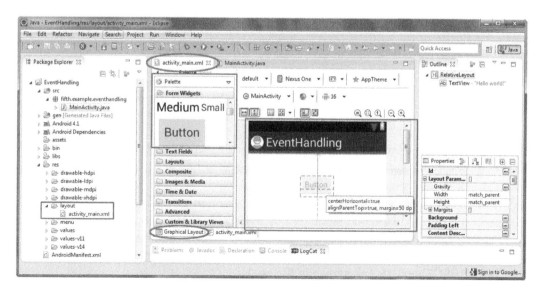

Figure 9-5. Creating a Button in /res/layout/activity_main.xml via the Graphical Layout Editor in Eclipse

Editing the activity_main.xml File

Now it's time to set up the XML mark-up in our *activity_main.xml* file in the /res/layout/ folder.

1. Select the *activity_main.xml* file under the */res/layout* folder and hit F3 to open it in the IDE in its own tab, or use right-click (on the *activity_main.xml* file) and the Open menu selection to open it that way instead.

2. Click the Graphical Layout Editor tab at the bottom of the IDE to show the layout visually (see Figure 9-5), Then drag the Button widget (shown selected and being dragged in Figure 9-5) onto the screen to the right, and drop it into place under the TextView widget. Make sure the tool-tip says centerHorizontal=true as well as alignParentTop=true and margin=50dp as shown in the screen shot in Figure 9-5.

3. Now click the *activity_main.xml* tab at the bottom of the IDE to switch the view from visual layout to XML coding view. Cut and paste the Button code so that it comes before the TextView code (but after the RelativeLayout tag). The Button should be the first thing at the top of the screen.

4. Now open the /res/values/ folder and right-click on the *strings.xml* file and select Open and then use the Properties Editor to change the Hello World default text string to use variable name button_caption and a text value of: CLICK TO GENERATE EVENT as shown in Figure 9-6.

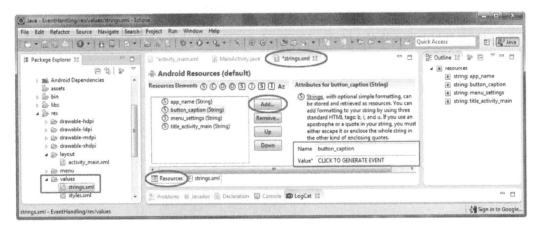

Figure 9-6. Editing the button_caption string property to read CLICK TO GENERATE EVENT

5. Now click the *strings.xml* XML editor tab at the bottom of the middle editing pane and duplicate the text string (or use the Add... button, shown in Figure 9-6, and add the second variable via the Visual Resources Editor) for the text output. Name the variable text_message and set its value to: NO EVENT RECEIVED YET as shown in Figure 9-7.

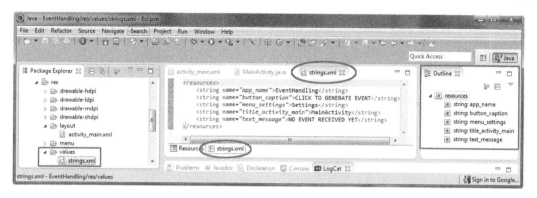

Figure 9-7. The strings.xml file after the EventHandling project's related text string tags have been added

6. Add the android:text @string XML variables, text message TextView object ID and the button1 Button object ID, and the centering attributes that you learned about in the previous chapters shown in Figure 9-8. Note that the Graphical Layout Editor added all of the android:layout_ parameters for you based on how you dragged and dropped the button earlier. Pretty cool. Here is what the final code should look like:

```
<RelativeLayout xmlns:android="http://schemas.android.com/apk/res/android"
    xmlns:tools="http://schemas.android.com/tools"
    android:layout_width="match_parent"
    android:layout_height="match_parent" >

    <Button
            android:id="@+id/button1"
            android:layout_width="wrap_content"
            android:layout_height="wrap_content"
            android:layout_alignParentTop="true"
            android:layout_centerHorizontal="true"
            android:layout_marginTop="50dp"
            android:text="@string/button_caption" />

    <TextView
            android:id="@+id/textmessage"
            android:layout_width="wrap_content"
            android:layout_height="wrap_content"
            android:layout_centerHorizontal="true"
            android:layout_centerVertical="true"
            android:text="@string/text_message"
            tools:context=".MainActivity" />
</RelativeLayout>
```

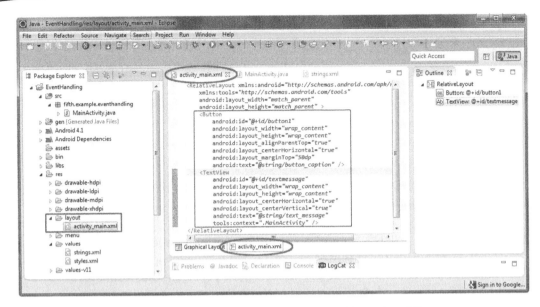

Figure 9-8. *Editing Button and TextView object parameters in our /res/layout/activity_main.xml file*

Updating MainActivity.java

Now let's go back into our Java code.

1. Click the MainActivity.java tab at the top of the code editor pane.

2. Add the code that responds to a click on the button, as follows (see Figure 9-9):

```java
public void onClick(View arg0) {
        TextView text = (TextView)findViewById(R.id.textmessage);
        text.setText("BUTTON HAS BEEN CLICKED. EVENT PROCESSED.");
}
```

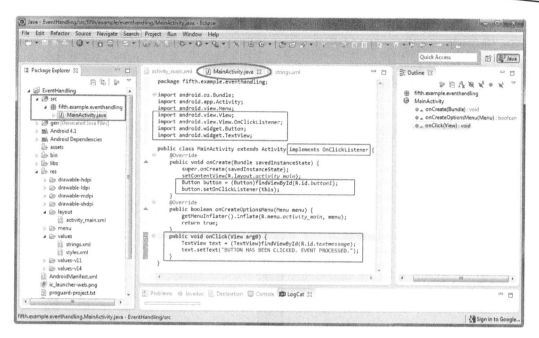

Figure 9-9. *Defining the onClick() event handler code for a TextView in MainActivity.java*

We add our TextView object declaration into onClick(). We also add a setText("BUTTON HAS BEEN CLICKED. EVENT PROCESSED.") call to the TextView object we named text, created in the previous line. Finally, we add an Import android.widget.TextView; statement, or we have Eclipse do it for us, via the error-warning icon mouse-over work process. You're getting pretty good at this, aren't you?

Running the Event Handling Examples App in the Emulator

To run this example, right-click your *EventHandling* folder in the Package Explorer pane and select **Run As ➤ Android Application**. We have our first UI that responds to the most common event handler out there: the onClick handler. Figure 9-10 shows the results.

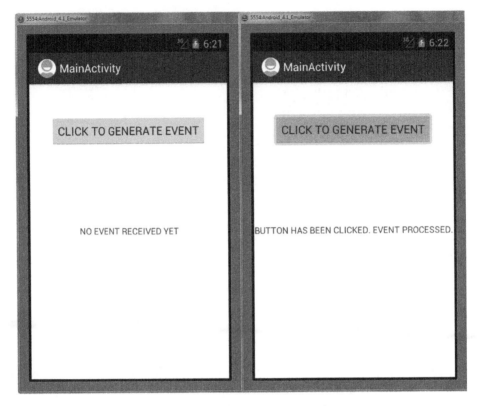

Figure 9-10. Running the onClick() event handling example in the Android 4.1 emulator

Android Touchscreen Events: onTouch

Android handsets that feature touchscreens—the vast majority of them today—can take advantage of advanced touchscreen features, such as *gestures*.

Note   *Gestures* are movements with the user's finger across the touchscreen that invoke certain program functions. They are popular for interaction on large screen smartphones and tablets. You will want to learn about implementing gestures when you become a more experienced Android developer. Gestures became available in Android 1.6, and thus they do work in Android 2.2, which is the recommended minimum SDK version that we are developing for in this book to provide a wider audience of user compatible devices. However, coding to the Gestures API is a bit too advanced for this Absolute Beginner book.

It is important to note that an onClick event handler also works on a touchscreen, but an onTouch handler does NOT work with the navigation keys or selector key (the center selector Enter key).

Therefore, it may well be wise to use the onClick() method for your apps for most UI operations for the widest compatibility, and use onTouch() specifically when working with more advanced touch events such as gestures that involve only the touchscreen.

Because we have already covered implementing onClick(), we'll continue here with the other important event handlers. These are the ones you will use most frequently in your application design and coding: onLongClick, OnKeyUp, onKeyDown, onCreateContextMenu, and onFocus, along with onClick as the most often used.

Android's Right-Click Equivalent: onLongClick

After OnClick, OnLongClick is the next most used interface event. It is generated by most input hardware and is also the basis for the context menu in Android.

The onLongClick() method works in the following scenarios:

- When the user touches and holds on the touchscreen for 1 second or longer

- When the user holds down the Enter key on the phone for 1 second or longer

- When the user holds down the center navigation key for 1 second or longer

- When the user presses and holds down the Trackball for 1 second or longer

Any of these will generate an OnLongClick event for whatever UI widget currently has the focus or, in the case of a touchscreen, is underneath the area of the screen being touched (or long-touched, in this instance!).

Because any View object can trap an onLongClick() callback, the most elegant way to show this event handling is to add it to our Button UI object in our current *EventHandling* example code. This also will allow you to see the common scenario of more than one type of handler being used right alongside other types of event handlers in the same View and class.

1. In *MainActivity.java*, add a comma after OnClickListener in the public class MainActivity definition and add OnLongClickListener, as shown in Figure 9-11. Then mouse-over the red-underlined OnLongClickListener and select the option to add the import statement (boom bam—there is our import code for this listener). Then mouse-over the red-underlined MainActivity class name and select the link to add unimplemented methods. Voila, we now have the following:

```
public boolean onLongClick(View arg0) {
    // TODO Auto-generated method stub
    return false;
}
```

Figure 9-11. *Implementing an OnLongClick listener in the MainActivity.java class*

2. Now copy the `text` object and `text.setText()` code from the `onClick` handler and paste it into the `onLongClick` handler, where the placeholder comment code is. Change the text message to reflect the hold and long-click, as shown in Figure 9-12. Note that we can use the same object name `text` in both handlers. Because it is a local variable to each handler, neither `text` object sees the other reference. Finally, wire the OnLongClick handler to the button using the button.setOnLongClickListener(this); method call just like we did with the setOnClickListener() method earlier.

Figure 9-12. Attaching an OnLongClick listener to our Button object in MainActivity.java

3. Now try the new functionality. Right-click the *EventHandling* folder and choose **Run As ➤ Android Project**. This time, you get an app that displays one message when you click and another when you hold the click. But when you release the long-click, the onClick message appears. The onLongClick message does not stay on the screen. Why is this?

4. Well, we forgot to change the default onLongClick() code, which returns false. This tells Android that nothing has been handled in that code block, so we are happy for Android to pass the event on to any other handlers that might be interested. But we don't want this to happen in our example. Instead, we need to return true when we handle the event, as follows (see Figure 9-13):

```java
public boolean onLongClick(View arg0) {
    TextView text = (TextView)findViewById(R.id.textmessage);
    text.setText("BUTTON HAS BEEN HELD. onLongClick EVENT PROCESSED.");
    return true;
}
```

Figure 9-13. *Returning a true flag from our EventHandling Project's onLongClick() method*

This tells Android that we have handled the event successfully, and sets the text that we wanted.

Some of the event handlers return a Boolean (true or false value) to tell the calling code whether your listener has handled the code (or *consumed* the event, as the programming terminology goes). So return true if you have handled the event (in our case, setText() has been done) and processing should stop here. Return false if you have not handled it, or if you want the event to "bubble up" — that is, to be passed on (up) to other event handlers, even if it has been handled.

Now compile and run our OnLongClick app version. It works perfectly. A click displays the proper message and stays on the screen, and a long-click displays the proper message that stays on the screen until a short-click changes it back again.

Now let's add an onKeyListener and trap some keystroke events.

Key Event Listeners: onKeyUp and onKeyDown

Events that will become familiar to you in Android app programming are onKey, or onKeyUp (key released) and onKeyDown (key pressed down). Key is short for keyboard, but more and more Android devices do not feature a traditional computer keyboard (unless you have a Bluetooth external keyboard as an accessory) but some still do have smaller sets of keys (a mini keyboard) or in the case of GoogleTV possibly some sort of remote control that has keys. Some iTVs may even come with a wireless keyboard, so this is an important event to handle for many Android applications.

These onKey() events are commonly used for games and to implement keyboard or keypad shortcuts in your application, much like the F5 shortcut that we use in Eclipse for **Refresh** or the F3 shortcut we use for **Open**.

To show how easy the keyboard event listeners are to implement, we are going to add a couple more lines (OK, a dozen more) to our Java code to listen for a key event (the center keypad hardware key, found on every Android Device).

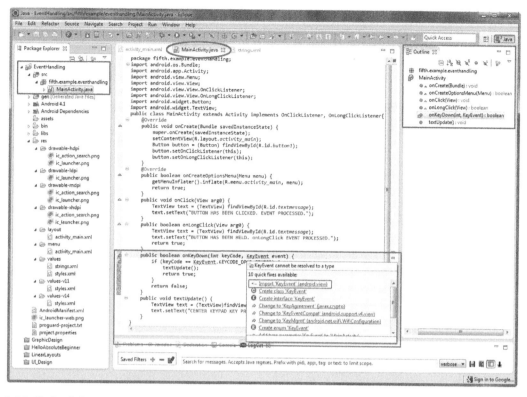

Figure 9-14. Having Eclipse Add our KeyEvent import statement for us

Adding the Java for Keyboard Events

In our *MainActivity.java* file, we want to add one simple import statement and two basic blocks of code that will allow us to handle keyboard events via the OnKeyDown handler. We will only add about a dozen lines of code to be able to handle key events in our current EventHandling Project. We are using one EventHandling project for all our code in this chapter to show how all the different types of Android Event Handling can coexist peacefully in a single application and so that you get experience writing more complex apps with more than one hundred lines of code.

Here is the code that we will need to add to the bottom of our current EventHandling Project's Java code (see Figure 9-15):

```java
public boolean onKeyDown(int keyCode, KeyEvent event) {
        if (keyCode == KeyEvent.KEYCODE_DPAD_CENTER) {
                textUpdate();
                return true;
        }
            return false;
        }
```

```java
    public void textUpdate() {
            TextView text = (TextView)findViewById(R.id.textmessage);
            text.setText("CENTER KEYPAD KEY PRESSED");
    }
}
```

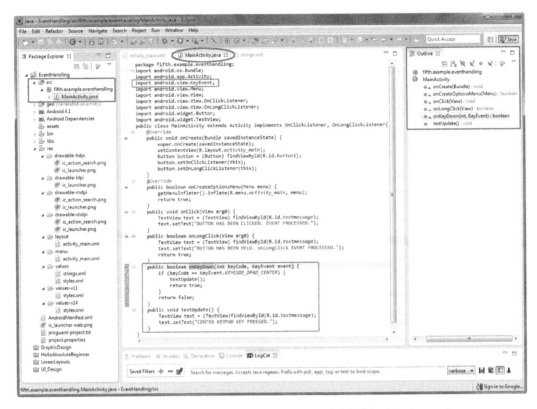

Figure 9-15. Adding an onKeyDown listener and textUpdate() method to our MainActivity class Java code

We need to import android.view.KeyEvent for the onKeyDown handler (first code block) or we can let Eclipse do it for us while we are writing the onKeyDown handler method (this is shown in Figure 9-14). We don't need to import android.widget.TextView for the textUpdate() method that we write in our second code block, because we are already using a TextView widget in our current application, and will use that TextView to display the text that our onKeyDown() handler sets.

We will leave the class declaration and the onCreate() and onClick event handling blocks of code exactly as they are.

The first block of code we write is the onKeyDown handler, which is a public method that returns a Boolean value that tells us if the event was handled (true), or not handled and needs to be passed along (false). The onKeyDown() method takes two parameters: the keyCode (the key that was pressed) and details of the event (event).

Our program logic inside the onKeyDown handler first looks at the keyCode passed into the handler. If it is equal to the center keypad hardware keyCode, signified by the KEYCODE_DPAD_CENTER constant, it runs the textUpdate() method, and then returns true to signify that we handled the event. Otherwise, onKeyDown() returns false to signify that an event was not handled.

This is the first time we have written our own method: the textUpdate() method that is called from inside onKeyDown(). This demonstrates some standard Java programming. The two lines of code that are in the textUpdate() routine could have been written where the textUpdate(); line of code is inside the onKeyDown() handler, like this:

```java
public boolean onKeyDown(int keyCode, KeyEvent event) {
        if (keyCode == KeyEvent.KEYCODE_DPAD_CENTER) {
                        TextView text = (TextView)findViewById(R.id.textmessage);
                        text.setText("CENTER KEYPAD KEY PRESSED");
                        return true;
        }
            return false;
        }
```

In actual programming practice the textUpdate() method can (and will) contain all of the various things that you want to do when someone clicks the center keypad hardware key. You can use this method to contain all of your code statements, rather than putting them all inside the onKeyDown handler, where they could be in among actions for other keys. Doing it this way simply makes things more organized and modular, and really comes in very handy when you get into more complex code constructs, so we are teaching you to write your own method (and call it) here for this reason.

Finally, you might be wondering why there is an onKeyUp and onKeyDown, rather than just one onKey listener. As you might imagine, onKeyDown is sent when the key is pressed down, and onKeyUp is sent when the key is released. The reason both are supported is because some applications need to know when a given key is being held down (like the repeating characters feature in a word processor) and for how long, thus in that application the code would look for both the onKeyDown (repeat these functions while onKeyDown) and onKeyUp (stop doing the functions now) events, and handle them with different code.

Now let's compile and run the application.

You'll see a text field that says "NO EVENTS RECEIVED YET" that changes after you click down the center keypad hardware key in the emulator (shown on the right in blue in Figure 9-16).

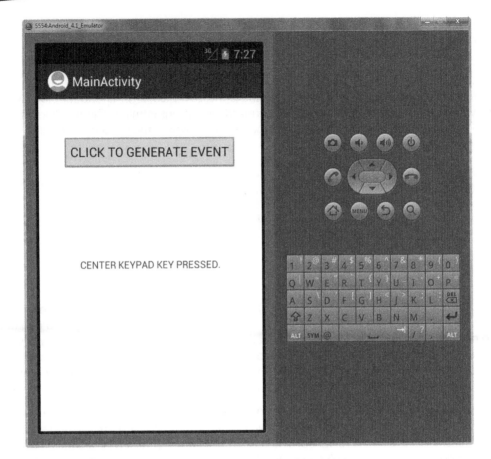

Figure 9-16. Pressing center keypad Button in 4.1 Emulator to send onKeyDown event

Tip   If you want to detect a range of keystrokes and send them to different custom methods, a good programming construct to use is the switch construct, which allows you to outline different cases from which to select. We used switch in Chapter 7's examples.

Context Menus in Android: onCreateContextMenu

The concept of the context menu is a very clever one. Unfortunately, it is often underutilized in PC, tablet, iTV, e-reader, and smartphone applications. Fortunately, Android provides us all the prebuilt classes we need, as well as a special event, to make implementing context-sensitive menus in our apps as easy as possible to code. Why does Android do this for us? It is because Google has a vested interest in making their Android OS and apps as easy to use and as standardized as possible.

A context menu should provide quick and easy access to all application functions related to a given UI object. For instance, when I right-click here in my word processor, I get a context-sensitive menu with options for cut, copy, paste, font, paragraph, bullets, numbering, styles, hyperlinks, lookup, synonyms, and translate.

The context menu in Android is always accessed by the LongClick event (covered earlier in the chapter), just as on a PC it is always accessed via a right-click of the mouse.

To demonstrate, we will add context menus to this chapter's example project. We'll add two classes, along with two custom methods, to implement our context menus. We'll take a look at the Android Toast widget, which is very handy to use to blast quick little messages to the user. This way, you don't need to use a full-blown dialog implementation, as we learned about in Chapter 7, and in this way we can learn about a different and new widget at the same time.

Adding the XML for Context Menus

First, let's add a second Button tag to our *activity_main.xml* RelativeLayout so that we have a UI element (button) to use to access our Context Menu.

1. Click the *activity_main.xml* file in the /res/layout/ folder and hit the F3 key to open it in the Eclipse central editing pane, and then click the Graphical Layout Editor tab at the bottom of that pane. Now drag a Button View out onto to the pane, and center it under the TextView, exactly as we did in Figure 9-5 earlier in the chapter, and with exactly the same parameters.

2. Once the button appears under your text, switch back into XML editing mode via the *activity_main.xml* tab at the bottom of the pane. Now we'll edit our Button tag attributes. The first one is android:text. Let's add a context_button_ caption name and a "Long-Click for Context Menu" value to a <string> tag in our /res/values folder *strings.xml* file and reference it with the Button tag parameter android:text="@string/context_button_caption" and we'll use the GLE generated Button object ID of button2 because it's our second button.

3. Let's also center our button using the android:layout_centerHorizontal = "true" attribute, as we have done previously. GLE can also do this for us via tool-tip feedback.

4. Make sure that the RelativeLayout positioning tag android:layout_below references the textmessage object.

5. Finally, make sure that the android:layout_marginTop is set to the same 50dp that the button1 object uses, so we keep our spacing even and professional looking.

Here is what your XML tags should look like (see Figure 9-17):

```
<RelativeLayout
xmlns:android="http://schemas.android.com/apk/res/android"
xmlns:tools="http://schemas.android.com/tools"
android:layout_width="match_parent"
android:layout_height="match_parent">
        <Button
            android:id="@+id/button1"
            android:text="@string/button_caption"
            android:layout_width="wrap_content"
```

```
        android:layout_height="wrap_content"
        android:layout_alignParentTop="true"
        android:layout_centerHorizontal="true"
        android:layout_marginTop="50dp"
        android:id="@+id/contextButton" />

    <TextView
        android:id="@+id/textmessage"
        android:layout_width="wrap_content"
        android:layout_height="wrap_content"
        android:layout_centerHorizontaltrue"
        android:layout_centerVertical="true"
        android:text="@string/text_message"
        tools:context=".MainActivity" />

    <Button
        android:id="@+id/button2"
        android:layout_width="wrap_content"
        android:layout_height="wrap_content"
        android:layout_below="@+id/textmessage"
        android:layout_centerHorizontal="true"
        android:layout_marginTop="50dp"
        android:text="@string/context_button_caption" />

</RelativeLayout>
```

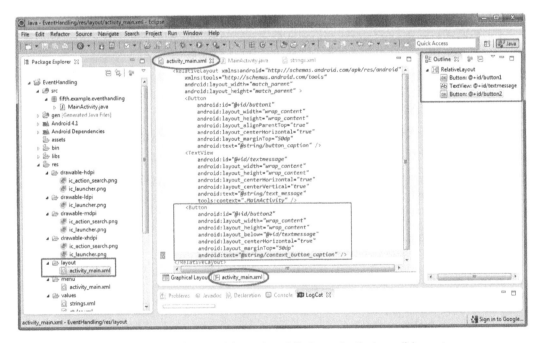

Figure 9-17. Adding a second Button object in our activity_main.xml file to receive the long-click event

We will reference the `textmessage` and `button2` inside our Java code.

Adding the Java for Context Menus

The main two Java methods that we override are onCreateContextMenu() and onContextItemSelected(), which replace Android's default methods of the same name. The use of the super object in the first one allows us to reference a method in the parent class that we are overriding. Note that overriding does not replace a class; it just allows us to customize it, leaving the original class that was extended intact and usable. This also leaves us a lot less code to write, as none of the code written in (for) the superclass is revisited.

Now let's add the code for our onContextMenu event handling in *MainActivity.java*. We'll add the new code in with the previous code that we wrote, right before the onKey() section we added to handle onKeyDown events.

First, we need to use an import statement to import the Java classes that we are going to reference in the code we are about to write, or we can just write the code into Eclipse and let Eclipse add the import statements. Three of the six relevant import statements for this code are related to our UI elements (android.view.View, android.widget.Button, and android.widget.Toast), and the other three are related to our implementation of our LongClick context menu. Some of the import statements relating to what we are going to do with Context Menus are already in our code so far. The four that will need to be added (or will be added by Eclipse, if you forget to add them) are:

```
import android.view.ContextMenu;
import android.view.ContextMenu.ContextMenuInfo;
import android.view.MenuItem;
import android.widget.Toast;
```

ContextMenu contains the methods that are related to the top level of the menu, such as what it is called, how it looks, and so forth. ContextMenuInfo relates to the information about any one given ContextMenu, which is really a collection of options. Within that container or level, we have the MenuItems, which are their own level of objects. Each MenuItem can have a name and styling, and can call methods once it is selected.

Now, let's see how Android attaches our UI element to a ContextMenu.

First, we need to add two key lines of code to our onCreate() method for our activity. The first declares and establishes a Button object, which we call Button2 and find by its button2 ID from the *activity_main.xml* file. The next line of code wires our newly created Button2 Button object to the ContextMenu system in Android.

```
    public void onCreate(Bundle savedInstanceState) {
        super.onCreate(savedInstanceState);
        setContentView(R.layout.activity_main);
        Button Button2 = (Button) findViewById(R.id.button2);
        registerForContextMenu(Button2);
    }
```

Tip   When I first started working with Android, I wondered which class contained the `registerForContextMenu()` method. To again demonstrate how to use Eclipse as a learning tool, I'll tell you how to answer a question like that. Place your cursor over the method you are interested in and a box full of information about the method in question will pop up in Eclipse including the class that contains the method. In Eclipse you will find that mouse-over and right-click are very helpful in researching what is going on, especially in relation to error flags and warning icons (left-click on these as well to reveal potential solutions).

Now let's get into our custom logic for creating our `ContextMenu` and its content. The first of the two menu methods is `onCreateContextMenu()`, which takes three objects as parameters:

- The `ContextMenu` object named `menu`

- The `View` object (UI widget) that called it

- The `ContextMenuInfo` object named `menuInfo`, which contains information about the menu configuration

The first line of code inside this code block simply passes our three parameters up to the parent class, which is referenced via the `super` keyword. The next three lines of code call methods against (or invoke methods on) the `menu` object, which is of type `ContextMenu`. This code is configuring our top-level `ContextMenu` object by giving it a title using `menu.setHeaderTitle()` and adding two menu items via the two `menu.add()` methods.

```
public void onCreateContextMenu(ContextMenu menu, View view,
                                ContextMenuInfo menuInfo) {
    super.onCreateContextMenu(menu, view,  menuInfo);
    menu.setHeaderTitle("Android Context Menu");
    menu.add(0, view.getId(), 0, "Invoke Context Function 1");
    menu.add(0, view.getId(), 0, "Invoke Context Function 2");
}
```

Shown in Figure 9-18 is the screenshot of Eclipse after adding the code, and the screenshot shows how Eclipse flags and then suggests and even adds our import statements for the ContextMenu and ContextMenuInfo classes. You should be getting used to this work process by now!

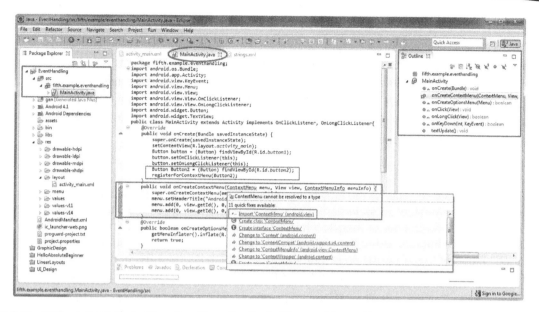

Figure 9-18. *Adding onCreateContextMenu() and importing ContextMenu and ContextMenuInfo classes via mouse-over*

The second context menu method is `onContextItemSelected()`, which is passed a single parameter of type `MenuItem` named `item`. Note that this method has a Boolean return type, which means we need to return a `true` (handled) or `false` (not done yet) reply.

To start with, we have an `if-then-else` loop that compares the title of each `MenuItem` to a string. If the title matches, it runs the appropriate `contextFunction1` or `contextFunction2` (which we will code next).

```
public boolean onContextItemSelected(MenuItem item) {
    if(item.getTitle().equals("Invoke Context Function 1")) {
        contextFunction1(item.getItemId());
    }
    else if(item.getTitle().equals("Invoke Context Function 2"))  {
        contextFunction2(item.getItemId());
    }
    else {
        return false;
    }
    return true;
}
```

Recall that the first code after the `if` in parentheses is the condition. It reads, "If the title that we are getting from the `item` object is equal to the text string `'Invoke Context Function 1'`, then perform the statements in the curly braces that follow this conditional statement." Note that this could also be written as: if(item.getTitle()=="Invoke Content Function 1"); however using the .equals() method is considered a better programming practice when comparing String values.

Note   Remember that == (two equal signs) means is equal to, and compares two integer or string values to each other, and = (one equal sign) means to set the value of a variable or constant to another value, so that is setting a value rather than simply comparing two values to see if they are the same or if they are different. What we are using here for ContextMenu is the .equals() method, which is considered "Best Practices" for comparing String values, and can also be chained, so we are using it here to show you both Java comparison operation solutions in a single chapter!

If this does not equate to true for the first if condition, then the next else block is encountered, along with a second (nested) if statement that is almost completely identical to the first, except that it is looking for the 2 option rather than 1. If this also is not satisfied or matching, the second else returns a false from the method to the calling code, telling it, "Sorry, no menu options here that match that!" If one of the if condition is met, the true, which is under the conditional code block is returned because we have not jumped out of the method by returning a value yet.

Type this code into Eclipse and when Eclipse flags the MenuItem class as needed to be imported, use the usual work process shown in Figure 9-19 to add the import statement, and then we'll be ready to write our own custom methods that are called in the onContextMenuItemSelected() method that we just wrote.

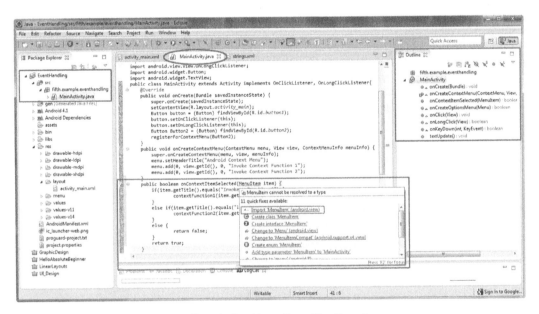

Figure 9-19. Adding an onContextItemSelected() method and importing a MenuItem class

Now we need to write our own methods for the two options, which we'll call `contextFunction1()` and `contextFunction2()`. We declare these methods as `public` and as `void`, as they do not return any values. They simply carry out a task with no result to report back. We name the first method `contextFunction1()` and define one integer data parameter to pass, in this case an ID.

```
public void contextFunction1(int id){
```

Inside this method, we make a call to the `Toast` widget, which allows us to send brief messages to our end users during their use of the application. To do this, we use the `makeText()` method and access it directly from the `Toast` class via the following one (admittedly dense) line of code:

```
Toast.makeText(this, "function 1 invoked!", Toast.LENGTH_SHORT).show();
```

This is another one of those "chaining" lines of code we talked about earlier in the book that does several things within a single code construct. Once you get really good at programming, this type of coding becomes a really great way to write more "compact" or dense code.

So we call the `.makeText()` method and pass it three parameters:

- The activity that is running the `Toast` alert, in this case the one it's contained in (this)

- What the message should be, contained between quotes

- How long (in this case, a short length of time) to show the `Toast` pop-up

After the `Toast.makeText()`, another `.show()` is appended. This displays (shows onscreen) the message that we just specified with `makeText()`. One line of code does everything. And the best part is, you can now use this same line of code to pop up little messages to your users whenever you want to do so. Grab that glass of wine on your left, and let's make a Toast to Toast!

Note that the context menu code that we learned about earlier has *nothing* to do with this one-line `Toast` construct, which will send a message to your screen anyplace you put it in your code. Some programmers use this for debugging, with messages like, "Setting X variable to 7 at (System Time)" or similar, so that you can see on the screen a visual progress of your app running through its code logic.

After our `contextFunction2` code construct, which is very similar to `contextFunction1`, we have our key event handlers from the previous section working at the same time as our `ContextMenu`. Once you write these two methods into Eclipse, be sure to note the flags that tell you that you need an import statement to use the Toast class, and use the usual work process shown in Figure 9-20 to have Eclipse insert the import statements needed for you.

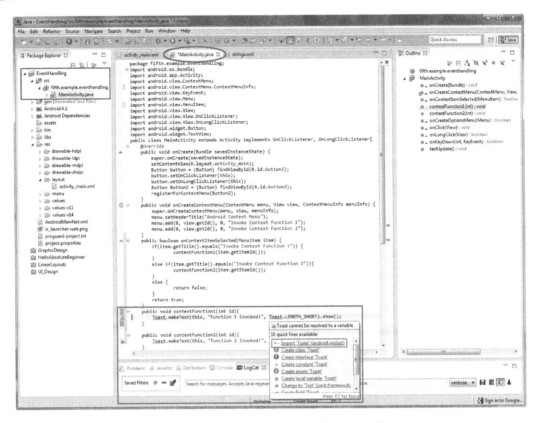

Figure 9-20. *Adding our two custom methods and having Eclipse import the Toast class for us*

The entire body of code in *MainActivity.java* should now look like the following (see Figure 9-21).

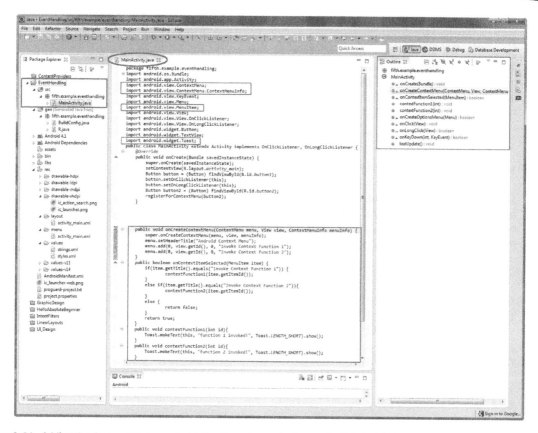

Figure 9-21. *Adding the Java methods needed to implement a context menu in MainActivity.java*

```java
package fifth.example.eventhandling;

import android.os.Bundle;
import android.app.Activity;
import android.view.ContextMenu;
import android.view.ContextMenu.ContextMenuInfo;
import android.view.KeyEvent;
import android.view.Menu;
import android.view.MenuItem;
import android.view.View;
import android.view.View.OnClickListener;
import android. view.View.OnLongClickListener;
import android.widget.Button;
import android.widget.TextView;

import android.widget.Toast;

public class MainActivity extends Activity Implements OnClickListener, OnLongClickListener {

    @Override
    public void onCreate(Bundle savedInstanceState) {
```

```
            super.onCreate(savedInstanceState);
            setContentView(R.layout.activity_main);
            Button button = (Button) findViewById(R.id.button1);
            button.setOnClickListener(this);
            button.setOnLongClickListener(this);
            Button button2 = (Button) findViewById(R.id.button2);
            registerForContextMenu(button2);
    }


    public void onCreateContextMenu(ContextMenu menu, View view,
                                    ContextMenuInfo menuInfo) {
        super.onCreateContextMenu(menu, view, menuInfo);
        menu.setHeaderTitle("Android Context Menu");
        menu.add(0, view.getId(), 0, "Invoke Context Function 1");
        menu.add(0, view.getId(), 0, "Invoke Context Function 2");
    }


    public boolean onContextItemSelected(MenuItem item) {
        if(item.getTitle().equals("Invoke Context Function 1")) {
                contextFunction1(item.getItemId());
        }
        else if(item.getTitle().equals("Invoke Context Function 2")){
                contextFunction2(item.getItemId());
        }
        else {
                return false;
        }
        return true;
    }

    public void contextFunction1(int id){
        Toast.makeText(this, "function 1 invoked!", Toast.LENGTH_SHORT).show();
    }

    public void contextFunction2(int id){
        Toast.makeText(this, "function 2 invoked!", Toast.LENGTH_SHORT).show();
    }
    public boolean onCreateOptionsMenu (Menu menu) {...}
    public void onClick (View arg0) {...}
    public boolean onLongClick (View arg0) {...}
    public boolean onKeyDown(int keyCode, KeyEvent event) {...}
    public void textUpdate() {...}
}
```

Now let's run our code with **Run As ➤ Android Application** and see how it all works together. A long-click on the button brings up the context menu. A touch or click on one of the buttons highlights it, as shown in Figure 9-22. Once it is clicked, a Toast menu tells us our method has been run. Also notice that our previous section code for onKeyDown() as well as for both onClick() and for onLongClick() all still works perfectly together.

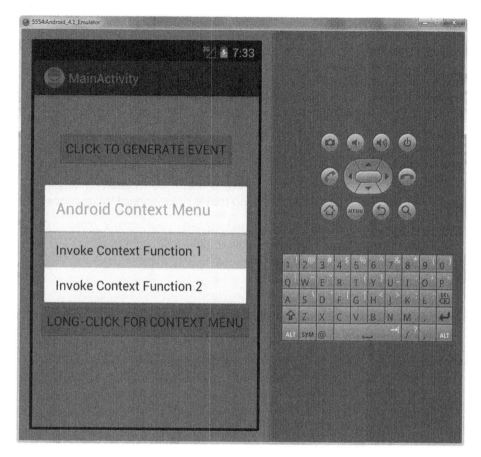

Figure 9-22. Running our application in the Android 4.1 emulator after adding a context menu

Controlling the Focus in Android

One of the most challenging aspects of UI design and programming is tracking and controlling the *focus* of your application. The focus is where the UI is paying attention, or focusing its attention currently, and this equates to representing which UI element the user is presently dealing with (or is using).

The tough part about focus is that you can't always see it visually. Even as an end user, it is sometimes difficult to see where the focus is currently at within an application. We have all experienced this with our computers at one time or another, most commonly while we are filling out forms, where the active text entry cursor for a field moves or "jumps" from one field to another as the form is filled out, or as the Tab key is used to jump (or progress) the input focus from one field to the next field.

It is even more difficult to control, track, and implement focus from a programming standpoint. Note that focus is typically not something that you need to specifically worry about (Android handles it automatically), unless it is somehow tripping up your application's user experience, or unless you want to implement finer or tighter control over how your users interface with your UI Design or Application's UX (user experience).

Android has an internal algorithm that decides how it hops from one UI element (View or Widget) to another, based on which View is closest to the previous View, but you can also control how the focus moves from one UI element widget to the next with your own custom code. Here we will go over the basics, to get you started and familiar with the concepts, in case you need to intervene with your own XML or Java code to manually control the focus inside of your application.

First, we will look at how to control focus via XML, as that is easier to understand and implement than the Java coding route. Later, we will go over which Java methods will allow you to take focus or otherwise control the focus, based on what the user is doing in the application.

Adding the XML for Focus Control

To start, let's add a couple more buttons to the bottom of the UI we've been developing in this chapter, and then we'll set the focus to do something that is not standard focus procedure in Android.

The easiest way to do this is to copy our existing button2 tag in our *activity_main.xml* file and paste it in twice right more underneath our existing button2 tag markup (see Figure 9-23). You can also use the Eclipse Graphical Layout Editor and drag a couple more button elements out onto the UI layout screen, if you'd rather do it that way.

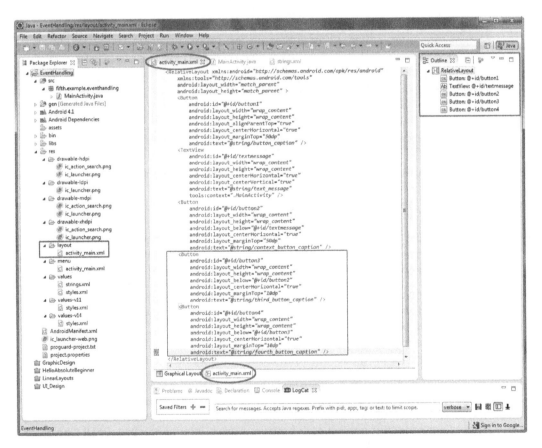

Figure 9-23. Adding a third and fourth UI button to the /res/layout/activity_main.xml file

```xml
<RelativeLayout
xmlns:android="http://schemas.android.com/apk/res/android"
xmlns:tools="http://schemas.android.com/tools"
android:layout_width="match_parent"
android:layout_height="match_parent">

        <Button
            android:id="@+id/button1"
            android:text="@string/button_caption"
            android:layout_width="wrap_content"
            android:layout_height="wrap_content"
            android:layout_alignParentTop="true"
            android:layout_centerHorizontal="true"
            android:layout_marginTop="50dp"
            android:id="@+id/contextButton" />

        <TextView
            android:id="@+id/textmessage"
            android:layout_width="wrap_content"
            android:layout_height="wrap_content"
            android:layout_centerHorizontaltrue"
            android:layout_centerVertical="true"
            android:text="@string/text_message"
            tools:context=".MainActivity" />

        <Button
            android:id="@+id/button2"
            android:layout_width="wrap_content"
            android:layout_height="wrap_content"
            android:layout_below="@+id/textmessage"
            android:layout_centerHorizontal="true"
            android:layout_marginTop="50dp"
            android:text="@string/context_button_caption" />

        <Button
            android:id="@+id/button3"
            android:layout_width="wrap_content"
            android:layout_height="wrap_content"
            android:layout_below="@+id/button2"
            android:layout_centerHorizontal="true"
            android:layout_marginTop="10dp"
            android:text="@string/third_button_caption" />

        <Button
            android:id="@+id/button4"
            android:layout_width="wrap_content"
            android:layout_height="wrap_content"
            android:layout_below="@+id/button3"
            android:layout_centerHorizontal="true"
            android:layout_marginTop="10dp"
            android:text="@string/fourth_button_caption" />

</RelativeLayout>
```

To make our `Button` tags unique, we also need to rename their IDs to `button3` and `button4`, which if you use the Graphical Layout Editor will be done for you automatically, as will the centering and margin spacing of 10dp parameters. This way, we can access the buttons in our Java code and also change their display text to reflect that they are the third and fourth buttons, respectively. Make sure to add their names and values to the /res/values/strings.xml file via the <string> tag, as we did in the previous sections, and as is shown in Figure 9-27 later on in this exercise.

We will leave all of the other `Button` tag attributes for scaling and centering the same, and use a android:layout_marginTop value of 10dp to keep the bottom three buttons closer together.

Now we will add our `android:nextFocus` attributes, so that we will have control over which UI elements our focus jumps to and from when the user navigates the UI with the up and down arrow keys on the front of the smartphone, iTV remote, e-reader or tablet.

For the existing `button1` tag attributes, we want to add an `android:nextFocusUp` attribute and point it to the fourth button. Then, if users hit the up arrow on their Android smartphone or tablet when they are on the first button, it will cycle back down to the last button, creating a seamless loop through the button stack.

Because the ID of the fourth button is `button4`, this tag attribute will read as follows:

```
android:nextFocusUp="@+id/button4"
```

This is done to reference the fourth button tag we have defined in our XML markup here as the destination UI element for the up arrow focus to go to if users hit the up navigation arrow when they are on (have focus on) the first UI button (`button1` from our first onClick and onLongClick examples).

To control advancement of focus from the `button1` to the `button2` button, we add this:

```
android:nextFocusDown="@+id/button2"
```

Now we have defined all of the focus movements that can happen for the first (top) Button UI element `button1`, and we are ready to define the focus movements for the next three user interface buttons.

This will be a very similar process. In fact, you can simply cut and paste the two lines of code that you wrote for the first Button (`button1`) tag and change the ID attributes after you paste them into the next three Button element tags for button2, button3, and button4.

For the second Button tag, we will add in another two `android:nextFocus` attributes. This time, these point to the buttons immediately above and below the second and third button, so the middle two buttons are the easiest to code. Their code will look like the following:

```
android:nextFocusUp="@+id/button1"
android:nextFocusDown="@+id/button3"

android:nextFocusUp="@+id/button2"
android:nextFocusDown="@+id/button4"
```

For the fourth Button tag, we will add in another two `android:nextFocus` attributes, which finally point to the buttons immediately above and back up to the top button in our loop of buttons, as follows:

```
android:nextFocusUp="@+id/button3"
android:nextFocusDown="@+id/button1"
```

The first attribute is pretty straightforward, as the button3 button is above our fourth button. For the nextFocusDown attribute because there is no button underneath the fourth button, we actually want the focus to wrap, or loop back, to our first button1 button, so that is the ID we use in the android:nextFocusDown attribute that we add to the final Button tag.

Note There are nextFocusLeft and nextFocusRight attributes available (one for each arrow key) if you are using a horizontal LinearLayout tag attribute, for instance, or if you have things arranged from side to side within a RelativeLayout container.

Here are the four blocks of nextFocus attributes that we added to our four buttons (we'll omit the dozens of other parameters, so as to show only the focus-related coding) so that you can check your work (also see Figure 9-24 for the complete XML code):

```
<Button
        android:id="@+id/button1"
        android:nextFocusUp="@+id/button4"
        android:nextFocusDown="@+id/button2"
        (other button parameters) />

<Button
        android:id="@+id/button2"
        android:nextFocusUp="@+id/button1"
        android:nextFocusDown="@+id/button3"
        (other button parameters) />

<Button
        android:id="@+id/button3"
        android:nextFocusUp="@+id/button2"
        android:nextFocusDown="@+id/button4"
        (other button parameters) />

<Button
        android:id="@+id/button4"
        android:nextFocusUp="@+id/button3"
        android:nextFocusDown="@+id/button1"
        (other button parameters) />
```

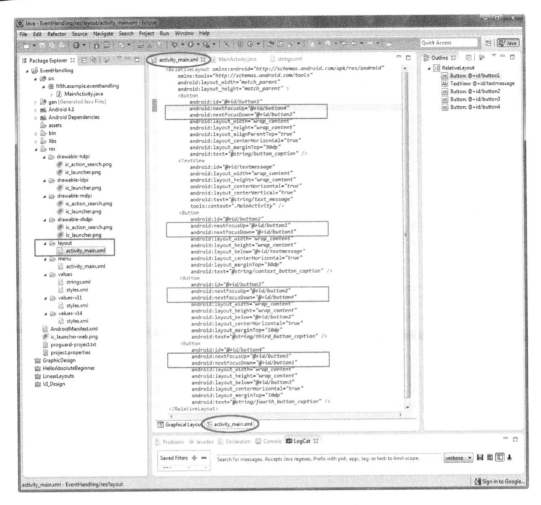

Figure 9-24. Controlling the focus via XML markup in /res/layout/activity_main.xml

Adding the Java for Focus Control

Now let's declare the two new buttons we defined in our *activity_main.xml* markup in our Java code, and point them toward our ContextMenu code that we wrote in the previous section, so that they actually do something useful, and bring up a Context Menu when we long-click on them.

Here are the four new lines of code that we need to write to support these new buttons (see Figure 9-25), which go in the end part of our onCreate() method as follows:

```java
public void onCreate(Bundle savedInstanceState) {
    super.onCreate(savedInstanceState);
    setContentView(R.layout.activity_main);
    Button button = (Button) findViewById(R.id.button1);
    button.setOnClickListener(this);
    button.setOnLongClickListener(this);
    Button Button2 = (Button) findViewById(R.id.button2);
```

```
registerForContextMenu(Button2);
Button Button3 = (Button) findViewById(R.id.button3);
registerForContextMenu(Button3);
Button Button4 = (Button) findViewById(R.id.button4);
registerForContextMenu(Button4);
}
```

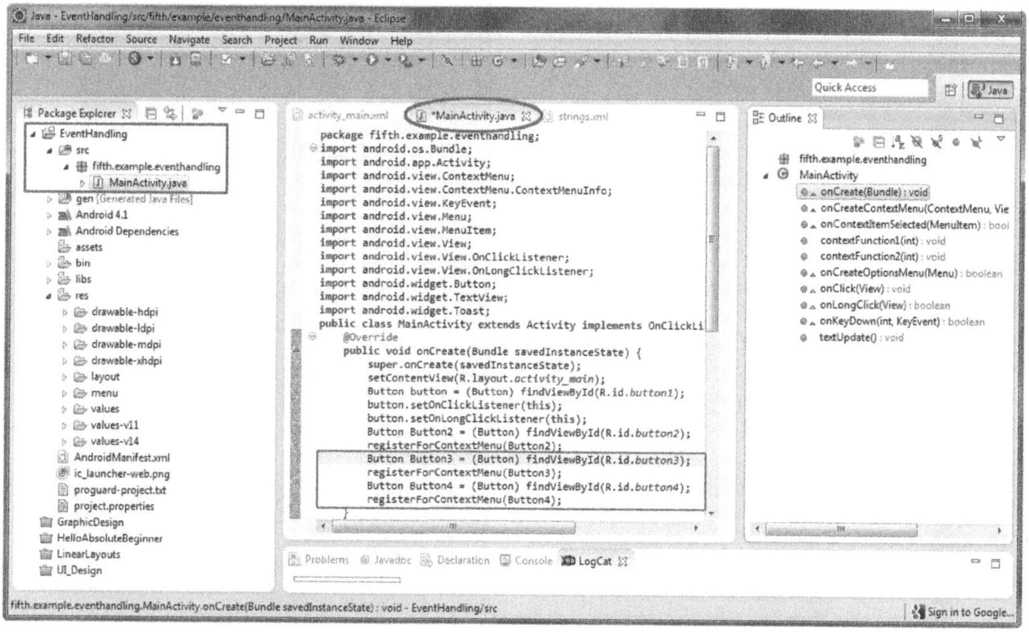

Figure 9-25. Registering our bottom two buttons for the context menu in MainActivity.java in Eclipse

To implement this in the quickest fashion, select the two lines of code that define and point our button2 object to the registerForContextMenu() method, and paste them twice below the original two lines of code.

Change the Button2 and button2 references to Button3 and button3 in the first two lines, and to Button4 and button4 in the last two lines. You have now declared all four buttons in Java and set them to actually do something in your code when they are either clicked or long-clicked on.

Now let's use our familiar **Run As ➤ Android Application** work process to compile and run this application, as shown in Figure 9-26. It now traps or handles onKey events, onClick events, and onLongClick events as well as handling onContextMenu events, and additionally implements control of focus among the usable UI elements, namely the four buttons.

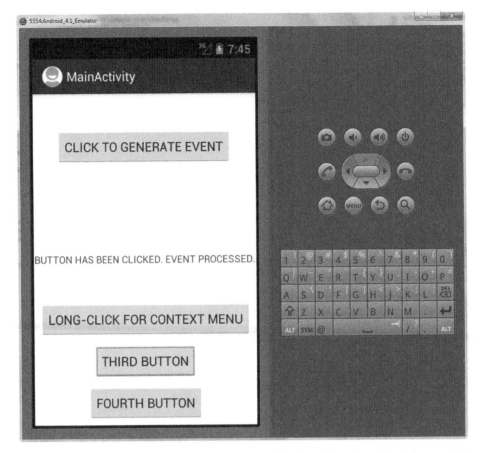

Figure 9-26. *Running our EventHandling project application in the Android 4.1 emulator after adding focus control*

You will notice now that when you compile and run this code, all three buttons at the bottom of the app will call up a ContextMenu. In your own apps, you may want all (or many) of your UI elements to bring up the same context menu selections (say the application default context menu), and this is the way that you would do that using just a very few lines of code.

If your code does not run for some reason, you can use the Eclipse **Project ➤ Clean...** option to "clean" your project. This regenerates the R.java class that lives in the /gen/ folder and that holds the generated (compiled) Java files for the application. Three key commands in Eclipse that you will use frequently are: Refresh, Validate, and Clean, usually in that order, to help Eclipse to troubleshoot code problems that you may be experiencing in the IDE.

The reason I mention this here is because when I first ran the focus code in this chapter, which I know is correct and bug-free, the activity would not run in the emulator, and I was getting an error in LogCat that said that I was "casting" a Button object into a TextView object. For this to have been true, I would have had to switch the FindById references for button1 (or button2, button3, or button4) with the FindById reference for textmessage in my Java code.

As this was not the case, I ran the Eclipse **Project ➤ Clean...** utility, which regenerated my R.java file, and fixed the problem for me. One of the tricky things about programming is that sometimes your code can be correct, and the code in the IDE or the Compiler (SDK) can have bugs in it too! Add to this the quick SDK revision cycles for Java and Android (between Version 1 and Version 2 of this book, Android went from SDK Level 3 to SDK Level 16) and programming becomes a "moving target" significantly more challenging than if it were inherently within a fixed or unchanging programming environment.

If the code still does not compile and run, you may have forgotten to add all of the string tags needed to the *res/values/strings.xml* file as shown in Figure 9-27. Also shown at the bottom of the screenshot is the successful running of the app in the emulator under the Console Tab at the bottom of the IDE.

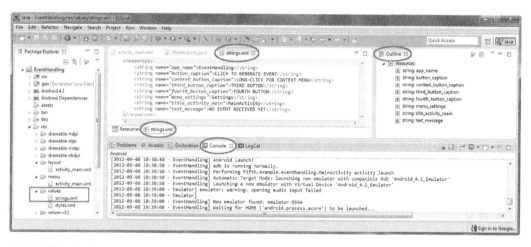

Figure 9-27. Adding the Button captions in the strings.xml file and view of the Android Console tab

It is important to test your applications vigorously, as some bugs will show up only after all of the features have been used already once or twice. Let's do that now.

To test the application, long-click on each of the buttons, and select either option. Everything should work as expected and pull up the context menu. To see the cycling focus that we have implemented, use the up or down arrow/keys in the middle of the Android smartphone or tablet (in this case, on the 4.1 emulator) to cycle the focus among the buttons (focus is shown in blue). You will notice no matter which direction (up or down arrow button) you choose, the focus cycles or loops through the buttons correctly and seamlessly.

> **Note**   Remember that Android will handle focus for you as a matter of routine. This includes jumping between UI elements on the screen and even jumping to the next logical UI element if a UI element (a View object) is hidden (or shown) or removed (or added) as a matter of the application programming logic.

Setting Focus Availability

View objects can be defined (in XML or Java) to be able to accept (or deny) focus using the isFocusable() method or the android:focusable (XML) attribute. If you define a View (UI object) to be focusable (or not focusable) in XML, and then want to change this later at runtime (while your application is running), there is also a setFocusable() method that can flip this (Boolean) switch. To switch Focus On .setFocusable(true); and Off would be .setFocusable(false); as you may have suspected. These focus methods control focus navigation via the smartphone, tablet, e-reader or iTV set navigation key hardware.

There are separate methods to control the focus in relation to the touchscreen, and these are named very similarly: isFocusableInTouchMode() and setFocusableInTouchMode(). For XML markup coding, you would use the format android:focusableInTouchMode, similar to nontouch focus.

Finally, if you simply want to ascertain if there has been a change of focus on a UI object, you can use the onFocusChanged() method. This method can be called to find out if there is a change in state from true to false, or focused to not focused, that you can use in more advanced programming endeavors that watch focus even more closely. With this method, your software can essentially watch what the user is doing with your UI and respond accordingly when the user is "on" each user interface element using onFocusChanged(true). As you can see, Android gives us a huge dose of control over our application's focus.

Summary

This chapter has covered some very important and advanced concepts in Java programming, as well as in Android app development. The topics ranged from setting up event listeners and event handlers to invoking context-sensitive menus to more ethereal topics such as controlling the focus of your UI design as the user moves through it, all of which represent important parts of your user experience design—interactivity, predictability, and responsiveness.

You now know how to handle clicks via hardware navigation keys or via the touchscreen, as well as handling long-clicks and keyboard use. We even covered more advanced features such as context menus, the Toast system widget for brief user message notifications, and controlling the focus in your XML or Java code, or via both.

You coded an app that used all the primary event handlers in Android all in one codebase (well over a hundred lines of XML and Java code was written—congratulations on coding your first major project) with no errors, warnings, or crashes. You also learned about the Eclipse **Project ➤ Clean…** utility; this can help "Clean" or regenerate generated Java files in the project's /gen/ folder as a way of "cleaning" (debugging) your code when there are no apparent logic or variable errors visible.

We covered a lot of important material in this chapter, so be sure to review it all again very soon. This chapter includes some clever and new ways to use the Eclipse IDE as well, and that is also important to master by the time you are finished with this book, so make sure to play around with the different "panes" in Eclipse such as the Properties, Overview, LogCat, and the Graphical Layout Editor. You should be exploring Eclipse (your IDE tool) as much as you are exploring the Java Classes, XML Tags, Android Libraries, and Method Functions.

Understanding Content Providers

In this chapter, we are going to take a look at how to provide content within your application. We'll cover how to share that content, and how to access, add, and display the data that represents that content.

We have gotten significantly more advanced as we have progressed from chapter to chapter, and this chapter is no different. Data access is significantly more complex than event handling and UI design. This is because it involves database design, and thus you also have to know how the database is structured (how it was originally designed) to be able to access the data correctly. Database use in Android also involves requesting security permissions for database access.

In Android, requesting permissions is done via the Android Manifest file that bootstraps every Android Application Launch, kind of like index.html does with a website. In fact, starting with this chapter, we will need to modify the application's *AndroidManifest.xml* file, so be warned that we are getting into some fairly complicated concepts and code here all the way around.

We'll begin with an overview of exactly what Android content providers are, and what they do for your Android user. After that, you will learn how to use these SQLite-based native Android OS content providers to read and write database content for your Android applications.

An Overview of Android Content Providers

Content provider is a term that is unique to Android development that means nothing more than a datastore of data values, most often found in the form of a SQLite database that is already part of the Android operating system (OS). You can also create your own content providers for your application.

An Android content provider provides you with access to sharable data structures commonly called *databases*. The basic procedure is as follows:

1. Get permission to read the database, and possibly to write to the database.

2. Query (find) the data.

3. Access (read) the data.

4. Modify (add, change (overwrite), append to, or delete) the data.

In accessing data, you might simply read the data, write to the data (i.e., change the values of the existing data); append (add) new data onto the database structure; or delete existing data, based on the type and level of security permissions that have been established in the *AndroidManifest.xml* file.

Data can be in Android internal (system) memory, in a SQLite database, or in external memory such as an SD card, or even on an external server that is remote to the Android device itself.

Databases and Database Management Systems

The usual way for content providers to provide data structures for Android applications is via a database management system (DBMS). A DBMS manages a database by providing ways for users to create databases, as well as to populate them with data via reading and writing operations.

There is a complete open source DBMS right inside the Android OS called SQLite. SQL is a relational DBMS (RDBMS). An RDBMS is based on relationships that can be drawn between data arranged in tables. Later in this chapter, you will see how to write data into these tables in the SQLite RDBMS. If you wish to research SQLite a bit more on your own, which would be a good idea if your application needs to use databases; it has its very own website located at: www.SQLite.org.

The SQL in SQLite stands for structured query language. The "Lite" or "Light" part delineates that this is a "lightweight" version of the DBMS, intended for embedded use in consumer electronics devices, and not a full blown version of SQL, as would be used on an advanced computer system such as a database server.

Later in this chapter, we will take a look briefly at how Android allows you to access the Android Contacts database data records and the data contained within their individual data fields. All you really need to know about SQLite is that it is a part of Android and that you can use it for data storage. Android takes care of the DBMS functions for you via classes that are already written for you and that do most of the work. All you have to do is learn how to use them properly, which is not a simple task, due to the database complexity (read: power) that has evolved in Android API Level 16 (also known as Android "Jelly Bean" version 4.1).

In a DBMS, the highest level of data storage is the database itself, which contains tables of data in rows and columns. Each table is two-dimensional, where a row is called a *record*. Within each record are *fields*, organized into columns, which contain the individual data items that make up the records. Fields can contain different data types, such as numbers, text, or even references to data that is stored somewhere else. However, each field must contain the same data type as the other fields in that same column (see Figure 10-1).

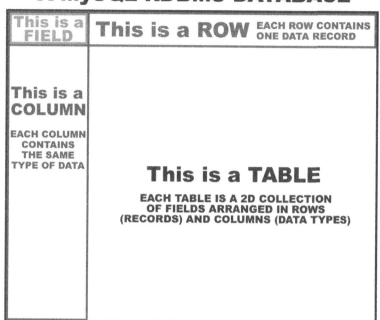

Figure 10-1. *A MySQL RDBMS database*

Note that there can be more than one table in a database (and there usually is, for both performance and for organizational reasons). As long as there is a key (a unique index) for each record in each table, information for a single data entry can span more than one table using that key, called an *ID* and designated via the constant "_ID" in Android SQLite databases. For instance, if your key or _ID value is 217, your personal information and phone information can be in two different tables stored under that same key value.

> **Caution**   After the record structure, and data fields that define this record structure, are set-up, don't change the record structure later, if you are designing your own databases. This is because the currently loaded records and fields may not fit into the new database structure definition correctly. So, it's best to ascertain and design what your database record structure will be up-front, making the DBMS design process especially critical to the success of any given project going out over time.

The content provider classes that are provided with the Android OS all use SQLite because it is compact and open source, and a part of the Android OS, so we are going to focus on those in this chapter. There is also an Android library of SQLite classes that can access SQLite directly, for more advanced use. If that is of interest, there are several books regarding using SQLite libraries inside of Android that focus only on this topic.

Android Built-In Content Providers

A significant number of SQLite-based database structures are "hard-coded" into the Android OS to handle things that users expect from their phones, iTVs, e-readers, and tablets, such as contact directories, address books, calendars, camera picture storage, digital video storage, music libraries, playlists, and so forth. The most extensive of these SQLite database structures is the Contacts database, which contains many different tables (subdatabases) for contact names, phone numbers, e-mails, preferences, social media settings, and so forth. This structure is very complex, and because this book is focused on programming for Absolute Beginners, and not database theory, we will only be working with the primary contact name database, to keep it more about Java programming and Android Content Providers, rather than about database structure and theory.

The base-level interfaces of the `android.provider` package allow us to access those data structures that define the setup and personalization of each user's Android device hardware. Obviously, the data within each of these data structures will be completely different for each user's smartphone, tablet, e-reader, or iTV set.

Contacts Database Contact Providers

Table 10-1 lists the Contacts database interfaces for Android 1.5, 1.6, and 2.0 that can be found on the Android Developer site (`http://developer.android.com/reference/android/provider/package-summary.html`).

Table 10-1. The Contacts Interfaces for Android 1.x and 2.0 Supports

Interface	Contents
`Contacts.OrganizationColumns`	Organization
`Contacts.GroupsColumns`	Groups
`Contacts.PeopleColumns`	People
`Contacts.PhonesColumns`	Phone numbers
`Contacts.PhotosColumns`	Contact photographs
`Contacts.PresenceColumns`	IM presences
`Contacts.SettingsColumns`	Phone settings
`Contacts.ContactMethodsColumns`	Contact methods
`Contacts.ExtensionsColumns`	Phone extensions

If you browse the current Android Developer documentation, you'll see that the interfaces listed in Table 10-1 are all described as "deprecated." *Deprecated* means that these classes, methods, or even database structures have been replaced by other classes, methods, or database structures in a newer version of the programming language (such as Java) or API (such as Android). The newer classes, methods, or database structures that replace the older ones are usually more robust or feature filled, or sometimes they differ only in how they are implemented, or in the case of a database, which fields of data they contain, and how those fields of data are organized.

This deprecation is exactly what has happened with the Contacts interfaces between Android versions 1.x and 2.0 (1.0, 1.1, 1.5, 1.6, and 2.0) and Android versions 2.1, 3.x, and 4.x (2.1, 2.2, 2.3, 3.0, 3.1, 3.2, 4.0, and 4.1). So, the database interfaces that work with Android 1.x and 2.0 phones are different than the ones that work on the Android 2.1 through 4.1 phones (more advanced or feature-rich database structures, in this particular case).

If you are going to support 1.5, 1.6, and 2.0 phones, you will need to use the database interfaces listed in Table 10-1. In this book, however, we have been taking the Android suggested application support default settings of API Level 8 (Android 2.2) through API Level 16 (Android 4.1) so we need to use the more advanced database structures that replaced the original database structures starting in Android API Level 7 (Android 2.1).

The good news is that deprecated does not mean disabled. It more accurately means in this case, "not suggested for general use unless you need to support pre-2.1 OS versions for your Android users." So, if you need to support Android 1.5, 1.6, and 2.0 phones, you can use the interfaces listed in Table 10-1, and they will still work on 2.1 (and 3.x and 4.x) smartphones. Note that inside of Eclipse, deprecated structures and program calls are "lined out" in the code, to show that they are deprecated, and that can be a bit unnerving, so because most devices these days are 2.3.7 through 4.1 compatible, we suggest that you take Android's "advice" and develop for API Levels 8 through 16.

You may not be able to access data from the new database fields or tables unless you add support for the new 2.1, 3.x, and 4.x DBMS structures in your code by detecting what OS the user is using, and have code sections that deal with each (1.x and 2.x vs. 3.x and 4.x) database access structure differently (using vastly different code).

> **Note**   If you want to be able to access every new feature, you can have your code detect which version of the OS the phone is using and have custom code in place that delivers the optimal functionality for each OS version, if you wish.

In the case of Android, deprecation (a common problem that developers need to get used to, hence we are covering it here, so that as an Absolute Beginner, you can learn all about it now, and not be blind-sided by this concept later) equates to different versions of the Android OS being able to do different things, and thus having different sets of functionality that can be used for each operating system level or version. With Android, this is especially prevalent, as different OS versions will feature support for different hardware features for newer phones, iTVs, e-readers, and tablets, requiring new APIs, and changing existing APIs to support the newest hardware features.

For instance, Android was initially created for smartphones. Then tablets (and e-readers) came along, and Android 3.x OS features added support for that type of consumer electronics (CE) device. Now iTVs are becoming popular, and GoogleTV (Android 4.x and Android 5.x) is adding even more features and APIs.

> **Note**   Over time, versional functionality gets more and more difficult to keep track of. Indeed, we already have sixteen (if you don't count Android 5.0 currently in beta as of the writing of this book) different OS versions (levels) that our code must work across. Keeping track of all the current programming constructs, database structures, and logic mazes is enough of a challenge for most, without another layer on top that involves remembering which constructs and interfaces work or do not work with any given OS API level version. This is one of many reasons why programmers are so very well paid.

Table 10-2 lists some of the newer versions 2.1 *through 4.1* compatible content providers for manipulating contact information. The vastly different content provider database structure differences solidified in API Level 7 and beyond may well be the primary reason that the default in the Android Application Project dialog suggests (defaults to) API Level 8 through 16 support.

Table 10-2. *Android 2.1 through 4.1 Content Providers*

Interface	Contents
ContactsContract.CommonDataKinds.CommonColumns	For subclassing databases
ContactsContract.ContactsColumns	Contact main information
ContactsContract.ContactOptionsColumns	Contact options
ContactsContract.ContactStatusColumns	Contact status
ContactsContract.PhoneLookupColumns	Phone numbers
ContactsContract.GroupsColumns	Group definitions
ContactsContract.PresenceColumns	IM presences
ContactsContract.SettingsColumns	Account settings
ContactsContract.StatusColumns	IM visibility

All of these replace the deprecated versions that are listed in Table 10-1 and are available from the same Android developer site link: (http://developer.android.com/reference/android/provider/package-summary.html).

Android MediaStore Content Providers

The other collections of content providers that you may find important for new media content within the Android OS are the MediaStore content providers. These are listed in Table 10-3.

Table 10-3. *Android MediaStore Content Providers*

Interface	Contents
MediaStore.Audio.AlbumColumns	Album information
MediaStore.Audio.ArtistColumns	Artist information
MediaStore.Audio.AudioColumns	Audio information
MediaStore.Audio.GenresColumns	Audio genre information
MediaStore.Audio.PlaylistsColumns	Audio playlist information
MediaStore.Files.FileColumns	Fields for master table for all media files
MediaStore.Images.ImageColumns	Digital images
MediaStore.Video.VideoColumns	Digital video
MediaStore.MediaColumns	Generic media store

In the rest of this chapter, we will look at how to declare content providers for use, access them, read them, and write to them. Because we are using the default OS support suggested in the New ➤ Project ➤ Android Application Project of API Level 8 (OS 2.2) through API Level 16 (OS 4.1) we will use the more modern (i.e., not deprecated) content providers in our code examples.

Defining a Content Provider

Before a content provider can be used, it must be *registered* for use by your Android application. This is done by using some XML markup in the *AndroidManifest.xml* file. The **<provider>** tag so aptly named, allows us to define which content providers we are going to access once our application is launched. Here's an example <provider> tag for the Images content provider:

```
<provider android:name="MediaStore.Images.ImageColumns" />
```

All Android content providers expose to developers a publicly accessible unique reference, or address, if you will, to each database. This address is called a URI, and the Android constant that points to the data location within the database table is always called CONTENT_URI. Providers built-in to the OS do not need a <provider> declaration (such as the examples we are using in this chapter).

A content provider that provides access to multiple tables will expose a unique URI for each table. Here are a couple examples of predetermined Android URI constants:

```
android.provider.ContactsContract.PhoneLookupColumns.CONTENT_URI
android.provider.ContactsContract.StreamItemPhotosColumns.CONTENT_URI
```

The first reads "android (the OS) dot provider (the component type) dot ContactsContract (the database) dot PhoneLookupColumns (the table) dot CONTENT_URI (the constant that points to the data location)." Yes, there is a logical method to the madness here.

> **Note**   URI objects are used for much more than just Android content providers, as you have seen in Chapter 8. All of the ones that are used to access Android content providers start with content://, just like a web address starts with http://.

Creating the Content Providers Example Project in Eclipse

Let's set up our *ContentProviders* project folder in Eclipse right now, so you can learn a little more about the Android Manifest Editor and how Eclipse can automate the Android Manifest XML coding process for us.

If you still have the *EventHandling* project folder open from the previous chapter, right-click that folder and select: Close Project.

1. Then select **File ➤ New ➤ Project** and choose **Android Application Project** to open the **New Android Application Project** series of dialogs.

2. Fill it out as follows (and shown in Figure 10-2).

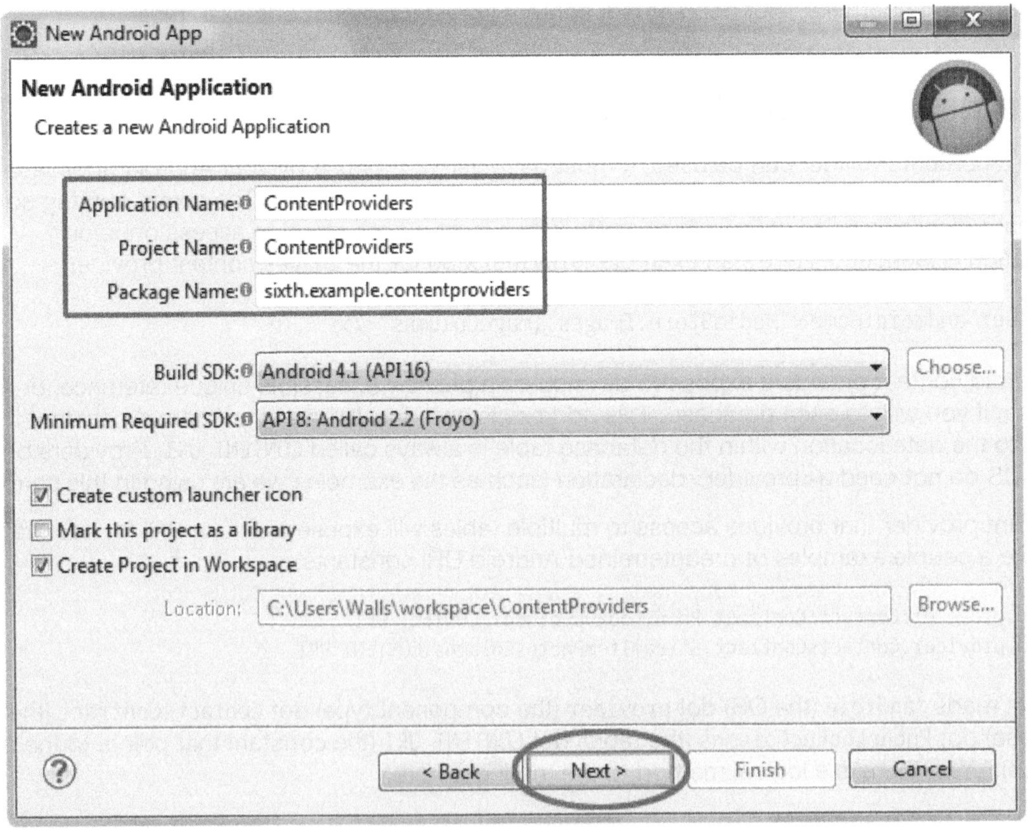

Figure 10-2. Creating the ContentProviders Android 4.1 project in Eclipse

- ▓ *Project name:* Name the project **ContentProviders**.

- ▓ *Build target:* Set this to Android 4.1.

- ▓ *Application name:* Name the application ContentProviders.

- ▓ *Package name:* Set this to sixth.example.`contentproviders`.

- ▓ *Create custom launcher icon:* Check this box and accept the defaults in the follow-on dialogs, as we have been doing in the earlier chapters.

- ▓ *Minimum SDK version* Enter 8, which matches the recommended minimum SDK version of 8, and thus supports Android 2.2 through 4.1 and thus the more modern (complex or detailed) database structures.

Defining Security Permissions

The *AndroidManifest.xml* file is usually referred to as the manifest for your application, and it tells the Android OS what you intend to do with your application. It is accessed during the initial launch of your application to set up the memory for the application, and to boot up any system resources or pointers (addresses to things that we are going to talk with, or connect to, that need to be ready in system memory) that are needed for the application to be run successfully.

In this case, that means we will be asking Android for permission to access, and possibly even change (depending on the tags we add), one of the Android databases outlined within the previous tables. The reason that we need to get permissions to use certain areas of the OS is so that Android can implement a robust level of data security within its OS infrastructure.

To define permissions, use the `<uses-permission>` tag:

```
<uses-permission android:name="android.permission.READ_CONTACTS" />
```

This tag allows the application to READ the CONTACTS database. Read-only operations are inherently safe, as we are only looking into these databases, and reading data from them. A read operation is thus termed to be a "nondestructive operation" to, or on, a database.

If we wish to change (overwrite or update, delete, or append to) data in a database, we need to use a different permission tag that tells Android that we are going to write data to an Android OS database. In this case, WRITE_CONTACTS represents the permission to change the Contacts database that we will be using. As you may have guessed, the WRITE version of the tag looks like this:

```
<uses-permission android:name="android.permission.WRITE_CONTACTS"/>
```

Permission for write operations is a bit more serious matter, due to the fact that we are now able to screw up the database, which is why the industry terms a database Write Operation to be "destructive." In this case, we are dealing with the Android device user's contacts data, and we might overwrite data that was there before our app ever accessed it.

> **Tip** There are different permission tags that control different levels of access to services or databases that are part of Android. To see a list of all of them, and to get an idea of what Android will let you access with regard to smartphone; tablet; e-reader; or iTV hardware, features, and databases, check out this link: developer.android.com/reference/android/Manifest.permission.html. You will be amazed and empowered and learn a heck of a lot about what features Android currently offers as well.

Now let's see how easy it is to use Eclipse to add the necessary permissions. Follow these steps:

1. Right-click the *AndroidManifest.xml* file in the Project Explorer navigation pane under your ContentProviders folder (near the bottom), as shown in Figure 10-3, and select **Open**, or just hit the F3 key on the keyboard once the file is selected.

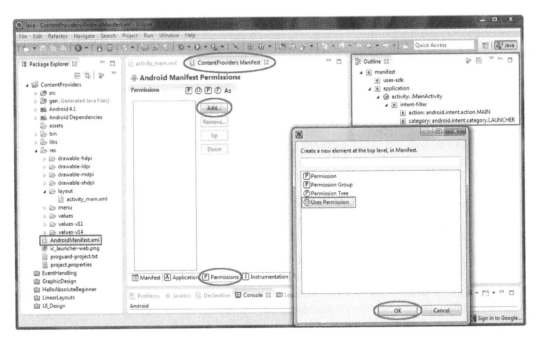

Figure 10-3. Adding a permission in the ContentProviders manifest using the Eclipse visual editor

2. In the ContentProviders Manifest tab, click the Permissions tab at the bottom of the window (see Figure 10-3).

3. Click the Add ... button in the right pane (also shown at left in Figure 10-3).

4. Select the Uses Permission entry at the bottom of the list, and then click OK (also shown on right in Figure 10-3; I get a lot of mileage out of my screenshots).

5. You'll now see the `uses-permission` tag in the Permissions pane (see Figure 10-4 just left of center). From the drop-down menu that lists permissions on the right, select `android.permission.READ_CONTACTS` (see Figure 10-4 on right side). Next click the Add ... button to add another Uses Permission Tag, which once you click on it will add the READ_CONTACTS Android Permission to the left pane list of tags.

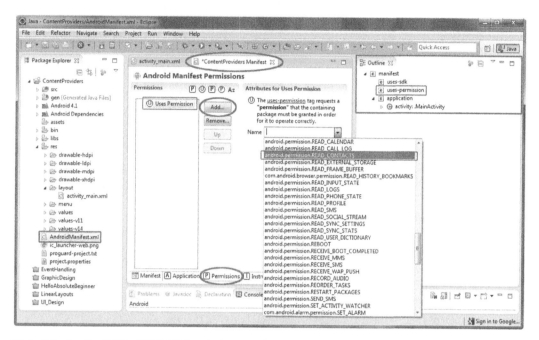

Figure 10-4. Selecting the READ_CONTACTS Permission entry from the drop-down menu

6. Selecting the Uses Permission type on the right should update the pane at the left, but currently it does not, so we go ahead and proceed to click the Add ... button to add another Uses Permission option and then the WRITE_ CONTACTS tag (as we did with the READ_CONTACTS just prior), which will force the visual manifest Permissions Editor to update the left pane with the proper `uses-permission` tag setting.

7. Once you select the WRITE_CONTACTS option from the drop-down menu, then click on the Up button to add the `android.permission.WRITE_CONTACTS` option (see Figure 10-5) to the permissions list pane. Alternately you could click the Add button and then simply not add another permission if you like.

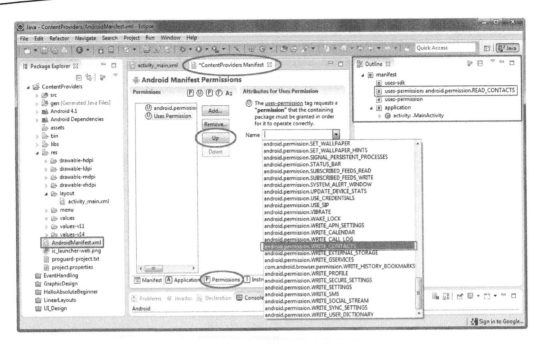

Figure 10-5. Selecting the WRITE_CONTACTS permission and UP Button to display

That's all there is to adding our read and write permissions. Figure 10-6 shows our *AndroidManifest.xml* file XML with the two permission tags at the bottom, before the closing tag:

```
<uses-permission android:name="android.permission.READ_CONTACTS" />
<uses-permission android:name="android.permission.WRITE_CONTACTS" />
```

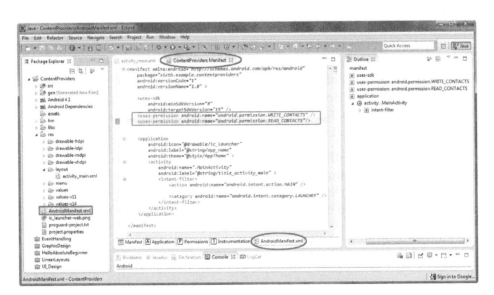

Figure 10-6. The XML output for the permission additions we made in the visual Permissions Editor

> **Tip**   Anytime you are working with the Eclipse Visual Manifest Editors, you can click the AndroidManifest.xml tab at the bottom of the window and see what this helper is doing as far as writing the actual XML markup code for your project's AndroidManifest.xml.

Now that we have permissions to read and write to the Contacts database, we can get started working with databases.

Adding Data to the Contacts Database

Android SQLite uses a table-based database model, where rows represent each data record and the columns represent the data fields, each with a predefined constant type used in Android to access the data. In this way, each piece of data in each column is the same exact type or classification, and each row is a unique collection of data of these types spanning across the row.

In this example, we are going to work with the **ContactsContract.Contacts** table. After we add some sample data to this table, it will look like Table 10-4.

Table 10-4. ContactsContract.Contacts Database Table (simplified) with Sample Data

_ID	_COUNT	DISPLAY_NAME_PRIMARY	PHONE
44	4	Bill Gates	212 555 1234
13	4	Steven Jobs	425 555 6677
53	4	Larry Ellison	201 555 4433
27	4	Mark Zuckerburg	213-555-4567

The column headers are the names that are used by Android to reference the data held in each column. These are what you use in your Java code to access each field of data within each record. For example, in some Java code we will write, we will refer to ContactsContract.Contacts.DISPLAY_NAME_PRIMARY.

The column names that are prefaced by an underscore character (_ID and _COUNT) are data fields assigned and controlled by Android; that is, you cannot WRITE to these values, you can only READ from them.

Now let's add the four data records shown in Table 10-4 into our Android emulator. (If you like, you can add more than four records.) We'll do this using the utilities that come with the Android OS. Follow these steps:

1.   Run the 4.1 emulator as usual by choosing **Run As ➤ Android Application**.

> **Note**   Another way to start the emulator is to select **Window ➤ AVD Manager** as shown in Figure 10-7. Select your 4.1 emulator and press the Start button and then the Launch button. Any contacts you enter should be saved for later, even if you close the 4.1 emulator, unless you specify otherwise within the Launch dialog settings.

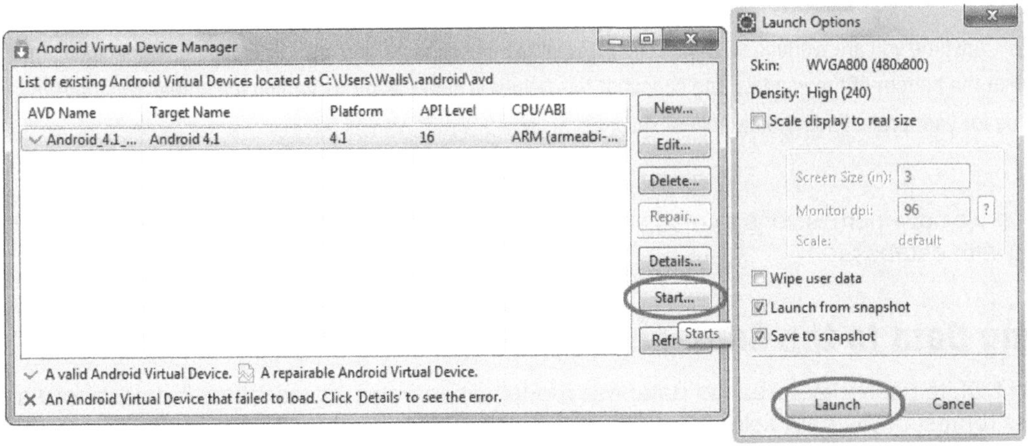

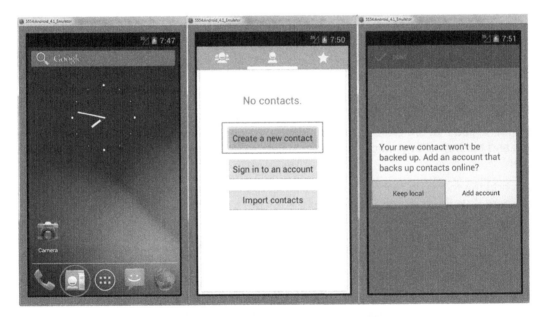

Figure 10-7. The AVD Manager Start... and Launch buttons used to start the Android 4.1 Emulator

2. Press the Home button. You will see four icons on the bottom of the home screen (shown in Figure 10-8 on the left side) with icons signifying Dialer (Phone), Messaging, Contacts, and Browser (Globe) in that order. The middle icon opens the desktop icon holder view. The icon called Contacts on the left (second one in) is a front-end to our Contacts database, and will allow us to add in the records shown in Table 10-4.

Figure 10-8. Adding new contacts to the Android Contacts database via the Contacts utility

3. Click on the Contacts icon to launch the Contacts database, which is initially empty. The screen tells us that we do not yet have any contacts. Click the "Create a new contact" button to add new contacts to the Contacts database (as shown in the middle of Figure 10-8). In the next screen select "Keep local" because we are doing this exercise in the IDE and emulator, and we do not want to influence your real Android account.

4. On the next screen, enter the first contact name (Bill Gates) using the onscreen keypad, and use the "Next" button at the bottom right when you are done, to advance to the Phone Number entry field.

5. Add a Phone Number just to practice adding contact info, and then click the "Done" button at the top right of the screen to see the record you created. Note that you can also use the Add New option to create multiple records at one time, if you like.

6. On the Data Record Display Screen, click the back arrow at the top left of the screen (shown in the middle of Figure 10-9) to see all your contact records by alphabetical order.

Figure 10-9. Adding a record to the Contact database

7. Select the Add New Record Icon (a+next to a new member head icon) to continue adding the other three records (as shown in the right side of Figure 10-9). Notice the Toast Notification telling us we are going to create a new entry! Even the Android OS uses Toast!

8. Repeat Steps 4 through 7 to add the three other names in Table 10-4, and maybe a few of own if you wish. When you are done, close the 4.1 emulator, there is no need to save or exit, as records are written to the Database as you add them, as long as you left the "Wipe User Data" option unchecked in the Emulator launch dialog shown in Figure 10-7 (if you even used that more complex emulator launch methodology).

Working with a Database

Let's get started writing our application that will access the Contacts database and Query, Add, and Display our Contact Name data. We'll do some data queries against the Contact name, query (read) the name data, add (write) some new name data, and display that name data.

Querying a Content Provider: Accessing the Content

First let's add a button to our example app's *activity_main.xml* file that will trigger our database query via an onClick event (as discussed in Chapter 9 regarding events processing).

1. Right-click the *activity_main.xml* file, which as we know is located under the */res/layout* folder. Then open the Eclipse Graphical Layout Editor and drag the TextView (HelloWorld) up to the top so that you get an AlignParentTop and centerHorizontal parameter added for you.

2. Next, add a button via drag-and-drop, as you have done in many of the previous examples. Make the button centered as well and aligned below the TextView with a 50dp marginTop parameter. Here is the code that shows the parameters for the Button and TextView that the GLE writes for us inside of our standard RelativeLayout tag (see Figure 10-10):

```
<TextView
        android:id="@+id/textView1"
        android:layout_width="wrap_content"
        android:layout_height="wrap_content"
        android:layout_alignParentTop="true"
        android:layout_centerHorizontal="true"
        android:text="@string/display_data"
        tools:context=".MainActivity"  />

<Button
        android:id="@+id/button1"
        android:layout_width="wrap_content"
        android:layout_height="wrap_content"
        android:layout_below="@+id/textView1"
        android:layout_centerHorizontal="true"
        android:layout_marginTop="50dp"
        android:text="@string/button_title" />
```

Figure 10-10. Adding a Button to the RelativeLayout in our activity_main.xml file

3. Next, right-click on the */src/sixth.example.contentproviders/MainActivity.java* file and select **Open**.

4. First, we will add in our Button object declaration and our onClick event handling code, as we did in the previous chapter. Later, we'll write our custom query method, once our UI is in place. To get things going, let's add the following three import statements (or allow Eclipse to do it for us later) that we need to define our Button:

    ```
    import android.widget.Button;
    import android.view.View;
    import android.view.View.OnClickListener;
    ```

> **Note**   Remember that you use the **import** statement to pull in the classes that you are going to leverage (utilize) within your code.

5. Now declare our Button object, like so, with some fairly standard code:

    ```
    Button queryButton = (Button)findViewById(R.id.button1);
    ```

6. Next, let's use a setOnClickListener() method to add the ability to handle events for this button, using the lines of code shown below (and shown in Figure 10-11). First, we will attach the new OnClickListener to our queryButton, and then inside the onClick event handler, we will assign the

queryContact() method (which we will code next), to be run when an onClick event is encountered. Note in Figure 10-11 that queryContact() is underlined in red in Eclipse, which tells us that the method we are calling does not (yet) exist.

```
queryButton.setOnClickListener(new OnClickListener() {

        public void onClick(View arg0) {
                queryContact ();
        }
});
```

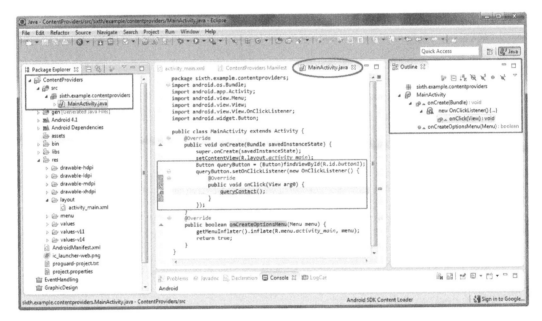

Figure 10-11. Adding a query button and setting an OnClickListener() method in MainActivity.java

Note that you can have the Eclipse IDE write most of this code for you, including all of the import statements and the onClick() container simply by mouse-overing red-lined elements in the IDE and selecting the import ... and add unimplemented ... options.

Tip As you've seen, when a method does not yet exist, Eclipse puts a red *X* in the left margin of the code-editing pane, as well as a red underline under the method name. If you want to remove those error indicators immediately, simply hover your cursor (mouse) over the red underline for a second, and select the Create Method option when the list of possible solutions pops up underneath it. Hovering your mouse over underlined (highlighted) code (either red for error or yellow for warning) in this way is a great technique for learning more about Java and Eclipse. Don't be afraid to explore and experiment with the Eclipse IDE as you work through this book.

7. Next, let's add the three new `import` statements that we need (shown at the top in Figure 10-12). Remember that you can also just write in your Java code, and let Eclipse insert these import statements for you automatically, if you prefer. The first brings in the database structure that we will be accessing via the `android.provider.ContactsContract` Class. The second imports the all-important database `Cursor` class `android.database.Cursor` that allows us to traverse (access or look at) the data within all of the Android databases. Finally, our familiar `android.widget.Toast` class needs to be imported to allow us to easily display our data via the `Toast` message broadcasting widget:

```
import android.provider.ContactsContract;
import android.database.Cursor;
import android.widget.Toast;
```

Figure 10-12. Java method for our queryContact() method and the database related import statements

8. Now we can write our **queryContact()** method, to query the database (also shown in Figure 10-12).

```
private void queryContact() {
    Cursor nameCursor =
getContentResolver().query(ContactsContract.Contacts.CONTENT_URI,null,null,null,null);
    while (nameCursor.moveToNext()) {
        String contactName =
nameCursor.getString(nameCursor.getColumnIndex(ContactsContract.Contacts.DISPLAY_NAME_PRIMARY);
```

```
        Toast.makeText(this, myname, Toast.LENGTH_SHORT).show();
        }
    nameCursor.close();
}
```

Let's decipher exactly what is going on in this queryContact() method that we have written. Our method is declared private (meaning it operates completely inside of the class that contains it) and void, as it returns no values. The first line creates a Cursor object called nameCursor and assigns it the results of the call to the getContentResolver() .query() method. This method uses the ContactsContract.Contacts.CONTENT_URI Uri constant and four nulls that represent more complex (and unused) SQLite operation options that are beyond the scope of an Absolute Beginners book.

```
Cursor nameCursor = getContentResolver().query(ContactsContract.Contacts.CONTENT_URI, null, null,
null, null);
```

The Cursor object that is now properly populated with our getContentResolver() .query() results (the ContactsContract.Contacts database that contains the Primary Display Name records that we added in Figure 10-9) will be used in our iterative code, a while loop that will traverse the records of our Contacts database table that getContentresolver().query() was used to access.

The while part of the statement is true whenever the nameCursor object is able to move to the next record, that is, whenever the next record is not an EOF (End Of File) marker. As long as this is true, and as long as there are more records to read, the contents of the while statement are executed.

```
        while (nameCursor.moveToNext()) {
```

As long as there is another record that can be moved to next this while statement will equate to true. When it cannot move to the next record (at the end of, or after, the last record in the results), it will equate to false, and will drop out of the loop, which will cease to function, just as we intended. In other words, as long as there is another record to process, we'll do another run of the code in the loop.

Now let's look at the two things done in the while loop while there are records to read.

First, we declare and set a String variable called contactName to the value of a fairly complex chained Java statement that gets the indexed data from the column of the ContactsContract. Contacts database record field (column) called DISPLAY_NAME_PRIMARY using the .getColumnIndex() function. That value is then turned into a String variable (made text compatible) value by passing the result of the nameCursor.getColumnIndex() function into the nameCursor. getString() function which then places that value into the contactName String object.

The data that is found in each current record of the results (on the first loop entry, this is the first record; on the second loop entry, this is the second record; and so on) is thus stored in the contactName string variable declared on the left side of the equals (=) sign as follows.

```
String contactName =
nameCursor.getString(nameCursor.getColumnIndex(ContactsContract.Contacts.DISPLAY_NAME_PRIMARY));
```

We do this via two key (no pun intended) methods of the nameCursor Cursor object:

- The .getColumnIndex() method gets the internal reference or index number for the ContactsContract.Contacts.DISPLAY_NAME_PRIMARY column for the current record.

- The .getString() method gets the string data from that location in the results and puts it into the contactName string variable that we declared on the left side of the equals sign.

Once our contactName string variable is loaded with the data value from the database record, we call our familiar Toast widget, and we display each record on the screen as it is read from the database during the execution of the while loop.

```
Toast.makeText(this, contactName, Toast.LENGTH_SHORT).show();
```

Note that this could also be written in two lines of code (if we were not chaining methods):

```
Toast.makeText(this, contactName, Toast.LENGTH_SHORT);
Toast.show();
```

Note that outside of the while loop once we are all done cycling through the database records, and drop out of the while loop at EOF, that we "close" our Cursor object with the contactName. close() method call. We don't want to leave open database access objects in memory, especially as they usually contain many records to be looked through, so this is what is termed "clean" (memory efficient) coding, as we clean out (up) memory space when we are finished utilizing it, freeing it up for a different use!

Now, right-click on your *ContentProviders* folder, and choose **Run As ➤ Android Project**. Try out the Click to Query Contacts Database button to see it trigger our query method, displaying the Primary Name data that we added earlier in the Chapter. Figure 10-13 shows the app in action.

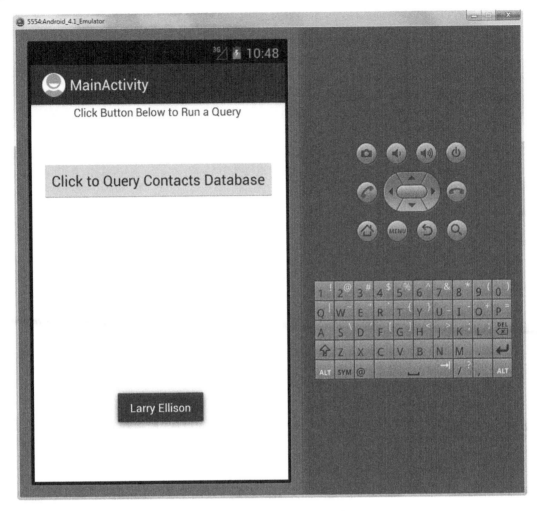

Figure 10-13. Running a Contacts Database Name query in the Android 4.1 emulator

Appending to a Content Provider: Adding New Content

Now you'll see how to add new content to a content provider database. In database terminology adding data records to the end of a database is called "appending" data records, but more important, now we're going to the next level (albeit a destructive one) and "writing" a new database record into the database. You've come a long way, Baby. Next, we will add a new contact name to the ContactsContract.Contacts database.

1. First, copy and paste the first `Button` tag in our *activity_main.xml* file or use the Eclipse Graphical Layout Editor to drag a second button onto your current UI, and center it 20dp underneath the first button. The text label of the button should be set to @string/append_data (see Figure 10-14).

```
<Button
     android:id="@+id/button2"
     android:layout_width="wrap_content"
     android:layout_height="wrap_content"
     android:layoutBelow="@+id/button1"
     android:layout_centerHorizontal="true"
     android:layout_marginTop="20dp"
     android:text="@string/append_data" />
```

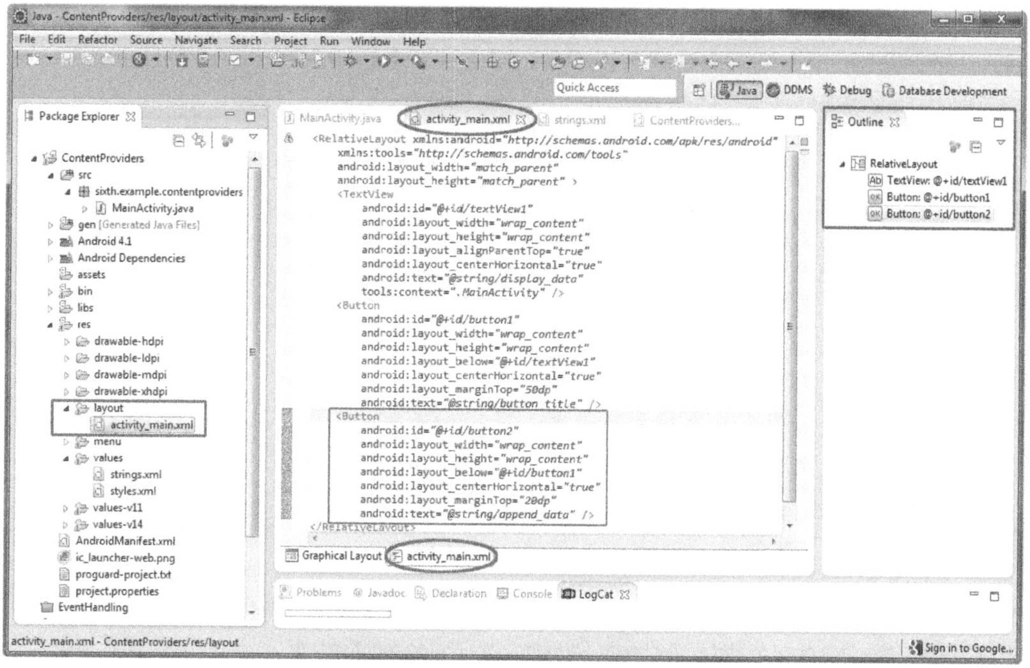

Figure 10-14. Adding in our second button tag in activity_main.xml *to use to add a new contact*

2. Next let's add in the<string>tag with a name value of append_data and
    its text value that specifies the text label for our second button that reads:
    "Click to add to Contacts Database."

3. Next, let's add in the code to implement the second button for our UI
    by copying the button1 Button object declaration and the onClick event
    handling code and pasting it immediately underneath the existing UI code in
    our MainActivity class to create our database Add button.

4. Change the queryButton variable name to read: addButton, and change the
    R.id to point to our new button2 ID. Also, set our method call to the new
    addContact() method that we are going to write (see Figure 10-15). Here is
    the new code:

```
Button addButton=(Button)findViewById(R.id.button2);

addButton.setOnClickListener(new OnClickListener() {
    public void onClick(View arg0) {
        addContact("Steve Wozniak");
    }
});
```

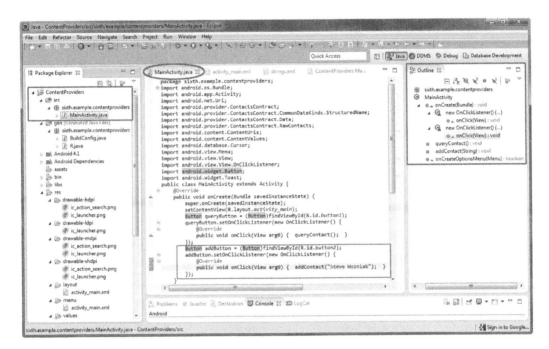

Figure 10-15. Adding the Java code to add in the second append data button functionality

Note This line of code calls our addContact() method and passes it a new database record Primary Name data value, so that a new contact entry will be added to the ContactsContract.Contacts database.

5.   Next, we are going to add the new method addContact().

```
private void addContact(String newName) {
    ContentValues myContact=new ContentValues();
    myContact.put(RawContacts.ACCOUNT_NAME, newName);
    myContact.put(RawContacts.ACCOUNT_TYPE, newName);
    Uri addUri=getContentResolver().insert(RawContacts.CONTENT_URI, myContact);
    long rawContactId=contentUris.parseId(addUri);
    myContact.clear();
    myContact.put(Data.RAW_CONTACT_ID, rawContactId);
    myContact.put(Data.MIMETYPE, StructuredName.CONTENT_ITEM_TYPE);
```

```
        myContact.put(StructuredName.DISPLAY_NAME, newName);
        getContentResolver().insert(Data.CONTENT_URI, myContact);
        Toast.makeText(this, "New Contact: "+newName,
                    Toast.LENGTH_SHORT);
}
```

We make sure that the addContact() private method is declared with the correct parameters, as follows:

```
private void addContact(String newName) {
```

This is quite different from our queryContact() method, as we are passing the method a string parameter: a name (in this case, Steve Wozniak). Because the addContact() method does not return any values, it is still a void method and is declared as such, just like the others.

Now we are ready to write the code that will add a new name to the Contacts database. The first thing that we need to do is to create a ContentValues object called myContact that defines the table, column, and data values that needs to be passed into the content provider. Because this is a new class that we are using in our code, we also need to add an import statement to our list of import statements (see Figure 10-16) or have Eclipse do that for us once we type in the new ContentValues() line of code that establishes a new ContentValues() object named myContact.

```
import android.content.ContentValues;
```

Figure 10-16. Writing the Java code for our AddContact() method

After we add the import statement, we can instantiate a new ContentValues object called myContact via the following declaration:

```
ContentValues myContact = new ContentValues();
```

Immediately after that, we need to configure that ContentValues object with a data pair via the put() method. This loads the ContentValues object with the table (RawContacts), the columns (or fields of data to operate on) ACCOUNT_NAME and ACCOUNT_TYPE, and the string variable with the name in it, newName.

```
myContact.put(RawContacts.ACCOUNT_NAME, newName);
myContact.put(RawContacts.ACCOUNT_TYPE, newName);
```

Next, we use the getContentResolver() method to insert the myContact ContentValues object into the RawContacts table, which is at the location specified by CONTENT_URI constant we discussed earlier in the chapter:

```
Uri addUri = getContentResolver().insert(RawContacts.CONTENT_URI, myContact);
```

This writes (inserts) the newName variable that we loaded (via myContact.put) into our myContact ContentValues object into the RawContacts.ACCOUNT_NAME database column that we specified in the same object. So, now our newName variable passed to our method has been taken care of. After this line of code, addUri will hold the location of the newly inserted record. Notice that we declared the addUri object as a Uri type of object and called getContentResolver.insert() all within a single line of compact code. Good job!

The next line of code takes our Uri object named addUri that appends the RawContacts.CONTENT_URI onto the addUri and creates a new, more detailed URI object for the next query. (We are basically setting the location of where to add the new name by using the location of the new name record as a reference.) Now all we need to do is parse the data in the myContact ContentValues object via the addUri for the final data-insertion operation. This is done by calling the parseId() method off of the contentUris Class and putting the value into the long variable rawContactId that we will use in our next line of code.

```
        long rawContactId = contentUris.parseId(addUri);
```

The next thing we want to do to the myContact object is to clear it, or basically turn it into an empty object with a clean slate. Then, in the next three lines, we use the put() method to load the myContact ContentValues object with the parsed ContentUris URI ID and table and column values for the DISPLAY_NAME field that we wish to write, and the newName primary name string variable data ("Steve Wozniak"), using the following lines of code:

```
myContact.clear();
```

```
myContact.put(Data.RAW_CONTACT_ID, rawContactId);
myContact.put(Data.MIMETYPE, StructuredName.CONTENT_ITEM_TYPE);
myContact.put(StructuredName.DISPLAY_NAME, newName);
```

Finally, we call our powerhouse getContentResolver() method to go into our content provider and insert the new name data into the correct table and data column (data field) location. This is done with the following code:

```
getContentResolver().insert(data.CONTENT_URI, myContact);
```

Once our data record is written by the two getContentResolver() operations, we can send a Toast to our users in the usual way, telling them that the write has been performed.

```
Toast.makeText(this, "New Contact: "+newName, Toast.LENGTH_SHORT);
```

Figure 10-16 shows the code as it appears in Eclipse with the import statements and our addContact() method highlighted.

Now right-click your *ContentProviders* project folder and select **Run As ➤ Android Application**. As you will see when you click the second button, the new name in our code is added to the Contacts database and a message confirming this is toasted (isn't that a cool term? Hope you're not toasted as well as trying to learn Java programming!) to the screen, as shown in Figure 10-17. Now let's go into our Android 4.1 emulator desktop and find the Contact Editor Utility so we can see the name data that we added.

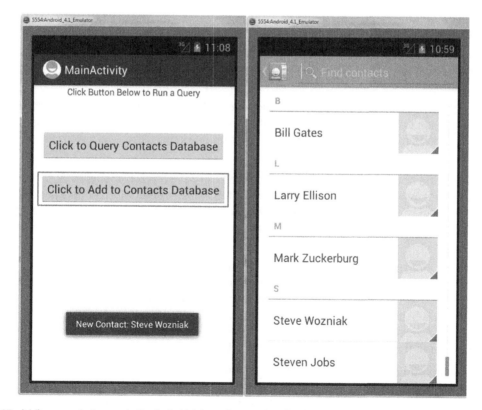

Figure 10-17. Adding a contact name in the Android 4.1 emulator and seeing it added in the Contacts Editor

To see the new data for Steve Wozniak, select the Contacts icon, hit the Menu button at the bottom of the screen (on the phone), and choose the Search function. Then scroll down the list until you see the Steve Wozniak entry (seen on the right screen in Figure 10-17). Even better, let's click the Top Query Button, once you've added Steve Wozniak, and see his name pop up in the end of the query code (that is Toasted to the screen) that you wrote earlier in this chapter! Pretty Cool.

Summary

This is probably one of the most complicated chapters in this book because it combines the following:

- Knowledge of SQLite database design, functionality, and access—in and of itself a topic that can easily span several books, and usually does

- The Android concept of content providers and setting up their permissions tags within the *AndroidManifest.xml* file

- The Java programming language iterative (looping) constructs that are necessary to access and manipulate these database structures

- How to read and write database records for the Android contacts database

You should feel a great sense of accomplishment from getting through all of this unscathed. You are learning how Android deals with advanced database concepts and structures. If you are really interested in database programming I suggest you get a book specifically on DBMS programming for Android, or at least go through some of the steps outlined in Chapter 12 regarding researching more complex SQLite database access coding, specifically using the SQLite library of classes included in the Android OS.

Most of the content providers that you will be working with in Android are already a part of the OS. They provide access to the common functions that users want in their phones, including contacts, music (audio), entertainment (video), and so on. The built-in content providers were listed in this chapter.

We also covered the concept of deprecation because after Android 2.1, the internal content provider database structures were enhanced, making pre-2.1 OS tables deprecated, although still usable, although it's not recommended that you do. Beware of code samples on the Internet using the older deprecated database table structures, as they will not work for anything other than Android 1.5, 1.6, and 2.0 support.

The primary Java classes in Android that handle content providers are (surprise!) the `ContentProvider` class, the `ContentResolver` class, and the `ContentValues` class. Each plays a critical role in defining (`ContentProvider`), accessing (`ContentResolver`), and addressing (`ContentValues`) a SQLite database structure. If you want to do really heavy SQL database programming in Android learn to use the SQLite database class libraries in Android, which are simply beyond the scope of this book, and probably have a book or two out there of their own!

Although there are other ways to pull in data to your Android application, such as off your SD card or off a remote server, the SQLite DBMS is the most robust approach and the only one that can be accessed between applications. Furthermore, this is the most useful content provider type to learn, because *all* of Android's user data is stored and accessed via these SQLite databases. Unfortunately, it's also the most difficult way to implement content providers (database access) in the Android OS.

Chapter 11

Understanding Intents and Intent Filters

This chapter will delve into *intents*, which are messaging objects that carry communications between the major components of your application—your activities, services, and broadcast receivers, which handle Android messaging. We have seen that Android development is highly modularized, and intents provide a way to wire these modules together to form a cohesive yet flexible application with secure, fluid communication among all of its components.

This is a fairly complex and important topic, and we are going to cover intents as they pertain to activities, services, and broadcast providers in detail. In fact, by the time we get to the end of the chapter, we will have an application that has four different XML files and four different Java files open in the Eclipse IDE. Lucky we are close to the end of the book because for a book on Android for absolute beginners, this chapter is going to seem a bit advanced. We'll chalk it up to a rapid learning process and dive right in.

What Is an Intent?

An intent is represented by the `android.content.Intent` class. It is in the `content` package because intents can be used to quickly access content providers, as we will see in this chapter. But its use is much broader than that; in fact, the Android Developer Reference says, "An intent is an abstract description of an operation to be performed," so intents can be used to quickly accomplish many tasks that would otherwise take more programming code. An intent is sort of a programming shortcut that's built into the Android OS and programming environment.

An Intent object is basically a passive data object (a bundle of instructions, if you will) that both provides a description of some sort of standard operating system or developer created "action" that needs to be performed and passes the data which that action needs to operate on to the code receiving the intent.

In addition to a specified action, the Intent object also can contain relevant data needed to complete that action, as well as data type specifications, constants, flags, and even extra data related to the data needed by the action.

Because intents provide a detailed data and process communication structure among Android application components, they also can be rather complex data structures (objects). We'll see the various parts of an intent's structure in the next section.

There are three types of Intent objects that can be used inside the Android OS to communicate with activities, services, and broadcast receivers. In fact, there is one intent type for each of these. None of these types of Intent objects are allowed to intersect with (i.e., interfere with, collide with, or mistakenly be used with or by) any of the other types of Intent objects. For this reason, we will cover each type of Intent object separately, so we can see how intent-based communication with activities, services, and broadcast messages differ from each other.

Android Intent Messaging via Intent Objects

Essentially, intents carry messages from one module of your application to another (activity to activity, activity to service, broadcast to activity, etc.). Intents can be sent to and from background processing services or intra-application activities or even inter-application broadcast messages. Intents are similar to the events that are found in other programming languages, except that intents can reach outside your application, whereas events can't. Events are used to process user interface elements, as we have seen in Chapter 9, and are internal to the blocks of programming logic you write. Intents can be passed to other applications written by other programmers, allowing them to be connected as modules of each other, if needed.

Intent object-based messages can contain up to seven different kinds of informational parts, as shown in Figure 11-1:

- **Component name**: The name of the class that the intent and its action are targeting, specified by using the package name and the class name.

- **Action**: A predefined type of action that is to be performed, such as ACTION_ DIAL to initiate a phone dialing sequence or ACTION_VIEW to view records in a database.

- **Data**: The actual data to be acted on, such as the address of the database records to view, or the phone number to dial.

- **Category**: Android has predefined intents that are part of the OS that are divided into various types or categories for easy access and use. The category name tells what area of the OS the action that follows it is going to affect. For instance, CATEGORY_HOME deals with the Android Home screen. An ACTION_MAIN following a CATEGORY_HOME would cause the Home screen to be launched in the smartphone, tablet, e-reader, or iTV.

- **Type**: This attribute specifies the type of the data using a MIME format. It's often left out, as Android is usually able to infer the data type from analyzing the data itself.

- **Flags**: This allows on/off flags to be sent with the intent. Flags are not used for typical intents, but allow more complicated intents to be crafted if needed by advanced developers.

■ ***Extras:*** This parameter allows any extra information that is not covered in the previous fields to be included in the intent. This allows very complex intents to be created.

Figure 11-1. *The anatomy of an Intent object*

With these seven different types of information, the messaging construct that an Intent object communicates can become quite an intricate data structure, if you need it to be, it can also be quite simple, depending on the application use that is involved.

The first thing an Intent object usually specifies is the name of the application component you are targeting (usually a class you create); this is specified via the package and class name, like so:

```
ComponentName(string package, string class)
```

The component name is optional. If it is not specified, the Android OS will utilize all of the other information contained within the Intent object to infer what component of the application or Android OS the Intent object should be passed to for further processing. It is safer to always specify this information. On the other hand, intents are intended to be used as programming shortcuts, and for many standard or common instances, Android is designed to properly infer how to process them.

The most important part of the Intent object is the action specification. The action defines the type of operation that the intent is requesting to be performed. Some of the common action constants are listed in Table 11-1, along with their primary functions, so you can get an idea of where these intents might be utilized in the Android OS.

Table 11-1. *Examples of Action Constants and Their Primary Functions*

Action constant	Target activity	Function
ACTION_DIAL	Activity	Displays the phone dialer
ACTION_CALL	Activity	Initiates a phone call
ACTION_EDIT	Activity	Display data for user to edit
ACTION_MAIN	Activity	Start up an initial task activity
ACTION_BATTERY_LOW	Broadcast Receiver	Battery low warning message
ACTION_HEADSET_PLUG	Broadcast Receiver	Headset plug/remove message
ACTION_SCREEN_ON	Broadcast Receiver	The screen turned on message
ACTION_TIMEZONE_CHANGED	Broadcast Receiver	Time zone has changed

It is important to note that in many cases the action constant that is specified determines the type and structure of the data of the Intent object. The data parameter is as important to the overall result of the intent resolution as the specified action to be performed. Without providing the data for the action to operate on, the action is as useless as the data would be without any action to be performed on it!

The ACTION_DIAL action constant is a good example; it targets an activity and displays the smartphone dialing utility with the phone number (the data passed to it) to be dialed. The data is the phone number the user entered into the user interface, and because the action constant is ACTION_ DIAL, Android can infer that the data passed to it is the phone number to be dialed.

Thus, the next most important part of the Intent object is the data component, which contains the data that is to be operated on. This is usually done via a URI object that contains information about where the data can be found.

As we learned in the previous chapter, this often turns out to be a database content provider; for instance, a SQLite database can be the target of an ACTION_VIEW or ACTION_EDIT intent action. So, to edit database record information about a person in your contacts list with the database ID of 1, we would use the following intent data structure:

```
ACTION_EDIT content://contacts/people/1
```

A closely related part of the Intent object specification is the data's MIME type, which explicitly tells Android what type of data the intent should be working with so that, for example, audio data doesn't encounter an image processing routine.

The type part of the Intent object allows you to specify an explicit MIME data definition or data type that, if present, overrides any inference of the data type by the Android OS. You may already be familiar with the MIME data type declarations, as they are quite common on web servers and other types of data servers.

MIME TYPES

MIME stands for "Multipurpose Internet Mail Extensions" and was originally designed for e-mail servers to define their support for different types of data. It has since been extended to other server definitions of supported data and content types, and to communication protocols (such as HTTP) data type definitions, and now to Android OS to define content data types as well. Suffice it to say that MIME has become a standard for defining content data types in a myriad of computing environments. Examples of MIME definition include the following:

- Content-Type: text/plain
- Content-Type: image/jpeg
- Content-Type: audio/mp3
- Content-Type: video/mp4
- Content-Type: application/msword

Another important parameter of an Intent object is the category, which is meant to give additional or more fine-tuned information about the action that is specified to execute. This is more useful with some actions than with others.

A good example of how categories help define what to do with a given action is launching the home screen on a user's Android phone via an Intent object. You use the Action constant `ACTION_MAIN` with a category constant `CATEGORY_HOME` and voila! Android launches the phone's Home screen and shows it on the display.

Finally, the extras parameter allows additional data fields to be passed with the Intent object to the activity, service, or broadcast receiver. This parameter uses a `Bundle` object to pass a collection of data objects.

This is a slick way to allow you to piggyback any additional data or more complex data structure you wish to pass along with the Action request/message.

Intent Resolution: Implicit Intents and Explicit Intents

Intents, like events, need to be resolved so that they can be processed properly. Resolution in this case means ascertaining the appropriate component to handle the intent and its data structure.

There are two broad categories of intents—explicit intents and implicit intents. We will look at explicit intent resolution first, as it is much more straightforward. Then, we'll cover implicit Intents and see how they need to be filtered so that Android knows how to handle them properly.

Explicit Intents

Explicit intents use the component portion of the Intent object via the `ComponentName` data field. You'll generally use these when working with applications you have developed, as you'll know which packages and classes are appropriate for the Intent object to send an action message and data to be acted on. Because the component is specified explicitly, this type of intent is also safer, as there is zero room for error in interpretation. Best programming practices dictate that you thoroughly document your code and thereby give other programmers using your intent code the proper component name information. However in the real world, this best case does not always happen, and thus Android also has implicit intents and intent filters to handle other scenarios.

Other developers may not know what components to explicitly declare when working with your application, and thus explicit intents are a better fit for private interapplication communication. In fact, developing your application so that other developers can use the intents is what implicit intents and intent filters are all about. As noted earlier, if there is a component name specified, it will override all of the other parts of the Intent object as far as determining which code will handle the intent resolution.

There are two ways to specify a component. One way is via the `setComponent()` method, which uses the `ComponentName` object:

```
.setComponent(ComponentName);
```

The other way is using the setClass(Context, Class) method to provide the exact class to use to process the intent. Sometimes this is the only information in the intent, especially if the desired result from using the intent is simply to launch parallel activities that are internal to the application when they are needed by the user.

Implicit Intents

Implicit intents are those that don't specify the component within the intent object. This means that Android has to infer from the other parameters in the intent object what code it needs to pass the intent message to for successful processing.

Android does this inference based on a comparison of the various actions, data, and categories defined in the intent object with the code components that are available to process the intent. This is usually done via intent filters that are defined in the AndroidManifest.xml file.

Although designing classes that utilize implicit intents and intent filters is beyond the scope of an introductory book on Android programming, we will go over the concept here just to give you an idea of what can be done in Android and in which situations you would use implicit intents and intent filters. You can find more information at:

developer.android.com/reference/android/content/IntentFilter.html

Intent filters are declared in AndroidManifest.xml using the <intent-filter> tag, and they filter based on three of the seven attributes of the Intent object—action, data, and category.

Intent filters provide a description of intent object structures that need to be matched as well as a priority attribute to be used if more than one match is encountered. If no action filters are specified, the action parameter of the intent will not be tested at all, moving the testing on to the data parameter of the intent. If no data filters are specified, then only intents that contain no data will be matched. Here is an example intent-filter definition from an AndroidManifest.xml file that specifies that video MPEG4 and audio MPEG3 can be retrieved from the internet via HTTP:

```
<intent-filter>
<data android:mimeType="video/mp4" android:scheme="http" />
<data android:mimeType="audio/mp3" android:scheme="http" />
</intent-filter>
```

For Intent filtering based on data characteristics, the data parameter gets broken down into four subcategories:

- **Data type:** This is the MIME data type, for instance, image/jpeg or audio/mp3

- **Data scheme:** This is written as scheme://host:port/path

- **Data authority:** This is the server host and the server port (see the data scheme format) specified together.

- **Data path:** A data path is an address to the location of the data, for instance, http://www.apress.com/datafolder/file1.jpg

Any of these you specify will be matched precisely to the content of the intent itself, for example:

```
content://com.apress.project:300/datafolder/files/file1
```

In this example, the scheme is `content`, the host is `com.apress.project`, the port is `300`, and the path is `datafolder/files/file1`.

Because we can specify intents explicitly, we can use intent objects productively via the methodologies outlined in the rest of this chapter without having to learn the convoluted hierarchy of how to match unspecified intents. If you wish to delve into the complexities of how to set up levels of intent filters for implicit intent matching, visit the Android developer site and get ready to wrap your mind around some intense global logic structures.

Using Intents with Activities

Enough theory, let's write an Android application that uses intents to switch back and forth between two different activities—an analog clock activity and a digital clock activity—so you can see how intents are sent back and forth between more than one `Activity` class.

1. First, let's close our `ContentProviders` project folder (via a right-click and Close Project) and create a new `IntentFilters` Android project with the following parameters, as shown in Figure 11-2:

    ■ ***Project name:*** IntentFilters

    ■ ***Application name:*** IntentFilters

    ■ ***Package name:*** seventh.example.intentfilters

    ■ ***Create custom launcher icon:*** Selected (checked)

    ■ ***Build target:*** Android 4.1 (API 16)

    ■ ***Min SDK version:*** Android 2.2 (API 8)

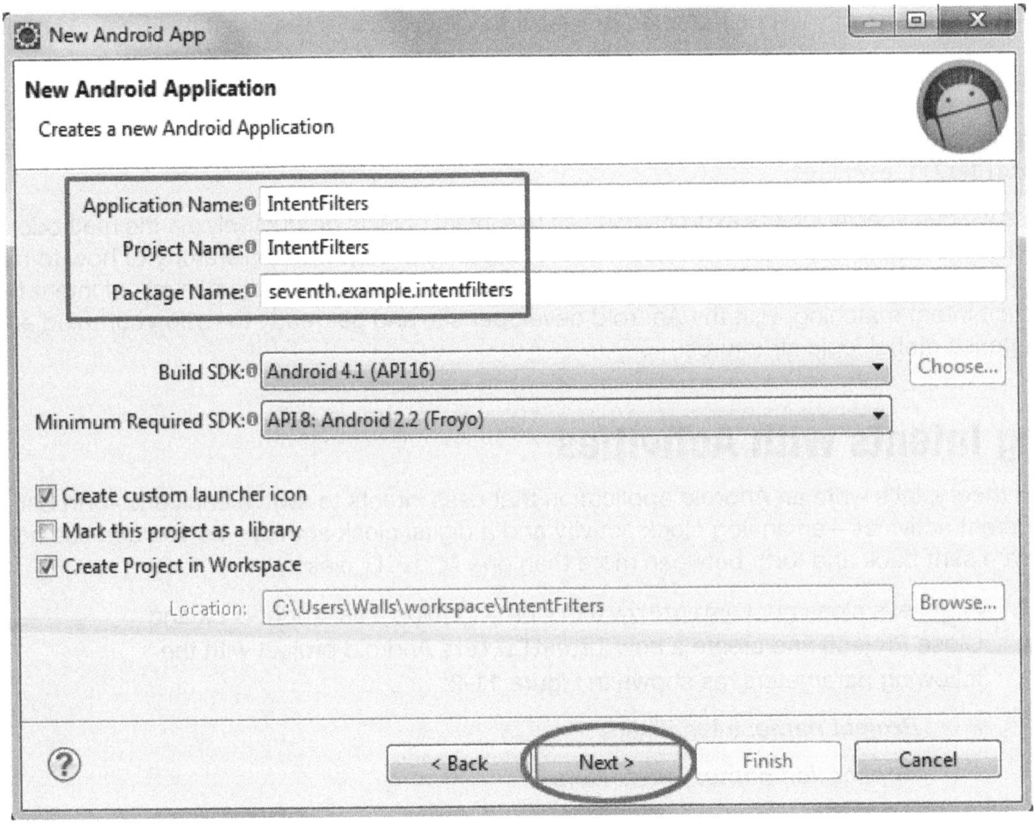

Figure 11-2. Creating our IntentFilters project in Eclipse New Android Application dialog series

2. Now we are going to create a second `Activity` class, so we can switch back and forth between the two activities using an intent. To do this, we need to right-click on the IntentFilters folder, and select **New ➤ Class**, which opens a dialog (Figure 11-3) that will create a new Java activity class in the same folder as the `MainActivity.java` class our New Android Application Project series of dialogs just created.

3. If you right-clicked on the IntentFilters folder to do the **New ➤ Class** operation, the dialog will already have the first field filled out, with the **Source folder** field set to `IntentFilters/src`. In the next field, you can either type in the `seventh.example.intentfilters` package name we created in our **New Android Application Project dialog**, or you can click the **Browse** button to the right of the field, and select this package from the bottom of the list.

4. Next we need to fill out the **Name** field, which will name our class. Let's use `AlternateActivity` as it's the alternate activity to the MainActivity that we'll use in this exercise.

5. Leave the **Modifiers** as set. Because we are creating an `Activity` class, we need to extend the superclass `android.app.Activity`. This is the full pathname to the `Activity` class, which is part of the `android.app` package in Android OS.

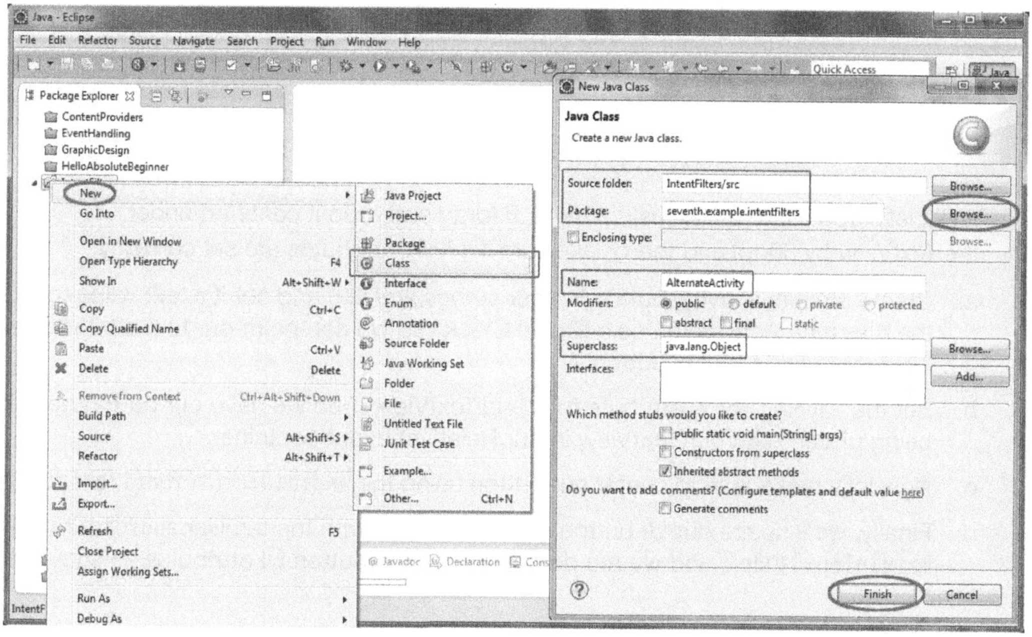

Figure 11-3. Creating new Java AlternateActivity class by right-click on IntentFilters project folder

Now let's create our user interface for our first activity, which we will leave in its default *activity_main.xml* file container (shown in Figure 11-4 on page 315).

1. Let's expand our `TextView` tag with some new attributes:

    a. Create a main_activity_text in your *strings.xml* file, which text value is set to: "You Are Currently in the MainActivity". Or you can edit the hello world string tag to serve this purpose, so that you don't have to delete it, as it will be unused in this exercise.

    b. Use the `android:text` attribute to set the pointer to the *strings.xml* file value via the "@string/main_activity_button" setting.

c.   Let's use the android:textSize attribute to increase the text size to 18 device-independent pixels, so it's large and readable. You can do this via the Properties Tab in Eclipse to the right of the bold TextSize parameter.

d.   Finally, let's use the android:centerHorizontal="true" attribute to center the text heading at the top of the screen. Note that the GLE and default XML TextView settings have done this for you, all you have to do is delete the android:centerVertical parameter to place the TextView at the top of the UI screen where it belongs.

```
<TextView
        android:layout_width="wrap_content"
        android:layout_height="wrap_content"
        android:centerHorizontal="true"
        android:text="@string/main_activity_text"
        android:textSize="18dp"
        tools:context=".MainActivity" />
```

2.   Next, let's add a Button tag using the GLE (drag and drop it centered under the TextView by 30dp) and then make sure it's XML attributes are set correctly:

a.   Create a main_activity_button in your *strings.xml* file, and set it's text value to: "Go To the Alternate Activity to use a Digital Clock" so we can point our text attribute to "@string/main_activity_button"

b.   Set the layout_below attribute to "@+id/textView1" so we have our button defined as being underneath our TextView in our RelativeLayout container.

c.   Now let's make sure to center our button using the android:centerHorizontal="true".

d.   Finally, we'll space our UI button down a little bit with the familiar android:layout_marginTop="30dp", and we are done creating the button UI attributes as shown below.

```
<Button
        android:id="@+id/button1"
        android:layout_width="wrap_content"
        android:layout_height="wrap_content"
        android:layout_below="@+id/textView1"
        android:centerHorizontal="true"
        android:layout_marginTop="30dp"
        android:text="@string/main_activity_button" />
```

3.   Now we'll add an AnalogClock tag, so we can create a cool watch. Use the Graphical **Layout Editor** tab at the bottom of the Eclipse editor (circled in Figure 11-4) and drag the AnalogClock View element icon out of the Views List on the left, and drop and center it 30dp underneath the Button element in the UI layout view.

4.   Then, either go into the **Properties** tab at the bottom of Eclipse, find the **Misc** section, and add in **Layout centerHorizontal** and **Layout marginTop** values of **true** and **30dp**, respectively, or click the *activity_main.xml* tab at the bottom of the editor, and add in these tags yourself by hand.

> **Note**   If Eclipse is not showing the **Properties** tab at the bottom, simply go into the **Window** menu and select **Show View ➤ Other** … and select Properties and then **OK**.

5. Next, let's use Windows Explorer to copy the image1.png file from our earlier UI_Design/res/drawable-xhdpi folder into the IntentFilters/res/drawable-xhdpi folder, then right-click on the IntentFilters folder and use the Refresh option so that Android can see this image file inside our project.

6. Go into the Properties tab again and find the image1 file using the Background option, then click on the search ellipses … to open a dialog where you can select image1.png in the drawable folder to use as a background. Here's the final AnalogClock tag:

```
<AnalogClock
                    android:id="@+id/analogClock1"
                    android:layout_width="wrap_content"
                    android:layout_height="wrap_content"
                    android:layout_below="@+id/button1"
                    android:layout_centerHorizontal="true"
                    android:layout_marginTop="30dip"
                    android:background="@drawable/image1" />
```

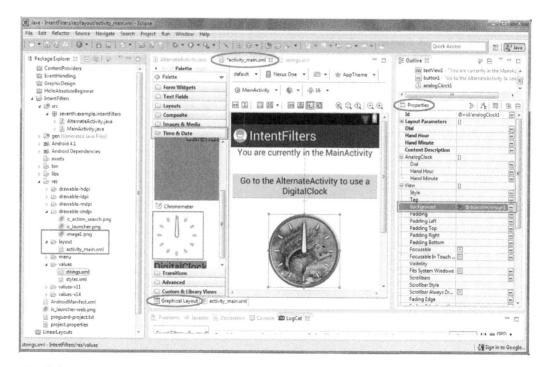

Figure 11-4. Using the Eclipse Graphical Layout Editor to add and configure AnalogClock

And here is the final code, which is also shown in Figure 11-5 for context:

```xml
<RelativeLayout xmlns:android="http://schemas.android.com/apk/res/android"
    xmlns:tools="http://schemas.android.com/tools"
    android:layout_width="match_parent"
    android:layout_height="match_parent">
    <TextView
            android:id="@+id/textView1"
            android:layout_width="wrap_content"
            android:layout_height="wrap_content"
            android:centerHorizontal="true"
            android:text="@string/main_activity_text"
            android:textSize="18dp"
            tools:context=".MainActivity" />
    <Button
            android:id="@+id/button1"
            android:layout_width="wrap_content"
            android:layout_height="wrap_content"
            android:layout_below="@+id/textView1"
            android:centerHorizontal="true"
            android:layout_marginTop="30dp"
            android:text="@string/main_activity_button" />
    <AnalogClock
            android:id="@+id/analogClock1"
            android:layout_width="wrap_content"
            android:layout_height="wrap_content"
            android:layout_below="@+id/button1"
            android:layout_centerHorizontal="true"
            android:layout_marginTop="30dip"
            android:background="@drawable/image1" />
</RelativeLayout>
```

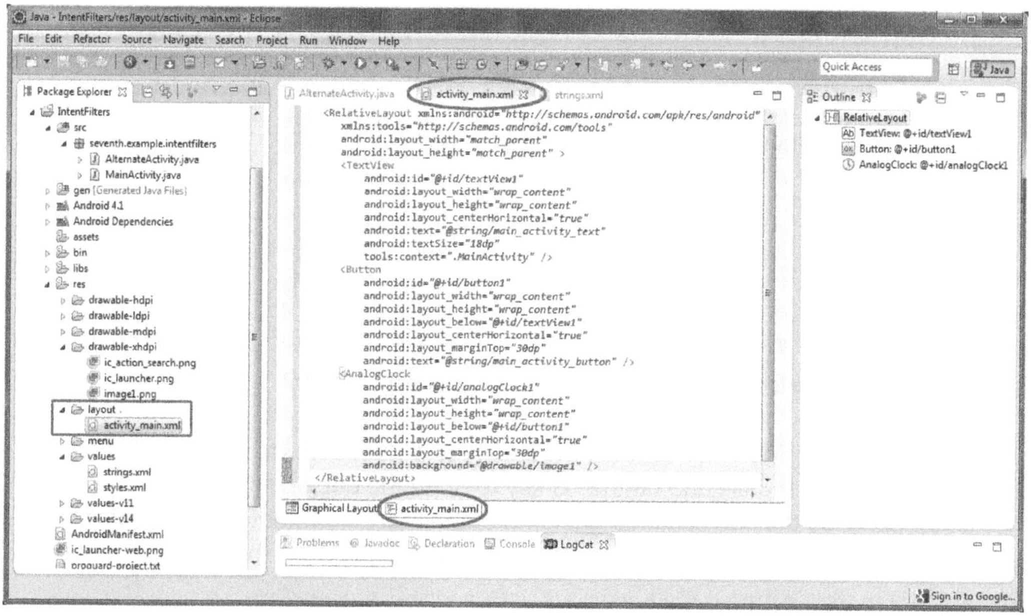

Figure 11-5. Adding user interface elements to our activity_main.xml file and image1 file to drawable-xhdpi folder

Writing a Digital Clock Alternate Activity

Now let's copy the user interface we have just developed in our *activity_main.xml* to use for our second activity, for which we've already created an AlternateActivity.java class.

1. The easiest way to do this is to right-click on the *activity_main.xml* file under the /res/layout folder and select **Copy** from the pop-up context menu, then right-click on the /res/layout folder in the Package Explorer pane (right above the file name) and select **Paste**, which will paste a copy of activity_main.xml right alongside activity_main.xml in the same folder. When you do this you will get a **Name Conflict** dialog, like the one in Figure 11-6.

2. Eclipse sees the duplicate file names and automatically provides a simple dialog box that allows you to change the name. Change it to *activity_alternate.xml* and click **OK**.

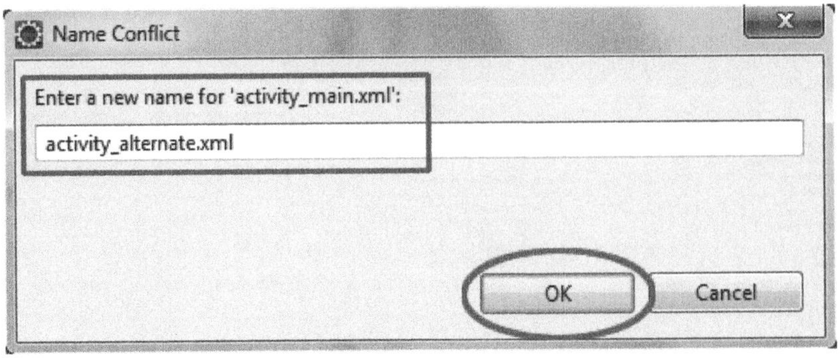

Figure 11-6. Specifying activity_alternate.xml as the new copy name for activity_main.xml

3. We are ready to right-click on the new `activity_alternate.xml` and select **Open**, or select the file and hit the F3 key to open the copied file in its own editor pane, so that we can change some of the key tag attributes and quickly craft a user interface for our second (digital clock) activity. Do this now.

4. Edit the `AnalogClock` tag as follows:

   a. Change it to a `DigitalClock` tag.

   b. Remove the background image reference to `image1.png`.

   c. Change the `id` to `digitalClock1`.

   d. Add a `textSize` attribute of `40dp`.

   e. Add a `textColor` attribute of #7AC to add some nice blue coloring. Note that #7AC is the same as (shorthand for) #77AACC.

   f. Finally, add an `android:typeface="monospace"` attribute for readability, and we're ready to change our `TextView` and `Button` UI objects.

   ```
   <DigitalClock
                   android:id="@+id/digitalClock1"
                   android:layout_width="wrap_content"
                   android:layout_height="wrap_content"
                   android:layout_below="@+id/button1"
                   android:layout_centerHorizontal="true"
                   android:layout_marginTop="30dip"
                   android:textSize="40dp"
                   android:textColor="#7AC"
                   android:typeface="monospace"/>
   ```

5. Change the button text to "@string/alt_activity_button" and leave the ID at `button1`. Why? Because these two different XML files are going to be called by two different Activity classes, and thus the ID does not conflict. If one Activity class referenced both these XML files, we might have a

naming conflict. Be sure and add the <string> tag to *strings.xml* that adds the alt_activity_button name and value of "Go to the MainActivity to use an AnalogClock" as well.

```
<Button
        android:id="@+id/button1"
        android:layout_width="wrap_content"
        android:layout_height="wrap_content"
        android:layout_below="@+id/textView1"
        android:centerHorizontal="true"
        android:layout_marginTop="30dp"
        android:text="@string/alt_activity_button" />
```

6. Finally, we change the TextView object text to read "@string/alt_activity_text" and change the android:textSize to the 17dp value so the text fits on a single line at the top of the screen.

```
<TextView
        android:id="@+id/textView1"
        android:layout_width="wrap_content"
        android:layout_height="wrap_content"
        android:centerHorizontal="true"
        android:text="@string/alt_activity_text"
        android:textSize="17dp"
        tools:context=".AlternateActivity" />
```

When you're done, the whole UI layout should look like this (also shown in Figure 11-7):

```
<RelativeLayout xmlns:android="http://schemas.android.com/apk/res/android"
    xmlns:tools="http://schemas.android.com/tools"
    android:layout_width="match_parent"
    android:layout_height="match_parent">

<TextView
        android:id="@+id/textView1"
        android:layout_width="wrap_content"
        android:layout_height="wrap_content"
        android:centerHorizontal="true"
        android:text="@string/alt_activity_text"
        android:textSize="17dp"
        tools:context=".AlternateActivity" />

    <Button
        android:id="@+id/button1"
        android:layout_width="wrap_content"
        android:layout_height="wrap_content"
        android:layout_below="@+id/textView1"
        android:centerHorizontal="true"
        android:layout_marginTop="30dp"
        android:text="@string/alt_activity_button" />
```

```
<DigitalClock
    android:id="@+id/digitalClock1"
    android:layout_width="wrap_content"
    android:layout_height="wrap_content"
    android:layout_below="@+id/button1"
    android:layout_centerHorizontal="true"
    android:layout_marginTop="30dip" />
</RelativeLayout>
```

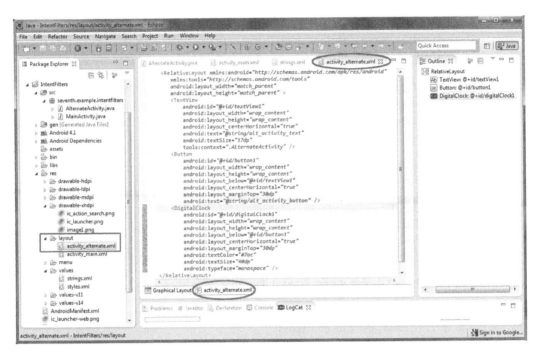

Figure 11-7. XML mark-up for activity_alternate.xml our second user interface activity shown in Eclipse

Wiring Up the Application

While we're working with XML files, let's add an activity tag in our *AndroidManifest.xml* file so that our second activity can be recognized by Android, before finishing off the configuration.

Right-click on the AndroidManifest.xml file name under your IntentFilters folder (at the bottom of the list), and select **Open**, or simply select the file name and hit F3. Add a second activity tag after the first tag (which our New Android Application Project series of dialogs has already created) that points to the new AlternateActivity.java class that we created earlier (see Figure 11-8). Here is the code:

```
<activity
        android:name=".AlternateActivity"
        android:label="@string/title_activity_alternate" >
</activity>
```

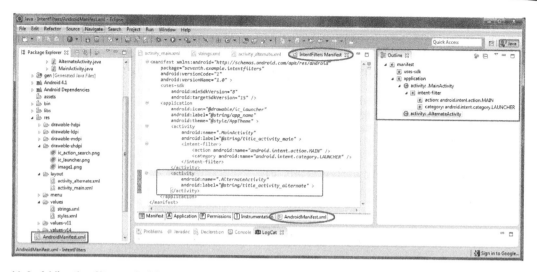

Figure 11-8. Adding the .AlternateActivity tag to our IntentFilters Project's AndroidManifest.xml file

Make sure to add the <string> tag to the *strings.xml* file by copying the MainActivity string tag and changing the "Main" to "Alternate" (and "main" to "alternate").

Now let's make sure both Activities have user interfaces. Thanks to our handy **New Android Application Project** dialog, our MainActivity class is ready and pointing to the *activity_main.xml* file so that the MainActivity side of the equation is already taken care of for us. So now, all we have to worry about is the AlternateActivity class.

Copy the three import statements and the onCreate() method over to the *AlternateActivity.java* class and then change the R.layout specification to point to the activity_alternate XML user interface specification. Now we've implemented our user interface logic for each of our two Activity classes as follows:

```
public void onCreate(Bundle savedInstanceState) {
    super.onCreate(savedInstanceState);
    setContentView(R.layout.alternate_activity);
}
```

Sending Intents

Now we need to add in our Button object and Intent object code to the onClick() event handler in each activity so each can send an intent to the other activity, allowing us to switch between the two activities using the button.

So let's get started with the primary MainActivity.java activity class first, and add in our familiar Button object instantiation and an onClick() event handler that will contain the code that creates our Intent object. Remember to also add in (or have Eclipse add in for you, using the hover-over-redline method we learned about earlier) the import statements for the android.view.View and android.widget.Button packages, as well as a new import we haven't used before called android.contact.Intent, which defines our Intent object class.

Because we've already covered adding a button and attaching it to an onClick() event handler routine, we'll get right into the two lines of code that create our Intent object and send it over to the second alternate activity. Here is the code, which you'll also see in Figure 11-9. The screenshot shows what your Eclipse editor pane for MainActivity.java will look like when we are finished.

```java
Button activity1 = (Button) findViewById(R.id.button1);
activity1.setOnClickListener(new View.OnClickListener() {
    public void onClick(View arg0) {
        Intent myIntent =
        new Intent(arg0.getContext(), AlternateActivity.class);
        startActivityForResult(myIntent, 0);
    }
});
```

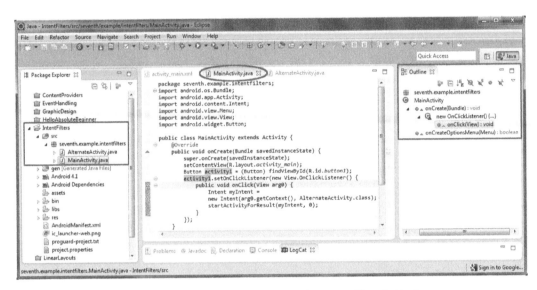

Figure 11-9. Adding the MainActivity Java code for the UI button, event listener, and Intent object

To create an Intent object, we use the now familiar structure where we declare the object type (Intent) and our name for it (myIntent). We set it equal to a new Intent object using the new keyword, along with a call to the Intent class's constructor. The constructor takes the context this intent is created in (in this case, from a button obtained from the View via a arg0.getContext() method call) and the activity class (AlternateActivity.class) into which we want to pass our Intent object.

We then use the startActivityForResult() method (part of the android.app.Activity class we imported) to pass the intent object we just created, myIntent, and a parameter of zero; this is what we are sending to the other activity to be acted on. This would typically consist of data that your application wants to pass from one activity class to another via the Intent object for further processing. In this case, we are simply calling (switching to) the other user interface activity.

Now let's look at the code in our AlternateActivity class and see how the second activity talks back to the first activity. We will skip over the Button instantiation and onClick() event handling explanations, and get right into the intent declaration and the Java code that returns a result to the calling activity class via yet another Intent object. Here's the code (also shown in Figure 11-10).

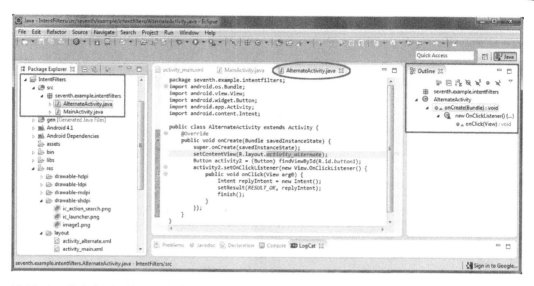

Figure 11-10. Java Code for the AlternateActivity, event listener, and intent object

```
Button activity2 = (Button) findViewById(R.id.button1);
activity2.setOnClickListener(new View.OnClickListener() {
    public void onClick(View arg0) {
        Intent replyIntent = new Intent();
        setResult(RESULT_OK, replyIntent);
        finish();
    }
});
```

In this activity class, in the `onClick()` listener we create a new (empty) intent object called `replyIntent`, then load it with the `setResult()` method, which loads a constant called `RESULT_OK`. When we have finished handling the intent (in this case by loading a new intent with the reply data), we call the `finish()` method to send the intent back, after the button in the second activity is clicked on to send us back to the first activity.

Now let's right-click on our IntentFilters project folder in the Package Explorer pane of Eclipse and then **Run As ➤ Android Application**, so we can see that we can now switch back and forth between the two activities that contain the two different time utilities we created in one application. As you can see in Figure 11-11, we can switch between the two activities by clicking on the respective buttons, and we can do this as many times as we like, and the application performs as expected and does not crash. That is important, by the way, that the app does not crash under repeated use.

Figure 11-11. Running our app in the Android 4.1 emulator and switching back and forth between activities

Next we will use an intent object to call a service, the MediaPlayer, to play some audio in the background, and allow us to start the audio and stop the audio.

To do this we first must learn what services are, and how they can help us do things in the background without affecting our application's user interface functionality. We will then get into an example that uses intents with both services and activities.

Android Services: Data Processing in Its Own Class

Android has an entire Service class dedicated to enabling developers to create services that run apart from the main user interface program logic. These services can either run in a separate process (known as a *thread* in Java programming, as well as in other programming languages) or in the same process as the user interface activities. With new Android devices featuring multiple processors, the preference would be to run processing-intensive services (such as 3D rendering via OpenGL ES or audio or video playback via the MediaPlayer class) in their own thread.

A thread is an area of the operating system's memory where a program function has its own resources and can run in parallel with other applications (termed: *multitasking*) or in parallel with other application components or processor-intensive functions. For instance, a video player can run in a different thread from the rest of the application, so that it doesn't hog all of the main application thread resources. If an Android device has a dual-core or quad-core CPU, it is also conceivable that a processing-intensive thread could even get its own processor allocated to it. Pretty cool!

Threads and Processes were originally devised for multi-tasking operating systems such as Mac, Linux, and Windows, so that if a program or task crashed, it would not bring down the entire operating system. Instead, just that thread or process could crash or lock-up, and the others that were running wouldn't be affected adversely. Because Android OS runs on top of a full version of the Linux OS kernel, it simply passes that capability through (up) to the Android OS.

A service is a type of Android application component that needs to run asynchronously (not in step with the usual flow of the user interface). For example, if you have some processing that takes a bit longer than the user is willing to wait for, you can set off that processing task asynchronously in the background, while the main program continues to respond to the user. When the processing has finished, the results can be delivered to the main program and then dealt with appropriately. A service can also be used by other Android applications, so it is more extensible (widely usable) than an activity.

To create your own service class to offload programming tasks like calculating things or playing media such as audio or video in real-time, you need to subclass the Service class and implement at least its onCreate(), onStart(), and onDestroy() methods with your own custom programming logic. You also must declare the Service class in your *AndroidManifest.xml* file using the <service> tag, all of which we'll get into in detail a bit later on.

Using Intents with Services

To see how to control a service class via intent objects, we will need to add some user interface elements to our IntentFilters project's MainActivity activity, namely two button objects that will start and stop our service. In this case, the service is the Android MediaPlayer, which needs to run in the background, independently of our user interface elements.

1. First, let's add a Button tag to our *activity_main.xml* file by using the Graphical Layout Editor to drag out a new button and center it horizontally underneath (android:layout_centerHorizontal tag) the AnalogClock tag by a margin of 20dp.

2. Change the android:text to "@string/start_media_button" and add a <string> tag to your *strings.xml* file setting that variable value to: "Start the Media Player Service" and leave the other attributes in the tag the same, as again the GLE has done all of the heavy lifting for you. Your tag should read as follows:

```
<Button
    android:id="@+id/button2"
    android:layout_width="wrap_content"
    android:layout_height="wrap_content"
    android:layout_below="analogClock1"
    android:layout_centerHorizontal="true"
    android:layout_marginTop="20dp"
    android:text="@string/start_media_button" />
```

3. Next, do the exact same thing with a third button UI element (button3) that we will use to stop the media player.

4. Change the android:text to read "@string/stop_media_button" and add a
   <string> tag to the *strings.xml* file that sets this variable to the value: "Stop
   the Media Player Service" so that we now have a stop button and a start
   button. Figure 11-12 shows both buttons in place in the **Graphical Layout**
   tab of Eclipse and Figure 11-13 shows the code in the XML Editor tab.

```
<Button
  android:id="@+id/button3"
  android:layout_width="wrap_content"
  android:layout_height="wrap_content"
  android:layout_below="button2"
  android:layout_centerHorizontal="true"
  android:layout_marginTop="20dp"
  android:text="@string/stop_media_button" />
```

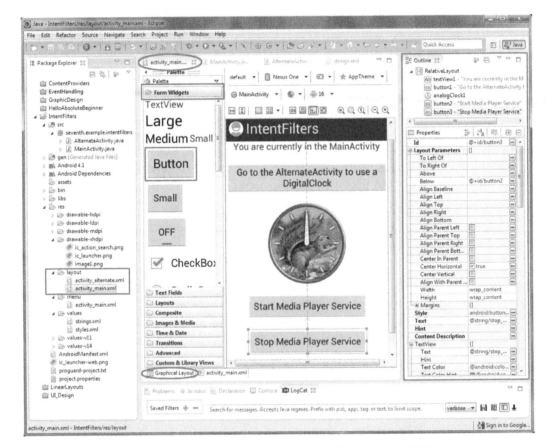

Figure 11-12. Designing a media player service user interface in the Eclipse Graphical Layout Editor

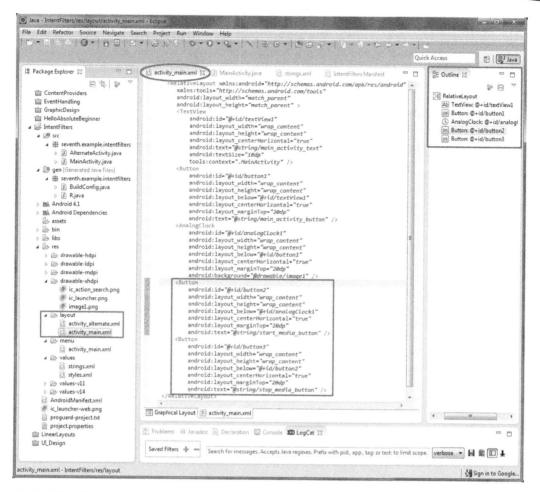

Figure 11-13. Adding the start and stop buttons for our media player service in activity_main.xml

5. Now let's change the AnalogClock tag attribute android:layout_marginTop to use 20dp rather than 30dp. Make the same modification for the first button (button1) so that all of our UI elements use a marginTop setting of 20dp.

    ```
    <AnalogClock
                    android:id="@+id/analogClock1"
                    android:layout_width="wrap_content"
                    android:layout_height="wrap_content"
                    android:layout_below="@+id/button1"
                    android:layout_centerHorizontal="true"
                    android:layout_marginTop="20dip"
                    android:background="@drawable/image1" />
    ```

6. Click the **Graphical Layout** tab at the bottom of the *activity_main.xml* pane to make sure the user interface layout looks good, and then check Figure 11-13 to see that your XML looks right.

Next we need to let our Android application know that we are going to be calling a service, and this is done via the *AndroidManifest.xml* file. We will edit that file next to add the service tag that points to our MediaPlayerService class, which we are going to code next. We will add this service tag right after the second activity tag that we added in the previous example (see Figure 11-14 for context). This is how the service tag is structured:

```
<service android:enabled="true" android:name=".MediaPlayerService" />
```

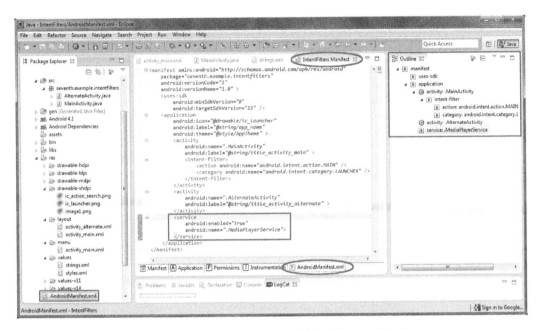

Figure 11-14. Adding a .MediaPlayerService <Service> Tag to the AndroidManifest.xml file in Eclipse

The first attribute of the service tag android:enabled indicates that the service is enabled for use. If you set this attribute to false, the service is still declared to Android for the application and can later be enabled via Java code. As we have seen, everything that can be done in XML can also be later accessed and changed inside of our Java code.

The second attribute, android:name , specifies the name of the service class that we will code. We are going to name it MediaPlayerService.java so we specify that in XML with a leading period, as .MediaPlayerService. Now we are ready to start coding the service that will play media files without interfering with the user interface code in our activity class.

If you haven't done so already, be sure to add the <string> tags for the Start Button and Stop Button labels as shown in Figure 11-15. We now have ten <string> tag entries in our *strings.xml* file and all of the UI and app labeling of activities and UI elements can be modified from one central location. The best part of all is that we have a "clean" IDE where our XML code is concerned, as Android does not like "hard coded" text values, and flags them in the IDE UI, which can be disconcerting, so we are doing things using the proper work process here for our string values.

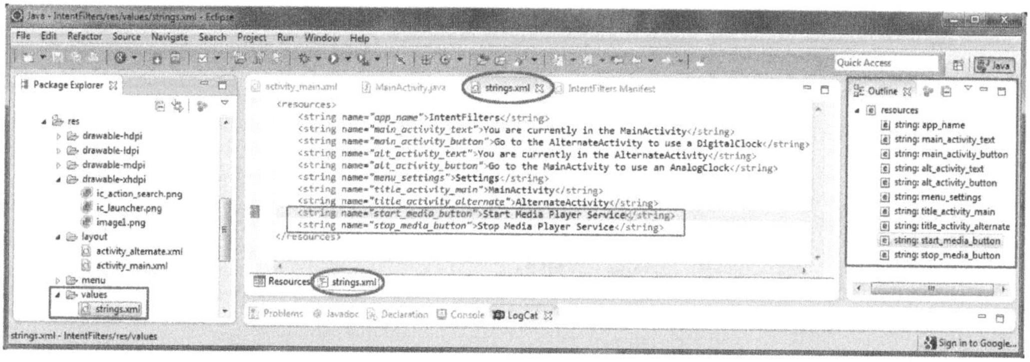

Figure 11-15. Adding the two new button labels to the strings.xml file in the XML Editor

Now that we've added the XML markup, let's create the `MediaPlayerService.java` class, extending the Android `Service` class to create our own custom service class that we'll call from our `IntentFilters` Project's MainActivity.java Activity class.

Creating a Service

To do this, we will use the same work process as before:

1. Right-click on your IntentFilters project folder in the Eclipse Package Explorer pane on the left and select **New ➤ Class**.

2. Fill out the **New Java Class** dialog as follows:

   - *Source folder:* IntentFilters/src Default entry, as auto-specified by Eclipse

   - *Package:* seventh.example.intentfilters. Click **Browse** button and select this from the bottom of the list

   - *Name:* MediaPlayerService

   - *Modifiers:* public

   - *Superclass:* android.app.Service

3. When everything is filled out, select **Finish**.

The completed dialog is shown in Figure 11-16. It will create an empty class where we can put our media player logic for creating, starting, and stopping the media player.

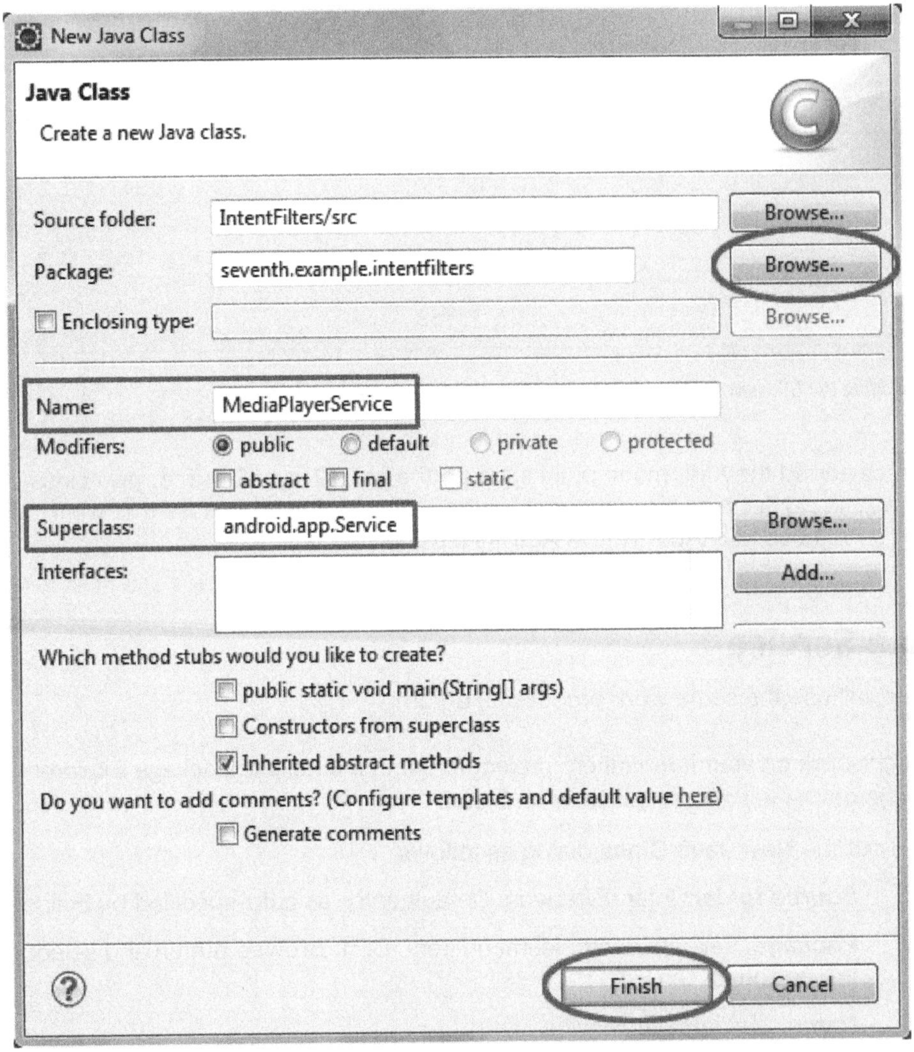

Figure 11-16. Creating the MediaPlayerService.java class via the New Java Class dialog in Eclipse

Here (and in Figure 11-17) is the empty class that the **New Java Class** dialog created for us, complete with the import statements that let us use the Service class, the Intent class, and the IBinder interface. We won't actually be using the IBinder interface in this example, but will leave it in the code. This won't affect how the app runs because it is used by a null method, onBind(). We need to keep this method here because Android expects it to be implemented when we extend the Service class, so we'll just leave it as is.

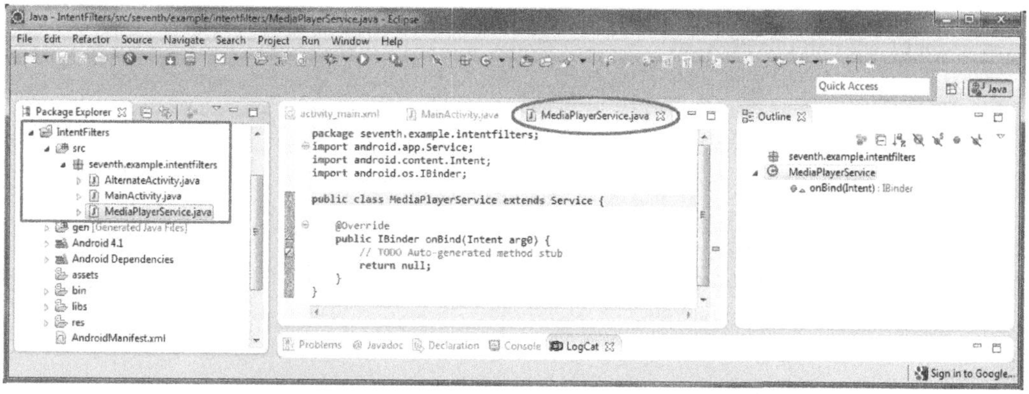

Figure 11-17. Eclipse-created MediaPlayerService base service class created by New ➤ Class

```
package seventh.example.intentfilters;

import android.app.Service;
import android.content.Intent;
import android.os.IBinder;

public class MediaPlayerService extends Service {
    @Override
    public IBinder onBind(Intent arg0) {
        // TODO Auto-generated method stub
        return null;
    }
}
```

> **Note** Binding is a concept in services where your activity can talk with the Service class while it is running and more than one time; but our example simply needs to start and stop the service, so the complexity of binding is not needed.

Here is the code that lets our MediaPlayerService class do things. I'll show you each of the sections in turn as I describe what they do, so you can type them in as we go:

```
package seventh.example.intentfilters;

import android.app.Service;
import android.content.Intent;
import android.os.IBinder;
import android.media.MediaPlayer;

public class MediaPlayerService extends Service {
  MediaPlayer myMediaPlayer;
```

```java
@Override
public IBinder onBind(Intent arg0) {
    // TODO Auto-generated method stub
    return null;
}

@Override
public void onCreate() {
    myMediaPlayer = MediaPlayer.create(this, R.raw.mindtaffy);
    myMediaPlayer.setLooping(true);
}

@Override
public void onStart(Intent intent, int startid) {
    myMediaPlayer.start();
}

@Override
public void onDestroy() {
    myMediaPlayer.stop();
}
}
```

The results are shown in Figure 11-18.

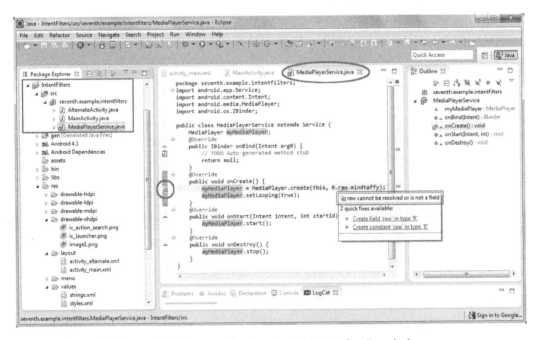

Figure 11-18. Adding our MediaPlayerService Class onCreate(), onStart(), and onStop() methods

The first code structure we always add to a new class is the `onCreate()` method, which tells the class what to do to set itself up when it is called the first time (i.e., created). This is where you would put initialization variables, for instance, if you were coding a game level. Then we'll add an onStart() method and finally an onDestroy() method. Here's a simple diagram of what happens when the startService(MediaPlayer) code we'll write later is called:

```
startService.Media.PlayerObject > onCreate() (Initialize) > onStart() (Do) > onDestroy (Clean Up)
```

We will use the `onCreate()` method to instantiate and configure our `MediaPlayer` object, and load it with our audio file. Because the audio file is an MP3 file and already optimized for compression, we will put it in the `/res/raw` folder. Files in the `/raw` folder are left alone by the Android app compression process and are simply put into the `.apk` file as is. As you can see in Figure 11-18 Eclipse will tell you if it cannot find the /raw/mindtaffy.m4a file referenced in your code. We'll add that file now before explaining the code in detail.

1. Let's create the `IntentFilters/res/raw` folder to hold the `mindtaffy.m4a` file that we will call in our `MediaPlayerService` class. You can either create the new `/raw` folder under the `/IntentFilters/res` folder using your operating system's file manager, or you can right-click on the `/res` folder in the Eclipse Package Explorer pane and select **New ➤ Folder** and enter **raw** in the **Folder name**: field.

2. Copy `mindtaffy.m4a` into the new `/raw` folder

3. Right-click on the `IntentFilters` folder and select **Refresh** and, if necessary, **Validate** to remove any error flags you might get in Eclipse. Usually if **Refresh** does not make something visible to Android and get rid of error flags in Eclipse, the **Validate** procedure will. If it doesn't, you may have a problem and may need to examine your overall application structure.

Implementing Our MediaPlayer Functions

Now it's time to go into the code so you can add the media player functionality to your own app:

1. First, at the top of the `MediaPlayerService` class, declare a public global variable called `myMediaPlayer` of object type `MediaPlayer`. This will be accessed in one way or another by each of the methods that we'll be coding, so we declare it at the top of the class to make it visible to the entire class full of methods.

   ```
   MediaPlayer myMediaPlayer;
   ```

2. In the `onCreate()` code block, let's set the `myMediaPlayer` object to contain the results of a `create()` method call with the `mindtaffy.m4a` file passed as a parameter using the `R.raw.mindtaffy` reference. The `create()` method call creates an instance of the media player and loads it with the audio file that we are going to play.

3. Next we call the `setLooping()` method on the `myMediaPlayer` object and set a true parameter so that the audio file loops while we are testing the rest of the code.

```
@Override
public void onCreate() {
    myMediaPlayer = MediaPlayer.create(this, R.raw.mindtaffy);
    myMediaPlayer.setLooping(true);
}
```

4. Now that our `myMediaPlayer` object has been declared, loaded with MPEG4 audio data, and set to loop when started, we can trigger it with the `start()` method, which we will code next in the `onStart()` method (`onStart()` is called when the service is started by our activity).

```
@Override
public void onStart(Intent intent, int startid) {
    myMediaPlayer.start();
}
```

5. In the `onDestroy()` method we use the `stop()` method to stop the `myMediaPlayer` object. The `onDestroy()` method is called when the service is closed and disposed of by Android, allowing the release of the memory locations (memory space) containing the media player and the audio file when we exit the application.

```
@Override
public void onDestroy() {
    myMediaPlayer.stop();
}
```

Wiring the Buttons to the Service

Now let's go back into our *MainActivity.java* class using the Eclipse Editor tab and add our Button objects, associated `onClick()` event handlers for each button, and the necessary calls to our Service class `onStart()` and `onDestroy()` methods, as shown in Figure 11-19.

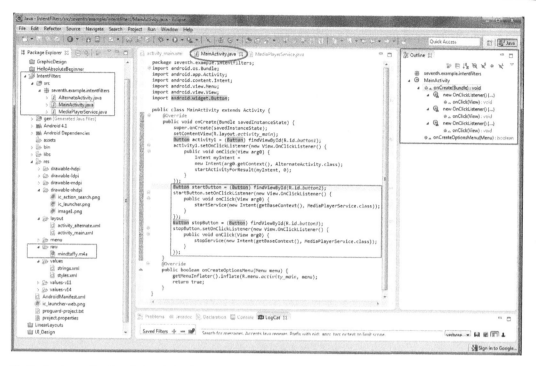

Figure 11-19. Implementing the start and stop buttons to control the media player

First we have the start button.

```
Button startButton = (Button) findViewById(R.id.button2);
startButton.setOnClickListener(new View.OnClickListener() {
    public void onClick(View arg0) {
        startService(new Intent(getBaseContext(), MediaPlayerService.class));
    }
});
```

As usual, we declare our startButton Button object with the button2 ID reference, then use the setOnClickListener() method to add onClick() event handling to the startButton. We are now ready to call the startService() method inside of the onClick() programming construct.

The startService() calls the onStart() method of the Service class we just wrote, and requires an intent object; this intent object tells Android what service to start and call the onStart() method on. We will get a little tricky here and create a new intent object inside of the startService() call using the following code structure:

```
startService(new Intent(getBaseContext(), MediaPlayerService.class));
```

To create a new intent object, we need to declare the current context as the first parameter and then pass the name of the service class we wish to call as the second parameter. In a third level of nesting (inside the new intent creation), we use another method called getBaseContext() to obtain the current context for the new intent object. As the second parameter, we will declare the name of the MediaPlayerService.class to complete the creation of a valid intent object.

Now let's go through the same procedure with the stopButton Button object, inserting the button3 ID reference and then using the trusty setOnClickListener() method to add onClick() event handling to our new stopButton. Now we're ready to call the stopService() method in our newest onClick() programming routine.

```
Button stopButton = (Button) findViewById(R.id.button3);
stopButton.setOnClickListener(new View.OnClickListener() {
    public void onClick(View argO) {
        stopService(new Intent(getBaseContext(), MediaPlayerService.class));
    }
});
```

The stopService() method calls the onDestroy() method of our Service class and requires an intent object that tells Android what service to stop (destroy) and call the onDestroy() method on.

We will create yet another new intent object in the stopService() call, using the following code structure:

```
stopService(new Intent(getBaseContext(), MediaPlayerService.class));
```

To create our final intent object, we will declare the current context as our first parameter and then pass the name of our MediaPlayerService()class as our second parameter.

Running the Application

Now we are ready to right-click our IntentFilters folder and **Run As ➤ Android Application** to run our app. You'll find when you test the application that everything works perfectly with everything else; you can start and stop the media player as many times as you like, the audio plays smoothly in the background without faltering, and you can switch back and forth between the two activities as many times as you want without affecting the media playback of the audio file. See Figure 11-20.

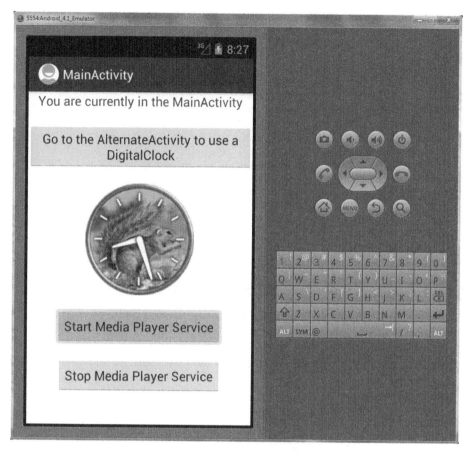

Figure 11-20. Running our media player service inside the Android 4.1 emulator

Next we are going to take a look at using Intent objects with broadcast receivers, and then we will have covered all three areas of Intent use within Android.

Using Intents with Broadcast Receivers

The final type of intent object we will look at in this chapter is the broadcast receiver, which is used for communication between different applications or different areas of Android, such as the MediaPlayer or Alarm functions. These intents send, listen to, or receive messages, sort of like a head's up notification system, to let your application know what's going on around it during the ongoing operation of the Android smartphone, tablet, e-reader, or iTV, whether that's a phone call coming in, an alarm going off, or a media player finishing a file playback.

Because we already have an analog watch and a digital clock, let's add a timer and alarm function to finish off our suite. Because our analog clock user interface screen is full of UI elements, let's add the alarm functions to our digital clock user interface screen in our AlternateActivity Class, as that's the most logical place to add an alarm anyway. Figure 11-21 shows a basic diagram of what we will do in XML and then Java to create the intent and implement the alarm in our next application segment.

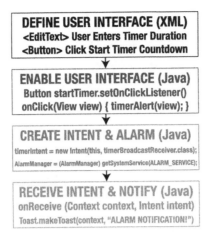

DEFINE USER INTERFACE (XML)
<EditText> User Enters Timer Duration
<Button> Click Start Timer Countdown

ENABLE USER INTERFACE (Java)
Button startTimer.setOnClickListener()
onClick(View view) { timerAlert(view); }

CREATE INTENT & ALARM (Java)
timerIntent = new Intent(this, timerBroadcastReceiver.class);
AlarmManager = (AlarmManager) getSystemService(ALARM_SERVICE);

RECEIVE INTENT & NOTIFY (Java)
onReceive (Context context, Intent intent)
Toast.makeToast(context, "ALARM NOTIFICATION!")

Figure 11-21. What we have to do in XML and then in Java to create the intent and alarm

Creating the Timer User Interface via XML

So, first, let's add an EditText tag via the Eclipse Graphical Layout Editor so that we can let users enter their own custom timer duration. Open the text field area of the GLE palette and find the numeric decimal text field (represented in the GLE UI as 42.0) and drag and drop it onto the existing UI, so that it centers both horizontally and vertically on the UI screen, as shown in Figure 11-22 below.

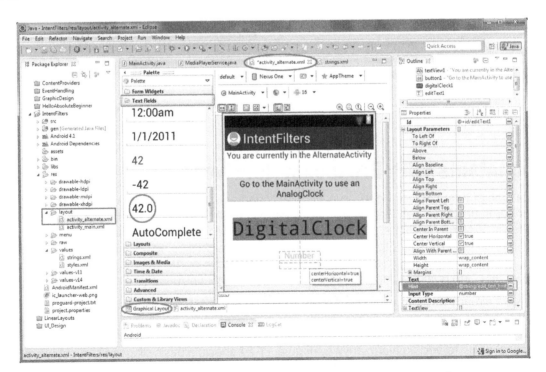

Figure 11-22. Using the Eclipse Graphical Layout Editor to add our EditText widget using the tool-tip guide

Now open up the *strings.xml* file and add a <string> tag with an edit_text_hint variable that points to the text value "Enter Number of Seconds" so we can add a "Hint" to our EditText field. Then use the properties editor as shown in Figure 11-22 (on the right side) to add a hint that points to the @string/edit_text_hint string (you can use the three ... ellipses to choose this variable once you add it to the *strings.xml* file and save it so that the entry is permanent).

This should place the following markup in your `activity_alternate.xml` file after the `DigitalClock` tag:

```
<EditText
        android:id="@+id/editText1"
        android:layout_width="wrap_content"
        android:layout_height="wrap_content"
        android:layout_centerHorizontal="true"
        android:layout_centerVertical="true"
        android:ems="10"
        android:hint="@string/edit_text_hint"
        android:inputType="numberDecimal" >
        <requestFocus />
<EditText/>
```

The `EditText` tag has an ID of `editText1` and a `layout_center` in both vertical and horizontal planes for consistency with our prior UI design. Because `EditText` is a new user interface object for us, we added an `android:hint` attribute that says "Enter Number of Seconds" so that you would have experience with that important EditText parameter.

Note   The `hint` attribute is text you enter to appear in the text field when it is created by Android and placed on the screen in the layout container. This hint tells the user what to type in the field, which in this case, is the number of seconds the timer should count down.

Next we have an important `android:inputType` attribute, which tells us what data type the field will contain, in this case a real number that is represented by the `numberDecimal` constant. The timer uses milliseconds, so if we want the timer to count 1,534 milliseconds, we can type 1.534 in this field and achieve this precise result.

We'll also add a `Button` that we will call `startTimer` in our Java code to, well, start the timer. Let's use the GLE to drag out a second button and center it and position it below EditText with a marginTop value of 30dp, all of which you will be able to see via the real-time tool-tip as you position the button via the GLE. We'll accept the GLE assigned ID of `button2` and edit the `android:text` value to read: "@string/timer_button_label" so be sure and add a <string> variable and value of "Start Timer Countdown" to the *strings.xml* file so we can prompt the user to action via the button label. Our *strings.xml* file now has a dozen variables defining all of our UI text elements as shown in Figure 11-23.

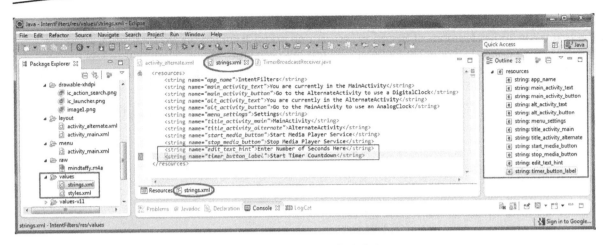

***Figure 11-23.** Adding string tags for our Timer Utility in the strings.xml file in Eclipse*

As usual, the GLE will use a now familiar android:layout_centerHorizontal="true" to center our button, and android:layout_below="editText1" so that the UI remains consistent and well defined. The Button tag and parameters should look like the XML code below:

```
<Button
        android:id="@+id/button2"
        android:layout_width="wrap_content"
        android:layout_height="wrap_content"
        android:layout_below="@+id/editText1"
        android:layout_centerHorizontal="true"
        android:marginTop="30dp"
        android:text="@string/timer_button_label" />
```

Figure 11-24 shows how our *activity_alternate.xml* file should look in the Eclipse IDE.

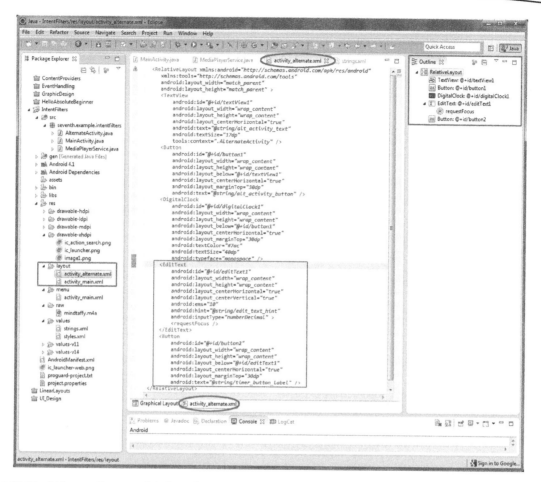

Figure 11-24. Adding our timer user interface elements to the activity_alternate.xml file

Creating a Timer Broadcast Receiver

Now let's create our `TimerBroadcastReceiver` class, which is a subclass of the `BroadcastReceiver` class.

1. As we are now used to doing, let's create a new class using **New ➤ Class**, and use the following parameters:

   ▪ *Source folder:* IntentFilters/src Default entry, as specified by Eclipse

   ▪ *Package:* seventh.example.intentfilters Click the **Browse** button and select from the bottom of the list

   ▪ *Name:* TimerBroadcastReceiver

   ▪ *Modifiers:* public

   ▪ *Superclass:* android.content.BroadcastReceiver

2. When everything is filled out, select **Finish**.

Figure 11-25 shows what your **New Java Class** dialog should look like when you've entered all of the relevant new Java class information.

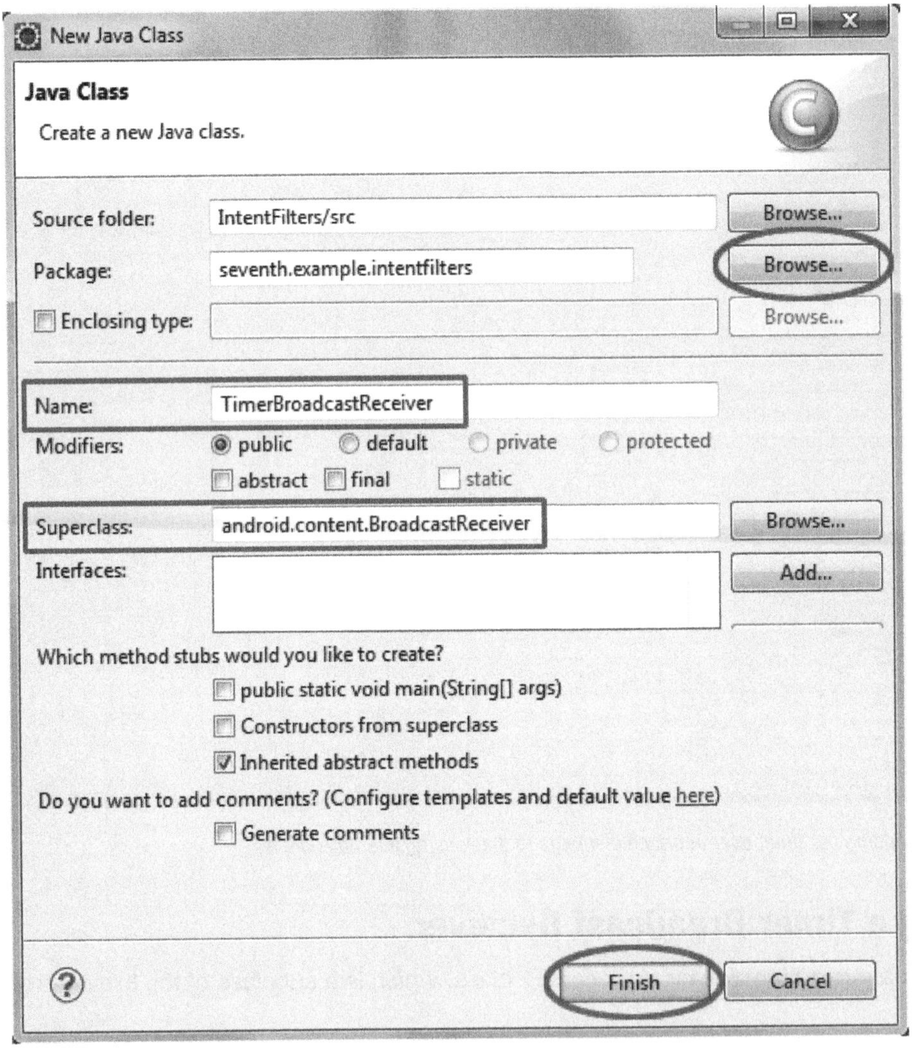

Figure 11-25. Creating a new TimerBroadcastReceiver class via the New Java Class dialog in Eclipse

Now we have an empty class shell with all of the `import` statements that we need for our `BroadcastReceiver` class and an empty `onReceive()` method for us to fill out with our programming logic. The `onReceive()` method will receive our intent and broadcast a message via the `Toast` class, which will notify us regarding the alarm status.

Let's add an `import` statement for the Toast widget, so that we can use it to broadcast a message to the user when the broadcast receiver is used. It is important to note that this Toast message could be replaced by anything we want to happen when our timer goes off, including but not limited to playing a song, playing a ringtone, vibrating the phone, playing a video, or anything else you can think of. As you know by now, you can add the Import statement below or let Eclipse do it for you when you code the Toast.makeText statement that follows.

```
import android.widget.Toast;
```

The Toast widget's makeText() method can be coded as follows:

```
public void onReceive(Context arg0, Intent arg1) {
Toast.makeText(arg0, "Alarm Notification", Toast.LENGTH_LONG).show();
}
```

We first pass the Toast widget the context parameter received along with the onReceive() call and then tell it what to write to the screen (our "Alarm Notification" string) and how long to show it on the screen (the LENGTH_LONG constant). We then append the show() method to makeText() to draw the message on the screen.

Figure 11-26 shows how all of this should look on the TimerBroadcastReceiver tab in the Eclipse IDE.

Figure 11-26. Our TimerBroadcastReceiver class

Configuring the AndroidManifest.xml file <receiver> Tag

Now we need to declare our broadcast receiver using the receiver tag in our *AndroidManifest.xml* file so it is registered for use with Android. We will do this right after the service tag that we added in the previous section, entering the following line of XML markup code:

```
<receiver
          android:name=".TimerBroadcastReceiver"
          android:enabled="true" >
</receiver>
```

This is fairly straightforward. We use the name attribute to assign our .TimerBroadcastReceiver class name to the receiver declaration tag and then enable it for use in our application by setting the android:enabled attribute to true so that the broadcast receiver is live (Figure 11-27).

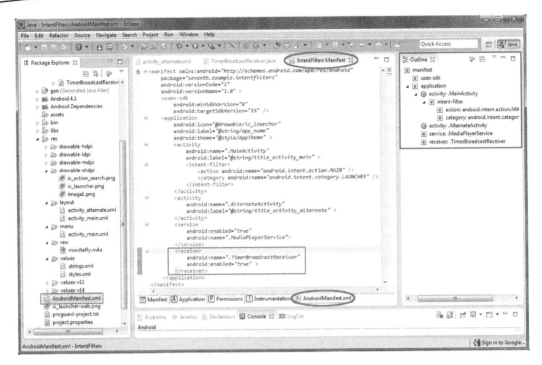

Figure 11-27. Adding a <receiver> tag to our AndroidManifest.xml file for .TimerBroadcastReceiver

Now our broadcast receiver is set up to notify users via a Toast message when the broadcast receiver is utilized. The next thing we need to do is add the code to our `AlternateActivity` class to implement an alarm clock function that triggers this Broadcast Receiver class via an intent object, so we can see how all this works together.

Implementing our Intent

The modifications to our `AlternateActivity` class will be done via several new `import` statements, an event handler for a click on our `startTimer` countdown button, and the `timerAlert()` method that we will write to do all the heavy lifting to implement the new timer functionality to our application and to trigger our broadcast receiver class using intent objects.

Let's start with the `onCreate()` method:

```
public void onCreate(Bundle savedInstanceState) {
    super.onCreate(savedInstanceState);
    setContentView(R.layout.activity_alternate);

    Button activity2 = (Button) findViewById(R.id.button1);
    activity2.setOnClickListener(new View.OnClickListener() {
        public void onClick(View arg0) {
            Intent replyIntent = new Intent();
            setResult(RESULT_OK, replyIntent);
```

```
            finish();
        }
    });

Button startTimer = (Button) findViewById(R.id.button2);
startTimer.setOnClickListener(new View.OnClickListener() {
  public void onClick(View arg0) {
    timerAlert(arg0);
  }
});
}
```

Now let's see how to add the highlighted code, starting with the `import` statements needed.

1. We need to import the two new widgets that we are going to use to implement editable text and a toast notification message, or have the IDE do it for us, either way. Both of these classes are from the `android.widget` package:

   ```
   import android.widget.EditText;
   import android.widget.Toast;
   ```

2. Next let's create our `startTimer` `Button` object for the start timer countdown button and use the `findViewById()` method to set it to the new `button2` button tag we previously added to our `activity_alternate.xml` file. Place the following in the `onCreate()` method after the existing button code:

   ```
   Button startTimer = (Button) findViewById(R.id.button2);
   ```

3. Now we'll add a `setOnClickListener()` method to handle events generated by the `startTimer` button. Inside of that construct we will create an `onClick()` method that calls a `timerAlert()` method, which holds all of the relevant program logic to set up intents and construct the alarm feature for our digital clock activity:

   ```
   startTimer.setOnClickListener(new View.OnClickListener() {
       public void onClick(View arg0) {
           timerAlert(arg0);
       }
   });
   ```

We will pass the `arg0` variable (the `onClick` View or Button that was passed from the `onClick()` method) to the `timerAlert()` method so that it has the context needed for the `PendingIntent`. Here is the code for the `timerAlert()` method, which we will go over line by line:

```
public void timerAlert(View view) {
    EditText textField = (EditText) findViewById(R.id.editText1);
    int i = Integer.parseInt(textField.getText().toString());
    Intent timerIntent = new Intent(this, TimerBroadcastReceiver.class);
```

```
PendingIntent myPendingIntent =
  PendingIntent.getBroadcast(this.getApplicationContext(), 0, timerIntent, 0);
AlarmManager myAlarmManager = (AlarmManager) getSystemService(ALARM_SERVICE);
myAlarmManager.set(AlarmManager.RTC_WAKEUP, System.currentTimeMillis() +
  (i * 1000), myPendingIntent);
Toast.makeText(this, "Alarm is set for " + i + " seconds!",
              Toast.LENGTH_LONG).show();
}
```

4. First, we need two import statements for two new classes from the android.app package.

    ▪   android.app.AlarmManager is a class that manages alarm functions for the Android OS.

    ▪   android.app.PendingIntent is a class that allows intents to be pending, which means they can be scheduled. This means they can be handled by classes in Android even if the calling class is paused, missing, asleep, stopped, or destroyed before the called intent has been processed. This is important for an alarm, especially if the timer is set to hours rather than minutes or seconds, because the phone could run out of charge before the Intent was ever satisfied.

    ```
    import android.app.AlarmManager;
    import android.app.PendingIntent;
    ```

5. The timerAlert() method is void because it just performs some tasks relating to setting up intents and alarm functions. It takes a View object named view as its passed parameter.

    ```
    public void timerAlert(View view) {
    ```

6. The first thing we do in this method's code block is to declare the EditText object, name it textField, and locate it in our *activity_alternate.xml* layout definition via its editText1 ID parameter.

    ```
    EditText textField = (EditText) findViewById(R.id.editText1);
    ```

7. Once we have the textField object we can use the getText() method along with the toString() method to get the string that the user types into the field. We then use the parseInt() method to convert that string value into an integer value and store it in the i variable of type int (or integer). Later we will use this integer value with our set() method to set the alarm duration.

    ```
    int i = Integer.parseInt(textField.getText().toString());
    ```

8. In the third line of code we declare an Intent object that we name timerIntent and set it to a new Intent object with the context of this and the class of TimerBroadcastReceiver.class as we have done in the previous sections of this chapter. We will use this timerIntent object in the PendingIntent object.

```
Intent timerIntent = new Intent(this, TimerBroadcastReceiver.class);
```

9. Now let's create a `PendingIntent` object called `myPendingIntent` and set it to the result of the `getBroadcast()` method call; this takes four parameters:

    ▩   The context

    ▩   Code

    ▩   The intent object we want to use as a `PendingIntent`

    ▩   Any constants

> **Note**   In this case we need no code or constants, so we use zeroes in those slots, and simply pass the current context, which we get using the `getApplicationContext()` method, and the `timerIntent` object we created just prior in the previous line of code.

```
PendingIntent myPendingIntent =
    PendingIntent.getBroadcast(this.getApplicationContext(), 0, timerIntent, 0);
```

10. Now we are ready to create our alarm using the `AlarmManager` class. To do this we declare an `AlarmManager` object named `myAlarmManager` and call the `getSystemService()` method with the `ALARM_SERVICE` constant to specify that we want to get the alarm system service and set it to the `myAlarmManager` object. Once we have defined `myAlarmManager` as an alarm service object we can use the `set()` method to configure it for our use in the application.

```
AlarmManager myAlarmManager = (AlarmManager) getSystemService(ALARM_SERVICE);
```

11. The next line in the code block is the one that ties everything else together. The `set()` method we will use on our `myAlarmManager` object has three parameters:

    ▩   **TYPE:** The type of alarm trigger we wish to set.

    ▩   **TRIGGER TIME:** The alarm will trigger when it reaches this system time.

    ▩   **OPERATION:** The `PendingIntent` object containing the context and target intent code we wrote in `TimerBroadcastReceiver.java`, as specified using the `getBroadcast()` method.

```
myAlarmManager.set(AlarmManager.RTC_WAKEUP, System.currentTimeMillis() +
    (i * 1000), myPendingIntent);
```

In our incarnation of the `set()` method on the `myAlarmManager` object, we first specify the `AlarmManager.RTC_WAKEUP`, which uses the Real Time Clock (RTC) method and wake-up constant to specify that we want to wake up the phone (if it is asleep) to deliver the alarm. The RTC method uses the system clock in milliseconds as its time reference.

Using RTC only (without the _WAKEUP) will not wake the phone up if it triggers while the phone is asleep, and thus will be delivered only when the phone wakes up again. This makes it not nearly as accurate as the RTC_WAKEUP constant. You can imagine how handy it is to be able to wake up your phone at a certain discreet time *even if it is asleep*, so it's a good thing we are exposing you to this handy constant here.

The next parameter we need to specify is the precise system time, in milliseconds, to trigger the alarm. We will wax a bit tricky here, and we will specify this middle parameter using a bit of inline programming logic.

We call the currentTimeMillis() method on the Android System object to get the current system time in milliseconds, then we add to the system time the number of seconds specified by our user in milliseconds, by multiplying the number of seconds in variable i by 1,000 because there are 1,000 milliseconds in one second. The system time is calculated in milliseconds since the calendar year 1970, so it is a discrete number that we can simply add our timer milliseconds value to.

This numeric result gives us the exact system time in milliseconds when the alarm needs to be triggered, and puts it into the set() method's second parameter, when our inline code is evaluated at runtime. As we have seen, Java allows some fairly powerful programming constructs to be created using just a single line of programming code.

Finally, we will specify the myPendingIntent object as our third parameter. This object, created earlier with two lines of code, was loaded with the current context and the timerIntent object that we created earlier with three lines of code. The timerIntent object references our TimerBroadcastReceiver class, which will ultimately be called when the alarm is triggered, and will send a Toast to the screen to tell our end user that the time is up.

The final line of code sends a familiar Toast message to the end user, confirming that the alarm has been set for the proper number of seconds. This is done by passing the Toast makeText() method the current context (this) along with the Toast.LENGTH_LONG constant and two strings with the i variable between them like this:

```
Toast.makeText(this, "Alarm is set for " + i + " seconds!", Toast.LENGTH_LONG).show();
```

As we've seen here, Java is very flexible in how it allows us to mix different data types. Figure 11-28 shows our newly enhanced AlternateActivity class with the new import statements, onCreate() method and timerAlert() method modifications shown. Notice in the Package Explorer pane that we now have *seven* actively used project files with XML and Java code that we have either modified or written. Actually, if you include the AndroidManifest we have eight files, four Java and four XML that we have customized for this project! This is the most robust application we've written so far! Now we will run and test our new app in the Android 4.1 emulator.

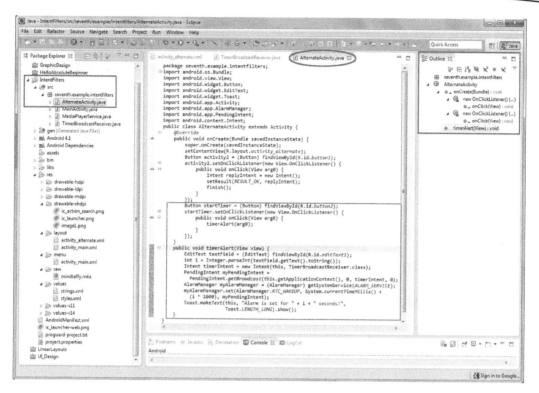

Figure 11-28. Adding the startTimer button UI code and timerAlert() method

Running the Timer Application via the Android 4.1 Emulator

Let's right-click on our IntentFilters folder, and select **Run As ➤ Android Application**, and get right into our final IntentFilters project application. You'll find that when you run this application that all three sections we've added work perfectly together.

This shows us that all of the different types of intents can work seamlessly together in Android, and that they don't interfere with each other, as we noted at the beginning of the chapter.

We can now go back and forth between the analog (main) and digital (alternate) activities using the intents we created; turn on the audio and go back and forth while it is playing; and use the timer function while the digital audio is playing back as a service.

In the digital clock alternate activity, we can use the editable text field to set our timer value and the start timer countdown button to trigger the broadcast intent, which broadcasts a Toast to the screen when the specified number of seconds has passed.

Figure 11-29 shows the application running in the Android 4.1 emulator displaying the digital clock, the timer function, and the button that allows us to switch back and forth between our two different activities and their user interfaces.

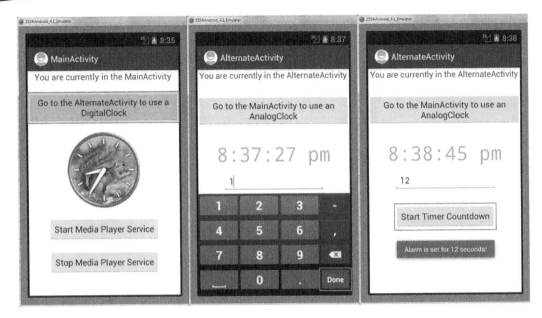

Figure 11-29. Running our timerAlert() method in the Android 4.1 emulator to show broadcast receiver intents

Summary

In this chapter, we've seen how different parts of the Android OS and the developer's application components communicate to form a cohesive and seamless application. From user interface activities to background processing services and systems utilities, intent objects are used in integral ways to pass requests for processing actions on data structures between different types of application components.

This serves to enforce a modular, logical programming work process on the Android applications developer, which ultimately increases security, decreases bugs and poorly constructed code, and attempts to facilitate the kind of optimization that will be needed in the mobile embedded environment of smartphones, tablets, e-readers, and iTV sets.

Ultimately, the proper use of intents and the creative structuring of application components is what set the successful Android developer apart from the crowd, so be sure to practice using intents and delve deeper into this area of the Android developer documentation whenever you get a chance.

12

Advanced Android Topics

There are a number of advanced Android topics that are beyond the scope of this book, but it's still good for you to know about them, so that you can continue learning on your own. I will try to expose as much of this information within this chapter as possible. This will be information that we were unable to cover in this book, outlined here just so that you know it exists, and that you should take a closer look at when you have a chance. Most of it is really amazing functionality that you can add to your apps to make them more marketable.

This chapter will cover how to research on your own the more specialized areas of programming for Android. It will provide a summary of what is available, where to find it, what it can do for your applications, and what classes it uses for its implementation, as well as provide some resources for finding more detailed information and tutorials on implementing these features and attributes in your future Android applications. Any code examples, where given in this chapter, will be very short and sweet, to give you a taste of what is to come if you take the initiative to go out there and find it.

Troubleshooting: Solving Problems on Your Own

I'd like to start out with troubleshooting problems in Android first because what's the use in researching new Classes if you can't get the Classes that you are already working with to function properly? We have already covered a number of commands in Eclipse that can be used to find and even fix the source of code errors and warnings that are being highlighted in your Eclipse IDE. These are as follows, in order of their logical application to the problem at hand:

- Right-Click (Project Folder) ➤ Refresh [F5] (look for missing files and resources)

- Right-Click (Project Folder) ➤ Validate (look for missing interrelationships in project)

- Project (Menu) ➤ Clean ... (delete and regenerate R.java runtime Java binary for project)

- Window (Menu) ➤ AVD Manager ➤ Start ➤ User Data Option (Emulator Reset)

- Eclipse LogCat Pane in the IDE (show exactly what errors are occurring)
- `http://developer.android.com/guide/faq/troubleshooting.html` (latest Android developer website troubleshooting information)

The last option is the Android Development website's troubleshooting web page section. Go there now and you will see that there are over a dozen of the most commonly encountered errors right there on the Troubleshooting "homepage." There also are over a dozen other areas on the left that expand to reveal dozens of subsections when the "down-arrows" next to them are clicked. Some of the subsections also will have down-arrows next to them that reveal sub-subsections as well.

The first 12 of these sections essentially cover things that we have learned about in this book, so if you want to go into further Android development documentation regarding these areas, this would represent a "one stop shop," and I highly recommend reading through it all when you have the time.

The next ten sections cover more advanced topics that we did not have the bandwidth (pages) to be able to cover in this book, but which cover some important features of the Android OS, including:

- Computation (Runtime API Reference, Advanced Renderscript)
- Media and Camera (Media Playback, Camera, JetPlayer, Audio)
- Location and Sensors (motion/position/environment sensors, maps)
- Connectivity (Bluetooth, NFC, Wi-Fi Direct, SIP, USB)
- Text and Input (Cut and Paste, Creating an IME, Spelling Checker)
- Data Storage (Storage Options, Data backup, App Install Location)
- Administration (Device Policies)
- Web Apps (Building, Debugging, Best Practices, Targeting Screens)
- Best Practices (Compatibility, Multi-Screen, Security, Performance)
- Google Services (In-App Billing, Licensing, Play, Cloud Messaging)

These areas of the OS may or may not be important to your particular application, depending on what its functionality entails, so you can pick and choose these topical sections based on the priority of your application development and what you want to do using the Android OS. I will cover a few of them in the next several sections of this chapter regarding your future research and development with the Android OS.

You also will find a lot of Android Developer forums online that are very useful, as well as sites such as StackOverflow that document a ton of questions and answers regarding Android programming. Simply go to Google.com and type in "Android Forums" or "StackOverflow" and you will find all of these great resources at your fingertips!

Finally, one last tip regarding research into troubleshooting any given Android programming issue: Learn How to Optimally Use Google! Yes, the Android Development website works well, and has a lot of information, as well as its own search functionality, but beware—they have a hard time keeping all of that information completely up to date for each API level. For that reason, I often use Google. com to research other websites that may have more recent solutions or programmers who are facing similar issues or problems.

To use Google effectively, make sure to use the Class and/or method names in the search parameters, or even cut and paste the error message right out of the Eclipse LogCat pane in the Eclipse IDE! If you do this, you will find that your search results will often return precise and highly relevant information that has already been asked on the Internet regarding that exact coding issue. Also, you can pose questions in the search bar, complete with a question mark at the end, such as: How do I register to use Google Maps in Android 4.1? Don't forget, Google is working on the Semantic Web (Internet 3.0), and searches such as this are going to work better and better each day as time goes on.

Widgets: Creating Your Own Widgets in Android

As we discussed in Chapter 7, Android has its own collection of user-interface widgets that can be used to easily populate your layouts with functional elements that allow your users to interface with the program logic that defines what your application does. These widgets have their own package called android.widget that can be imported into your application and used without further modification.

Android extends this widget capability for its programmers by allowing us to also create our own widgets that can be used by Android as mini-application portals or views that float on the Android home screen, or even inside other applications (just like the standard UI widgets).

If you remember, user-interface elements are Widgets that are subclassed from View objects. Widgets can be used to provide cool little extras for the Android homescreen, such as weather reports, MP3 players, calendars, stopwatches, maps, or snazzy clocks and similar micro-utilities.

To create an app widget, you utilize the Android AppWidgetProvider class, which extends the BroadcastReceiver class. The documentation on the App Widget Development can be found at:

http://developer.android.com/reference/android/appwidget/AppWidgetProvider.html — and — http://developer.android.com/guide/topics/appwidgets/index.html#AppWidgetProvider

To create your own app widget, you need to extend this class and override one or more of its key methods to implement your custom app widget functionality. Key methods of the AppWidgetProvider class include the following:

- onUpdate(Context, AppWidgetManager, int[])
- onDeleted(Context, int[])
- onEnabled(Context)
- onDisabled(Context)
- onReceive(Context, Intent)

To create an app widget, you need to create an AppWidgetProviderInfo object that will contain the metadata and parameters for the app widget. These are details such as the user interface layout, how frequently it is updated or refreshed, and the convenience class that it is subclassed from (AppWidgetProvider). This can all be defined via XML, which should be no surprise to you by now.

The AppWidgetProvider class defines all of the methods that allow your application to interface with the app widget class via broadcast events, making it a broadcast receiver. These broadcast events, as we discussed in Chapter 11, will update the widget, with some frequency if required, as well as enabling (turning it on), disabling (turning it off), and even deleting it if required.

App widgets also (optionally) offer a configuration activity that can launch itself when the user first installs your app widget. This activity adds a user interface layout that allows your users to modify the app widget settings before (or at the time of) its launch. The app widget must be declared in the *AndroidManifest.xml* file, so that the application has registered it with the OS for communications, as it is a broadcast receiver.

More information on widget design can be found at the App Widget Design Guidelines page located at:

```
http://developer.android.com/guide/practices/ui_guidelines/widget_design.html
```

Location-Based Services in Android

Location-based services and Google Maps are both very important OS capabilities when it comes to a smartphone or tablet device. You can access all location and maps related capabilities inside of Android via the android.location package, which is a collection of classes or routines for dealing with maps and locations, and via the Google Maps external library, which we will cover in the next section.

The central component of the location services network is the LocationManager system service. This Android system service provides the APIs necessary to determine the location and (if supported) bearing of the underlying device's GPS and accelerometer hardware functionality.

Similar to other Android systems services, the LocationManager is not instantiated directly, but is instead requested as an instance from the system by calling the getSystemService(Context) method, which then returns a handle to the new LocationManager instance, like this:

```
getSystemService(Context.LOCATION_SERVICE)
```

Once a LocationManager has been established inside of your application, you will be able to do the following three things in your application:

- Query for a list of all LocationProviders for the last known user location.

- Register (or unregister) for periodic updates of the user's current location.

- Register (or unregister) for a given Intent to be fired once the device is within certain proximity of a specified latitude or longitude specified in meters.

Google Maps in Android

Google provides an external library called Google Maps that makes it relatively easy to add powerful mapping functions to your Android applications. It is a Java package called com.google.android.maps, and it contains classes that allow for a wide variety of functions relating to downloading, rendering, and caching map tiles, as well as a variety of user control systems and display options.

One of the most important classes in the maps package is the MapView class, a subclass of ViewGroup, which displays a map using data supplied from the Google Maps service. Essentially this class is a wrapper providing access to the functions of the Google Maps API, allowing your applications to manipulate Google Maps through MapView methods that allow maps and their data to be accessed, much as though you would access any other View object.

The `MapView` class provides programmers with all of the various user interface assets that can be used to create and control Google Maps data. When your application passes focus to your `MapView` object, it automatically allows your users to zoom into, and pan around, the map using gestures or keypresses. It can also handle network requests for additional map tiles, or even an entirely new map.

Before you can write a Google Maps-based application, you must obtain a Google Maps API key to identify your app:

1. To begin with, you need to provide Google with the signature of your application. To do so, run the following at the command prompt (in Windows the Command Prompt Utility is located in the Start Menu under the All Programs menu in the Accessories folder):

```
keytool -list -keystore C:\users\<username>\.android\debug.keystore
```

> **Note** The signature of your application proves to Google that your application comes from you. Explaining the niceties of this is beyond the scope of this book, but for now, just understand that you are proving a guarantee to Google that you created this application.

2. When prompted, the password is **android**. Here is what you should see:

```
Enter keystore password: Keystore type: JKS
Keystore provider: SUN
Your keystore contains 1 entry
androiddebugkey, 21-Jan-2011, PrivateKeyEntry,
Certificate fingerprint (MD5): <fingerprint>
```

3. Select and Copy (CTRL-C) the fingerprint string value. You'll need it in the next step.

4. Go to `http://code.google.com/android/maps-api-signup.html` and enter the fingerprint data you copied into the "My certificate's MD5 fingerprint:" box.

5. Accept the terms and conditions, and then click: Generate API Key.

6. On the next page, make a note of your API key.

Now that we have our key, here are the basic steps for implementing a Google Maps app:

1. First you would want to create a new project called `MyGoogleMap`, an Activity called `MainActivity`, with a Project Build Target of **Google APIs** for default version support for 2.2 through 4.1. We need to do this to use the Google Maps classes.

> **Note** You may have to install the Google APIs using the Android SDK and AVD Manager. They are listed as Google APIs by Google Inc.

2. In the AndroidManifest.xml file, within the `<application>` tag use the `<uses-library>` tag to point to the Google Maps library address specified above as follows:

```
<uses-library android:name="com.google.android.maps" />
```

3. Also in the *AndroidManifest.xml* file, and within the `<application>` tag, use the `<uses-permission>` tag to request permission to access the Internet as follows:

```
<uses-permission android:name="android.permission.INTERNET" />
```

4. Next you would want to define some simple user interface elements within your *activity_main.xml* layout definition, using a basic linear layout with a vertical parameter specified, and then a Google Maps `MapView` user interface element with the `clickable` parameter set to `true`, allowing the user to navigate the map, as follows:

```
<LinearLayout
    xmlns:android="http://schemas.android.com/apk/res/android"
    android:id="@+id/linearLayout1"
    android:orientation="vertical"
    android:layout_width="match_parent"
    android:layout_height="match_parent" >
    <com.google.android.maps.MapView
        android:id="@+id/mapview"
        android:layout_width="match_parent"
        android:layout_height="match_parent"
        android:clickable="true"
        android:apiKey="Your Maps API Key Goes Here"
    />
</LinearLayout>
```

5. Now enter your unique Google Maps API key that was assigned to you in the `apiKey` parameter in the last parameter of the `MapView` tag.

6. Next open your `MainActivity.java` activity and extend your class to use a special subclass of the `Activity` class called the `MapActivity` class, as follows:

```
public class MainActivity extends MapActivity {...}
```

7. One of the primary methods of the `MapActivity` class is the `isRouteDisplayed()` method, which must be implemented, and once it is, you will be able to pan around a map, so add this little bit of code as follows to complete your basic map:

```
@Override
protected boolean isRouteDisplayed() {
    return false;
}
```

8. At the top of your `MainActivity` class instantiate two handles for the `MapView` and the `ZoomTool` controls (`LinearLayout`) we are going to add next, as follows:

```
LinearLayout linearLayout;
MapView mapView;
```

9. Next in your `onCreate()` method, initialize your `MapView` UI element and add the `ZoomControls` capability to it via the `setBuiltInZoomControls()` method as follows:

```
mapView = (MapView) findViewById(R.id.mapview);
mapView.setBuiltInZoomControls(true);
```

Note that we are using the built-in `MapView` zoom controls so we do not have to write any code, and yet when we run this basic application, the user will be able to zoom the `MapView` via zoom controls that will appear when the user touches the map and then disappear after a short time-out period (of nonuse).

10. Compile and run to test your `MainActivity` in your `myGoogleMap` project application in the Android 4.1 emulator.

It is important to note that the external Google Maps library is not an integral part of the Android OS, but is actually something that is hosted externally to the smartphone/tablet environment, and which requires access externally via a Google Maps key that you must apply for and secure before your applications utilize this service from Google. This is the same way that this works when using Google Maps from a website; it's just that the `MapView` class fine-tunes this for Android usage. To learn more about the Google Maps external library visit:

```
https://developers.google.com/android/add-ons/google-apis/
```

Google Search in Android

Google has built its business model on one major service that it has always offered: search. It should not be a surprise that search is thus a well-supported core service in Android. Android users can search for any data that is available to them on their Android device or across the Internet.

Android, not surprisingly, provides a seamless, consistent search experience across the board, and Android provides a robust search implementation framework for you to implement search functions inside of your Android applications.

The Android search framework provides an interface for search that includes both the interaction and the search itself, so that you do not have to define a separate Activity in Android. The advantage of this is that the use of search in your application will not interrupt your current Activity.

Using Android search puts a search dialog at the top of the screen, pushing other content down on the screen as it is utilized. Once you have everything set up to use this capability in Android, you can integrate your application with search by providing search suggestions based on your app or recent user queries, offer you own custom application specific search suggestions in the system-wide quick search function, and even turn on voice search functions.

Search in Android is handled by the SearchManager class; however, that class is not used directly, but rather is accessed via an Intent specified in XML or via your Java code via the context.getSystemService(context.SEARCH_SERVICE) code construct. Here are the basic steps to set up capability for a search within your AndroidManifest.xml file.

Specify an <intent-filter> in the <activity> section of the AndroidManifest.xml:

```
<intent-filter>
    <action android:name="android.intent.action.SEARCH" />
</intent-filter>

<meta-data android:name="android.app.searchable"
        android:resource="@xml/searchable" />
```

1. Next, create the *res/xml/searchable.xml* file specified in the <meta-data> tag in Step 1.

2. Inside *searchable.xml*, create a <searchable> tag with the following data:

```
<searchable
        xmlns:android="http://schemas.android.com/apk/res/android"
        android:label="@string/search_label"
        android:searchSuggestAuthority="dictionary"
        android:searchSuggestIntentAction="android.intent.action.VIEW">
</searchable>
```

3. Now in *res/values/strings.xml*, add a string called search_label via text value: "Search" or whatever you want it to say next to the search data entry field.

Now you are ready to implement a search in your application as described here:

```
http://developer.android.com/guide/topics/search/search-dialog.html
```

Note that many Android phones, tablets, iTVs, and e-reader devices come with a search button built in, which will pop up the search dialog. You can also provide a button to do this, in a menu maybe, or as an icon. That's for you to experiment with, so have some fun with Search.

Data Storage in Android

Android has a significant number of ways for you to save data on your smartphone, from private data storage for your application, called shared preferences, to internal storage on your smartphone device's memory chips, to external storage via your smartphone device's external storage (SD card or Micro-SD), to network connection (Network Accessed Storage) via your own network server, to an entire DBMS (database management system) via open source SQLite private databases.

Shared Preferences

Shared preferences are persistent data pairs that remain in memory even if your application is killed (or crashes), and thus this data remains persistent across multiple user sessions. The primary use of shared preferences is to store user preferences for a given user's Android applications and this is a main reason why they persist in memory between application runs.

To set your application's shared preferences Android provides us with the SharedPreferences class. This class can be used to store any **primitive data types**, including Booleans (1/0, on/off, true/false, or visible/hidden), floats, integers, strings, and longs. Note that the data created with this class will remain persistent across user sessions with your application even if your application is killed (the process is terminated, or crashes).

There are two methods in the SharedPreferences class that are used to access the preferences; if you have a single preference file use getPreferences and if you have more than one preference file, you can name each and use getSharedPreferences(name) and access them by name. Here is an example of the code in use, where we retrieve a screen name. The settings.getString call returns the screenName parameter, or the default name Android Fan if the setting is not set:

```
public static final String PREFS_NAME = "PreferenceFile";
...
    @Override
    public void onCreate(Bundle savedInstanceState) {
        super.onCreate(savedInstanceState);
        setContentView(R.layout.activity_main);

        SharedPreferences settings = getSharedPreferences(PREFS_NAME, 0);
        String screenName = settings.getString("screenName", "Android Fan");
        // do something with the screen name.
    }
```

We can set the screen name with the following:

```
SharedPreferences settings = getSharedPreferences(PREFS_NAME, 0);
SharedPreferences.Editor editor = settings.edit();
editor.putString("screenName", screenName);
editor.commit();
```

Internal Memory

Accessing internal memory storage on Android is done a bit differently, as that memory is unique to your application and cannot be directly accessed by the user or by other applications. When the application is uninstalled these files are deleted from memory. To access files in memory use the openFileOutput() with the name of the file and the operation needed, which will return a FileOutputStream object that you can use the read(), write(), and close() methods to manipulate the data into and out of the file. Here is some example code showing this concept:

```
String FILENAME = "hello_file";
String string = "hello world!";
FileOutputStream fos = openFileOutput(FILENAME, Context.MODE_PRIVATE);
fos.write(string.getBytes());
fos.close();
```

External Memory

The method that is used for accessing external memory on an Android device is getExternalStorageState. It checks to see whether the media (usually an SD card or internal micro SD) is in place (inserted in the slot for an SD card) and available for usage. Note that files written to external removable storage media also can be accessed outside of Android and its applications by PCs or other computing devices that can read the SD card format. This means there is no security in place on files that are written to external removable storage devices.

Using SQLite

The most common way to store data for your application, and the most organized and sharable, is to create and utilize a SQLite database. This is how Android stores and accesses its own data for users who utilize its internal applications such as the Contacts list or Database. Any private database you create for your application will be accessible to all parts of your application, but not to other parts of other developer's applications unless you give permission for them to access it.

To write and read from a custom database structure, you would utilize the getWritableDatabase and getReadableDatabase methods, which return a SQLiteDatabase object that represents the database structure and provides methods for performing SQLite database operations.

To perform SQLite database queries on your new SQLite database you would use the SQLiteDatabase query() methods, which accept all common data query parameters such as the table to query and the groupings, columns, rows, selections, projection, and similar concepts that are mainstream in database programming. This is a complex topic, so I suggest getting a book on SQLite for Android from Apress if you want to master this database technology inside of Android.

Device Administration: Security for IT Deployments

As of Android version 2.2 (API Level 8), Google has introduced support for secure enterprise applications via its Android Device Administration API. This API provides developers with employee device administration at a lower system level, allowing the creation of "security aware" applications that are necessary in MIS enterprise applications that require that IT maintain a tight level of control over the employees' Android Smartphone devices at all times. Support for this feature between API Level 8 and 16 may be yet another reason why these are the default API Level support (Minimum and Target) recommendations that are set as default values in the New Android Application Project series of dialogs that we have seen throughout this book.

A great example of this is the Android e-mail application, which has been upgraded in OS version 2.2 to implement these security features to provide more robust e-mail exchange security and support. Exchange Administrators can now implement and enforce password protection policies in the Android e-mail application spanning both alphanumeric passwords and simpler numeric PINs across all of the devices in their organization.

IT administrators can go as far as to remotely restore the factory defaults on lost or stolen handsets, clearing sensitive passwords and wiping clean proprietary data. E-mail Exchange End-Users can now sync their e-mail and calendar data as well.

Using the Android Camera Class to Control a Camera

The Android Camera class is used to control the built-in camera that is in every Android smartphone and in most tablets. This Camera class is used to set image capture settings and parameters, start and stop the preview modes, take the actual picture, and retrieve frames of video in real-time for encoding to a video stream or video file format. The Camera class is a client for the camera service, which manages the camera hardware.

To access your Android device's camera, you need to declare a permission in your *AndroidManifest.xml* that allows the camera features to be included in your application. You need to use the <uses-feature> tag to declare any camera features that you wish to access in your application so that Android knows to activate them for use in your application. The following XML AndroidManifest.xml entries allow the camera to be used and define it as a feature along with including the autofocus capabilities:

```
<uses-permission android:name="android.permission.CAMERA" />
<uses-feature android:name="android.hardware.camera" />
<uses-feature android:name="android.hardware.camera.autofocus"/>
```

The developer.android website has plenty of Java code for you to experiment with at the following link locations:

```
http://developer.android.com/reference/android/hardware/Camera.html
http://developer.android.com/guide/topics/media/camera.html
http://developer.android.com/reference/android/hardware/Camera.Parameters.html
```

3D Graphics: Using OpenGL ES 2.0 in Android

One of the most impressive capabilities of the Android OS is its ability to "render" 3D graphics in real-time using only the open source OpenGL (open source graphics language) ES 1.x API prior to API Level 8 (2.2), and in later releases of Android after 2.2, the OpenGL ES 2.0 APIs. OpenGL ES stands for OpenGL for embedded systems. OpenGL ES 3.0 was recently ratified, and OpenGL ES 4.0 is under consideration and should be available soon as well. Apress has several books covering Android 4 game development using OpenGL including *Beginning Android Games*.

OpenGL ES is an optimized embedded devices version of the OpenGL 2.0 API that is used on computers and game consoles. OpenGL ES is highly optimized for use in embedded devices similar to the way Android Dalvik Virtual Machine optimizes your code by making sure there is no "fat" that the smartphone CPU and memory need to deal with, a streamlining of sorts. OpenGL ES 2.0 is a feature parallel version to the full OpenGL 2.0 standard version, so if what you want to do on Android is doable in OpenGL 2.x, it should be possible to do it in OpenGL ES 2.0.

The Android OpenGL ES 2.0 is a custom implementation but is somewhat similar to the J2ME JSR239 OpenGL ES API, with some minor deviations from this specification due to its use with the Java Micro Edition (JavaME) for cell phones.

To access the OpenGL ES 2.0 API, you need to write your own custom subclass of the View Class and obtain a handle to an OpenGL Context, which will then provide you with access to the OpenGL ES 2.0 functions and operations. This is done in the onDraw() method of the custom View class that you create, and once you have a handle to the OpenGL Object, you can use that object's methods to access and call the OpenGL ES functional operations.

More information on OpenGL ES can be found at: `www.khronos.org/opengles/`

Information about version 1.0 can be found at: `www.khronos.org/opengles/1_X/`

Information about version 2.0 can be found at: `www.khronos.org/opengles/2_X/`

Information about version 3.0 can be found at: `www.khronos.org/opengles/3_X/`

Android Developer Documents do in fact exist for OpenGL ES 1.0 and 1.1 at

```
http://developer.android.com/reference/javax/microedition/khronos/opengles/
package-summary.html
```

FaceDetector

One of the coolest and most advanced concepts in the Android SDK is a facial recognition class called FaceDetector.

FaceDetector automatically identified faces of subjects inside of a Bitmap graphic object. I would suggest using PNG24 (24-bit PNG) for the highest quality source data for this operation, as FaceDetector uses 16-bits of RGB data (5-6-5 bits of R-G-B channel values respectively) currently in its algorithm (so don't use GIF or PNG8 format indexed color images).

You create a FaceDetector object by using the public constructor FaceDetector:

```
public FaceDetector (width integer, height integer, maxFaces integer)
```

The method you use to find faces in the bitmap file is findFaces(Bitmap bitmap, Face[] faces), which returns the number of faces successfully found.

SoundPool

The SoundPool class is great for game development and audio playback applications on Android because it manages a pool of Audio Resources in an optimal fashion for Android Apps that use a lot of audio, or where audio is a critical part of the end-user's overall experience.

A SoundPool is a collection of audio "samples," such as sound effects or short songs that need to be loaded into Android memory from an external resource, either inside the application's .apk file, or from an external file or from the internal file system.

The cool thing about the SoundPool Class is that it works hand in hand with the MediaPlayer Class that we looked at earlier to decode the audio into a raw PCM mono or stereo 16-bit CD quality audio stream. This makes it easier for an application to include compressed audio inside its APK, and then decompress it on application start-up, load it into memory, and then play it back without any hiccups when it is called or triggered within the Android application code.

It gets even more interesting. It turns out that SoundPool can also control the number of audio assets that are being simultaneously "rendered" or turned from data values into audio sound waves. Essentially this means that the SoundPool is an audio "Mixing Console" that can be used to layer audio in real-time to create custom mixes based on your gameplay or other application programming logic.

SoundPool defines a maxStreams parameter that limits the number of parallel audio streams that can be played, so that you can put a "cap" on the amount of processing overhead that is used to mixdown audio in your application, in case this starts to affect the visual elements that are also possibly rendering in real-time on the screen. If the maxStreams value is exceeded, then the SoundPool turns off individual audio streams based on their priority values, or if none are assigned, based on the age of the audio stream.

Individual audio streams within the SoundPool can be looped infinitely (using a value of –1) or any number of discreet times (0 to …) and also counts from zero, so a loop setting of three plays the audio loop four times. Playback rates can also be scaled from 0.5 to 2.0, or at half the pitch to twice the pitch, allowing real-time pitch shifting, and with some clever programming, one could even simulate effects such as Doppler via fairly simple Java code. Samples can also be pitch-shifted to give a range of sound effect tones, or to create keyboard-like synthesizers.

SoundPool also lets you assign a Priority to your individual audio samples, with higher numbers getting higher priority. Priority only comes into play when the maxStreams value specified in the SoundPool Object is hit and an audio sample needs to be removed from the playback queue to make room for another audio sample playback request with a higher priority level. Be sure to prioritize your audio samples, so that you can have complete control of your audio and effects mixing during real-time playback.

MediaRecorder

In Chapter 11 we discussed the Android `MediaPlayer` class, which is commonly used to play back audio or video files. Android also can record audio and video media files at a high level of fidelity and the counterpart to the `MediaPlayer` class for this is, logically, the `MediaRecorder` class. It is important to note that `MediaRecorder` does not currently work on the Android smartphone emulators.

There are five main `MediaRecorder` classes that control the process of media recording. They are as follows (note that these are defined inside the `MediaRecorder` class, hence the dot notation):

- `MediaRecorder.AudioEncoder`
- `MediaRecorder.AudioSource`
- `MediaRecorder.OutputFormat`
- `MediaRecorder.VideoEncoder`
- `MediaRecorder.VideoSource`

You construct a `MediaRecorder` object and operate on it using the public methods such as start(), stop(), `prepare()`, `release()`, `reset()`, `setAudioChannels()`, `setCamera()`, `setOutputFile()`, and a plethora of other methods that control how the new media data is captured and stored on your Android device.

More information on the `MediaRecorder` class can be found at

`http://developer.android.com/reference/android/media/MediaRecorder.html`

VideoView: Playing Video in Your Android Apps

As our final topic, just to make sure we cover everything major you will want to do in your Android apps in this book, we'll look at how to simply and effectively play digital video files in your Android applications. You do this through a very handy class called VideoView. We are going to show the ability to play video in our application using only three lines of XML code and eight lines of Java code, or less than a dozen lines of code in total.

Adding a VideoView Object

For video playback, we would use the VideoView class. As with TextView and ImageView objects, VideoView objects make it easy to access MPEG-4 H.264 or WebM (VP8) video in your Android applications. Your video can either be in your /res/raw folder or streamed from a remote server, keeping your application download size to a minimum.

To add a VideoView to our activity_main.xml, place the following tag in your UI layout container:

```
<VideoView   android:id="@+id/videoView1"
             android:layout_height="match_parent"
             android:layout_width="match_parent" />
```

This names our VideoView and tells it to match its parent container size using match_parent. The match_parent value does the opposite of wrap_content. It sizes the content up to fill the layout container, rather than scaling the layout container down around the content.

Adding the Java for Video

First, add three new import statements for the classes we need:

```
import android.net.Uri;
import android.widget.VideoView;
import android.widget.MediaController;
```

To get the video from our server, we also need to define its path using a Uri object, so we must import the android.net.Uri class. We next import the VideoView widget (android.widget.VideoView). Finally, to play the video in the VideoView, we will use a MediaController object, so we import the android.widget.MediaController class as well.

Next, add the following to your MainActivity.java onCreate() method to create our VideoView object:

```
Uri vidFile = Uri.parse("http://commonsware.com/misc/test2.3gp");
VideoView videoView = (VideoView) findViewById(R.id.videoView1);
videoView.setVideoURI(vidFile);
videoView.setMediaController(new MediaController(this));
videoView.start();
```

First, we create the Uri reference object, which holds the path, or address, to the video file on the server. The uniform resource identifier (URI) can use the familiar HTTP server paradigm or a more advanced real-time streaming protocol. As you can see, here we are using the HTTP protocol, which works fine, and is the industry standard, thanks to the Internet. We create a Uri object called vidFile using the parse() method with the HTTP URL to any valid path and file name in quotes. Here, the Uri object points to the content at http://commonsware.com/misc/test2.3gp, so that we have some video to play.

Now we have an object called vidFile that contains a reference to our video file. Next, we set up our VideoView object, calling it videoView and using findViewById() to locate the videoView1 ID we created in our XML layout file. This is the same thing we have been doing with the other View types, and should be very familiar to you at this point.

Now that we have a VideoView object, we use the setVideoURI() method to pass the vidFile Uri object to the videoView VideoView object, so that the VideoView is loaded with the file path to use to retrieve the video. Now our Uri is wired into our VideoView, and we need only to wire the MediaController into the VideoView so that the video can be played.

Finally let's declare a new MediaController object named mediaControl and in the next line of code connect that MediaController to the videoView object using the .setMediaController() method.

```
MediaController mediaControl = new MediaController(this);
videoView.setMediaController(mediaControl);
```

Finally, to start our videoView object playing, we send it a .start() method call, like this:

```
videoView.start()
```

New Features in Android 4.2

Right before we went to press (the holiday weekend before, actually) Android 4.2 was released, with a lot of operating system level features that will automatically make your apps better without your intervention, which is a boon to absolute beginners, so we're covering them here. Some of these include a new user interface element style treatment, performance (speed) optimizations, international language optimizations, dozens of security enhancements, HDR Camera support, and support for multiple users on a single Android device. Other features that we cover in this book, such as SoundPool and 3D Rendering via hardware GPUs, were also greatly enhanced with new code and features. I will point out some of the other new Android 4.2 API Level 17 (called: Jelly Bean Plus, or JellyBean+) additions in this section, so that you know about them and can further investigate their relevance to your Android application development on your own.

Presentation is a big area of enhancement in Android 4.2, in fact, there is a new Presentation Dialog UI element that you can code to, as well as support for Miracast technology. Using Miracast, users using Miracast-certified Android devices can connect to external displays (even non-Android displays) using Wi-Fi via Miracast, a peer-to-peer wireless display standard created by the Wi-Fi Alliance. When a wireless display is connected to an Android device, Android users can stream any type of new media content to that external screen, including: images, photos, videos, maps, audio, and much more. Your applications can now take advantage of wireless displays in a similar way as it can currently with direct-wired external displays, and no extra programming work is needed. Hey! That's another absolute beginner's feature! The Android operating system manages all of the network connections for you, and even automatically streams your Presentation or application content over to the wireless displays as needed. So be sure and research the new Presentation Classes and the Wi-Fi Alliance Miracast technology soon.

Two more areas you will want to take a look at if you are into widget development are Lock Screen Widgets and the new Daydream Interactive Screen Saver Mode. Lock Screen Widgets are fairly self-explanatory; they are widgets that display on your user's Locked Screens! This is a really cool new feature, as it essentially allows developers to provide custom Lock Screens. Android users can have up to five Lock Screen Widgets, each of which can have its own panel in the five screen panel navigator that became so popular via the Android RAZR. Lock screen widgets can display any kind of content, and they can accept direct user interaction. Lock Screen Widgets can be entirely self-contained, such as a widget that controls audio playback and can even allow users to jump straight inside an application Activity (after unlocking, of course). Daydreams merge the capabilities of live wallpaper with home screen widgets; they are essentially an interactive screen saver mode which starts-up when an Android device is docked and charging. Daydream is really a remote content service that is provided to the user via an installed application, only in the form of an Android device screen saver. Your users can turn on Daydream mode using their Settings controls and also choose the daydream that they wish to utilize. Both of these new capabilities allow developers to increase the user engagement impact of their application significantly, so be sure to check out these new Android 4.2 features when you have a moment. More information about Android 4.2 Jelly Bean Plus features and APIs can be found via the following two links:

`http://developer.android.com/about/versions/jelly-bean.html`

`http://developer.android.com/about/versions/android-4.2.html`

Summary

There are a lot of really great features in Android that we simply do not have enough time to cover in one book, or that are too complex for an absolute beginners' book. That doesn't mean that you should not investigate all of the cool features that Android has to offer on your own, however, so this chapter introduced some that are very powerful and advanced for a mobile phone, tablet, iTV, and e-reader operating system.

We started out covering the most important area that you will want to research: troubleshooting. Fortunately, Android has a troubleshooting section for Android development research, and this page has references on the left-side to some on the most key areas that you will want to research further once you are finished with this book. Please make sure that you do so, it will increase your overall knowledge of what Android is currently capable of considerably.

Widgets are another key part of Android, and something that you may well want to create at some point in time, as they are like mini-apps that users can use on their desktops. They are so important, in fact, that Android has given them their own Class and section of the Android Developer website.

Location based services and Google Maps are another ideal way to add really cool features to your apps with relatively little programming effort, and Google Search is another great way to leverage things that Google has already mastered and is offering on its servers and generously allows you to offer these features to your users again with almost zero coding effort on your part.

Where graphics are concerned, there is no more powerful open source graphics library than OpenGL, and Android 2.2 through 4.1 implements the latest OpenGL ES 2.0 technology, just like

HTML5 does currently. Because Android phones have built-in GPU (graphics processing unit) hardware, this means that you can "render" real-time 3D on the fly, to visualize just about anything that you want to within your application, and in three dimensions to boot! This is another very logical reason to use that default (suggested) API Level 8 through 16 support that is set as a default in the New Android Application Project series of dialogs in Eclipse and that we have been using throughout this book.

There are many other interesting areas to be discovered in Android as well, from creating your own Audio Mixing App using the SoundPool Audio Engine to creating your very own SQLite databases to using the Smartphone or Tablet Camera and MediaRecorder class to using the Face Recognition class to identify unique people within your content. All of this is covered in fine detail on the Google developer.android.com website, so be sure to go there to explore at length to enhance your knowledge of the literally thousands of interesting features in Android OS, with many more to come soon in the Android OS Version 5.0!

Index

CPSIA information can be obtained at www.ICGtesting.com
Printed in the USA
LVOW022124150513

334046LV00006B/64/P